# EARTHKEEPING

# EARTHKEEPING
## CHRISTIAN STEWARDSHIP
## OF NATURAL RESOURCES

*By the Fellows of the Calvin Center
for Christian Scholarship, Calvin College*

Peter De Vos     Vernon Ehlers
Calvin De Witt     Derk Pereboom
Eugene Dykema     Aileen Van Beilen
Loren Wilkinson

WILLIAM B. EERDMANS PUBLISHING COMPANY
GRAND RAPIDS, MICHIGAN

*Copyright © 1980 by Wm. B. Eerdmans Publishing Co.*
*255 Jefferson Ave., S.E., Grand Rapids, Mich. 49503*
All rights reserved
Printed in the United States of America

*Reprinted, November 1981*


**Library of Congress Cataloging in Publication Data**

Main entry under title:
Earthkeeping: Christian stewardship of natural resources.

   Includes bibliographical references.
   1. Natural resources.   2. Environmental protection.
3. Stewardship, Christian. I. De Vos, Peter.
II. Wilkinson, Loren. III. Calvin Center for
Christian Scholarship.
HC55.E27    261.8'5    80-15900
ISBN 0-8028-1834-X

All Scripture quotations are taken from the Revised Standard Version unless otherwise noted.

*This book is printed on recycled paper. Appendix C provides an analysis of the factors involved in a decision to use recycled paper.*

# CONTENTS

# LIST OF FIGURES AND TABLES

# PREFACE

In 1977 Calvin College began an ambitious new enterprise: the establishment of the Calvin Center for Christian Scholarship. This undertaking arose from a recognition that our calling as Christian scholars and our responsibility as a Christian institution oblige us to contribute, from within the vantage point of the Christian faith, to the solution of the complex problems facing humankind today. The purpose of the Calvin Center for Christian Scholarship is stated well in its constitution:

> The purpose of the Center is to promote rigorous, creative, and articulately Christian scholarship which is addressed to the solution of important theoretical and practical issues. More specifically, the scholarship promoted shall be of the sort:
>
> a. that goes beyond what is usually expected of an undergraduate faculty whose primary responsibility is to students;
> b. that goes beyond the specialized disciplinary research interests of individual members of the faculty;
> c. that can best be conducted by a group of Calvin College scholars working together, supplemented whenever feasible and desirable by scholars and others from outside the Calvin College community;
> d. that would be of benefit to a broad spectrum of the Calvin community and of the world beyond;
> e. that is focussed on areas of life and thought in which it is reasonable to expect that a distinctively Christian position can be worked out; and for which traditional Christian positions have been too parochially expressed, too superficially developed, or too little in accord with the Christian faith.

The topic of study selected for the initial year of operation of the Calvin Center for Christian Scholarship was "Christian Stewardship and Natural Resources." Those scholars selected to participate in this study were: Peter De Vos, Professor of Philosophy, Calvin College; Calvin De Witt, Professor of Environmental Studies, University of Wisconsin-Madison; Eugene Dykema, Assistant Professor of Economics, Calvin College; Vernon Ehlers, Professor of Physics, Calvin College; and Loren Wilkinson, Professor of English, Seattle Pacific College (currently at the Oregon Extension of Trinity College, Deerfield, Illinois). In addition, two Student Fellows were selected:

Derk Pereboom, philosophy major; and Aileen Van Beilen, history major. During the 1977–78 academic year this group actively studied the topic of Christian stewardship and natural resources.

However, the 1977–78 Fellows wished to do more than their assigned task of scholarship followed by the customary publication of their thought in scholarly articles and journals. It was also their desire to discuss, in a general yet scholarly way, the broad issues surrounding Christian steward-ship of natural resources, and to do so at a level appropriate for the intelligent layperson. This book is the result of their study.

It was our desire to take a holistic approach to the problems discussed in this book, and not merely to produce an anthology which would deal with bits and pieces of them. This thrust us into an intensive project which entailed many group discussions and countless more individual conferences. We have attempted to bring to this enterprise the collective knowledge of our disciplines in a joint endeavor to address, in the broadest terms possible, the resource-use problems faced by the world today. We have not attempted to be so specific as to tell you what kind of car to buy, how to set your home thermostat, or what legislation your government must pass. Nor have we analyzed in detail which alternative energy approaches are best, least costly, or most environmentally suitable. There are others more capable of doing that. Furthermore, the value of this book, as we perceive it, is not that it is produced by a team of scholars from different disciplines, though the mutual insight and the correction of disciplinary narrowness generated by that com-bination is, we think, important. Nor is its strength that we have spent a year devoted specifically to understanding our use of resources; there are other think-tanks, with bigger budgets, which have done that. The distinc-tiveness of this book is rather that we have approached the problem in an in-depth and integrated way from within the framework provided by biblical principles. Thus, in this book we consider the enormously difficult and im-portant problem of how human beings should use the world, guided by the knowledge that in the gospel of Christ, God shows people not only how to attain eternal life, but also how to care for the creation in which he has placed us as stewards.

The writing of this book has indeed been a joint endeavor, and no person can be singled out as having been the major driving force. However, it should be mentioned that Loren Wilkinson served as the principal writer, performing the Herculean task of taking six disparate writing styles and combining them into one. Aileen Van Beilen spent many hours writing, editing, and tending to the minutiae, such as footnotes and references, and Judy Nydam efficiently and unerringly converted illegible handwriting and garbled dictation into polished typewritten pages. Lastly, Vernon Ehlers served as editor-manager of the project.

# HUMANITY AND THE PLANET EARTH: TWO FUTURES

> *. . . two hundred years ago almost everywhere human beings were comparatively few, poor, and at the mercy of the forces of nature, and 200 years from now, we expect, almost everywhere they will be numerous, rich, and in control of the forces of nature.*
>
> —Herman Kahn, *The Next Two Hundred Years*

> *There is a question in the air, more sensed than seen, like the invisible approach of a distant storm, a question that I would hesitate to ask aloud did I not believe it existed unvoiced in the minds of many: "Is there hope for man?"*
>
> —Robert Heilbroner, *An Inquiry into the Human Prospect*

**WE LIVE IN THE PRESENT:** shaped by the past and shaping the future, it is nevertheless *now* that we make the choices which shape our world. This has always been true for humans. For us, every point is a turning point. Nevertheless, some times seem more crucial than others, and we live in such a time. We may merely be suffering from what one futurist called "future shock"—the too-rapid approach of the future and the changes it brings—but in any case, we are obsessed with the total shadow which our present actions cast across the future. A handful of typical concerns illustrates this compulsive "tomorrow-mindedness":

—We live (though by now it has become almost a cliché to say it) under the "shadow of the mushroom." The mere possibility of war keeps us aware that everything we take for granted might be canceled by the radiant zero of nuclear energy. Though the conscious fear of nuclear war may have receded somewhat in the decades since Hiroshima, it has been supplanted by a panic over the dark side of "peaceful" nuclear power. The hundreds of demonstrators who in recent years have been arrested at nuclear installations

**1**

around the country are acting out of no present pain or damage, but out of a vague sense of the danger *to the future* which those harnessed energies pose.

—Throughout much of his administration, an American president has begged a placid people to use less energy. The remarkable thing about the Carter energy plan was not, however, the President's failure to convince a Congress or a constituency of the correctness of his analysis (political careers are littered with such failures). It is, rather, that he banked his political career on an event which has not yet happened, and which even the most pessimistic analysts say will not happen for a decade or two: the exhaustion of cheap petroleum.

—A vocal minority of North Americans have changed their way of life at the prospect of various kinds of future chaos: a "population explosion" which might threaten our well-being, a worldwide famine which would starve millions, the melting of the polar icecaps (from too much air pollution), the destruction of the ozone layers (from too many aerosol cans). In addition to those who have made some sort of token attempt to avoid such an assortment of catastrophes, there are millions more who live unchanged lives, but do so in a vague uneasiness of approaching calamity.

Predictions of such disasters no longer cause headlines and conferences as they did a few years ago. But the fears have been repressed, not removed. And they have in common an uneasiness about the consequences of human action for the whole earth. Individuals have been at a turning point before. But, for the first time in history, large numbers of people are beginning to see that what we do affects not only ourselves, but the whole world. (Indeed, with our tentative explorations into space, we can dimly sense the possibility of affecting not just our planet, but the whole solar system, and beyond.) Phrases like "world hunger," "global awareness," and "the ecosphere" were strange a generation ago; now they are common vocabulary. And whether these new words issue in new actions is not, perhaps, as important as the new awareness which they point to. Like it or not, we now know that we are involved with the planet's life—with the health of an Indian child, the dwindling population of the blue whale, the thickness of the polar icecaps.

Appropriately, this new planetary awareness is the gift (or curse) of those who have the greatest ability to actually affect the earth. The hungry child in India knows far less about his or her involvement in the world community than does the American businessperson; he or she also has far less chance to change it. Thus our new knowledge is bitter: the more we understand that we are managers of the planet, the more we recognize that we have not managed it well. Our obsession with the future, then, is a painful consequence of the consciousness of our involvement in the life of the earth.

This growing awareness of our obligation to the earth (particularly in the wealthy West, where we are haunted by both consciousness and conscience) places Christians in a difficult position. On the one hand, we affirm that God made the world, called it good, and directs its course. And we believe that God continues to care for the world. The word translated "world" in the New Testament is usually *kosmos*, which means, in its broadest sense, "cosmos," the universe. When Christians affirm that God loved the world and that Christ died for the life of the world, they are speaking not just of humanity, but of the whole planet—indeed, the whole created universe. Thus, of all the people, Christians should be concerned for the future health of the planet—both for the narrow "world" of humankind and the broader "earth" of a complex and living ecosphere.

And yet, with a few important exceptions, Christians have not shown much concern for the world's health. For the emphasis in Christian thought has been much more on personal than on cosmic salvation. Indeed, one narrow use of the word "world" is in declarations that Christians have been saved *out of* the world. That idea has been interpreted by many to be a sort of license to neglect the world in order to care for the soul. This interpretation, when combined with a radically individualistic trend in Western thought, has produced what is the prevailing mood among Christians with regard to their involvement in the planetary environment: we are concerned first of all with the relevance of the gospel for our own salvation; second, with its relevance for the salvation of the rest of humankind. But for most, the concern stops there: that vital human center is also the circumference of any feeling of responsibility for the rest of creation. We have seen the rest of the world merely as background for the human drama of salvation.

But quite apart from both a man*-centered theology and the threats of various crises—pollution, overpopulation, resource shortage, and so forth—the findings of biologists in the last few decades make it impossible to act any longer as though humankind could be considered apart from the rest of nature. We have discovered traces of synthetic materials (such as DDT) in creatures as distant from human habitation as the Antarctic penguin. And (to reverse the picture) we know that our own bodies are made up of live entities which could exist independently elsewhere. As one contemporary biologist puts it:

> We are shared, rented, occupied. . . . My centrioles, basal bodies, and probably a good many other more obscure tiny beings at work inside my cells, each with its own special genome, are as foreign, and as essential, as aphids in anthills. My cells are no longer the pure line entities I was raised with; they are ecosystems more complex than Jamaica Bay.[1]

We simply cannot escape from our embeddedness in nature or nature's embeddedness in us. Therefore, our knowledge seems to indicate that we can no longer speak of humanity being saved out of nature: we are redeemed

*Throughout this book, we sometimes refer to human beings as "man." This is a generic term and includes women, men, and children.

*in* nature, not apart from it. In some way, the Christian must include the rest of creation in his or her own salvation.

At this point the bewilderment for the thoughtful Christian increases. For there are, in our time, plenty of non-Christian thinkers around who are quick to see humans as lords or saviors of nature. Yet their ideas are difficult for the Christian to affirm. At one extreme, we find those who regard nature merely as raw material for the building of human civilization, the perfecting of human comfort. Thus, an armchair philosopher asserts, man should

> wipe out the jungles, turn deserts and swamps into arable land, terrace barren mountains, regulate rivers, eradicate all pests, control the weather, and make the whole land mass a fit habitation for man.[2]

Another picture of human mastery is provided by Buckminster Fuller, whose argument is that it is the destiny of man to do increasingly more and more with less and less. Thus man steadily increases his control over nature, and by doing so, frees his mental powers for the unique sort of management he can give to the processes of the planet. Fuller's viewpoint is perhaps best suggested in the title of one of his books: *Operating Manual for Spaceship Earth.*

But that popular modern picture of the earth as a spaceship, though it expresses a much needed recognition of the unity of the planet, is in some ways inappropriate. As one contemporary historian puts it, "The metaphor is, in fact, ecologically terrifying. A spaceship is completely a human artifact, designed to sustain human life and for no other purpose."[3] The Christian knows that the earth is the Lord's, not man's; thus, sustaining human life is not its only purpose.

A logical conclusion of this man-centered view of man's relationship to nature is that of Herman Kahn, whose 1976 bicentennial study of the future called *The Next 200 Years* concludes with the gloriously optimistic prophecy that in 200 years, "almost everywhere" humans will be "numerous, rich, and in control of the forces of nature." Kahn predicts a leveling out, in 200 years, of the earth's population at 15 billion, with a per capita income (in today's dollar values) of $20,000.

On an even more exalted level is the opinion of a Christian thinker, Pierre Teilhard de Chardin. Teilhard writes glowingly of

> this sudden deluge of cerebralisation, this biological invasion of a new animal type which gradually eliminates or subjects all forms of life that are not human, this irresistible tide of fields and factories, this immense and growing edifice of matter and ideas—all these signs . . . proclaim that there has been a change on the earth and a change of planetary magnitude.[4]

And Teilhard goes on to speak with hope of a time when the earth shall become "a solid sphere of hominized substance."

Here too, as with the pessimists, we find an obsession with the future. There are many—like Kahn, or Fuller, or Teilhard—who see man moving into a place of confident and benign dictatorship of the life of the universe. Despite the appeal of such a future, however, there are many who see in such a humanization inevitable disaster for both humanity and the rest of creation.

And there is in that body of truth at the center of the Christian's faith justification for both views: on the one hand that humanity is bound for destructive crisis, and on the other that it is growing toward an Edenic Utopia.

In support of the first view, Christians have it on high authority that humans are destructively wicked creatures. From Eden on, we have tried to make ourselves gods, and in the attempt we have consistently misused creation (from Eve's fruit to Cain's club to Babel's bricks). We have always brought pain or death to other persons, and we have as often brought destruction to the wider world—whether in flood sent to punish the human race or fire that fell on Sodom. But of course we do not have to look to biblical history to find evidence of man's destructive sinfulness; any place or period of our past is filled with examples of such dead-end malignancy: Roman soldiers salting the fields of conquered enemies, Nazis cremating millions of Jews, Americans slaughtering billions of passenger pigeons, the scorched-earth policies of a thousand petty tyrants. The contemporary Christian finds in these episodes good reason to despair at the present state of human stewardship and the future prospects for humanity. Anxiety would seem the only response to a future governed by such a creature, whose heart is "deceitful above all things, and desperately wicked."

But there is another biblical picture of human possibility and the earth's future. Man is not solely evil: he was made good in God's image, and the twisted path of his goodness is made straight in Christ. Great portraits of *shalom*, peace, abound in the Bible. They present humans as living in harmony with each other, the world, and with God. Such is the ideal picture of Psalm 104, in which God is portrayed as causing

> . . . the grass to grow for the cattle,
> and plants for man to cultivate,
> that he may bring forth food from the earth,
> and wine to gladden the heart of man,
> oil to make his face shine,
> and bread to strengthen man's heart.
> The trees of the Lord are watered abundantly,
> the cedars of Lebanon which he planted.
> In them the birds build their nests;
> the stork has her home in the fir trees. . . .

We find such a picture of harmony between people and their environment in the apocalyptic future of Isaiah, in which they

> shall plant vineyards and eat their fruit. . . .
> They shall not labor in vain

Or bear children in calamity. . . .
The wolf and the lamb shall graze together. . . .
They shall do no evil or harm in all My holy mountain.

Thus the Christian understands the greed, the voraciousness, the evil that seems to be turning the world toward destruction; but he or she also understands the possibility of a redeemed—and redemptive—humanity, at peace in a garden earth.

How then should the Christian think and act? This book is an attempt to answer that question by looking carefully and thoroughly at the nature of the problems which face us, at the nature of humanity itself, and at the significance of the gospel of Christ for Christians who seek to live wisely in the present and carefully for the world's future.

Should the Christian side with the doomsayers or with the Utopians? What kind of tomorrow should the Christian work toward? How should Christians live their lives in the face of the obvious needs of their fellow creatures—both human and nonhuman?

There have been two main answers in the history of Christendom. One has stressed the separation of the church from the world—and even from the earth. From Tertullian to Ellul, those who have held this position have asserted the tension between Athens and Jerusalem. They have maintained that the wisdom, powers, and techniques of corrupt man can only lead to slavery and destruction, and that any attempt to build a future on human foundations will produce Babel, Babylon, or Sodom—but not Zion. Today, those who hold this view stress the evil of technology, the corruption of the political process, and the need for Christians to live in radical tension with the fallen order—if necessary, letting it destroy them to thus reveal its fallenness.

The other response to the dilemma is made by those who see the institutions and abilities of humans as gifts of God, redeemable along with humankind. In various ways—from Justin Martyr, through Calvin and the Eastern Orthodox tradition, to many contemporary Reformed or Sacramental thinkers—these have maintained that for Christians to build the city of man, however haltingly, in an awareness of God's working in the world is to build Zion and that ultimate kingdom of peace.

The consequences of these traditional answers are magnified today by the enormous forces which humans have learned to exercise. The extent of those human powers seems to confirm those who give the first answer: for they are clearly powers misused. We see their misuse in exploitative trade relationships, destructive mining, devastation of the habitat of nonhuman creatures. But that enormous human power confirms also those who give the second answer: they see in it, in the very technology which can be so destructive, a potential to care for, to *steward*, the earth.

How then should Christians live on the earth? In these pages we seek to give information which will help to answer that question. The answers are at times complex and difficult, and to find them we will explore many paths, both in the contemporary affairs of man and nature and in that complex past which has shaped human thought and action. But there are answers; of this we are confident. This book develops the possibility of a careful Christian stewardship of creation.

# THE STATE
# OF THE PLANET

"You can't miss them—just above the slag pile and left of the clearcut scar."

From *Audubon*. Used by permission of Herbert Brammeier, Jr.

### CHAPTER 1

# THE LAND ENTRUSTED TO US __

*. . . when we look at the patterned landscape we are looking at a very complicated structure of cover, within and to a large extent outside and around which are living a very large number of animals, with populations interspersed to form communities, highly dependent on the kind of structure that the cover provides. Within this pattern of cover the species network is maintained as an enormous production machine in which the members of most food-chains meet in staccato contact. It seems most probable that without the damping effect of cover upon all these feeding contacts the whole system would soon break down or at any rate become very simplified. And insofar as this cover structure is in itself partly edible, we must suppose that there must be some limiting arrangements that do prevent animals from eating themselves out of house and home.*

—Charles Elton,
**THE PATTERNS OF ANIMAL BEHAVIOR**

In December 1977, the Voyager I space probe, outward bound on a voyage past Jupiter, Saturn, Uranus, and finally beyond the solar system entirely, sent back a photograph. From seven million miles out, the picture shows the earth and the moon hanging like twin planets against the black backdrop of space. From that distance the difference in size is not appreciable. The remarkable difference, however, is in the colors: the moon shows bone white and dead, while the earth is a living jewel of blues, whites, and greens, and its whites, unlike those of the sun-blasted, meteor-scoured face of the moon, are the whites of shifting mist.

Seeing the earth and moon together, small but whole, emphasizes what we have suspected for some time and are learning from our exploration of space: the earth's life is unique in the solar system, and perhaps in the universe. For we increasingly understand that blue, white, and green sphere to

**11**

be a highly ordered system in which more than a million species of living things are maintained by the sun-powered cycling of liquid, solid, and gas.

Those processes which support the earth's life take place in a thin film of land, water, and air: the ecosphere. Every living creature lives within this ecosphere, and draws from it the materials necessary for its life. And whether those resources are used for shelter, food, or other basic needs, they are, after being used, returned to the ecosphere for use by others in a complex and perpetual cycling of materials.

Even when we study the ecosphere, most of this life-sustaining cycling of resources is not very evident. Some of those processes have been discovered only recently, and more are unknown or uncomprehended. Only recently, for example, have we learned of the strong likelihood that the earth's oxygen-rich atmosphere not only makes life possible, but is itself made by life, specifically by the photosynthesis, over many years, of green plants. Without that continual cleansing of the air, the atmosphere would be a lethal mixture of methane and carbon dioxide.

We are learning slowly how the ecosphere is made and maintained. In the pages which follow, we would like to review some of the fragile features of that ecosphere. To begin such a study, it will be helpful first to consider the meanings of a few terms. The most important is *ecosystem*. An ecosystem is any set of interacting plants, animals, and nonliving things (such as earth, water, wind) which can be viewed as a functioning unit. Thus a lake, a marsh, a forest, or a stream can be viewed as an ecosystem. So also can the entire ecosphere—that envelope of all living things and their sustaining environment.

In any given ecosystem, the interacting set of plant and animal species is called a *biotic community*, or simply a *community*. The forests of northeastern North America contain the beech-maple community: an intricate system of plants and animals such as beech trees, sugar maples, box turtles, and Jacks-in-the-Pulpit. All are living parts of that forest ecosystem.

One way to explore the design of ecosystems is to look in detail at several of them. Such in-depth consideration is quite possible: major studies have been made on such large ecosystems as the lakes, grasslands, and eastern deciduous forests of North America. The result of such studies is a detailed understanding of the way the sun's energy flows through an ecosystem. In general, the energy is caught and stored by the photosynthesizing plants, which are eaten by herbivores, which are eaten in turn by carnivores, which may be eaten by yet larger carnivores. And even those top carnivores, be they eagle, grizzly, or human, are broken back down into soil by microscopic organisms which specialize in decomposition. Such ecosystem studies also show how nonliving substances—water, oxygen, carbon dioxide, carbon, phosphorus, iron—are caught up and cycled by the network of life.

But from such a study one learns not only the contents of the ecosystem; one also learns what is even more important: the relationships. Those relationships, among the living things and between them and the nonliving environment, are highly complex. Such complexity is essential to the perpetuation of the health and beauty of ecosystems. When disturbed by drastic environmental change—fire, floods, or destructive storms—most healthy ecosystems are resilient enough to restore themselves. Their complex design tends to be self-sustaining.

In this ability to sustain itself over a long period of time, an ecosystem is like an individual organism. However, though large in comparison to a single organism, and more resilient than any single organism, an ecosystem is nevertheless *finite*. When we see from outer space the thin blue haze at the margins of the earth, we realize how finite the total of those ecosystems are in comparison to the extent of the universe, the solar system, or even the earth itself. From both that distant vision provided by space flight and our own study of ecosystems, we know that living things live and move within definite limits. In no way can they use more energy, more food, and more nutrients than are available. They must "live within their means." And, of course, they do.

But the very fact of those limits within which creatures must live says much about the design of the ecosphere. For living things rarely exploit their resources to the limits, collapsing after futile attempts to live beyond them. If this were the case, we would expect to see weak and hungry animals. But normally we do not—starving animals are rare in nature, except perhaps during an especially severe winter. Most of us have probably never seen a starving robin, rabbit, or squirrel.

The design of animal social systems is such that resources usually are *not* exploited to the limit. They have the potential to reproduce themselves so abundantly that within a few years, or a few decades, they could cover the earth. But, in fact, they do not. Their high potential for reproduction is normally not realized. Rather than pressing the limits of needed resources by increasing their number, populations are usually kept well below those limits. The cardinal singing in the backyard usually has more food than it needs. So it is with other organisms. Consequently, organisms in nature are normally healthy and vigorous.

This regulation is accomplished by many different means. The availability of food may affect the number of eggs laid; the sight or sound of an increasingly dense population may diminish the number of breeding animals; the disturbance of a large population may affect fertility; predation may keep population down; and so forth. But, for the purpose of our study of human use of the earth's resources, it is mainly important to understand not the mechanism itself, but the *fact* that population size among animals is successfully controlled. Other creatures tend to stay within the limits set by their resources. And with very few exceptions, starvation is normally *not* one of those means. We do not see a starving and emaciated natural world.

This balance in the ecosystem is, to the Christian, an indication of a

Creator who does all things well. For the life-sustaining beauty of the created earth declares the glory of God, as God declares its goodness. Thus the more we understand of the intricacy of a healthy ecosystem, the more we learn of the Creator. Nevertheless, that intricacy reminds us of our creatureliness: for, despite the fact that starvation does not generally occur within ecosystems, the balance is maintained by death. And death—of a plant, an animal, or of another person—reminds us that we too are creatures. We are a part of that ecosphere.

*Man also is a creature.* It is true that man has a personal relationship with God, is made in his image, and thus stands apart from creation. But it is also clear that God has created *us* as he has all other creatures. We, too, are organisms, living within a rich but limited world. We share with all creatures fundamental biological needs: the need for energy and minerals, for food, for air, for water. We can now get so far away from the earth that we can see earth and moon as two small spheres against blackness; nevertheless, we are bound to earth, still enmeshed in its cycles of life. The life of the earth is *our* life, and we depend upon it. Thus the Christian respect for creation has a twofold source: believers delight in it as God's work and respect it as they respect their own bodies—for in a sense the ecosphere *is* our extended body.

This dual nature of human respect for creation suggests that there are two ways in which we can study man's use of resources. First of all, as man is another organism in the ecosystem—a large, omnivorous mammal—we can study this organism as a part of the ecosphere. But man, made in the image of God, is also apart from the ecosphere. We can, therefore, study the modifications he makes in the ecosphere, modifications of a different sort than those made by other resource-using creatures.

## HUMANS AS PARTS OF ECOSYSTEMS

In the distant past, all humans were part of natural ecosystems (this is still true today for a few remote human communities). Such early humans harvested animals from the naturally occurring food chains, and made little effort to cultivate the plants they used as food. Like animals, they were "hunters and gatherers." They harvested and ate only the food provided by the natural functioning of the ecosystem. Uneaten food and body wastes were returned to the soil not far from their origin. Under these circumstances, humans meshed well with their ecosystems, fitting into natural flows of energy and materials. They affected those cycles no more than would any large mammal. They were nonmanipulative parts of the ecosystem, taking their places within it without altering its major processes or parts.

## HUMANS AS MODIFIERS OF ECOSYSTEMS

It seems at one time to have been possible for humans to function harmoniously in an ecosystem without deliberate manipulation. But that is no longer an alternative for us. For thousands of years, people have been living in tension with their supporting ecosystems. In fact, it is likely that the ideal of an animallike harmony with the ecosphere is only that: an ideal which neither can nor should be attained by contemporary humans. From their beginning, humans have been able to manipulate the natural world to a degree that no other animals have achieved. It is likely, for example, that the extinction of many large mammals at the end of the last ice age is the result of human hunters.

Usually such changes have been to the benefit of human populations, resulting in improved conditions and better living—for humans. Unfortunately, human modification of natural ecosystems has seldom, if ever, improved the condition of the ecosystem itself. Sometimes, human disruption of ecosystems has resulted in the lowering of the quality of life even for humans. All too often throughout history, well-functioning ecosystems have been converted into deserts, dust bowls, and cesspools. Clearly, though man may once have been simply a part of the ecosphere, and though he still depends upon it, he is capable of altering it drastically. There is something different about man. The anthropologist Loren Eisely sums up the grim side of that difference:

> It is with the coming of man that a vast hole seems to open in nature, a vast black whirlpool spinning faster and faster, consuming flesh, stones, soil, minerals, sucking down the lightning, wrenching power from the atom, until the ancient sounds of nature are drowned in the cacophony of something which is no longer nature, something instead which is loose and knocking at the world's heart, something demonic and no longer planned—escaped, it may be—spewed out of nature, contending in a final giant's game against its master.[1]

Though the Christian is not likely to agree completely with the picture of universal chaos which Eisely's words present, it is nevertheless important to understand the nature of those increasing disruptions of the ecosystem. And one of the greatest comes from our manipulation of ecosystems in order to grow food efficiently.

## AGRO-ECOSYSTEMS

Humankind has largely replaced prairie and forest ecosystems with systems of its own design: the "agro-ecosystems" of our farmlands, and the urban complexes of our towns and cities. This replacement of naturally balanced systems by ones which are man-managed has, in some cases, been successful. Soils have been maintained, and harvests have been sustained over centuries. Much of Europe and Japan has traditionally been farmed this way. Most of the plants and animals are under human care and control, but the resulting system is fertile and stable, without the need for large amounts of commercial fertilizers or fossil fuels.

But more often, our attempts at replacing natural ecosystems with synthetic ones end in failure. This is depressingly true of the current highly mechanized agriculture in North America. Increasingly, the principles which sustain the productivity of a natural ecosystem are ignored. They are replaced instead by an agriculture which draws largely on a diminishing supply of fossil fuel in order to produce crops more economically. As a result, nutrients once returned to the fields are now lost to creeks and rivers. As contour farming is abandoned, soils are exposed to wind and rain—a problem furthered when protective fencerows and windbreaks are removed to allow for more efficient mechanized farming. The traditional farm, which produced a variety of crops and maintained a variety of animals, is now replaced by farms which grow only one crop in great amounts.

In the United States, we already learned the painful consequences of carelessly replacing natural ecosystems with synthetic ones. But those lessons learned in the dust bowl days of the 1930s are being set aside once more in an attempt to produce ever more food with ever less labor. Increasing costs of labor and a steadily growing human population seem to justify such short-run measures. But the long-term costs are the declining fertility and stability of the soil.

This gradual decline in the productivity of agricultural land is world-wide. On marginal land good only for grazing—which makes up eight billion acres of the earth's thirty-two billion acres of land—over-grazing is rapidly transforming pasture into desert. And our record with the four to five billion acres of land most suitable for agriculture has not been much better. About 3.5 billion acres of such land are already under cultivation. The rest could be cultivated only at very high cost, largely because of the need for drainage and irrigation (see Figure 1).

In our replacement of natural with agricultural systems we have shown little concern for stability and longevity. The land has been cleared of its natural vegetation and planted with crops which leave soils exposed to wind and rain. In order to make up for the resulting loss of nutrients, we have had to use fertilizers on an increasingly large scale. The result, almost without exception, is that we have replaced ecosystems which had a yearly gain in topsoil with systems which have a yearly loss in topsoil. The complex natural system made up of many plants and animals has been replaced by simple systems with only one or two components. Self-regulating features have thus been destroyed; vital nutrients no longer recycle within the system, but escape to rivers, lakes, oceans, and the atmosphere.

This is not an overstatement of the situation. The United States, which as a result of the dust bowl years has been more sensitive to erosion than many other nations, still loses an average of twelve tons of topsoil per acre each year, while the annual rate of soil formation, under normal conditions, is only one-and-a-half tons per acre. Consequently, some fifty million tons of plant nutrients—nitrogen, phosphorus, potassium—are lost each year

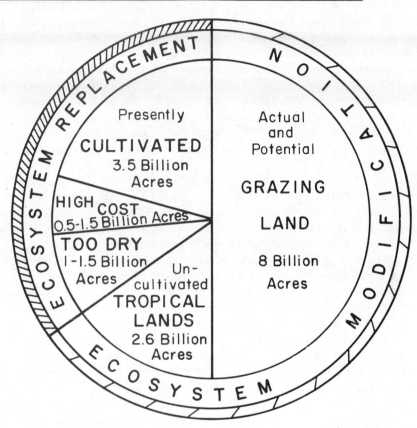

Figure 1:1 Breakdown of the earth's land areas suitable for food production. Some 4 to 5 billion acres, including a presently-cultivated 3.5 billion acres, is available for agriculture by replacement of natural ecosystems with synthetic ones. Based on data from Miller (1975) and National Academy of Sciences (1969).[2]

from U.S. cropland, at a yearly replacement cost of some seven billion dollars. And that loss of nutrients from the land produces too much fertility in the water—lakes eutrophy through excessive fertilization, and become choked with plant growth.

In any one year, the loss of topsoil does not result in a very significant crop loss. Thus people with short-term interests in land—land speculators and tenant farmers, for instance—may not notice the continuous erosion of the cultivated soil, and may do nothing to stop it.

This loss in a corn field amounts to about a half bushel of corn per acre—worth less than one percent of the total production cost and insignificant relative to the total. Since the total production cost per acre is about

$190, the loss is insignificant in any one year. In time, however, those continuing losses add up. Figure 2, which is based on data from field studies, shows that a field of corn with a typical twenty-ton-per-acre soil loss decreases steadily in yield, so that after a century the yield is only half. Whether the farmer applies large or small amounts of fertilizer, yield still decreases. For those who have only a short-term interest in the land, these decreases are unimportant. Persons who expect to pass the farm on to their children, on the other hand, are likely to take better care of the soil—but by doing so, they will not be able to compete with those who farm the land for maximum short-term yield.

There is, however, a way of farming which sustains the soil's productivity—thus duplicating the effect of the natural ecosystem. If corn is grown only twice during a five-year period, as part of a corn–corn–oats–pasture–pasture sequence, the result is a slight *increase* in topsoil (Figure 3). The middle curve in the diagram, which describes continuous corn–cropping and declining yields, is the one which appears to be most feasible, but which, in the long run, represents very poor management of resources. Even poorer is the intensive cultivation represented by the bottom curve. Yet for those who hold land near a city, expecting to sell it soon for industrial or residential development, such destructive agriculture is all too common. Reinforcing the trend is the fact that the poorer the land becomes for food production, the more reasonable it seems to convert it to urban uses.

The consequences of these agricultural policies are grim. Agriculture in the United States is, in most regions, more than a hundred years old. The average depth of the American topsoil is seven or eight inches, down from an original average of more than twelve inches. By 1935, erosion had already ruined about 100 million acres of cropland, some of which has now been restored to forests. When we consider that the total present cropland area in the United States is about 400 million acres, such vast and continuing losses give great cause for worry. It is clear that we have replaced self-perpetuating natural ecosystems with short-term, destructive human ones. Our agriculture increasingly operates on principles different from those of the rest of the ecosphere. Consequently, good stewardship is rare. And where it is practiced, it usually requires economic sacrifice, because current economic principles often operate within too short a time horizon to encourage the long-term preservation of those very soils we depend upon for food.

## THE THREAT OF URBAN EXPANSION

Thus far we have spoken of the *quality* of the land entrusted to us. And, whether we speak of the disruption of natural ecosystems or of the declining productivity of agricultural land, it is clear that human activity has affected that quality adversely. But the *quantity* of productive land is also threatened, particularly by the expansion of cities onto agricultural land. It

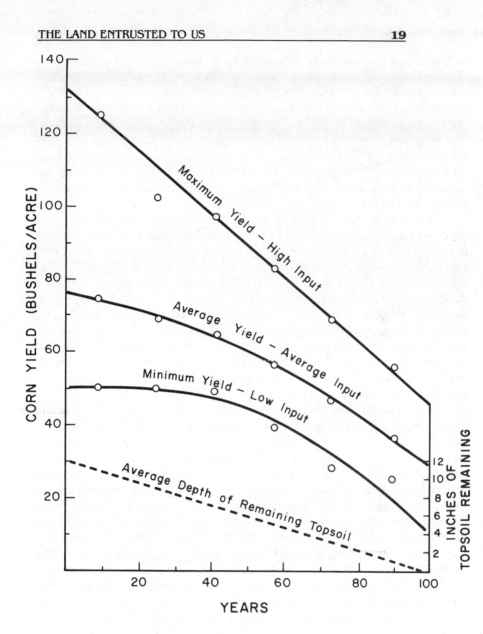

Figure 1:2 Decline of corn yields and topsoil under three different levels of management: high fertilizer and other technology, low fertilizer and other technology, and an intermediate case. Graph constructed on the basis of (1) data for corn yields as a function of topsoil depth and technology input and (2) data on acreage loss of U.S. topsoil. Based upon data compiled by Pimental (1976).[3]

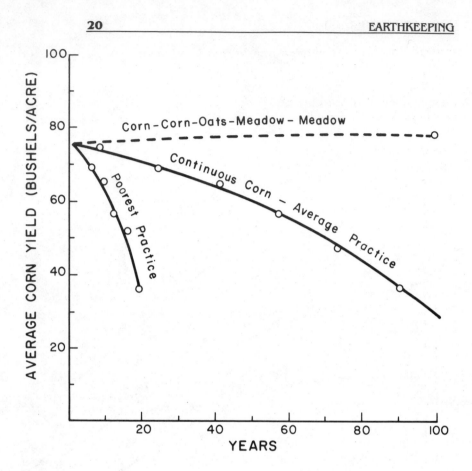

Figure 1:3 Corn yield under three management programs. Based upon data compiled by Pimental (1976).[4]

will be helpful to review briefly the pressures which cities place upon productive land. We will do so by concentrating on the situation in America—though similar pressures are present all over the world.

The towns and villages of the American Midwest—the world's most productive agricultural area—were built to serve agriculture. The farmers of the great plains and the newly cleared forest lands of the Midwest needed places to which they could bring their harvests, buy provisions, seeds, and implements, and attend church. Thus as farms spread across the Midwest, villages sprang up, spaced about a day's wagon-journey apart and usually arranged along the major routes from the farmland to the marketplaces of large cities. Where agriculture is limited, by poor soil or low rainfall (as is the case further west), towns and villages are sparse.

But the towns which once served agriculture exclusively have since diversified. With the coming of labor-saving farm machinery, fewer people were needed to work the farms. Instead, new industries and new jobs were created in town. As these commercial and industrial enterprises grew, new residential areas grew to serve their employees. Towns which were once placed on agricultural land in order to serve the farmers have turned away from agriculture, spreading out over the adjacent fertile soil which once nourished a farm town. So it is that the finest agricultural land in America is often the first to be consumed by the growth of the cities. Though this pattern is most evident in the Midwest, it is characteristic of most American cities. Around Seattle, for example, the only Class I soil in the county is long since buried under a shopping center.

The pattern of consuming cropland near cities was intensified by the invention of the automobile: the resulting cheap transportation has put most of the best U.S. cropland within commuting range of large cities. And since most Americans want to live in a suburban or rural setting, the spreading suburbs are rapidly devouring good farmland.

Other factors encourage this rapid conversion of farms to cities. Although the U.S. population rate is growing less rapidly, and is likely to stabilize within a few decades, the amount of land used per family for residential purposes is steadily increasing. Young cities reveal this fact by their low population densities; cities which grew large before the automobile have a much higher density. And within the commuting zone of any large city the trend is clearly evident: lot sizes grow progressively larger as one moves from the city to the suburbs. In most cases, that increased space is bought at the price of decreased farmland.

At least one other factor affects this rapid conversion of agricultural land to urban purposes: the number of households. Though the average family size in the United States is indeed declining, the demand for housing does not decline proportionately. Each family, whether it has eight members or two, needs a place to live. Thus the demand for housing remains very high. And since most people prefer to live on the fringes of the cities, that growing fringe is devouring farmland.

The result of this growing demand for residential land is the estimated yearly displacement of a million acres of the best cropland from a base of about 400 million acres. And this estimate is probably too low; the U.S. Soil Conservation Service puts the loss at 1.7 million acres a year.

There is usually not much concern for the problem on the part of city councils and chambers of commerce. Macomb County, Michigan, for example, recently boasted in its promotional materials that over forty acres of farmland every week were elevated to urban use. That attitude of welcoming "higher" uses and discouraging farming is typical of the "growth mentality" shown by most cities.

Obviously, such pressure on farmland threatens our base for food production. But it is indirectly responsible for another problem. We are compensating for disappearing farmland by putting new lands into production. This new farmland comes from draining marshes, irrigating the dry soil of the west, clearing still more forests, and putting marginal lands back into production. In most cases, the expansion of agriculture into these new areas means less room for dwindling wildlife. And in all cases, it means greater expenditure in dollars and energy for transporting, irrigating, and fertilizing, often resulting in higher food prices.

How long can such a trend continue? United States Soil Conservation Service data indicate that 112 million acres not presently in production could be used for agriculture, but such conversion would be at the expense of 82 million acres of pasture and 24 million acres of forests, which together include 23 million acres of wetlands.

The value of forests and wetlands in maintaining the quality of soil, water, and wildlife is so great that the acceptability of such losses must be seriously questioned. So too must the advisability of using marginal lands which were, in many cases, removed from production in the first place because of erosion problems.

Our record of learning from the structure of divinely created ecosystems is not a good one. Natural ecosystems are characterized by diversity; we replace them with systems which contain but a single species. Natural ecosystems match gains with losses; our agro-ecosystems lose more than they gain, and make little use of recycled materials. Natural ecosystems continue over centuries; man's replacement ecosystems are short-lived.

The solution to these problems is not to give up agriculture. It is rather to develop enough humility to learn from the functioning of the created world. And we must have the economic foresight and courage to apply responsibly what we learn.

### CHAPTER 2

# THE CREATURES UNDER OUR CARE

*To most people, talk of "endangered species" evokes images of tigers under siege in Asia and cheetahs losing ground in Africa, of whales hunted to scarcity in the Antarctic and whooping cranes clinging to life in North America. . . . At risk, the scientists say, are not just hundreds of familiar and appealing birds and mammals. Examination of the survival prospects of all forms of plant and animal life—including obscure ferns, shrubs, insects, mollusks, as well as elephants and wolves—indicates that huge numbers of them have little future. Not hundreds, but hundreds of thousands of unique, irreplaceable life forms may vanish by the century's end.*
— Erik Eckholm, DISAPPEARING SPECIES: THE SOCIAL CHALLENGE

I n the foregoing chapter we considered mainly the land—or, more precisely, the ecosphere. There our concern was with the overall health of ecosystems, from the stable complexity of a forest to the precarious simplicity of a wheat field. In either case, the emphasis thus far has been on the whole pattern, not on individual parts of it. In these next two chapters, however, we will narrow our consideration to the particular creatures supported by that ecosphere and to the effects of human activity on those creatures. There are two chapters in this discussion of the earth's creatures because there are, at least from the human viewpoint, two sorts of creatures: humans on the one hand, and plants and animals on the other. And, as the foregoing survey of our uses of the land suggests, we humans have not been hesitant to shove other creatures aside when we feed at the planet's wealth. In this chapter, then, we will consider the health of nonhuman creatures on an increasingly human-dominated planet. And in the following chapter we will consider the physical welfare of humanity itself on the planet which it dominates.

We began the previous chapter by recalling the now-familiar sight of the earth from space. There is no better way to reflect on the marvel of the planet's life. But, in one sense, that blue green vision of vitality is misleading, for the sizeable human disruptions of the ecosystem are invisible from a distance. Had there been observers on the moon for the thousands of years of human history, they might not have known we were here. To such observers, the colors of the planet would still be blue, green, and shifting white; the seasons would tint the continents; the great white spirals of storms would still move slowly across the surface; and the edges of the crescent earth would be smudged, now as ten thousand years ago, with the blur of atmosphere. Despite many millennia of agriculture and a century and a half of industry, the main features of our ecosphere are unchanged. Despite erosion, smog, and creeping cities, the planet is still green and living—at least from a distance. Even from a low earth orbit—say, a hundred miles up—the difference between natural and agricultural systems is hard to notice.

In the past chapter we catalogued some of the consequences of our alterations to the ecosphere, more visible to us than to an observer on the moon: the substitution of wheat fields for prairies, for example, or lawns and shrubs for beech-maple forests. But apart from some unpleasant economic consequences (like higher prices for food) the differences between a natural ecosystem and a farm, or between a soil-sustaining farm and a soil-destroying one, are increasingly inconsequential to those humans for whom the ecosphere is mainly irrelevant background. So long as we have air, water, and food, the changes in the ecosphere over the last ten thousand years—and especially over the last century—are hardly more visible to us than they would be to an observer on the moon. The fine points of the ecosphere are too often not our concern.

In the same way, the average dweller in London or Paris sees that all is well on the skyline of his city. It is only the eccentric or the specialist who notices that the saints and gargoyles of the cathedrals have, in the past few decades, dissolved like leprous flesh in the automotive air. It is just as difficult, at first, to notice the changes in the great cathedral of creation. The outline is the same; the ecosystems still function. But in the niches and cornices of the ecosphere, the fine work blurs and crumbles. Whole species dwindle and vanish. And though the outline of the system may be roughly the same, creation, like a cathedral in the city, becomes more and more like a vast hollow shell, stripped of its original intricacy.

It is our purpose in this chapter, then, to move beyond the main features of the ecosphere and to look at some details, particularly at some instances of the threatened and dwindling diversity of those million species of living things that fill the niches of our temple, the earth.

What the Psalmist exclaimed about himself is true of all creatures: they are "fearfully and wonderfully made." Indeed (as we will see in a later chapter), God answers Job's complaints about his management by pointing out the intricacy and strangeness of the world he made. He says of the hippopotamus (or "behemoth"):

Behold, Behemoth,
   which I made as I made you;
   he eats grass like an ox.
Behold, his strength in his loins,
   and his power in the muscles of his belly.
He makes his tail stiff like a cedar;
   the sinews of his thighs are knit together.
His bones are tubes of bronze,
   his limbs like bars of iron.
He is the first of the works of God;
   let him who made him bring near his sword!
                (Job 40:15–19)

Whether or not we have marveled thus at a hippopotamus, the principle is clear: cedars, whales, dragonflies—and hippopotami—are of value for themselves and for what they declare of the Creator. Their use to humans is not particularly important, nor even is their importance to the creation as a whole. They are not just parts of a system, but are exultantly unique and individual. They are works of God, which he made and we can only destroy. And when we destroy the last individuals of a species, we cannot recreate them. Instead, the splendor of creation as a whole is diminished.

To be sure, extinction is a natural process; that is, it takes place apart from human influence. Creation is a continuing process, and it involves change not only in the physical environment, but in the creatures who live in that environment. And if creation is a dynamic and changing work of divine art, Christians should not understand their task to be freezing that flux at one particular point. Yet neither should they accelerate that change by eliminating a habitat for cranes, hunting pigeons to extinction, or rendering all remaining sea mammals into oil. All of these things we have done, or are in the process of doing. For the pressing needs of the human population for food, minerals, energy, and living space are inexorably reducing the chances for life of most other creatures on the planet.

As we shall see in a later section, Christians have strong biblical reasons for developing a way of life which treats the rest of creation with great care. But there are other reasons even apart from those which Christians hold because of a personal relationship to the Creator. Humans should be concerned for the maintenance of the full diversity of created things, for those things make up an irreplaceable genetic reservoir from which to draw new sources of food and other materials in the years to come.

If we should succeed in eliminating from the earth all life except what we have an immediate use for, the tragedy would not be only for that other life and a few "nature lovers." For in so doing we would eliminate most of that source of living potential which enables us to breed new plants and animals. One source of hope in an otherwise discouraging long-range outlook for world food production is the improvement of food crops for higher yield, more resistance to disease and drought, higher food value, and so forth. For example, the purpose of the International Crops Research Institute for the Semi-Arid Tropics, situated in India, is the making of such improvements of food plants. One of its main ways of doing so is to search out undiscovered, undomesticated species of pigeon peas, chickpeas, sorghum, or millet. Such new strains increase the genetic resources from which human food crops can be improved.

A second reason for maintaining plant and animal diversity is that such a variety allows us to gain knowledge of our own bodily functions—particularly through study of creatures in which those functions are exaggerated through response to a particular environment. For example, the function of the kidney in desert kangaroo rats, adapted as they are to the scarcity of water in desert environments, has contributed much to our knowledge of the functioning of the normal human kidney. In the same way, the giant nerve cells of seagoing squids provide an excellent tool for understanding the function of human nerves.

There are many other human-centered reasons for preserving various forms of life: possible new drugs such as quinine and antibiotics; biological pest control; a fuller understanding of how ecosystems function in order to maintain the livability of increasingly manipulated systems; and so on. And, of course, there is wide interest in preserving species on aesthetic grounds.

Despite the merit of all these reasons for preserving animal and plant life, for the Christian the fundamental reason is still unselfish: humans are designated as stewards, or guardians, over creation. And today we, like Noah, are presented with a threat to the earth's life and are given the task of preserving it.

On the whole, we have done poorly at that task, and there is little to indicate that the Christian vision has improved the generally destructive human attitude toward the rest of creation. Humankind has exploited much life to extinction, or near it. The catalogue of examples is not a pleasant perspective on human history. In North America, the list of endangered animals is long and depressing. There are perhaps 800 grizzly bears left in the country and 400 timber wolves. Despite their important role as "top carnivores" in the food chain, they have been regarded as "varmints" through most of our history—"critters," not creatures—and only recently, by removing the bounty, have we stopped paying people to exterminate them.

The Atlantic salmon, which once thronged up pure Eastern rivers, is rarely seen. The great ivory-billed woodpecker—once hunted for food and feathers—has not been sighted for twenty years. Bald eagles are scarce, and the peregrine falcon is extinct south of Canada. Elsewhere, the once-expansive forests we know as the cedars of Lebanon have been reduced to twelve small and scattered groves (Figure 1). And even these few remaining stands would have perished if it had not been for the stewardly care given the

From *The New Yorker*, September 17, 1979. Drawing by H. Martin; © 1979
The New Yorker Magazine, Inc. Used by permission.

"For your own good I'm telling you that I'm loaded with pesticides."

From *Audubon*. Used by permission of Jan van Wessum.

species by a few monks who preserved the trees near their chapels. An even grimmer story is that of the whale. There are perhaps 400 blue whales—the largest of all animals—left in the oceans. It is doubtful now that the members of this decimated and intelligent species will even be able to find each other to reproduce. Many Americans deplore the fact that Japan continues to hunt the whale, yet it was largely the efficiency of Western factory-ship whaling earlier in this century which brought the great whales so close to extinction.

The extinction or near extinction of whales, wolves, great auks, bison, and passenger pigeons is something we can all abhor. It was for the most part blatant and deliberate, and the animals were attacked directly. But such conscious exploitation is only a small part of the problem. Much more serious than such direct actions is the destruction of the animals' habitat. And for such destruction we are all responsible: in our increasing use of land for homes, in our increasingly efficient agriculture, in our mining and processing of mineral resources, we are diminishing the living space of nonhuman creatures.

In building homes, we alter the landscape. Some of the land is covered with buildings; rainwater runoff increases, due to large areas of impervious materials on rooftops and roadways. Homeowners in wooded areas remove trees to allow sunlight for lawns; plants and animals are thus left with no habitat, and die. Drainage patterns are altered to remove unpleasant wetness; creeks are replaced with storm sewers, and moisture-dependent species are eliminated. Gradual marsh borders are replaced with sharp, neat banks, destroying the moisture gradient on which a complex of plants and animals depend—each with its slightly different water level requirements. Thus herons no longer have a place to fish. And mosquitoes multiply in the absence of dragonflies, which depend on marsh-edge vegetation for metamorphosis from aquatic nymphs into flying, mosquito-eating adults.

Threats to natural habitats occur on every continent, especially in those areas of heavy rain forests where an incredible diversity of nature is manifested. The variety of woody plant species growing on the slopes of a single volcano in the Philippines is greater than that of the entire United States. The Amazon Basin, with Southeast Asia close behind, may contain up to a million plant and animal species. Such areas are biologically the richest regions on earth.[1]

In providing for our food needs, we have replaced prairies and deciduous forests with agriculture. Consequently, we have moved many creatures near extinction by taking away their habitat. As the pressures for more efficient food production increase, seminatural areas on the farm become more costly to maintain; consequently, fencerows, marshes, and woodlots are removed. And, as we saw in the previous chapter, the removal each year of a million acres of land from agriculture for roads and suburbs places ever greater pressure on remaining wild areas; woods are eliminated, marshes drained, and arid lands are irrigated for crops.

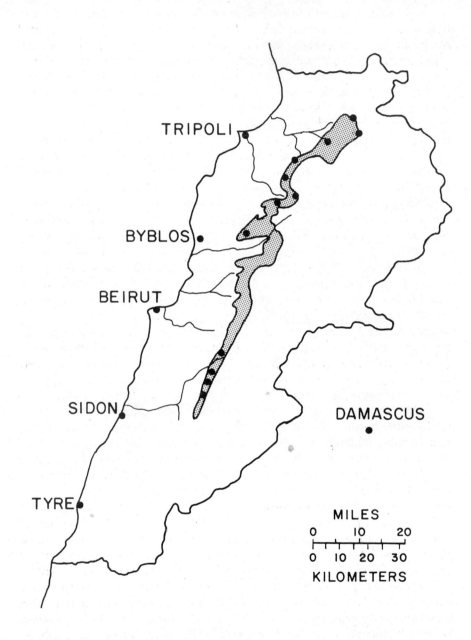

Figure 2:1 Cedars of Lebanon groves today (black dots) compared with original distribution (shaded areas). Based upon the article, "The Deforestation of Mount Lebanon" by Mikesell (1969).[2]

The destruction of wildlife habitat extends to our use of forests. Though large tracts of first, second, and third growth forest remain in the United States, there is an increasing need for wood—for lumber, paper, and fuel. Old policies of selective cutting are being abandoned—especially in the West—for "even-age management." Such practices turn forests into tree farms. The danger in such a move is not in the concept of farming—and hence, harvesting—trees, but rather, that some of the destructively single-purpose methods of modern agriculture are being applied to forest management, with the same grim consequences for the diversity and health of the ecosystem. Increasingly, tree farms are planting one species of tree, which is bred for maximum wood production in a short period of time. There is no room in such "forests" for trees which grow slowly or produce unusable wood. Underbrush is discouraged. Nothing is done to encourage nonusable wildlife, and it is tolerated only if it does no damage. Black bears, for example, are a nuisance in the tree farms of the West because they tend to destroy seedlings. Where possible, the bears are being removed. Obviously, the consequences of such a silviculture leave little room for nonuseful species. Yet there are more subtle effects. Since all of a tree is viewed as a crop, dead and rotting trees or fallen, unused limbs are seen as an economic crime. No wood should be wasted—that is, nothing should rot. But that rotting, as we saw in the previous chapter, is the first stage in a process that supports not only the health of the very soil, but the worms and insects which are the foundation of the whole complex pyramid of an ecosystem. It is little wonder, then, that there is little room outside wilderness areas for creatures for which we have no immediate use.

The wealth of mineral resources—coal, peat, sand, metal ores, and so forth—have become as crucial to human needs as food itself. Yet the extraction of these materials also places pressures on living space for nonhuman life. In many places such materials are strip-mined. And in order to get at the deposit, the "overburden" must be removed. "Overburden" is a conveniently vague term, for it includes not only "worthless" rock, but also the soil, the bacteria, the plants, the animals which live in it. In short, to remove the "overburden" is to remove a piece of the ecosystem. In some cases, a kind of ecosystem has been established in an area after it has been mined. But even in these rare cases, the life that was there before was incomparably more complex and resilient than the agriculturally managed replacement.

There are many of these trade-off situations: marshes and swamps are being seen as valuable tertiary sewage treatment plants; sand dunes, with their vibrant cover of life, as raw material for making glass; and trees, from cedars of Lebanon to redwoods, are understood as lumber in the rough. In none of these solutions to human problems is there any room for the creature—bird, beast, tree, or flower—which has no value as a crop.

There are, of course, some exceptions. The Endangered Species Act in the United States prohibits destruction of the environment of an endangered species. This admirable law has enraged and amused many people in recent years, having halted a power plant in the Northeast for threatening the furbish lousewort and a similar project in the Southeast for threatening the snail darter.

Such situations present us with a real dilemma. How much right does a species have to live? A dam may (through flood control) save hundreds of human lives, and may also provide jobs and power for human well-being and happiness. What if the only price of such a project is the loss from the planet of the two-inch snail darter? Would it not be worth it? What if our own life were at stake, or our children's? Would we not choose their lives over the perpetuation of a small fish? We may justly criticize the destruction of ecosystems and the dwindling or extinction of animal life. But our own standard of living—at least in Western society—has risen as the vigor of many species has declined. Does the benefit to us equal the cost to the nonhuman? These are difficult questions, which we will not attempt to answer until we have looked at the situation from several other perspectives. But one thing is clear: the dynamics of human civilization leave little room for plants and animals for which we have no use.

The impact of our activity on natural ecosystems is often not very obvious, however. As we noted at the beginning of this chapter, an observer from the moon would see the earth as green now as it was a thousand years ago. But again, it is the quality of the life which has diminished. This is particularly obvious when one considers the kinds of creatures that surround the average North American dwelling place. On the farm, they are corn, wheat, rice, sheep, and cattle. In suburbs and on farms there may be dandelions, chickweed, plantains, cats, rats, cockroaches, European house sparrows, European rock doves, and European starlings. Such plants and animals—wanted or not—form part of a human "ethno-ecosystem"—a pattern of life which accompanies human settlement, and which, in our case, has followed us to the New World from Europe and Asia.

Now European dandelions are as worthy a flower as an American counterpart—say, an orange hawkweed. Likewise, a starling is a bird as interesting and worthy as a red-winged blackbird.* The problem is not that alien species—be they weeds, trees, or songbirds—are inferior; rather, what is of concern is the displacement of native species. The more their living space is taken over by alien species, the more likely we are to see a diminishing of the carefully designed harmony of the ecosphere. Sometimes, as on the disturbed floodplains of rivers (which is a preferred location for many

---

*The starling got its start on this continent when a wealthy American developed a hobby of introducing into the country all the birds mentioned in Shakespeare's plays. Nightingales and cuckoos, alas, did not prosper. But the starlings thrived so much that they have become a colossal nuisance, requiring large-scale efforts at extermination. Millions at a time have been killed by spraying on the birds a mixture which renders them susceptible to cold.

American towns), we use native trees: American elm, or sycamore, or silver maple. Some native birds and animals have prospered, too, especially those which like the continuous edge between trees and lawn—robins, cardinals, and squirrels—or those which like human garbage—raccoons, for example. But in the majority of cases, native species diminish rather than prosper as human civilization brings with it the plants and animals which have made a more successful adaptation to the activities of man the steward.

But of course we must ask the question whether this diminishing of all life that does not fit in with human activity is indeed good stewardship. The answer would seem to be "no," and from the perspective of nonhuman life, human activity is beginning to look like a new deluge. And there is an ever greater need for new Noahs.

"We just ran a test on your river water, . . . it *will* support life, in fact, you can walk on it."

From *Industrial Research*, January 1971. Copyright 1971, *Industrial Research*. Used by permission.

### CHAPTER 3

# THE HUMAN TIDE ___

*It is just one of the stark facts of this century that man is not only getting more numerous, but wanting more. Hs is pressing harder than ever in the history of the world into what used to be unexploited, or lightly exploited habitats. And every time he makes a move of this kind, there are new ecological disturbances.*

—Charles Elton,
**THE PATTERNS OF ANIMAL BEHAVIOR**

The relationship between the health of man and the health of the land is as old as Eden. But in the past, the earth was vast enough and humans scarce enough that poor human stewardship of resources did not seem very consequential. At worst, a people could always move to undisturbed land and start over. This illusion of endless resources was encouraged by the first two centuries of North American experience in the New World.

But the vast increase in human population in recent years has suddenly brought the limits of the earth's productivity—as well as the decline in the earth's environmental health—home to us with startling suddenness. There are now 4.4 billion people on the earth—an increase of some 2 billion beyond the population just 35 years ago. But it is not only the unprecedented increase in population which threatens the continuing health of the planet. It is also that the human use of machines and fossil fuels has enormously multiplied our ability to dominate the earth. It is now common for a single person to wield the power of a hundred men. Though it is true that only a relatively small percentage of the earth's population have such power available, so spectacular have the consequences of that power been that the rest of the earth's peoples either fear it or seek it. Today when we speak of development in the Third World, we frequently mean development which will give individuals of other nations an equivalent power.

The result of this dramatic increase in both the number of humans and in the power available to them is (as we saw in the previous chapters) a great increase in demands for land, food, and other resources. The demands for land have resulted in human expansion into almost every habitable area—usually at the expense of the ecosphere. Grazing of marginal arid land in Africa and the attempted clearing of the Brazilian jungle are only two large-scale instances of this expansion. Demands for food result in drastic alteration of ecosystems and threats to the stability of the whole natural order; alien species are introduced, and native species are diminished, replaced, and destroyed.

Thus it is necessary for us to consider the increasing human impact on natural resources, which is in turn a consequence of our increasing population and our increasing technology. And it is necessary to consider the worldwide need for that basic resource, food. For it is mainly because of our need for food that we have made such unprecedented demands on the fabric of the earth's ecosystems.

## BASIC HUMAN FOOD NEEDS

Apart from superficial differences owing to physical size and level of activity, adult humans all over the world require about the same amount of food. We need that food for two reasons: to provide the energy necessary for work, and to provide materials to build, maintain, and repair our bodies.

The need for energy is measured in calories. A calorie is the amount of heat needed to raise the temperature of a kilogram of water one degree Celsius. Ultimately, then, the world food need is an energy problem. Food is fuel, burned in the organic furnace of our bodies. Each person in the world needs, on the average, about 2200 calories a day of that organic fuel, food.

The other food need—materials for growth and maintenance—is measured in weight units: grams, milligrams, ounces. Of these materials, proteins are of particular interest. These complex substances, derived from animals and plants, are essential for human life. Proteins are made up of amino acids. Some of these amino acids can be synthesized from other substances, but others cannot be made by our bodies, and must therefore be part of our diet. The body's need for protein is not related to how active we are, as is our caloric need. Rather, these needs are a result of the biological demands for raw materials needed for growth, maintenance, or repair. Persons who have a particular need for protein, therefore, are growing children, nursing mothers, and those undergoing healing processes.

Proteins vary in quality—in suitability for the body's needs. Thus, in addition to differences in people's need for protein, there are differences in the capacity of various foods to meet those needs. Animal protein is more accessible to the body's metabolism than is most plant protein; therefore, it usually is necessary to eat more plant protein than animal protein to provide the same amount for the body. There are exceptions, however, as some kinds of plant protein, when combined with others, complement each other and are adequate substitutes for meat. For example, a diet of rice provides inadequate protein, as does a diet of beans, but a diet of rice and beans *eaten together* will provide all the amino acids necessary for the body's needs. On the average, the body needs about seventy grams, or 2.5 ounces, of protein per day.

### Food Needs Per Person

The immediate reason for inadequate food in the world is the lack of the resources—money, land, and so forth—for obtaining food. The ability to purchase food increases as the standard of living rises. As a country becomes wealthier, the per-person demand for food increases. Unfortunately, however, that demand for food often exceeds—by large margins—those basic minimal requirements for calories and protein.

One result of this excessive food demand on the part of the wealthier countries is simply that people eat too much—overweight is a major problem in North America. A more serious problem is not that people demand extra helpings of things, but rather that they demand high-quality protein—specifically, beef. To meet the world's protein needs we could use our land to grow protein-rich crops, which, when eaten in the proper combination, would provide the bulk of our protein requirements. Instead, we use a large percentage of our cropland in North America to grow feed for livestock. Ultimately we eat the livestock, but by the time grain gets converted into beef, about 90 percent of the original protein has been lost.

This is not to say, of course, that it is wrong to eat beef. Nor does it imply that it is wrong to raise beef. Much range land can grow no other crops besides those suitable for grazing. But for millions of acres of cropland in North America we have the choice: do we grow crops for food or crops for feed?

Obviously, when human food needs are met by eating the protein-rich crops directly, instead of by eating the animals to which they are usually fed, a given amount of land can feed many more people. The result is less pressure on those dwindling wild areas we discussed in the previous chapter; it is also more food for the increasingly hungry human population. It is important not to oversimplify the problem here. There is a good deal to be said for the high-quality protein of livestock, which can be maintained as a kind of buffer. Excess grain can be fed to cattle in "fat" years; those cattle can be killed and eaten in "lean" years. Agricultural societies have operated this way for centuries. Nevertheless, it is clear that the demand of affluent countries for a high-meat diet is a great drain on the availability of both food for other humans and habitat for the earth's nonhuman creatures. Figure 1 provides a good summary of the impact of different diets on the amount of real food eaten. The consumption of animal products, as shown in the shaded area, has an impact on the food-producing system many times greater than it would be if the land producing feed were used instead to produce food

"Give us this day our daily meat. . . ."

From *Christianity Today*, April 27, 1973. © 1973 by John Lawing. Used by permission.

"Their breeding rate is incredible."

From the *Grand Rapids Press*, April 4, 1969. Used by permission of Bill Mauldin and Wil-Jo Associates, Inc.

directly for humans. Though it is not possible for a person to sustain a food consumption of 10,000 calories per day, we effectively do so when we eat a high-meat diet, for we are eating animals fed from land which could feed people.

Pointing out the intrinsic wastefulness of a high-beef diet is likely to make most of us uncomfortable about our eating habits. And it probably should. But at this point, we are not concerned with arousing feelings of guilt over last night's dinner or the contents of the family refrigerator. Our purpose is rather to provide an understanding of the worldwide need for adequate food and of the pressure which that demand places on the earth's productivity. At least a half billion of the world's 4.4 billion people are starving or severely malnourished. At least that many more people are barely able to eat enough to supply their basic bodily needs. These people lack food because they lack resources. An increase in resources would multiply their demand for food, but it would place even greater pressure on both our food supplies and on the dwindling natural ecosystems of the earth. Even if there were no further increase in world population (and there unavoidably will be a great increase, as the last part of this chapter makes plain), to bring all people in the world to our level of diet would require a fourfold increase in the land's productivity. It is questionable—in view of the destructive tendencies of modern agriculture outlined in an earlier chapter—whether man's managed ecosystems can survive such an increase even if it were possible. Clearly, then, a concern both for the world's poor and for the maintenance of the healthy diversity of the ecosphere suggests that large-scale changes are needed in the diet to which most North Americans have become accustomed. Are we willing to reduce our own personal impact on the food production system? For reasons of economic and political survival, we, or our children, might *have* to. But for reasons of compassion, love, and stewardly responsibility—not to mention for reasons of personal health—we might *want* to reduce our consumption. In either case, some sort of change in diet seems inevitable for North Americans in the near future. As Christians, we must determine whether that change will be forced upon us, or whether we will be leaders in effecting it.

## HUMAN POPULATION GROWTH

A cloud on the horizon of any discussion of resource use is the awesome, inexorable increase in human population. All of the problems of resource use that we have discussed thus far—whether we speak of energy needs, mineral needs, food needs, or impact on the ecosphere—are already problems under present levels of population. But the increase in population means that the problems can only become more severe. And that increase is magnified in turn by the efforts of poorer nations to achieve the scale of

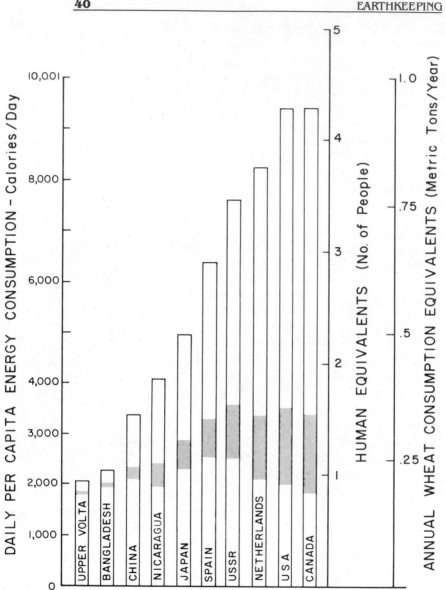

Figure 3:1 Food consumption per person for various nations, showing the effects of consumption of grain-based animal products. The length of the clear area containing the name of the nation indicates the daily per-capita consumption of non-animal foods, while the shaded area represents the consumption of animal-product calories. The total length of each bar represents the total equivalent calorie consumption of each nation, based on the conservative assumption that the average calorie input in grain fed to animals is five times greater than the number of calories delivered as usable animal-derived food. Data from various U.N. sources.

consumption established as a model by the industrialized world, particularly by North America.

Despite all that has been said recently in books, newspapers, and on television, not many of the world's burgeoning billions understand the unprecedented scale or danger of the current population increase. In 1950, a time well within the memory of many readers of this book, there were 1,800,000,000 fewer people on earth than there are today. When we consider that this number is (for example) 450 times greater than the population of the entire state of Wisconsin, nine times the population of the United States, and twice the population of China, we begin to realize the magnitude and speed of the increase.

We have spoken in the previous chapter of the impact of expanding agricultural land on the remaining natural ecosystems. Population growth figures make us see that destructive expansion is understandable, if not inevitable. For if we allow the bare minimum of one acre (208 feet by 208 feet) for the production of each person's food needs, the amount of land needed to feed that increase from 1950 to 1980 would require more than four times the area of existing U.S. cropland.

This enormous increase in population is disturbing enough. It took all of human history—from the beginning of humanity to about 1940—to reach the first 2 billion people. The next 2 billion was added in a scant 35 years. If our present rate of increase continues, another 2 billion will be added in less than 20 years.

The current time taken for the human population to double in size is about 38 years. Thus a population of 4 billion becomes 8 billion in 38 years; in the succeeding 38 years it becomes 16 billion. This rate of increase is remarkably high for any human population at any time in human history. One can readily test this by reducing in half the present world population of 4.4 billion to 2.2 billion, and halving it again and again, as is shown in Table 1. It takes only 31 "halvings" to reduce the population to two people. Put the other way around, a population of 2 becomes a population of 4.4 billion after doubling 31 times. If we assume that each of those previous doublings of the human population took place in our current time of 38 years, we find the date of Adam and Eve to be 802 A.D.! Even if we take a doubling time of 100 years, we press the beginning of humanity back to only 1120 B.C., 3100 years ago.

Obviously, humanity has been around much longer than 3100 years. This exercise is only a way of illustrating that the present doubling time of 38 years—or less—is highly unusual. It has not long been in effect in the past, and cannot be in effect very long in the future. For all practical purposes, then, ZPG (Zero Population Growth), an idea which seems radical to many today, was the norm throughout most of human history, when birth rates were nearly equal to death rates.

At least in the developed, industrialized nations there has been an im-

Table 1.
Population Levels for 31 Doublings

The population figures shown below were produced by halving the 1980 estimated population time after time, rounding off appropriately, until an initial population of two persons was reached. The column labeled "Year" gives the date for each doubling, using the present doubling time of 38 years. Note that if population had always increased at its present rate, Adam and Eve would have to have been created in 802 A.D.!

| Doubling Period | Year (A.D.) | Population |
|---|---|---|
| 31 | 1980 | 4,400,000,000 |
| 30 | 1942 | 2,200,000,000 |
| 29 | 1904 | 1,100,000,000 |
| 28 | 1866 | 550,000,000 |
| 27 | 1828 | 275,000,000 |
| 26 | 1790 | 137,500,000 |
| 25 | 1752 | 68,750,000 |
| 24 | 1714 | 34,375,000 |
| 23 | 1676 | 17,187,500 |
| 22 | 1638 | 8,593,750 |
| 21 | 1600 | 4,296,875 |
| 20 | 1562 | 2,148,437 |
| 19 | 1524 | 1,074,218 |
| 18 | 1486 | 537,109 |
| 17 | 1448 | 268,554 |
| 16 | 1410 | 134,277 |
| 15 | 1372 | 67,138 |
| 14 | 1334 | 33,569 |
| 13 | 1296 | 16,784 |
| 12 | 1258 | 8,392 |
| 11 | 1220 | 4,196 |
| 10 | 1182 | 2,098 |
| 9 | 1144 | 1,049 |
| 8 | 1106 | 524 |
| 7 | 1068 | 262 |
| 6 | 1030 | 131 |
| 5 | 992 | 65 |
| 4 | 954 | 32 |
| 3 | 916 | 16 |
| 2 | 878 | 8 |
| 1 | 840 | 4 |
| 0 | 802 | 2 |

plicit recognition of this problem of population increase, and in those countries moves to control it are meeting with some success. But the most serious problem is in the developing countries (Table 2). In these areas, even though agricultural production is (by a variety of means, some of them destructive and expensive) steadily increasing, that increase is only enough to maintain the already low level of food per person. In those countries, tremendous efforts are necessary simply to keep on feeding the people at the same low level—in some cases at a starvation level. The increase in population means that the number of tilled acres per person in these countries will inevitably be reduced to one-half the present area in less than a lifetime. A further consequence of that population growth is that even the Gross National Product per person will, despite large increases in the country's total GNP, show little increase—a fact which reflects the diminishing resources available to each person for obtaining food.

Why is it that the less-developed countries have such explosive rates of population growth when compared to industrialized nations like the United States and Japan? Without going into the immediate personal reasons for why people choose to have a certain number of children, we can find a helpful explanation simply by looking at the relationship of the birth rate to the death rate. In the developed countries, largely as a result of various applications of medical and food-producing technology, both death rates and birth rates have shown significant declines in the past hundred years.

In the less-developed countries, on the other hand, only death rates have shown a recent significant and rapid drop, while birth rates remain high. This transition from high birth and death rates to low birth and death rates is called by students of population "the demographic transition." It is, as study of the population of many nations reveals, a process in which declining death rates are followed—a few generations later—by declining birth rates. But this phase of the transition, in which birth rates are high and death rates are low, shows an explosive increase of population—and that increase may continue from a few years to many decades, depending on the values of the people involved.

Of course, what population stability requires is not simply declining birth and death rates; what is required is that the birth rate and the death rate be made essentially equal—as they appear to have been through most of

Table 2.
*Regional Populations, Doubling Times, and Birth and Death Rates.*
(From Population Reference Bureau, 1977. Literacy Rates and Births per Woman from the Environmental Fund, 1977.)

|  | Population Estimate (millions) | Doubling Time (years) | Projection to Year 2000 | Births per Woman | Infant Mortality Rate (per 1000 live births first year) | Per Capita GNP U.S. 1974–75 | Literacy Percentage |
|---|---|---|---|---|---|---|---|
| Africa | 423 | 27 | 811 | 6.3 | 154 | 400 | 22 |
| Asia | 2,325 | 35 | 3,584 | 4.9 | 116 | 530 | 49 |
| U.S. and Canada | 240 | 116 | 294 | 2.2 | 16 | 7,020 | 99 |
| Latin America | 336 | 26 | 608 | 5.3 | 78 | 1,030 | 65 |
| Europe | 478 | 173 | 539 | 2.3 | 22 | 4,090 | 96 |
| USSR | 259 | 77 | 314 | 2.4 | 28 | 2,620 | 98 |
| Oceania | 22 | 53 | 32 | 3.4 | 55 | 4,490 | 84 |
| World | 4,083 | 38 | 6,182 | 4.4 | 103 | 1,530 | 59 |

human history. The sheer limitations of the ecosphere will impose such equality sooner or later, and all humans would like to avoid the usual means of achieving that stability: war, starvation, and disease. Yet already, through the starvation of millions of people in countries with high birth rates and low death rates, we can watch that deadly type of equalization beginning to take place. Certainly a task arising from the Christian gospel is to bring about such stability, and to do it through means other than starvation and warfare. Those tasks are our Christian obligation, not only for the sake of other humans, but also for the sake of this Eden of a planet placed in our trust. For it clearly will become a kind of man-made desert unless we can control the exploding population, and the exploding demands, of the people of the planet.

### Prospects for the Populations of Developing Countries

In developing countries, the prospects for success in humanely reducing birth rates to match the relatively low death rates are not at all clear. We know that as affluence increases, in most cases, birth rates decrease. The reasons for this relationship are not clearly understood. Whatever the reasons, it is likely that an increasing affluence in crowded countries may limit the birth rates to some extent. But there are problems with increased affluence as a solution. In the first place, we noted that the increasing population itself is likely to use up the increase in a country's total affluence. Thus, though productivity may increase and more food may become available, the multiplication of hungry mouths cancels out those gains. But even if affluence could overtake population, we have seen many examples of the fact that increasing wealth causes our demands for food—and other resources—to rise far beyond the level needed for a comfortable existence. In fact, we are, in North America, the world's most dramatic example of the principle that increasing affluence increases waste. Simply increasing affluence in hopes that it will decrease the birth rate does not seem a wise choice. It is more important to get at the reasons for high and low birth rates, and to change them without destroying the worth and freedom of individual persons. Such a solution requires more wisdom than most members of affluent countries have been able to exercise. More important, it requires the kind of understanding love which Christians ought to demonstrate.

Ultimately, the goal of population control must be to prevent population size from exceeding the carrying capacity of the environment. It is very difficult to determine what the carrying capacity of an environment is, particularly when we are speaking of the whole ecosphere as the environment of humans and millions of other species. But what the preceding chapters have shown is that the carrying capacity at which we arrive must leave room for the diversity and intricacy of the rest of creation. The reasons for that accommodation are both selfish, for we know we cannot survive apart from the supporting life of a healthy ecosphere, and stewardly, for it is the human responsibility to care for creation.

In some cases, even when the carrying capacity is understood, to arrive at a stable population will not be enough. For, in places adversely affected by climatic change or by the lingering effects of human overuse (as in the dry areas of the world being taken over by deserts), it may even be necessary to *reduce* the population size by letting the birth rate fall below the death rate.

A number of nations have already achieved zero population growth. They have usually done so by slowly recognizing the limits to their continued growth. In nations such as the United States, however, that "demographic transition" took place very slowly. But in the developing nations it must take place much more rapidly. One result of the rapidity with which demographic transition is coming to other nations is the fact that even if birth rates were to equal death rates—that is, if each couple were to have, on the average, only two children—there would still be a sizable increase in population in those nations.

This is largely due to the ages of the people within those various populations. Developing countries, due to the suddenness with which modern medical technology has been introduced, have a very large proportion of young people. This youthful age structure is reflected in the pyramidal shape of the age-structure diagram for developing countries shown in Figure 2. The youthfulness of the population in developing countries is further dramatized by the fact that in North America only 27 percent of the people are under age 15; in Europe, only 26 percent. But in Latin America, 43 percent of the people are under the age of 15; in Africa and Southeast Asia, 44 percent.

A hidden consequence of this youthful population in developing countries is that, even if the number of children per family were steadily and dramatically reduced, the size of the population would continue to increase as those who are now children approach child-bearing age. The long delay in humans between birth and reproduction builds a lag into population dynamics, so that the effects of changes in birth rates are not evident until several decades later.

This fact is illustrated in Figure 3. It shows that if the average number of children per family dropped to replacement levels (NRR—Natural Replacement Rate) by the year 2000 (which means dropping from 2.6 down to 2.1 children per family in developed countries, and from 5.7 to 2.7 children per family in developing countries), world population still would increase from its present level of 4.3 billion to 5.8 billion in the year 2000. It would eventually stabilize, shortly before 2100, at a level of 8.2 billion (curve C). That possibility is perhaps the best we can hope for, given the present ethos of Third World countries. But if the population in developed countries reached replacement levels by the year 2000, and those of developing countries by 2045, world population would not stabilize until about 2145, at a level near

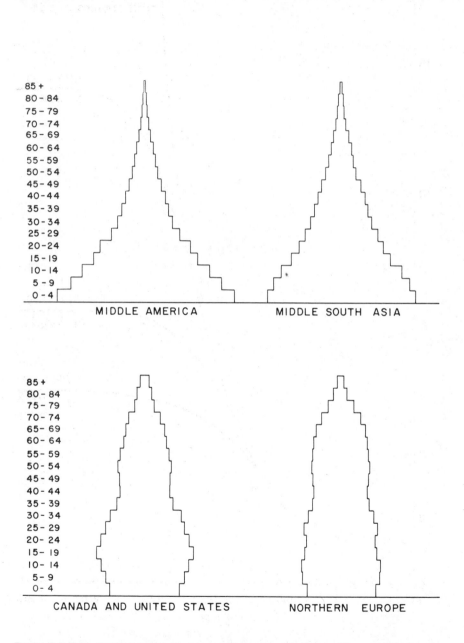

Figure 3:2 Age structures of various populations showing those with prospects for continuing explosive growth (pyramid-form) and those with prospects for relatively stable levels (steep-sided form). Based upon data compiled from the *Demographic Yearbook* of the United Nations (1977, 1978).

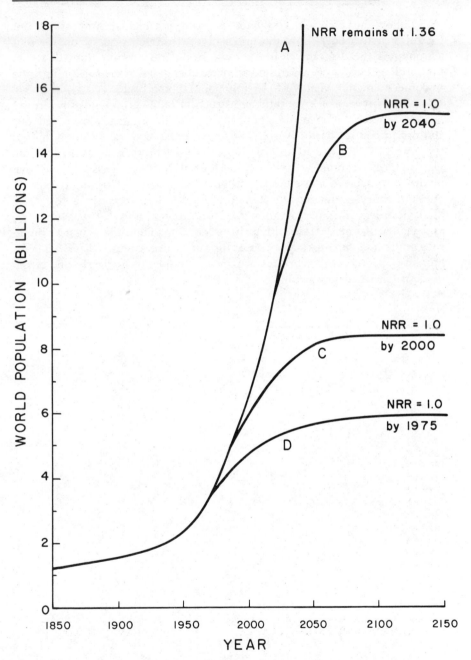

Figure 3:3 World population past and future, under various assumptions (see text). Based upon data from Frejka (1974) and estimates of past populations by Carr-Saunders (1964).[1]

15.5 billion (curve B). Curves D and A (both of which are impossible, but for different reasons) show the limits of the consequences of our present actions. As the diagram clearly shows, population momentum due to a youthful age structure will result in increasing populations for a long time to come, no matter what we do to slow population growth.

The problem of a youthful age structure only compounds the already serious problem of increasing population. We have already exercised our abilities to control death. It is clear that we must also exercise our abilities to control birth. If we are to exercise care for each other, as well as for the planet entrusted to us, we must temper our abilities with wisdom and love in order to achieve consciously what has been the case through most of human history—a relatively stable population. The alternative is to let the blind destructiveness of starvation, war, and disease do what we should do as a matter of careful stewardship. In order to maintain the planet as home to a million different kinds of creatures, it is necessary to have a *limited* human population. To work toward such a population is clearly one of the tasks of Christian stewardship.

### CHAPTER 4

# THE EARTH
# AND ITS FULLNESS _

*"Then you keep moving around, I suppose?" said Alice.*
*"Exactly so," said the Hatter, "As the things get used up."*
*"But when you come to the beginning again?" Alice ventured*
*to ask.*
*"Suppose we change the subject," the March Hare inter-*
*rupted, yawning. "I'm getting tired of this. . . ."*
—From Lewis Carroll, ALICE IN WONDERLAND

*It is difficult to make predictions, especially about the future.*
—Niels Bohr, quoted in Amory B. Lovins,
SOFT ENERGY PATHS: TOWARD A DURABLE PEACE

I n these past chapters we have sketched the basic structures of life on
this great gift of a planet. We have seen first the complexity and
delicacy of the relationships between plants, animals, and humans.
We have seen also the serious ways in which those relationships, and
the organisms themselves, have been disrupted or destroyed by human activity.

But underlying all this activity, from the industry of fungi breaking a
fallen tree into soil to the industry of humans breaking a mountain down
into coal, are two basic nonliving resources: minerals and energy. When we
consider the world of God's creation we are likely to think first not of this,
but of the world of living things—perhaps because we are living things
ourselves. But without the energy of the sun, and without carbon, calcium,
nitrogen, oxygen, iron, all those substances which we first encounter in the
blossoming flesh of the world—none of that life would live.

Likewise, apart from the energies of sun and atom and our own abilities
to apply those energies to the bedrock of creation—coal, iron, copper, oil—
all our civilization, and human life itself, would cease. Thus it is our purpose

in this chapter to consider the state of those nonliving resources on which both human and nonhuman life depend so totally. We are not concerned now with the complex and marvelous ways in which the plant world turns earth and energy into the food which sustains all life; rather, we are concerned with *human* use of earth and energy. In this sense, our discussion is one step removed from the previous chapters, for we are not discussing the operation of the planet as it takes place in "nature," apart from human intervention. Rather, we are considering the *human* use of "natural resources": how *man* uses things. And though man, like plants and animals, uses energy to transform minerals for his own purposes, his energy use is different. First of all, it differs in scale: no other creature has the ability to change the earth so radically and quickly. Nor does any other creature have the ability to turn so many things to his own use. For this reason, the analysis of our resource use in the future is particularly difficult. For what is not a resource today may become one tomorrow—and vice versa.

There is a little fable about a man condemned by fate—like the Wandering Jew or the Flying Dutchman—to carry through the ages a rock from a mountain. He had to carry the rock until a use was discovered for it. It (and the mountain of its origin) was useless stone for millennia; but in the twentieth century the man's quest ended, for the process of nuclear fission was discovered, and the rock was found to be from a deposit of uranium ore.

The same sort of story could be told of coal, oil, iron ore. The earth is a storehouse of wealth, but until we learn to use it, it is worthless. Careful use of the earth's treasure is a legitimate human activity. Unfortunately, in many cases we have not managed the storehouse well; we have regarded it *only* as a storehouse, raided it unwisely and indiscriminately, and often used its treasure carelessly.

In the middle of this century, uranium had become a treasure—but it has also become a curse. The same sort of thing has taken place with other resources. Ranchers in Wyoming, for example, discovered not long ago that their land lay atop a treasure house of coal—but that their ranches would have to be destroyed in order to remove the coal.

It is our purpose in this chapter to take a close look at these ambiguous treasures of energy and minerals, at the way in which we have used them (and may yet use them), and the implications of our use for the human task of stewardship.

We have divided our discussion of these resources into two categories: "energy" and "minerals." But this is not a very precise distinction. For example, we use 95 percent of all petroleum and natural gas for fuel, but the other 5 percent is our main source of raw materials for petrochemicals. However, though many have argued that it is unwise to burn up a mineral treasure like petroleum on our freeways and in our furnaces, we will nevertheless consider resources under their principal current use. Thus, in our discussion, petroleum is an energy resource.

In trying to get an overall picture of our mineral and energy resources, it might be helpful to look at this wealth by analogy with the wealth of an individual.* People ordinarily have three sources of wealth: *income, savings,* and *inheritance.* By analogy, in the earth's resources we have only one source of *income*: the vast but neglected flood of solar energy. We also have *savings*: a fraction of that solar income, caught by plants through the marvelous process of photosynthesis and stored in food, wood, coal, oil, and natural gas. Most of the energy we currently use, both in our bodies and in industry, comes from these savings. Finally, we have an *inheritance*: the nonliving planet itself—the heat of the earth's core, and its rock and mineral wealth, of which radioactive ores are particularly important for energy.

In the human use of natural resources, just as in an individual's use of financial resources, it is wise to live within one's income, though for a short time that income may be supplemented by drawing on savings and inheritance. The wealth of personal savings and inheritance may either be wasted or invested in order to yield a return. In the same way we may waste our savings of fossil fuels and our inheritance of mineral wealth, or we may use them so as to yield a return. A useful, long-term principle for resource use is that our inheritance of mineral wealth should be recycled: we should live within our solar energy income, and draw cautiously on the savings of fossil fuels or the inheritance of nuclear energy (which can only be used once). We ought to use our savings and inheritance only to set up better ways of using our energy income or of recycling our mineral inheritance. When we reflect on the way in which the ecosystems described in the previous chapter operate, we see that such a pattern is implicit in the natural world. All of nature lives within its income of available food or sunlight. And eventually the savings of fibre or protein are "recycled" in the earth or taken up into the food web. But ultimately, nothing is wasted, except the unused energy which is radiated back into space.

## ENERGY RESOURCES

Against this background of personal and "natural" finance, let us consider energy, our energy resources, and the use we make of them. First, we must understand what energy *is.*

Energy is unique among natural resources. It has properties which no other resource has. These characteristics point out why energy is our most important resource, why it is so important in contemporary human civilization, and why the "energy crisis" is of such great concern.

*To make the analogy more appropriate, we will prohibit borrowing.

We can summarize these unique characteristics of energy very simply by saying that energy:

—is intangible;
—is the capacity to do work;
—is the most basic natural resource;
—is the only nonrecyclable resource;
—is the biggest factor in changing how we live.

Let us consider why each of these claims is true.

*Energy is intangible.* Despite the abundance of talk about energy, few people understand what it is—and no one has seen it or touched it. We have all seen the *effects* of energy or the *sources* of energy, but never the energy itself. When we lie in the sun on a warm day, we can see the source of the energy—the sun—and feel the effect of the energy—the sun's warmth on the skin—but we do not experience the energy itself as it is transmitted between the sun and the body. For energy itself is intangible.

*Energy is the capacity to do work.* Energy's great importance to us comes from its ability to do work; humans have always tried to minimize the work they do. In earlier days, this was done by slaves; today it is done by machines—but both slaves and machines apply energy to a particular job. Likewise, for millennia people have realized that heat energy is useful and have used fire for heating and cooking. It took them much longer to recognize that other forms of energy—particularly mechanical energy—could also be useful. Once this discovery was made, the industrial revolution was upon us. Today, most people in industrialized societies live lives of relative leisure, because energy-consuming machines do their work for them.

*Energy is our most basic natural resource.* This claim might at first seem extravagant, but consider the following: if we wish to make an object out of iron, whether it be an automobile or a can, we must first mine the iron ore, then transport it to a smelter, smelt it, form an ingot, transport the ingot to a rolling mill, roll the steel, transport it to a factory, and then make the car or the can, which must finally be transported to the consumer. Energy is required at every step. Without energy, we could not dig the iron ore out of the ground, smelt it, form an ingot, transport it, roll it, or form an end product. This is the reason energy is the most basic natural resource, for without it we could not use our other natural resources. Until we learned how to use nonanimal sources of energy effectively, we were unable to tap most mineral resources. And many other mineral resources such as oil shale or the uranium in granite are at this time effectively inaccessible to us because of the tremendous energy which would be needed to process them.

*Energy is our only nonrecyclable resource.* Most metal resources—iron, for example—could, with the right kind of effort, be recycled. We have not done so in the past, but in principle there is nothing to prevent us from doing so. The same could be said of most of our nonfuel mineral resources. But energy is different. Even if we wanted to recycle it, we could not; it is simply impossible to do so. The second law of thermodynamics states that any transformation of energy results in a lower quality of energy—that is, in energy which can do less useful work. Energy is degraded in all natural processes. Furthermore, virtually all energy used or transformed is eventually converted into heat energy, which ultimately is radiated into space, never to be recovered. There is no way of stopping this. The more energy we use, the more energy we radiate outward. This necessary and irrevocable loss makes energy intrinsically nonrecyclable.

*Energy is the biggest factor in modifying our lifestyle.* Because energy is the capacity to do work, the application of energy for our own purposes means that we have less work to do or at least a different kind of work. Energy's ability to do work affects even what we call play—as when we use a golf cart to move us around a golf course. The consequences of the application of energy to necessary tasks have been so great in the last century as to almost totally transform the shape of everyday life. We have no way of knowing what changes energy use will produce in our future. There is one of which we can be certain, however: energy has a price. In the past, that price has been the depletion either of solar "savings" in coal and oil or of the "inheritance" of nuclear fuels. We may not be able to pay that price indefinitely; and this would result in catastrophic changes in our way of life— particularly in North America, where that life has been transformed so thoroughly by cheap energy.

## The "Energy Crisis"

So much for what energy is. We must consider now the availability of energy. Specifically, what is the "energy crisis"? Or is there such a thing?

There is a crisis in availability of energy, but it is not what many people think it is. In 1973, out of disapproval of American support of Israel in the "Yom Kippur" war, the Arabs declared an oil embargo. The result was an immediate shortage of petroleum products in the United States, which meant we had to wait in line for gas at service stations, and sometimes we could not get gas at all. This short-term problem first brought the term "energy crisis" into everyday language. But the 1973 shortage of oil was not absolute; it was artificially contrived. The Arabs turned off the valve, and our gas stations ran dry. The oil was still under the ground, however, waiting to be pumped up and distributed. When the political problems were worked out, the valves were opened, and oil from Arabia flowed again to the U.S. In fact, though America was importing less than 25 percent of its oil before that temporary crisis, it is importing nearly 50 percent now, and thus is much more vulnerable to the same sort of politically motivated cut-off. This hard lesson was learned once again in 1979 as a result of, among other things, Iranian political unrest.

When we speak of an energy crisis in this book, however, we are referring to a much more serious problem: the approach of a time when most of the oil will have been pumped out and used. And by all indications, that day is not far off. The real energy crisis has not yet begun. The temporary shortages of a few years ago and of today serve as a reminder of our dependence on oil, and the consequences of its coming depletion.

The reasons for this approaching *real* energy crisis are all around us. At any supermarket, for example, we can look in the parking lot and notice rows and rows of 5,000-pound automobiles which have been driven there by 150-pound persons to pick up ten pounds of groceries. It takes very little energy to transport ten pounds of groceries from the store to the home. It does not even take much energy to carry a person from his or her home to a store—most people could walk it without much trouble. But it takes a great deal of energy to transport a 5,000-pound automobile to and from the store. A little experiment can dramatize the difference. On your next trip to the store, instead of driving your car, try pushing it!

Such an experiment might cause us to reflect on the history of our use of energy. When Abraham was wandering about the Near East, he used very little energy: wood for heating and cooking, and pasture for his camels and horses. His own personal use probably amounted to about 2,500 calories per day. This basic human energy consumption—the food it takes to keep an active person healthy—is indicated on the accompanying chart (Figure 1).

Already in Abraham's day, some civilizations were making the transition from an economy based on nomadic existence to one based on agriculture. But this agricultural revolution did not succeed until domesticated animals were used to work the fields. In other words, it was not until humankind learned to harness energy other than its own that the effects of the agricultural revolution became permanent. Cities came into being and the capacity of the earth to support humans increased dramatically. The first major revolution in human use of energy had a major impact on the history of humankind. The typical agricultural person used (or uses—there are still some agricultural societies) approximately 20,000 calories of energy per day, as we have shown on the accompanying chart. The added 17,500 calories were consumed not by the person directly, but by the animals whose muscles he had used to assist him in his work.

The next major increase in our use of energy occurred in the industrial revolution. When we learned how to tap nonanimal sources of energy and to develop machines to use it, both energy use and our way of life changed more dramatically than ever. At the beginning of the industrial revolution, when we were burning mainly wood and coal, the energy consumption per person rose to about 75,000 calories per day. It was then that we began to draw heavily on the "savings" of solar energy. Today, in North America, we use approximately 250,000 calories per person per day.

The figures on this chart illustrate the point we made earlier: energy

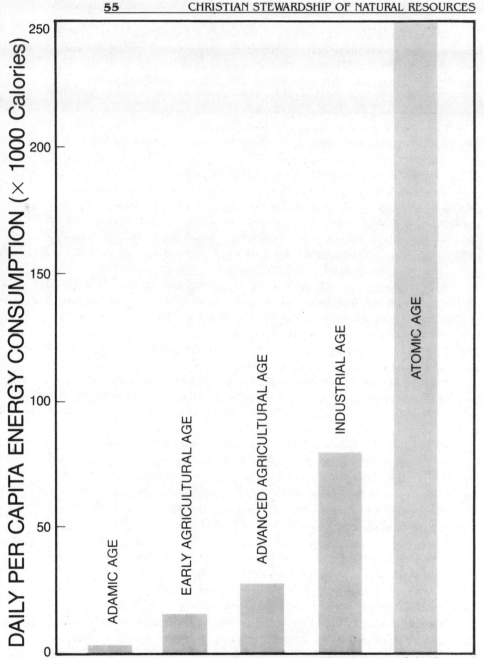

Figure 4:1 Daily per capita consumption of energy at different stages of development of civilization. The energy consumed by primitive civilizations consisted only of the food necessary to sustain life. As humans began using wood and other fuels, as well as animal energy, energy consumption increased. Today vast quantities of energy are used in transportation, heating and cooling, and industrial production.[1]

use is the major factor in changing our way of life. The two greatest changes in the way humankind has lived on the earth were the agricultural revolution and the industrial revolution. In both cases, these revolutions were the result of changes in our ability to use energy. With each change, the amount of energy use increased manyfold. As a result, each of us in North America uses approximately 100 times the amount of energy per day that a person of Abraham's time would have consumed. Because energy represents the capacity to do work, the effect is like having 100 slaves working for each of us.

From our previous discussion of human population growth, we can rightly conclude that the drama of the increase in energy consumption per person is outstripped by that of the growing number of people using that energy. To be sure, the bulk of that population increase is occurring in nations which have a relatively low consumption of energy per person. But that only suggests two other unpleasant realities. One is that we already use far more than our share of the earth's resources. The other is that our excessive use has been adopted as a model for the developing world; the Third World countries are trying, as rapidly as they can, to catch up with our number of energy slaves. All our policies and attitudes reinforce the idea that it is only through such high rates of energy use that we can achieve happiness. The consequence is that the exponentially rising world population, multiplied by the exponentially rising per-person energy use, is placing a very great demand on our energy resources. And that demand is being met almost entirely out of energy savings and inheritance—very little out of energy income. There is a very real possibility that we may use up those great reserves before we are forced to develop means of effectively harnessing energy income— and by that time, we may not have sufficient energy resources to do so.

Such predictions may seem unnecessarily alarming. Indeed, there is still much oil in the Middle East, and new discoveries are being made elsewhere every year. But simply because we have plenty of oil now does not mean that we will have plenty in the future. Odd as it may seem, we have a glut of oil now, but can foresee severe shortages in fifteen years and a real crisis in thirty.

We seem, then, to be nearing the end of an era. Our desire for energy, particularly for the cheap energy of solar "savings," is likely to surpass our ability to fulfill it before the end of the century. The alternatives we face in such a system are two: we must either increase our energy supply, or reduce our demand. Let us consider the possibilities for both of those alternatives.

### Can We Increase Our Supply of Energy?

There are only three sources of energy available to us: the sun, which provides our energy income and is the source of those fossil fuel savings which have been so important in the past hundred years; the moon, which produces a small energy income; and the earth, whose heat and minerals make up our energy inheritance. Of these three, through all of history, virtually all energy used has come from the sun. We have used its energy from the beginning to fuel our bodies, to keep us warm, to enable us to work. By means of photosynthesis, plants are able to transform and to store in themselves the radiant energy of the sun. Our most immediate way of using these energy savings is to eat and digest the food; the plant's stored chemical energy is released in heat energy and in the movements of our muscles. In addition to providing our food energy in this way, the sun heats our entire planet, enabling it to support life. Thus our very existence depends on the sun's incoming energy.

Even when we begin using energy other than food, we find that it still comes from the sun. Whether we harness the energy of animals or burn wood to cook our food, we are releasing, either as work or as heat, the photosynthetically stored energy of the sun. Since the industrial revolution, and the massive use of fossil fuels which accompanied it, we have increasingly turned away from using the short-term savings of wood and food to the long-term savings of coal and oil; but still we are using the energy of the sun. This ancient solar energy, stored for eons in the hydrocarbons of old jungles and river deltas, has fueled the industrial revolution. But supplies are running out, and we must seriously ask what will happen to our industrial society when that ancient stored sunlight is no longer available.

We tap solar energy in many other ways. One of the simplest and cleanest is to hold water behind dams and to let it spin the turbines of electric generators on its way back to the sea. By doing this we are capturing solar energy, for it was the sun which first evaporated the water from the seas and lifted it into the sky, from where it fell again on the high watersheds behind the dam. The elegance of such a method is suggested in a poem by Wendell Berry called "Falling Asleep":

Raindrops on the tin roof.
What do they say?
We have all
    been here before.

There are yet other ways of using the sun. Some cities are beginning to burn refuse to provide steam heat and electricity: again, the energy in refuse originates almost entirely in solar energy caught by plants. With windmills we tap wind energy, energy which is generated by the unequal heating of the earth's surface by the sun. Making use of the temperature differential between the surface and depths of oceans is a more exotic proposed method of tapping solar energy.

We also use solar energy directly by means of roof-mounted heat absorbers, which are used either to heat (or cool) buildings or to provide hot water for the occupants. Photovoltaic cells produce energy directly from sunlight. Plans to use them on a large scale have been proposed: orbiting satellites, for example, equipped with solar collector panels would convert the sunlight into electricity and beam the energy back to earth by means of microwave radiation.

With these abundant resources of solar energy, it would seem that we should have little need for worry. But there are many problems with living on solar income. We are already outstripping the energy which can be provided through food and forest. Nor can hydroelectric power supply much more; excellent as it is, there are only a limited number of good dam sites, and some of those sites threaten important natural environments.

Direct generation of electricity or heat holds much promise, as does wind power. But serious problems arise here, the most serious of which is their intermittent nature: what happens to a solar power plant when clouds obscure the sun? What happens to an economy which depends on wind energy when the wind stops blowing? Clearly, there must be either a standby source of power or an adequate storage system. Either greatly increases the cost and reduces the efficiency of the whole system. The serious proposals for orbiting satellites would avoid the problem of the intermittent nature of earthbound systems. But the expense of such installations is great, and no one is sure about the effects on the ecosphere of massive amounts of incoming microwave radiation. Yet despite these problems, the fact that solar energy uses energy *income* makes it look very attractive—if not inevitable—for the future.

What of the fossil fuels, that solar savings account on which we are drawing so heavily today? Apart from the increasing pollution which the production and consumption of fossil fuels causes, the biggest problem is that they are energy savings, and thus are limited. The accompanying graph (Figure 2) is a production curve typical for all fossil fuels, although this particular curve describes only petroleum. As the curve shows, production begins slowly. As persons demand more and more energy, new production facilities are built, and use and production increase. At some point, however, the supply of fuel is depleted to the point that production must decrease— because no savings account is infinite.

The most startling feature of this graph is its prediction (based on the most reliable data available) that by the year 2000 we will have reached the peak of the petroleum production curve. Thereafter, despite all our efforts, petroleum production will decrease. And, as the graph shows, even if optimistic predictions about the amount in the fuel reserves are correct, the increased supplies will make little difference in the time when the peak in production is reached and must begin declining.

The curve for natural gas, in Figure 3, is even less comforting; at current rates of usage, we are likely to run out of natural gas even before we run out of petroleum.

The curve for coal (Figure 4), on the other hand, is considerably more comforting: there were great forests in the carboniferous era, and they

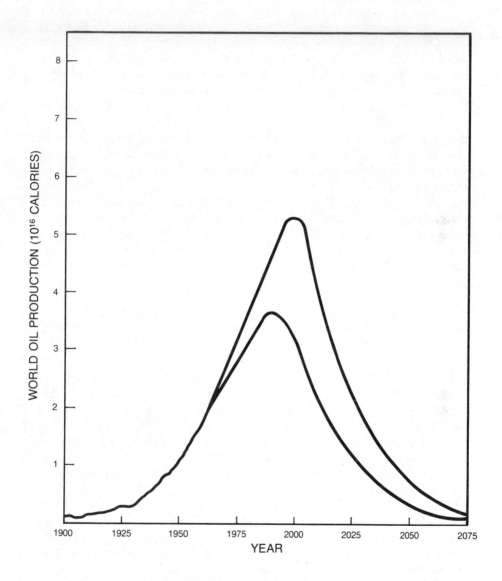

Figure 4:2 Actual and projected world oil production as a function of time. The upper line is based upon an optimistic estimate of the earth's total oil reserves; the bottom line reflects a pessimistic estimate.[2]

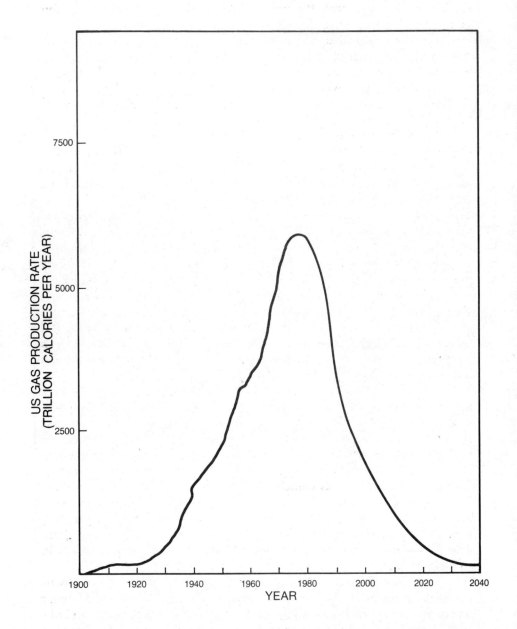

Figure 4:3 Actual and projected United States natural gas production as a function of time. Note that, although world natural gas production is still increasing, United States natural gas production has already begun to decline.[3]

trapped vast amounts of sunlight. But serious problems are connected with the large-scale use of coal. Burning coal releases into the air large amounts of sulphur dioxide, which forms an acidic and destructive rain; coal also produces much particulate matter. Even more serious problems come from mining the coal, particularly from strip-mining. Furthermore, coal is inconvenient for individual use. This problem could be solved if proposals to liquify and gasify coal were successful, but such processes consume energy, and would have the likely net result of making the whole process more inefficient.

Perhaps even more important, ultimately, is the fact that coal, oil, and natural gas are chemical treasures and our main source of synthetic materials. To burn them would be foolish if there were alternatives to doing so; it is likely that future generations would be grateful for our conserving oil and coal—not for fuel, but for use in producing synthetics.

We have not yet considered the large reserves of petroleum contained in oil shales or tar sands. However, their extraction would take large amounts of energy, and (especially in the case of oil shale) probably leave large amounts of waste. In any case, the use of these low-grade energy reserves would only increase by another few decades the time until the oil is effectively depleted.

No matter how wealthy one is, one cannot draw indefinitely on a savings account. The main problem with our use of fossil fuels is that we are drawing on savings which were deposited over many, many years, and which we are burning up in a few centuries (see Figure 5). Obviously, such a pattern cannot continue; yet the majority of the world's people assume that it can and will continue.

We mentioned earlier that the sun, moon, and earth are our only basic sources of energy. We do not normally consider the moon as an energy source; it neither radiates nor generates energy. But, if we could tap it, the energy stored in its relative motion around the earth would provide the earth's energy needs for a billion years, at our present rate of consumption. Tidal energy is the one way in which we can make use of this kinetic energy, for the energy in the tides comes from the energy of the moon's motion. The mouth of the Rance River in France is one place where tidal energy is being used. However, since the type of site required—a large bay, a narrow inlet, and a great difference between high and low tide levels—is not abundant, it is unlikely that we will be able to tap the moon's kinetic energy to any large extent.

The other probable source of energy is that major part of our inheritance, the earth itself. The earth contains (besides the stored solar energy mentioned earlier) only two known sources of energy: geothermal and nuclear. Geothermal energy is the heat energy stored in the earth's interior. Hot springs, geysers, and volcanoes are manifestations of this hot center; anyone who has observed a lava flow must be impressed with the rock-melting potential of the earth's inner heat. However, though the heat energy

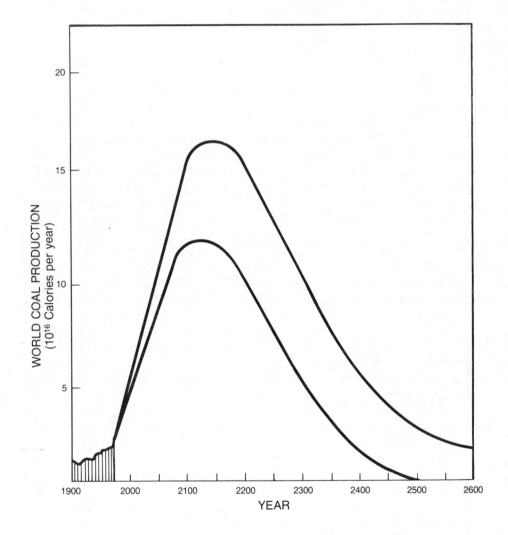

Figure 4:4 World actual and projected coal production as a function of time. The upper curve reflects an optimistic estimate of the supply of mineable coal; the bottom curve reflects a pessimistic estimate.[4]

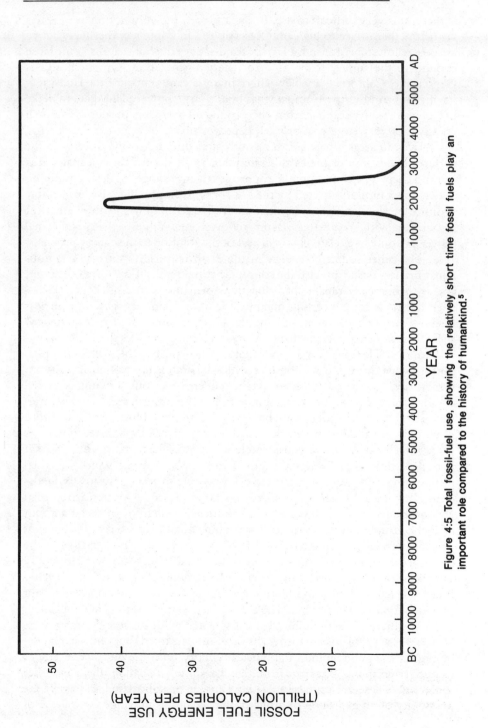

Figure 4:5 Total fossil-fuel use, showing the relatively short time fossil fuels play an important role compared to the history of humankind.[5]

is there, it is very difficult to use. In most places, the very hot material is too far below the surface to be readily accessible. Only in a few thermally active areas—Yellowstone, Iceland, New Zealand—does the hot magma come close enough to the surface to be used for energy generation. One such area is Geyserville, California, a valley where many steam vents dot the landscape. Pacific Gas and Electric Company has built a large power plant there to make use of the steam escaping from the ground. That plant produces as much energy as a very large coal or nuclear power plant.

Even in areas where steam or hot water does not come directly to the surface, the energy of the earth's interior may be used if the hot material is not too deep. There are a number of proposals for doing so, such as pumping water down until it is heated by the hot rock. Although there is considerable promise in such energy sites, their uneven distribution and their frequent association with scenic areas, as in Yellowstone, suggests that geothermal power can only be a relatively small part of the solution to the energy problem.

The other source of energy in the earth is nuclear. Einstein's famous equation, $E=mc^2$, expressed the concept that matter itself is a form of energy, and is theoretically capable of being transformed into useful energy. However, methods for converting one into the other—nuclear fission or nuclear fusion—are neither obvious nor simple. Unfortunately, we first experienced these forms of energy (apart from the fusion which provides the sun's energy) in weapons. Thus the best-known example of fission is the nuclear (atomic) bomb, while the hydrogen bomb provides a grim example of nuclear fusion. Obviously, we do not wish to obtain our energy from such uncontrolled explosions, and have found it possible to build a nuclear reactor which uses the fission process to obtain usable energy. By assembling a large quantity of uranium (or plutonium) inside a reactor, a controllable chain reaction takes place which can release a considerable amount of heat energy over a long period of time. This heat can be used to generate steam, which can then drive turbines to generate electricity. The whole process is relatively inefficient. But since nuclear reactions release far more energy per reaction than chemical ones do (that is, convert more mass to energy), the total amount of fuel consumed in a nuclear reactor is quite small compared to the amount of coal burned in an ordinary coal-fired power plant. And therein lies the beauty of the nuclear reactor. If we use uranium-235 fuel only, we can supply our electrical energy needs for a century or more. If, instead, we develop breeder reactors, which use plutonium fuel made from the more abundant uranium-238 isotope, we should be able to meet our needs for a few millennia.

Yet there are serious problems associated with nuclear power plants. In part, these problems are the results of an unwarranted (but understandable) linking in the public mind of all nuclear energy with the destructive power of nuclear weapons. But apart from that fearsome association, there are other problems. These are primarily: 1) the disposal of radioactive wastes; 2) the possibility of an explosion or a meltdown, resulting in dangerous release of radioactive material into the atmosphere (such as was threatened in the Three Mile Island incident); and 3) diversion of nuclear material for use as weapons material by terrorist groups or nation-states. These problems have been widely and hotly debated, and are, as yet, unsolved. We can summarize the prospects and problems of nuclear energy in the words of Alvin Weinberg, former Director of Oak Ridge National Laboratories: "We nuclear people have made a Faustian compact with society: we offer . . . an inexhaustible energy source . . . tainted with potential side effects that, if uncontrolled, could spell disaster."[6]

In some ways, the nuclear fusion process shows more promise. The fuel supply, deuterium, is abundant in the ocean, replacing the hydrogen atoms in one out of every 5,000 gallons of seawater. Even though (in our present knowledge of fusion) the process would draw on "inherited" energy sources, the fuel is so abundant that we would not have to worry about depletion for thousands of years. Also, the problem of radioactive waste appears to be much less with fusion. However, though the hydrogen bomb has proved that the fusion process does, indeed, release enormous amounts of energy, we have not yet succeeded in slowing the reaction down to a point where it can be controlled and usable energy can be released. Much research is being done on fusion power, but each problem resolved suggests more which need to be solved. We are unlikely to have a fusion reactor which shows a net energy gain before the year 2000, and perhaps not for a long time after that. The promise of inexhaustible power from nuclear fusion is a very uncertain one.

As this short summary has shown, there are a variety of possible ways of increasing our energy resources. But all of them are deficient in one way or another. Thus it seems clear that energy costs are likely to rise substantially in the future. These rising costs and dwindling energy supplies will inevitably affect the way we live and the way our industrial processes are carried out. These changes will, in turn, have great economic and political consequences. No alternative to our limited supply of fossil fuels shows much promise for enabling us to maintain the way of life we now know.

There is, however, an alternative to increasing our supply of energy. It is one which Christians, in particular, should act on, for reasons which will become clearer later in the book. That alternative is to use less energy: this we can do by conserving energy or by using it more efficiently. The energy we do use should come, where possible, from income, not from savings or inheritance resources. In our use of energy, at least, we have been prodigal; we have "wasted our substance in riotous living," and need to take better care of a rich inheritance.

## MINERAL RESOURCES

As we indicated earlier, minerals are another part of that inheritance contained in the earth. But apart from a few large meteorites, there is no mineral income similar to the energy income from the sun. There are, to be sure, slow processes of concentration taking place in seabed rifts. But these processes take place over eons. We must, for practical purposes, consider the supply of minerals unchanging—they are an inheritance, not income. What this indicates, of course, is that one of the ways in which we should use our energy income is to set up means for ensuring that our mineral inheritance will be recycled and not wasted. Unfortunately, we have—with the exception of a few rare and very precious metals like gold—done very little to conserve and recycle mineral resources. But the need for doing so should be obvious from a brief discussion of the mineral wealth of the earth.

Traditionally, man has extracted most minerals from the land, but recently it has become apparent there are substantial resources on the seabed as well. In this section we will briefly examine our mineral resources on both land and sea, review the known reserves and patterns of our usage, and then consider some of the effects of that usage on the earth's energy supply and on the earth's life.

## Land Resources

From early in history, people have extracted minerals and metals from the earth to make tools and implements. This early mining was mainly for gold, iron, silver, and copper, and took place near the surface. As the human race gained technical knowledge, the mining and use of minerals became increasingly sophisticated. In today's industrialized world, mining is a major industry, and mines descend ever deeper into the earth. Furthermore, increasingly sophisticated materials and alloys are being developed from the various minerals which are extracted.

However, most minerals do not occur abundantly, and mining is economical only where there is a substantial concentration of a specific material. With continued use, the high quality reserves are disappearing. Thus we must continually improve our mining practices as we search for new deposits. This is particularly true in North America; the United States has only 6 percent of the world's population but consumes approximately one-third of all the world's resources. If we continue our exponential increase in the use of the world's resources, or if the remainder of the world even begins to approach our level of resource consumption, we are likely to face shortages of minerals very soon.

How much is yet available for our use? The answer to this difficult question depends on many factors. As reserves of a particular material become depleted, the price tends to rise. This rise in price naturally slows down the rate at which the material is used. Furthermore, the increase in price encourages recycling or the development of substitute resources.

The best estimates of resource depletion are obtained by analyzing current usage patterns, making reasonable predictions about future usage and discovery of resources, and plotting resource depletion curves like those shown earlier in this chapter for petroleum and natural gas. Because depletion curves approach zero as time goes on (but reach it only in infinity), it is impossible to say that one ever really "runs out" of a resource. Use simply decreases as availability decreases and prices rise. A useful way of measuring the effective size of the reserves is to calculate the estimated number of years until 80 percent depletion. The accompanying chart (Figure 6) illustrates the currently estimated 80 percent depletion time of several resources, based on two different sets of assumptions.

This chart indicates that we will reach the 80 percent depletion level for most important minerals sometime within the next century or two. Thus our situation with mineral resources appears to be little better than our situation with fossil fuel resources. However, the problem is actually much more severe in the case of mineral resources, for minerals are part of an irreplaceable inheritance—there is no "income" of minerals.

### Seabed Resources

Fortunately, the picture is not as bleak as Figure 6 suggests. It has been known for some time that there are substantial amounts of minerals in ocean water, but they are extremely diffuse and in most cases it is not economically feasible to recover them. Recently we have learned, however, that the spreading of plates in the earth's crust allows mineral-rich waters to well up from below the ocean floor and to create layers of minerals near continental rifts. Scattered about the ocean floor in a number of different places are manganese nodules, which contain not only manganese, but numerous other important metals such as copper, iron, aluminum, nickel, and magnesium. These nodules and sea floor deposits represent a most important resource to us. Table 1 indicates that if we consider these sea floor resources, the depletion time for many key minerals should be expressed not in centuries, but in millennia.

From this one might get the impression that the problem of mineral resources is solved; however, several words of caution must be inserted here. First, the chart shows depletion times which are calculated strictly by taking present consumption levels and extending them at the same rate. But our use of most minerals, as we saw earlier, is increasing exponentially. Figured on the basis of that increase, the chart would yield appreciably shorter depletion times. Second, there are many unsolved problems involved in mining the deep seabed, and these must be overcome. Third, the environmental effects of deep seabed mining are unknown at this point, and deserve very careful study. Present proposals involve dredging the ocean bottom with large suction dredges. This would involve sucking up many ocean plants and animals, as well as sediment, and redistributing them in the process, unless extreme care were exercised. This disruption would have major environmental consequences. A fourth unknown at this point is the international legal situation

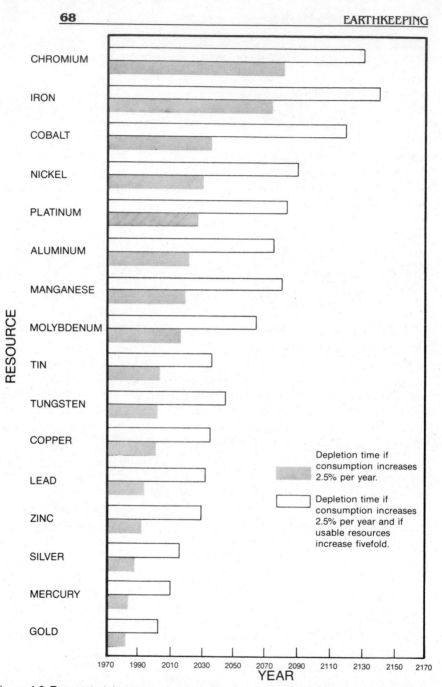

Figure 4:6 Two materials reserve indices, showing the estimated number of years to reach 80 percent depletion of key resources under two different sets of assumptions. Our present long-range plans should probably be based on a future somewhere between these two predictions.[7]

Table 1.
Reserves of Metals in Manganese
Nodules of the Pacific Ocean

| Element | Amount of element in nodules (billions of tons)[1] | Reserves in nodules at consumption rate of 1960[2] (years) | U.S. rate of consumption of element in 1960[3] (millions of tons per year) | Ratio of (world consumption) (U.S. consumption) |
|---|---|---|---|---|
| Magnesium | 25 | 600,000 | 0.04 | 2.5 |
| Aluminum | 43 | 20,000 | 2.0 | 2.0 |
| Titanium | 9.9 | 2,000,000 | .30 | 4.0 |
| Vanadium | 0.8 | 400,000 | .002 | 4.0 |
| Manganese | 358 | 400,000 | .8 | 8.0 |
| Iron | 207 | 2,000 | 100. | 2.5 |
| Cobalt | 5.2 | 200,000 | .008 | 2.0 |
| Nickel | 14.7 | 150,000 | .11 | 3.0 |
| Copper | 7.9 | 6,000 | 1.2 | 4.0 |
| Zinc | .7 | 1,000 | .9 | 3.5 |
| Gallium | .015 | 150,000 | .001 | — |
| Zirconium | .93 | +100,000 | .0013 | — |
| Molybdenum | .77 | 30,000 | 0.25 | 2.0 |
| Silver | .001 | 100 | .006 | — |
| Lead | 1.3 | 1,000 | 1.0 | 2.5 |

1. All tonnages in metric units.
2. Amount available in the nodules divided by the consumption rate.
3. Calculated as the element in metric tons.
(From Mero, J. L. "Potential economic value of ocean-floor manganese nodule deposits." In *Ferromanganese Deposits on the Ocean Floor*, Horn, D. R., ed., IDOE, National Science Foundation, Washington, D.C. 1972:191–203.)

with respect to mining. The Law of the Seas has historically assumed the ocean to be a common heritage of all humankind. There has been considerable controversy during the past several years regarding deep seabed mining and its relationship to the Law of the Seas. Some people believe that any nation with the technological ability should be free to begin mining the ocean bottom. But many others believe that mining should be carried out by international consortia, or that, at the very least, the profits of mining should be distributed to all nations equitably.

In summary, although the ocean appears to offer substantial mineral resources for our use, it is unclear at this point what the economic, political, and environmental effects of deep seabed mining will be. Some who were originally optimistic about deep sea mining are now pessimistic. It is too early to say that we have solved the problem of mineral resources.

## Resource Recovery

Even if seabed mining should be as good as its most enthusiastic and optimistic supporters claim, we still would not have solved some basic issues. As we have mentioned, the earth's minerals are an inheritance for humankind and for the planet. Even if we had enough of them to supply all our needs for one or two thousand years, our current usage levels and patterns would be difficult to justify. We do not know what the future will bring, but we must take into consideration the needs of future generations. For this reason, we should use such inherited resources conservingly. In fact, the ideal situation would be to recycle all materials for which we have no income. Such recycling would allow the mineral resources in the earth or on the ocean floor to continually circulate from one use to another. It is ironic that in today's world we transport iron ores from Europe to Japan for smelting, transport the steel from Japan to the United States for manufacture, and then throw the product into a landfill after we finish with it! Some of our landfills have a higher iron content than some of the iron ores currently being mined. Yet our government persists in subsidizing mining operations. In addition, regulated freight rates on American railroads are preferentially weighted toward virgin materials rather than recycled materials. As a result, it is economically more advantageous to bury our steel cans in a landfill than it is to recycle them.

Clearly this trend has to be reversed. There are encouraging signs in industry; many companies are now making major efforts to recycle as many of their waste products as possible. The biggest offenders at the moment are the average homeowners. Thus it becomes absolutely essential for all of us to recycle as many materials as possible. Glass bottles, steel and aluminum cans, and even yard wastes or other organic wastes should be separated and recycled. Such work takes little time or effort on the part of the individual homeowner, but it can accomplish a great deal of good. In future years our trash may be our best resource.

### Environmental Effects

An important part of our analysis of mineral resources and their use must be our concern with the earth's environment. As some have observed, pollution is usually a misplaced resource. If we used our resources wisely and properly, seeking to minimize environmental effects, we would go far toward solving present or future resource shortages and at the same time minimizing pollution.

We have mentioned recovery of steel and aluminum cans and glass bottles as an important example of recycling our resources. But there are many other instances where we could recycle valuable materials. For example, we spend large sums mining and isolating tungsten, a rather scarce material. Then we carefully form it into filaments, ingeniously incorporate it into light bulbs, and transport the bulbs long distances to the consumer. Yet we think it not worth the trouble to recycle the light bulbs in order to recover the scarce and expensive tungsten, as well as the brass, lead, and glass in the bulb. Such recycling is considered troublesome and economically unrewarding. But why do we not think it troublesome and economically unrewarding to mine the materials, produce the light bulbs, and transport them to our homes?

What is needed in handling mineral resources is not only research in developing new resources, but also—and especially—a transformation of our attitudes. It is important for us to get away from the attitude that proper resource use simply involves digging materials out of the ground, using them, and throwing them back in the ground. We need a new perception of our role and responsibility as *stewards* of the earth.

### The Role of Energy

As we pointed our earlier in this chapter, energy plays a crucial role in materials handling. All our use of mineral resources depends upon the availability of nonhuman sources of energy. The flow of energy is essential to insure the flow of materials. However, materials are recyclable and energy is not. Fortunately, God has provided his creation with a continuous income of energy. In the distant future our energy may come primarily from the sun, with a supplement from our "inheritance" of nuclear and geothermal energy. This energy would be used, among other things, to maintain the flow of mineral resources from one capital stock to another, in a continual closed-loop recycling pattern, similar to the flow of materials and energy in the whole ecosphere. Because we are only in the beginning stages of energy and resource use on a worldwide scale, we have not yet established that pattern. But we need to model it after the way in which the creation itself cycles matter and energy through its intricate web of life. We need then to bring our industry and our individual way of life into conformity with that pattern of "living within income" which is established by the economy of creation.

### CHAPTER 5

# THE RICH, THE POOR, AND NATURAL RESOURCES

*. . . what we call Man's power over Nature turns out to be a power exercised by some men over other men with Nature as its instrument.*

**—C. S. Lewis, THE ABOLITION OF MAN**

There are two emphases to this book: earth and humanity. In the discussion thus far we have moved gradually from one to the other, from a consideration of earth—the ecosphere and the creatures which it supports—to a consideration of man—that one particular creature with such enormous capabilities for affecting the rest of creation. It should be evident by now that there is some tension between these two concerns. One tension is obvious: man takes from nature what he needs, and nature seems to resist—with storms, famine, disease, and death. But there is another sort of conflict between the twin centers of this book which can be stated in a question: are we concerned here with the welfare of man, or with the welfare of nature? And can we be concerned with both? When we speak of the damaged ecosphere, of scarce whales and diminishing wildlife, we seem to be concentrating on the welfare of nature. But when we speak of energy shortage, human malnutrition, and the extraction of seabed minerals, we seem to be speaking of human welfare. At first the two concerns seem incompatible; indeed, many have considered them so. Those from developing countries speak with understandable suspicion of First World concern for controlling pollution. Such control is necessary, they say, largely because of the profligacy of nations now rich, and it seems to them like a clever way of keeping the poor nations poor. Arthur Simon, in *Bread for the World*, sums up well this conflict:

> The campaign to save our environment mounts pressure against poor countries to pay an extra price as they industrialize: the cost of pollution control. For that matter, the pressure is felt on low income people in our own country and at times has surfaced in public clashes between those fighting for jobs and those fighting to conserve nature.
>
> In reality *two* environmental campaigns are going on. One centers primarily on protecting nature and its ecosystems. The second concerns itself with social ecosystems that produce hunger, disease, and crowded hovels. . . .
>
> The first campaign is being waged by those who are not so poor, some of whom are more indignant about smog than about slums, more worried about the mistreatment of animals and lakes than about mistreated people. This tends to pit the rights of nature against human rights. . . .
>
> The poor of the world would probably like to breathe better air and keep their waterways pure, if they had decent jobs and enough to eat. But pollution-free hunger does not appeal to them.[1]

We have already suggested the resolution of this dilemma: broadly speaking, the health of humankind depends upon the health of nature. It is thus in the human interest to preserve the ecosphere. But it is a divinely given responsibility to care not only for the whole fabric of creation, but for one's human neighbor as well. We will discuss those biblical principles more clearly in Section III, but for now, it is enough to assert that "the two environmental campaigns" cannot be kept separate; to try to do so would only worsen problems in both spheres. Simon also says in *Bread for the World* that these two campaigns ought to unite and strengthen each other. It is as shortsighted to limit our concerns to human well-being as it is to limit them to the well-being of the rest of the created world. For that reason, the opening part of this book, with its emphasis on the health of ecosystems and on the effect of our activity on other creatures, is a necessary prelude to this final part of our analysis of the health of the planet. Our concern in this chapter is with the structures which provide, and limit, human accessibility to the world's wealth.

## HUMAN STRUCTURES AFFECTING RESOURCE USE

Questions about the ownership and use of natural resources are inseparable from many questions about the structures of human society. On the one hand, we confess that natural resources are God's property—he created them, he has retained ownership of them, and he cares about their use. On the other hand, we recognize that the exercise of stewardship requires some degree of human power and freedom to administer the resources. Insofar as stewardship is a test of their faithfulness, human beings must presumably have some freedom to demonstrate whether or not they are good stewards.

God has granted humanity the possibility of organizing its collective

life through social, political, and economic structures. The positive role of
these structures is outlined in the Bible, and should be affirmed and celebrated
by all Christians. It is difficult to imagine an orderly, secure life of any sort
without nation, family, law, commerce, and so on. At the same time, we
must confess with humility that: 1) not all human structures have been affected by Christians or Christian principles; 2) not all Christians have felt or
exercised any mandate to improve structures; and 3) not all that Christians
have done with those structures has been ethically or biblically correct. As
a result, the very structures that support our struggle to live as members of
God's kingdom, restraining the influence of sinful acts, are themselves tainted
with human sin. And that, unfortunately, is evident in the lives of both the
redeemed and the unredeemed.

Christians wish to reform the structures under which they live as a
testimony to the transforming power of Christ's love and as a way of bringing, in part, God's *shalom* to their own lives and to the lives of others on this
earth. It is not that good structures are themselves the instruments of man's
salvation; they are rather the evidence of it—evidence of Christian faithfulness and stewardship to those who are not redeemed. Even if structures
cannot be perfected in this life, they can surely point in the right direction—
they can, for example, be more, rather than less, just.

This justice applies both to how we use creation and to how we share
the fruits of creation with other people. While he granted man dominion and
stewardship rights, God has demonstrated his continued interest in his creation by warning his own people Israel that the land—their most important
natural resource—was his, that they were only sojourners with him, and that
they were to recognize this fact by refraining from selling the land in per-
petuity. That prohibition amounts to a divinely given structure affecting
human use of the land. Although Israel's theocratic structure and her failure
to keep this commandment are part of a particular historical experience, there
is no evidence that God has changed his attitude toward his creation or ceded
his ownership. Thus we may legitimately seek other biblical guidelines for
the structures which control our use of natural resources.

Humans have devised, or perhaps stumbled upon, various methods for
allocating the resources God has made. Squatters' rights are an example—
the right of ownership or administration based solely upon the presence of
the owner. Military conquest, treaties, international agreements, transfer
through sale—all of these explain some part of who has what and why. Not
all of these means of allocation are equally admirable. The terms usurper and
exploiter come to mind too frequently during a mental review of the history
of man's relationship to natural resources and his fellow man. But in any
case, through various structures, the created resources have been and still are
being divvied up. We shall comment briefly on some of these structures.

## Ownership

If all belongs to God, then, in the Christian view, if not in Christian practice, the basis on which humans possess things is a conditional one. For the Bible is clear that we are *stewards* of the earth, not owners. Even so, the stewardship responsibility must be assigned to or seized by someone. God cares for his creation and may intervene with man's care, but man himself has an important responsibility for exercising that care.

The responsibility for administration of goods which we call ownership may be delegated to individuals or it may be held by groups, large or small. Even where use is ultimately a matter of individual consumption, the administration of resources—decisions about their allocation, production, and distribution—can be a matter of collective will. In some sense, virtually all systems for the administration of resources and their products have a collective character to them, since even the assignment of private rights to property must have the overarching consent of the group. Otherwise an individual property right would depend only on the power of the individual to hold his or her claim against the competing claims of other individuals. In general, this state of anarchy has been avoided and people have organized their lives in a more orderly fashion. Within nation-states at least, the dominant form of property rights, be they individual or collective, are legal rights, which may well be backed by the power of the sword wielded by the state in the name of law and order. In the case of international property rights, the legal basis is somewhat more tenuous, and the power of the sword proportionately more visible and supreme.

## Social Organization

For a variety of reasons, not merely the maintenance of property rights, the human population of the world is organized into sub-groups called nation-states. Within each of these nation-states, some form of "sovereignty" is presumed to hold. In nation-states which are weak militarily, economically, or in other ways (for example, in the wills of their people or leaders), this sovereignty may be little more than a name. The destinies of the peoples of these states are shaped more from without than within. But in all cases, there is some tension between a concern for global justice and the power of a state to realize its supposed sovereignty in the face of other powerful and "sovereign" states. This tension is an important background in our consideration of the possession, administration, and exchange of the world's resources.

## Distribution of Resources

Another major background for our consideration of human use of the earth's resources is the distribution of finite resources on a limited planet.

Whether we call the planet spaceship earth, global village, or ecosphere, we have all become acutely aware of limits. The basic limitations of the planet—symbolized so beautifully in those views from space—remind us of more specific limitations: finite resources, finite capacity to absorb waste, finite living space, and finite capability to cope with the demands of a growing world population.

In one sense this global vision of the earth's finiteness and interrelatedness does little to indicate one of the most basic problems for the creatures within it: the needs and resources of the planet's creatures cannot be considered *en masse*. There is a physical oneness to the planet and its cargo of life, but there is not a oneness to the distribution of the earth's resources to meet the needs of the earth's creatures. And since the distribution of those resources among human beings is the basis for human impact on nonhuman life, it is necessary, in order to understand the health of both man and nature on the planet, to speak of the radical differences in the wealth and incomes of the world's peoples.

## DISPARITIES BETWEEN RICH AND POOR NATIONS

### Income

For most of us, the facts about the relative incomes in the world, no matter how much we qualify them, are like a plunge into icy waters. The data are shocking and are likely to leave us numb. What would it be like, for example, to live in a nation whose income per person was only 2 percent of that of United States citizens? How would we survive, what could we do in life, how could we, under those circumstances, exercise stewardship over the earth? Yet twenty-one nations, with a combined population of 815 million people, do have an average GNP per person of less than two one-hundredths of that of the U.S. per capita GNP. Moreover, the situation in those nations is not improving very rapidly. Their average annual growth rate in GNP per capita was only 1 percent for the period 1965–72, half that of the United States growth rate. This is why they, together with twenty-one other nations which averaged 3 percent of the U.S. GNP per capita, have become known as the "Fourth World." They are distinguished from the poor Third World both by the despair of their present situation and by the bleakness of their outlook.

There are other ways of making comparisons. North America contains about 6 percent of the world's population, but has almost 35 percent of the world's combined GNPs. Asia and Africa, on the other hand, have about 63 percent of the world's population, but only 11 percent of the combined GNPs. In other words, our share of aggregate GNPs is about six times our share of population, while Asia and Africa have a share of aggregate GNPs only two-tenths their share of population. These and comparable data for other areas of the world are shown in Figure 1.

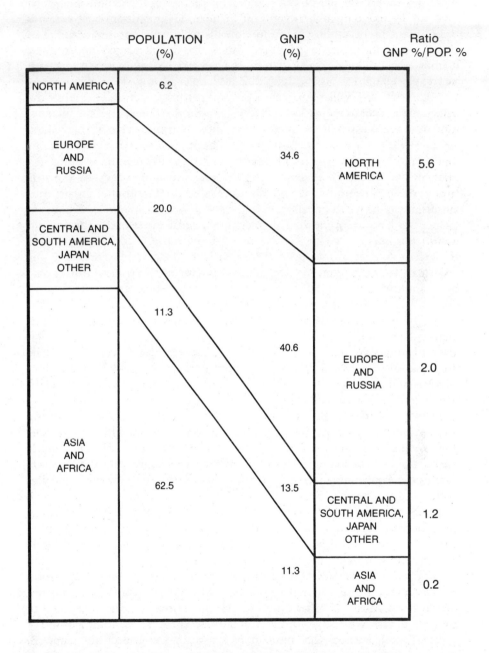

Figure 5:1 Aggregated GNP shares compared to population shares. (From James W. Howe et al., *The U.S. and World Development, Agenda for Action 1975* [New York: Overseas Development Council, Praeger, 1975], p. 210).

But these facts still do not give a clear picture of the conditions which many of the world's people experience, because they give the *average* incomes or GNP in a given nation; they ignore the distribution *within* a nation. When we consider that internal distribution, we see that the inequalities within poor nations are frequently greater than those within rich nations. In nations such as Kenya, which has an average GNP per capita of only $170, the poorest 40 percent of the population receives only 10 percent of the income while the richest 20 percent of the population receives almost 70 percent of the income. Under conditions of such dramatic inequality, statistics about average GNP per capita become almost meaningless. To be sure, some very poor nations, such as Pakistan, Sri Lanka, and Chad, do better at internal distribution. All of these nations have less than $130 GNP per capita, but they have distribution patterns more like that of the U.S. (though distribution in the U.S. is, of course, far from equal).

Another way of viewing the very poorest of the people of the world is to define a "poverty line," as we have done in the U.S. This method is somewhat arbitrary, since it does not consider all the living conditions for the poor, but once again the data are so dramatic as to preclude most quibbling about the meaning. If we take $75 per person per year as the poverty line, and apply that criterion to Latin America, Asia, and Africa, 578 million people fall below it—over half a billion people have an income under $75 per year.

The facts we have for measuring the economic well-being of citizens of various nations are quite crude. It might be more desirable, therefore, to measure inequality as something like the resources which are available to people in relationship to their needs. But no such precise measure is available, so we will have to make do with what we have now and what we can gather in the future. Despite these difficulties in precise measurement, we do know that the differences in GNP are awesome, and that these differences affect the possibilities for living a full and meaningful life. Significantly, too, these differences in income affect a person's ability to exercise stewardship of the earth.

## Wealth

We have amazingly little data on the actual wealth of the people of the world or even on the size of the wealth stock in the United States. Although we know that wealth tends to be more unequally distributed than income, this doesn't get us very far. Nevertheless, we can at least list some of the things which make up wealth in varying nations of the world.

1. *Natural resources.* Some nations are sitting on top of abundant resources which are indigenous to their territory, while others have little of this kind of wealth. Oil is one example of such indigenous wealth; metals and minerals are another. The list is far larger; it includes the character of

the soil, the climate, the topography, water power, forest resources, and the geographic position of the country in relationship to other countries and markets. Large amounts and fortunate combinations of these resources, as well as some degree of control over their use, lead almost inevitably to wealth and income, at least for some members of the society. Their absence leads almost as inevitably (with some significant exceptions) to poverty.

*2. Capital goods.* Capital goods are the nonhuman means of production: the tools, factories, and vehicles necessary for that production. It is not just the size of these stocks of capital goods that counts, but also their age, their location by geography and by industry, and their efficiency or technological sophistication. Wooden hand looms and old Singer foot-treadle sewing machines are capital goods, but they are much less efficient than a modern textile plant.

*3. Human capital.* "Human capital" refers (rather crassly) to the fact that the potential for production lies not only in tools, but also in some of the characteristics of the people. Their skills, education, health, strength, motivation, attitudes, and religion all have an impact on productivity, and can be thought of as a form of wealth.

*4. Technology.* Technology (as we shall discuss it in Chapter 12) refers to the techniques necessary to accomplish a task. Techniques should be efficient in achieving the purposes most important for the people. Because it is meant to complement man's fulfillment of the cultural mandate, and not to violate it, misplaced technology can be disastrous. Even the substitution of capital-intensive technology for labor-intensive technology, a transition usually thought of as a part of normal economic "development," can work great hardship on the people of a poor nation who desperately need jobs and income now. But technology can also greatly increase those jobs and income, and thus falls under the category of wealth.

### Consumption Patterns

The disparity between rich and poor nations can also be illustrated by a comparison of consumption patterns. Consider, for example, the percentage of disposable income paid for food among the following nations:[2]

| | | | |
|---|---|---|---|
| United States | 17% | Indonesia | 50% |
| Great Britain | 22% | Peru | 52% |
| Japan | 23% | Zaire (Congo) | 62% |
| USSR | 38% | India | 67% |

The average person in India or Zaire obviously has little left over after he has obtained his food. When we consider further the gluttony and the frivolity of food consumption in the countries which spend only a little of their income on food, and the malnutrition and scarcity in the countries which spend most of their income on food, we see an even greater contrast. Not only do we in the rich countries tend to eat too much, but we also buy a great deal of unnecessary services with our food dollar. We buy food which is overly processed, cosmetically perfect, and (for our convenience) wastefully packaged.

In the Fourth World, the energy consumption per person, important because it indicates by what energy other than the strength of their hands people are able to live, is only about one-hundredth of the U.S. average. The U.S. consumes 33 percent of nonrenewable energy and mineral resources. Incredibly, it consumes 63 percent of the natural gas produced, 33 percent of the petroleum, and 42 percent of the aluminum. Yet the population of the U.S. is only 6.2 percent of the total world population. Moreover, the average American consumes 2.4 times that of the average Russian, 8.8 times that of the average Mexican, and 63.6 times that of the average Indian. Canadians are almost as profligate.

Certainly there are two implications of such figures. One is that those in poor nations are not consuming enough. But another, surely, is that those in rich nations are consuming too much. Overconsumption in rich nations not only deprives the poorer nations of wealth, but it also sets up a model of happiness-through-consumption which all other nations seek to imitate. Thus the great disparity in resource consumption between the rich and poor nations is itself a major cause of the rapid consumption of natural resources and of the negative impact on the ecosphere outlined in earlier chapters.

## RELATIONS BETWEEN RICH AND POOR NATIONS

These great inequalities might seem more tolerable if each nation were economically isolated from the others. But we cannot consider the wealth or poverty of one nation by itself, because the uneasy community of the world's nations is bound together in a complex pattern of trade, tradition, and economic compulsion. In general, this complex of relationships works to the advantage of the richer nations, not to that of the poorer.

To satisfy their demands, rich nations look to other nations to supply food, energy, and mineral resources. Much food consumed by Americans, for example, is obtained from sources outside of the United States. The U.S. depends on foreign countries for 99 percent of its coffee, 100 percent of its cocoa, 99 percent of its bananas, and 43 percent of its sugar. With respect to mineral and energy resources, the U.S. depends on other nations for half of its oil, 90 percent of its bauxite, 35 percent of its iron ore, 85 percent of its tin, and 59 percent of its zinc ores. Let us consider briefly the two main ways in which these unequal relations among nations are maintained: direct trade and the transnational corporation.

### Trade

Most of the demands of the rich nations for resources are met through international trade, which theoretically should work to the advantage of the poor nation as well as the rich. However, the terms of trade usually limit the possibilities for the poor countries. To any nation, international trade represents the possibility of selling products which it can produce cheaply and buying products which other nations produce cheaply. For example, a nation might sell its tin ore, which it has in abundance, and buy a variety of food and manufactured products produced cheaply by other nations. In order to buy what it needs in world markets, a nation must sell *something* in those same markets in order to generate foreign exchange to pay for what it buys. Balance of trade and balance of payments are thus crucial considerations for any country. The tragedy for the poor countries is that the *terms* of trade usually do not permit such a balance. An important exception is OPEC— the oil producing and exporting nations. The ability of these nations to get higher prices for oil has roused great hope in other developing nations.

Poor countries (again with the exception of OPEC) have suffered a dramatic decline in their share of world exports and a dramatic rise in trade deficits. The trade deficit was accelerated by the increase in oil prices, but both trends were established before that price rise which, despite its ray of hope for developing countries, did great damage to their balance of payments. It is not always obvious why the trading positions of the poor countries are so inferior, but we can summarize at least some of the reasons.

1. Poor countries often depend very heavily on the export of only one or, at most, a few commodities. The principal export product of poor nations typically accounts for about 45 percent of their total exports; the three main export products together account for about 75 percent. Changes in climate or market conditions can thus have disastrous effects on export earnings and on the entire economy.

2. Poor nations depend heavily on the export of unprocessed products. The nature of the demand for these products, together with the above-mentioned concentration on a few exports, seems to work against the possibility of significantly increasing export earnings by increasing output. Suppose that to pay for its imports a country must increase its earnings from exports. Suppose also that, lacking several kinds of things to export, this increase could only be achieved by exporting a single product: coffee, for example. As the export of coffee is increased, the price of coffee on world markets falls rapidly, leaving the country little better off—and, potentially, even worse off. This vicious cycle is a serious consequence of a one-crop economy.

3. Rich countries, which are the largest markets for exports from the poorer countries, frequently can substitute other products for the ones purchased from poor nations if the price rises too high. For example, synthetic materials can be substituted for cotton, wool, or rubber. Thus the rich nation can avoid trade with the poor nation completely. The poor countries, on the other hand, usually lack this flexibility to substitute the products they buy from other countries. They must pay the price or do without.

4. Perhaps the most significant set of influences on the terms of trade are the specific trade policies pursued by various countries. There are three main models for understanding these international interactions.

  a. The first stresses that trade is intrinsically beneficial, and that therefore all barriers to trade should be removed. Some who hold this view concede that it may occasionally produce undesirable effects, such as unequal distribution of benefits. But these are seen to be minor drawbacks. In this view, trade is usually understood to be interaction between equals, without acknowledgment of substantial differences in power or wealth among the trading nations. Because this view is a restatement of the "classical" *laissez faire* (or "hands off") capitalism of Adam Smith, it is sometimes called the *neo-classical* view.

  b. The second model affecting international trade policies assumes that there are structures which limit the effective operation of the "free market" assumed in the neoclassical view. Those who hold this position maintain that trade should take into account differences in bargaining power which result from differences in wealth, income, and technological capacity. Because of their emphasis on the structure of the trading relationships, those who hold this position are called *structuralists*.

  c. The third model of international trade sees international relationships as the systematic exploitation of the poor nations by the rich nations. Trade thus amounts to an international class struggle. The best-known proponents of this theory are the Marxists, but the basic idea is broader than Marxism. Because this understanding assumes that some nations will be dominant and others dependent, it is called the *dominance/dependence* view.

Each of these models is important because each implies different causes for the inequalities between nations. Consequently, they each call for radically different solutions to the inequity.

Most rich nations, the United States in particular, have formally adhered to the neoclassical view, which stresses the virtue of free trade. In practice, however, this loyalty to free trade is distinctly less than complete. While the recent "General Agreement on Tariffs and Trades" (GATT) talks have had some effect in reducing tariffs, the rich nations have not opened their own markets to the poor nations to the extent that their economic theory calls for. The U.S., for example, has shown itself very ready to work toward the exclusion, through tariffs or quotas, of products deemed damaging to the interests of the U.S. domestic industry. Because of "cheap labor" in Brazil, South Korea, and Hong Kong, for example, shoes and radios from those countries are not welcome in U.S. markets. Such action is not necessarily in the best interest of all of the citizens of the U.S. It tends, rather, to benefit special groups. The steel manufacturers want limits on steel imports, the farmers on beef, the cotton growers on cotton. The overall effect is the protection of markets for the predominantly manufactured products of rich countries. Significantly, markets for U.S. agricultural products are protected in the same way. Such market protection effectively denies both the markets and the facilities for production to the poor countries, and makes it difficult or impossible for them to diversify their exports, develop an efficient manufacturing sector, and earn adequate foreign exchange. The enormous inequity of this system is indicated by the fact that poor nations get $30 billion for twelve main export commodities (excluding oil), while final consumers pay $200 billion. Obviously, most of the wealth is being kept in the rich countries.

5. Raw materials are worth less than the products manufactured from them. As a result of the foregoing factors and the limitations of available capital and technology, some poorer nations have been prevented from benefiting from the extra value that manufactured goods have over raw materials. When poor nations attempt to manufacture such goods themselves, they are faced with high tariffs, low quotas, and high shipping charges, making such ventures economically infeasible.

In a speech given at Howard University in Washington, D.C., Julius K. Nyerere, President of Tanzania, cited an example of the discrimination against those labor-intensive goods which can be made more cheaply in the developing nations. He said:

> . . . the poor nations have to ship both their imports and their exports in ships owned and managed by the developed countries. The freight rates are mostly fixed by a shippers' cartel. . . . This cartel has an apparently ineradicable bias against carrying processed goods away from East Africa; for a ton, it costs $41 to ship raw sisal and $73 to ship twine to and from the same port, with similar differentials between cotton lint and textiles, hides and leather, and so on.[3]

The result is that while developing nations are forced to depend for income on raw materials and primary products, the prices of many of the manufactured goods produced by developed nations rise proportionately faster. In Tanzania's case, it takes more and more sisal to buy the increasingly expensive agricultural machinery needed for its production.

Overarching all of these trade problems for developing nations is the need to reform the international monetary structure. Unquestionably, this structure is outdated. But because it is their creation and continues to be dominated by them, rich nations have been relatively slow to open up the operation of the money structure, including credit access, to the needs of the poor countries.

## Multinational Corporations

Most of the relationships described thus far take place between nation-states. A different kind of force operating between rich and poor nations is the multinational or supranational corporation. Even though our knowledge of these corporations is obscured by poor information and many accusations, several things seem clear: 1) Multinationals are usually very large and powerful; 2) they pursue their own self-interest in an enlightened or unenlightened fashion; 3) to the extent that they are supranational, they may also be supralegal institutions, since no effective international law governs their activity; 4) in most poor nations, multinational firms are big fish in small ponds and, inevitably, exert a great deal of economic and political influence; and 5) contrary to the popular belief that multinationals bring a windfall of financial capital to underdeveloped countries, they in fact frequently siphon off local capital for their own use.

Given all of the above, it seems clear that the present activities of the multinationals are not entirely good for poor countries. Increased control of their operation is a major objective of the "New International Economic Order" (NIEO), a program for the reform of relations between nations.

Some of the issues with which the NIEO is concerned include the following:[4]

1. Whether the multinationals protect monopolistic power by entering foreign countries and cutting off possible foreign competition.

2. Whether they introduce products and technologies inappropriate to the people of the developing countries. (Coca-Cola, for example, is a capital-intensive industry located in areas which are long on labor and short on capital.)

3. Whether they manipulate transfer prices among nations so as to take advantage of national tax and tariff structures.

4. Whether they worsen foreign exchange problems by manipulating money markets. (To sell large holdings of weak currencies, for example, tends to further weaken them.)

5. Whether they reinvest much of their profits in developing countries.

6. Whether these corporations exercise decisive control of the economies of poor nations.

Thus far we have been considering those relationships between rich and poor nations which cause such a great gap between them. Julius Nyerere, the eloquent and perceptive president of one of those poor nations, sums up the problem:

> Poverty is not the real problem of the modern world. For we have the knowledge and resources which could enable us to overcome poverty. The real problem—the thing which creates misery, wars and hatred among men—is the division of mankind into rich and poor.[5]

Our focus in this book as a whole is on the stewardship of natural resources. And that "division of mankind into rich and poor" of which

Nyerere speaks is a direct consequence of our use of natural resources. For it is what we mine, grow, and pump from the earth which creates wealth. When we use that wealth unwisely, we injure not only the earth from which it is drawn, but the people for whom it should be used. Ultimately, that same selfish use of resources that creates the gap between the rich and the poor on earth is responsible for the problems of the health of the whole ecosphere, including the human race. We should keep in mind these connections between the welfare of the ecosphere and the welfare of the poor as we turn now to consider the prospects for changing relationships between rich and poor nations.

## DEVELOPMENT

### Background

In discussing what can be done about the plight of the poor nations, we should keep in mind the history of many of the poor nations' relationships with the rich nations. Although it is not always true that being a colony yesterday means being a poor nation today (for some poor nations were not colonies, and some former colonies are now rich), a large number of the poor nations were once part of colonial empires.

The driving force for the establishment of colonial empires was the self-interest of the rich nations; thus the poor nations have usually suffered from being colonies. The self-interest of rich, powerful nations meant not only that the economic relationships were one-sided, but also that there was no deep concern for the integrity of the poor nations. In attitudes and practices of rich nations toward the poor, a predominant element has been cultural domination—the imposition of values, systems, policies, and practices which are not necessarily appropriate for the poor countries. This has been done for a variety of reasons, including a feeling of superiority on the part of the rich or a paternalistic feeling toward "backward" peoples. The rich have sometimes observed that the indigenous practices and institutions of poor countries are inefficient for economic accumulation, and have set about to "improve" them. This has frequently been done without an adequate understanding of the traditions, cultures, or even of the circumstances of the poor nations. A clear distinction has not always been made between the aspects of the culture which are the cause *of* poverty and those which are caused *by* poverty. If the poor do not spend what money they have wisely, this is assumed to be the reason for their poverty and proof that they are unworthy of more because they would not use it responsibly. The more complex relationships between poor stewardship and inexperience, ignorance, or insecurity—themselves all likely to be caused *by* poverty—have seldom received adequate consideration. Rich nations sometimes indeed have better ideas and better institutions than poor nations, but these things should be offered and accepted with great wisdom and with a recognition that the rich might also learn from the poor.

The age of colonies has ended. But, in considering what to do about the plight of the poor nations, it is all too easy to retain a colonial mentality and to assume that their development must be modeled after that of the rich nations, that what they need are the values, policies, systems, and institutions possessed by the rich nations. However, as the preceding chapters have shown, those values and policies of the rich nations have often led to serious problems with the earth's resources. "Development" in the United States, for example, has eliminated wildlife, fouled air and water, halved our topsoil, and depleted our mineral reserves. Can one even imagine the consequent environmental problems if India and China used natural resources in the same way and at the same per-capita rate as we do? It is not at all clear what kind of development is best for the "developing" nations. One of the central questions becomes, therefore, "What is development?"

For too many years, development was thought to be equivalent to sheer economic growth, a growth that was measured in aggregate terms. A country was considered to be developed when its GNP per capita reached a certain level and when its annual growth rate hit a certain percentage. Unfortunately (as we pointed out earlier), a nation may reach a high level of aggregate income and still have wide gaps between the rich and the poor. U Thant recognized the shortcomings of such aggregate definitions of development when, at the start of the United Nations' "First Development Decade," he defined development as economic growth *plus social change*. Dudley Seers comments on such development:

> The questions to ask about a country's development are . . . : What has been happening to poverty? What has been happening to unemployment? What has been happening to inequality? If all three of these have declined from high levels, then beyond doubt this has been a period of development for the country concerned. If one or two of these central problems have been growing worse, especially if all three have, it would seem strange to call the result "development," even if per capita income had doubled.[6]

Even this view of development, however, is not accepted by some. For example, liberation theologians, Third World Christians concerned for social justice, argue against thinking that the problem of the poor is merely a matter of alleviating problems of poverty, unemployment, or inequality. Rather, it is a matter of *liberation*. As Denis Goulet summarizes their position:

> For liberationists, therefore, success is not measured simply by the quantity of benefits gained, but above all by the way in which change processes take place. Visible benefits are no doubt sought but the decisive test of success is that, in obtaining them, a society will have fostered greater popular autonomy in a non-elitist mode, social creativity instead of imitation, and control over forces of change instead of mere adjustment to them. The crucial question is: Will "underdeveloped" societies become mere consumers of technical civilization or agents of their own transformation?[7]

And again:

> Such liberation arises at freeing oneself from nature's servitude, from economic backwardness and oppressive technological institutions, from unjust class structures and political exploiters, from cultural and psychic alienations—in short, from all of life's inhuman agencies.[8]

## Development Considerations

Whatever the proper view of development (and surely those views are better which recognize the worth of the individual as well as of society, and which include the health of the ecosphere), certain factors which impede development within poor nations need to be taken into consideration. The first part of this list is obviously parallel to our earlier listing of what makes a nation "wealthy."

1. *Lack of natural resources.* Some countries (those of the Fourth World) lack the stocks of resources within their territorial boundaries which are necessary for accumulating wealth. Without such resources, they are not in a position to trade with other nations.

2. *Lack of capital goods.* Poor nations often lack the capital goods—those nonhuman means of production—which are needed for development.

3. *Lack of appropriate knowledge.* Some nations lack the technical knowledge necessary for increasing production. Other nations do possess certain technical knowledge and technological products, but both are often inappropriate, given the needs and culture of the people. This technology is often capital- and energy-intensive and labor-saving, and thus is inappropriate in societies which have plenty of labor, but little energy or capital.

We have dealt with the preceding factors briefly because we touched upon them earlier. The following deserve more attention.

4. *Attitudes.* Piero Gheddo suggests three attitudes of poor nations which have hindered development:[9]

    a. A concept of life and work which is directed toward subsistence rather than improvement. Enough to eat is enough, period.

    b. An absence of any idea of progress and an orientation solely to the past or to the status quo.

    c. Religions whose teaching on the relationship between man and nature impedes the use of nature for human needs.

These attitudes undoubtedly underlie problems in development.

It is ironic, however, that the opposite extremes of all three are causes of environmental problems in the "developed" nations: an idea of "improvement" which encourages wasteful affluence, an idea of progress which encourages continual growth of consumption, and an idea of nature which sees this planet only as raw material. Nevertheless, since in the modern world these nations have to compete in markets dominated by the Western ideas

of values, their attitudes on improvement, progress, and nature only perpetuate their own poverty. But the problem can be dealt with as much by
the rich nations learning from the poor as by the poor learning from the
rich. As we shall suggest in a later chapter, there is a middle ground between
progress and poverty which is suggested by the Christian gospel.

5. *"Inadequate" social structures*. Piero Gheddo also considers the social
structures, such as tribal and caste systems, of some poor nations to be further
hindrances to development. Tribal systems are typically centered around land
and agricultural resources, and caste systems tend to keep a large proportion
of people working to serve a smaller proportion. Development would seem
to require breakup of both tribal and caste systems. Prosperity would be
determined no longer by tradition or birth, but by the money obtained from
jobs in industrial cities. Again, however, the problem is not so much in the
social structures per se of the developing nations; it is rather in the difficulty
of fitting those structures into rich-nation ideas of development.

6. *Unequal distribution*. In many poor nations where development has
begun, the resulting benefits and wealth are distributed over a fairly small
fraction of the population. Such distribution leaves a large group—consisting
chiefly of landless peasant farmers, rural artisans, and what has come to be
called the urban informal sector—with little (if any) improvement in income
and almost no connection to the development process. This problem is magnified by the tendency for the internal distribution of income to become even
more unequal as poor countries begin to increase their total GNP.

7. *Population growth*. Population expansion is a critical problem for
poor countries, because hard-gotten economic gains can be effectively canceled out when they are spread over larger populations. Nevertheless, the
solution so easily summarized as "population control" is not easy at all.
Intervention in the family is not a light matter—as should be obvious to all
Christians, and as India found out in the people's resistance to a mandatory
sterilization program. And poor nations, though they do recognize the problem, resist the rich nations' demands that they institute population control
as a precondition for aid. We, in turn, must be cautious about a self-righteous
attitude toward population growth for several reasons. First, a large part of
the plight of the poor nations is the absence of possibilities for territorial
expansion—and such expansion played a vital role in the development of
most of the presently rich countries. Second, we have worsened the population problem by helping to decrease mortality rates without at the same
time increasing economic security. In most cultures, having many children
has traditionally been an economic advantage. Even in our own past, large
families were the source of many farm hands. Likewise, the role of large
families in poor countries appears, at least to the people of those countries,
to be closely related to economic security. Though it is true that the birth
rate falls as the result of economic growth, such a decline would not be the
*cause* of economic growth. And the "transition period" is longer than most

poor nations can tolerate. Third, we in rich countries may be more directly responsible than we think for the inability of poor nations to provide work for larger populations. As our own population movements from farm to city took place, the cities were able to employ the additional people because of the manufacturing operations going on there. But today, we take much of the raw material resources from the poor countries in order to do the manufacturing ourselves. Thus we take their potential for urban employment, but not their people.

   *8. Urbanization.* Rising unemployment rates in agrarian societies are often caused by the sale of small farms to large landholders and by the introduction of labor-saving technology. No longer able to work on farms, many go to the cities to seek work, armed with limited savings and no skills but farming. And, as Arthur Simon says,

> Too often the jobs aren't there. Families settle in shantytowns, and if unemployment persists, broken homes, alcoholism and crime may follow. In the poor countries urbanization is taking place at a far more rapid rate than it ever did in Europe or the United States. . . . To find something like it in the United States you turn to the migration from the rural South of several million impoverished blacks, who arrived in the cities when unskilled hands were no longer in demand. . . . Still, it is microscopic compared to the migration now going on in the underdeveloped countries.[10]

   But why do the causes of this forced urbanization (large landholdings and high-level technologies) occur? Part of the problem is caused by the consumption patterns described earlier. To satisfy the demands of rich countries for luxury foods—pineapples and bananas, for example—larger farms and more "efficient" farming methods are needed. And, ironically, the "Green Revolution," with its capability for producing more food through hybrid grains, is also more amenable to mechanized agriculture, thus providing fewer jobs.

   A further consequence of urbanization is that, while their food needs had previously been supplied by their small farms, in the cities the landless poor are forced to rely on money to obtain the food they had previously grown themselves; only those with enough money can feed themselves adequately, and money comes from jobs, which are simply not available.

   Shifts from agriculturally based to industrially based economies occurred in the developed countries as well. But such changes were gradual. In poor, developing nations, there has simply not been enough time to make the adjustments required by the rapid introduction of labor-saving machinery and death-reducing medical technologies.

### Efforts for Change

   *1. Aid.* Perhaps the effort for development which comes most readily to mind is that of foreign aid. Most people use the term "foreign aid" to indicate one-way transfers between nations. Before saying more about such transfers, we must make several qualifications. First, the term "aid" suggests an act of charity freely given because of the conscience of the giver. But not all "aid" transfers fall into this category. If the transfers are mandated out of justice, then they are not aid so much as they are the paying-up of an obligation. Second, not all aid is actually intended as a transfer. We frequently give aid expecting very explicit returns, such as buy-back requirements, or at least implicit returns, such as the expectation that the recipient country will refrain from criticizing us, will allow us to establish a military base in their country, or will vote with us in the United Nations. Aid given with these expectations is not a transfer or grant, but a transaction—a way of buying favors. Third, aid is frequently given for specific purposes: we can, and often do, choose to give weapons rather than food. Correspondingly, the type of aid has an effect on internal balances, including the distribution of income within the recipient country. Depending upon the sort of aid, and the mechanism for its delivery, some people will be made relatively better off than others. We have not always demonstrated a concern for this problem; sometimes we have knowingly aided the rich instead of the poor. At other times, because of the internal power structures, we have found it very difficult to get past the rich in order to reach the poor. Finally, not all dollar figures stated for aid are transfers. Some are loans which demand repayment, though perhaps on favorable interest terms.

Aid figures can be deceptive. Though total aid from all sources was about $20 billion in 1972, this amount represents a very small net transfer of wealth in the world. Even using the gross aid figures, this is only about one twenty-fifth of the military budgets of the industrialized nations and only about half of the 0.7 percent of the GNP figure recommended for aid by the Pearson Commission. The U.S. figure is about .26 percent of GNP; for Canada it is .58 percent. What is worse, aid as a percentage of GNP is falling.

If we rank countries according to the percentage of GNP which they give away as foreign aid, Canada lies in the eighth position and the United States in the twelfth. Sweden, giving .80 percent, and the Netherlands, giving .69 percent, rank first and second respectively.

Even adding private aid to governmental aid does not change the figures much. In 1975, the U.S. gave the equivalent of .06 percent of its GNP in private aid, while Canada gave only .04 percent.

In any case, it seems clear that foreign aid: 1) has suffered from a lack of support by the rich nations, especially the U.S.; 2) has been an instrument in the power struggle between nations; and 3) has not been at an adequate level to solve all problems. Reforms are therefore needed to increase the level of true aid to the poor. And, given the level at which rich nations have exploited the resources and the people of poor nations, that aid should be given as much out of justice as charity. If justice demands the transfers, there should ideally be no resistance to giving them and no stigma associated with receiving them. Aid will also have to be freed from political and economic power struggles. Perhaps this can be accomplished by moving away from the domination displayed by two spheres of influence: Russia and the United States. Already the amount of aid given by the oil-rich Arab nations is changing that old bilateral picture.

2. *Strategies of Internal Development*. With only temporary setbacks, increases in consumption, capital accumulation, innovation, and industrialization have all proceeded steadily in the recent history of most of the GNP countries. In the poor countries, on the other hand, growth tends to be minimal. When almost all effort is directed toward survival, there is little effort available for longer-term gains. Conversely, the lack of such gains keeps the poor in a fight for survival in the future. To those who may not live, long-run solutions are nonsolutions. The economist Keynes' dictum, "In the long run we are all dead," has special meaning for these people. This lack, in many poor nations, of any hope for the future is an especially cruel aspect of poverty.

As we have seen, past development strategies have failed to take into consideration some of the problems faced by the poor nations that are trying to begin development. For example, when wealth begins to come into poor nations, it often accumulates in small sectors of those societies. Some say that this wealth will eventually "trickle down" to the poorest groups. However, the lack of integration of the groups in a society usually impedes such "trickling down" of wealth. And even if there were such an effect, we might well wonder what the poor are to do while they are waiting for this to happen. Critics of this theory point out that poor countries lack the institutions to facilitate this "trickle down." Gunnar Myrdal warns also that instead of "trickle down" effects, the opposite, or "backwash effects," can occur when inequalities exist.[11] When this happens, wealth and talent tend to flow from the poorer to the richer regions, where returns are both higher and more secure. The "brain drain" experienced by many poor countries is an example of this problem. It has also been observed that the wealthy citizens of poor countries frequently invest their savings outside of their native land in order to earn a higher return or to insure greater safety of their funds.

In response to this difficulty in distributing wealth, many poor countries are beginning to reassess their own growth strategies. They are trying to design programs which aim not just at gross economic growth, but at social justice. These programs would try to avoid too early a transition to a low-labor industrialized economy, would seek to give control of the land to more of the people, and would attempt to integrate the urban underemployed into small businesses or train them in the skills needed by larger businesses. These are strategies directed toward the immediate needs of the people, but which promise long-term growth as well. The change in attitude is summed up by Mahbub ul Haq: "We were taught to take care of our GNP as this will take care of poverty. Let us reverse this and take care of poverty as this will take care of the GNP."[12]

3. *New International Economic Order.* Perhaps the most important strategy which the poor nations have adopted to promote their development is the determination to effect international economic reform. Accordingly, a group of poor nations, primarily from the Third World, have presented to the U.N. proposals for a "New International Economic Order." The NIEO's platform includes the following principles:

   a. Nations shall have permanent sovereignty over natural resources and the right to nationalize according to national law.

   b. Developing countries shall have the right to establish commodity producers' associations (such as OPEC).

   c. The export prices of commodities from developing countries shall be linked directly to the prices of imported manufactured goods.

   d. The operation of multinational corporations shall be subject to international regulation.

The intent is to stabilize the prices and earnings for poor nations, and to gain additional control over the operations of multinational firms. The U.S., however, has responded to each of these proposals by expressing confidence in the virtues of the market system as an efficient allocator of wealth, or by suggesting that the role of private capital in the development process be enlarged. Both responses reveal little inclination to change past policies. The U.S. has also asserted that improvement in the Third World is dependent upon the continued growth of the industrial economies. But, as we have seen, increased industrialization will not necessarily improve the situation of the poor and hungry, nor will it lessen pressure on natural resources and on the welfare of the ecosphere.

4. *Law of the Seas.* Establishment of a new international economic order is not the only hope for the future of poor nations. We noted earlier that there are substantial amounts of recoverable minerals deposited on the seabed floor—so much, in fact, that the depletion times for many key minerals (given current rates of use) are greatly increased. Moreover, these deposits, like the water and its life, lie outside of national territorial limits, and have been regarded as a global "commons." These commons are the areas and resources that are not under the sovereignty of any nation and that have been traditionally regarded as belonging to all nations together or to no nation at all. Since these ocean mineral deposits, like the ocean waters and their inhabitants, belong to us all (or to no one in particular), poor nations, and especially resource-poor Fourth World nations, have claimed at least a share of the ocean deposits.

Of course, such a claim would have little significance unless it were possible to extract these deposits. But their extraction is indeed possible.

Governments of various countries are already involved in or are supporting various activities in deep seabed mining; Australia, Japan, the Federal Republic of Germany, France, New Zealand,the U.S.S.R., the United Kingdom, Canada, and the United States all participate in these endeavors to greater or lesser degrees. Within the past few years, enterprises within these nations have been forming international consortia for the purpose of mining. Since these enterprises are all in the rich nations, and since most poorer nations lack the capital and technology necessary for seabed mining, the poorer nations fear that they will miss out on their share in the wealth of a common heritage.

And they have cause to fear. Those nations which have been able to harvest the ocean's fish and other creatures normally claim that what they have harvested is, by that very count, theirs. Moreover, attempts to put limits and restrictions by international agreement on how much and what can be harvested, although sometimes successful, are often difficult to achieve and even more difficult to monitor.

The poorer nations have not let this precedent deter them. In 1969, the U.N. General Assembly adopted a moratorium resolution which declared that,

> . . . pending the establishment of . . . [an] international regime: a) states and persons, physical or juridical, are bound to refrain from all activities of exploitation of the resources of the area of the seabed and ocean floor, and the subsoil thereof, beyond the limits of national jurisdiction; b) no claim to any part of that area or its resources shall be recognized.[13]

The following year the Assembly unanimously declared, among other things, that,

> 1. No state . . . shall claim, exercise, or acquire rights with respect to the [ocean floor] or its resources incompatible with the international regime to be established. . . .
>
> 2. All activities regarding the exploration and exploitation of the resources . . . shall be governed by the international regime to be established.
>
> 3. The exploration of the [ocean floor] and the exploitation of its resources shall be carried out for the benefit of mankind as a whole, irrespective of the geographical location of states, whether landlocked or coastal, and taking into account the interests and needs of developing countries.
>
> 4. The [international] regime [to be established] shall insure the equitable sharing by states in the benefits derived therefrom, taking into consideration the interests and needs of the developing countries, whether landlocked or coastal.[14]

After eight consecutive Law of the Sea conferences, however, no treaty to establish the regime has yet been set up. Meanwhile, pressure has built in the U.S. to begin mining without a treaty. A report of a House Subcommittee on International Organizations says:

As a country in the forefront of the technologically sophisticated free enterprise undertaking, the United States and U.S. companies view the prospect
of deep seabed mining with the same zeal and imagination as they did the
Alaska North Slope oil discovery. Similarly, U.S. companies have anticipated
free access to all deep seabed resources, protection against price and production controls, coverage by U.S. laws—tax, customs, safety, and antipollu-
tion—and U.S. diplomatic protection. The absence of such elements in our
internationally negotiated treaty has introduced pressures for either 1) uni-
lateral legislation to insure the acquisition of deep seabed mining interests; 2)
no treaty; or both.[15]

Two things are clear in the ominous optimism of this report. One is that
there are powerful forces in the United States which have no intention of
regarding seabed resources as the common heritage of humankind. The
other, exemplified in the opening phrase describing the United States as "a
country in the forefront of the technologically sophisticated free enterprise
undertaking . . . ," reveals the attitude that the *power* to use a resource is the
*right* to use a resource.

### The Stewardship of Structures

As this chapter has made all too clear, we cannot discuss the problems
of resource use without considering the structures through which individuals
and nations act. And when we consider those structures, we are faced with
a complexity as deep and tangled as the human soul. Whether we speak of
ownership, capital, cities, or multinational corporations, we are considering
the social tools whereby we use—or misuse—both nature and other persons.

Certainly some of these structures seem to be "negative resources"—
the dominance of rich nations over trade relationships, for example, or the
elusive accountability of transnational corporations. But the structures of
human society are as much a resource as the earth and sea. In a sense, these
resources of human institutions are even more basic to our stewardship of
the earth than the earth itself, for it is through them that we affect the earth,
for good or for evil.

Implicit in all that follows, then, is our assumption that our exercise
of stewardship extends to the earth *through* human institutions; one cannot
speak of "nature" without speaking also of human societies. For the range
of resources over which we are called to be stewards includes not only forests,
floodplains, oceans, and ores, but also tariffs, technologies, legislatures, and
corporations.

# JOY OR DESPAIR?

**SO THAT, BRIEFLY, IS** the state of the planet. These first five chapters have given us some understanding of the wealth in minerals, fuels, animals, and soil of this rich world. They have also sketched what we are doing with that wealth: the patterns of our use and our ways of structuring trade, labor, and our very freedom to act on and with the earth. But at this point it will be helpful to recall the puzzlement with which this book opened. What is our future going to be? Do we act with those who see that future as a disastrous struggle by burgeoning mobs for dwindling resources? Or do we follow those who see the future opening into a bright world of cheap energy, inexhaustible resources, and limitless human opportunity? Do we face the future with joy or despair?

Though we yet have much to consider before attempting to sketch specific attitudes and acts, we have, in these past chapters, seen enough of the wealth of the earth and its resources to suggest, if not joy, at least optimism. It might be helpful to summarize that wealth.

First, there is the nonliving stuff of the earth: that planetary given of rock, water, and air around a core of hidden heat. And though we call that mineral sphere nonliving, it changes with a dynamism that suggests life: tides pull its oceans daily around a basalt crust; and that crust itself, we are learning, shifts and flows in a vast, slow cycle that brings metal-rich rock from the molten core, shifts and lifts it across seafloor and continent, and, after unimaginable time, conveys it down again to the planet's heart. We have quite literally only scratched the surface of that mineral sphere; and of its total resources we know very little.

A second kind of wealth is the steady flood of energy through which our planet moves. We circle a star that every second transforms more than four million tons of its mass into energy and beams it into space. Turning in this torrent of radiance, the earth receives only about a billionth of the total, yet so great is that earth-impinging energy that, if it could be harnessed, each person on earth would have for his or her personal use over 3,000 times the energy consumption of each citizen of the United States; the total solar energy striking the earth in only one week is greater than the energy contained in all the oil, coal, and natural gas ever stored in the earth. That great wealth of energy moves the currents of the sea, and brings a vast (and often violent) movement to the atmosphere. As the surface of the world turns steadily from its shadow into light, the unevenly heated air circles and flows in breezes, gusts, and hurricanes; each day the sun's energy in the atmosphere causes thousands of thunderstorms, each with the energy of many atomic bombs. More important: each day the sun's heat evaporates and condenses billions of gallons of water into clouds, which rain down on the land and flow from it in a great wealth of waterfall and river. And, most important of all, the daily turning of the planet into the sun's light drives the silent chemistry of photosynthesis. Thus the sun is the physical source of our life.

Then there is the third great kind of treasure on our planet: that fecund wealth of living cells, ordered in patterns we call redwood, spider, trillium . . . and human being. Catching the sunlight in chemical nets, trillions of organisms breathe, eat, multiply, and die; the very breathability of the atmosphere is a result of countless sun-catching lives; so, also, is that stored intensity of sunlight in oil and coal. The soil in forests and fields owes its fertility to living things, as we owe the food which sustains us to that life-supported, and life-supporting, fertility. What that intricate interdependence recalls for us, lest we forget, is that we too are organisms. Not only do we depend on this tissue of life, we are part of it—not simply because we affect other life, and life affects us, but because we *share* its life. Such thoroughness of participation in the natural world is disturbing: how can such coinherence of nature and ourselves be understood as *wealth*? But it is disturbing only if we are chauvinistic about our distinctness from nature.

If we understand that our bodies are inseparable from the rest of organic life, and that we cannot say, with the Psalmist, "I am fearfully and wonderfully made," without including the fox, the paramecium, and the oak tree, then we will have learned an essential lesson about how to live on the planet. We will have understood that the intricate diversity of organic life is our own diversity. Every time we eat or breathe we participate in that created network of sun-catching life which is fertile, tough, resilient, and which its Creator—and ours—calls good.

And yet, we are more than that life. To the mineral wealth of the planet, the torrent of energy which bathes it, and the rich diversity of organic life in which our bodies are enmeshed, we must add the fourth, and (apart from our knowledge of God) greatest kind of wealth we have: that is, our own ability to stand apart (in our consciousness) from the planet—to know it, to name it, to use it, and to see it whole. Nothing better symbolizes that ability than the photographs of the earth from space. They not only reveal the earth as a rich and vulnerable planet, but also demonstrate an ability to use the planet's wealth to transcend it. Ultimately, then, it is that human capability to *know*, and to create new things and methods with that knowledge, which is our greatest resource. Without it, none of the planet's other wealth—its mineral capital, its stored and incoming solar energy, its blooming and beautiful life—is wealth at all. The greatest resource is humanity itself, and the capabilities to know, structure, create, and accomplish which seem to distinguish humanity from the rest of creation.

As this quick summary of our resources suggests, there is cause for joy in being human at this difficult time—joy at simply being present, alive, responsive, and responsible in this diverse kingdom of a planet. There is cause for joy, too, in the task given to the unfallen Adam, but which is no less ours: to *cultivate* the fertile earth—somehow to use, and serve its great wealth.

And yet there is cause for despair. For though the planet's wealth is undeniably great, its greatest wealth—that human capacity to know, change, and manipulate—is also the planet's greatest danger. For all of the problems referred to in the earlier chapters—the forced urbanization, the wasting of energy, the loss of our topsoil, the human starvation, the decline of wildlife— are the consequences of that great gift of intelligence and creativity. Clearly it is that wealth of manipulative and reflective ability which enables us to use the rest of the world's wealth. But clearly, too, that manipulative ability is monstrous—even suicidal—unless it is guided and controlled. For, as the problems of the planet show, the values that guide our humanity and that inform our structures of use and exploitation need redeeming. And such redemption comes not from the earth, for all its wealth and beauty; it comes from beyond it, from its Creator.

If, then, we are to choose among different ways of using the planet's wealth, we must, as Christians, consider more broadly the consequences of that salvation we have understood too often as a private and otherworldly gift. For we are saved not only *from* the consequences of our sinning, but *for* that continued task of stewardship once given Adam. Unless our understanding of redemption extends to our stewardship of the earth, it is incomplete; and without redeemed persons, humanity will only destroy the rich and beautiful planet it inhabits.

It is not easy for us to think of the relevance of Christianity for our treatment of natural resources. There are clear historical and structural reasons for that blindness which we will consider in the next section; in the section following it, we will explore the biblical bases of a concern for the planet and its wealth. But a brief reflection on a familiar biblical story, from a perspective provided by the foregoing material, may serve as a good introduction to a consideration of our *attitudes* toward the earth. To see the relevance of the story we must digress briefly.

It could be objected that a concern for the whole planet's life, an attempt to apply human intelligence and creativity to the development of the whole earth and its resources, is a task for God, not man. The last edition of that counter-cultural Bible, *The Whole Earth Catalogue*, has as a preface the declaration, "We *are* as gods and might as well get good at it." Such an attitude rightfully seems somewhat blasphemous. The consequences, for both man and nature, of the full use of the unredeemed manipulative powers of humanity are likely to be disastrous indeed. This potential tragedy has been seen clearly by many thoughtful Christians. C. S. Lewis, for example, in a novel that explores the problems of an unregenerate power over nature, writes of a time and situation much like our own, when

> dreams of the far future destiny of man were dragging up from its shallow and unquiet grave the old dream of Man as God. . . . There was now at last a real chance for fallen Man to shake off that limitation of his powers which mercy has imposed upon him as a protection from the full results of [his] fall. If this succeeded . . . Nature, all over the globe of Tellus, would become [his] slave; and of that dominion no end, before the end of time itself, could be certainly foreseen.[1]

The story of Babel is one record of the consequences of that "old dream of Man as God." Impelled by their efficiency, the cleverness of their hands, and their power over nature, men said, "Come, let us build ourselves a city, and a tower with its top in the heavens, and let us make a name for ourselves, lest we be scattered abroad upon the face of the whole earth" (Gen. 11:4). Certainly there are today many equally clever schemes for applying ever greater skill and efficiency to our power over both humanity and nature. Indeed, any awareness of the need—and ability—to master the earth and its wealth could easily become a Babel-like hubris.

God's response to this example of human creativity and endeavor has seemed to many to make of God a sort of anti-Promethean killjoy: " . . . this is only the beginning of what they will do; and nothing that they propose to do will now be impossible for them. Come, let us go down, and there confuse their language, that they may not understand one another's speech" (Gen. 11:6, 7). But that response should not be taken as divine timidity, nor should it discourage Christians from exercising godlike powers in their care and use of the planet's wealth. For it is not the divine intention to limit human endeavor or accomplishment. The Psalmist speaks of man as "a little lower than God," and a frequently repeated New Testament teaching is that redeemed man is to be a "joint heir" with Christ—Christ, the sustaining *logos* of the world, in whom all things consist. The idea that man—redeemed man—is to share in that creatorly task is clearly the implication of Romans 8:19, in which Paul writes that "the creation waits with eager longing for the revealing of the sons of God."

There are, as we shall see in the chapters which follow, great longings in man to restore the foundations of Babel, to make himself master on his own terms. Such unredeemed mastery would indeed be the occasion for despair. But there are also, as we shall see in subsequent chapters, good reasons for Christians to care for the world as Christ cares for it. And the consequence of *that* kind of mastery is one at which the very trees will clap their hands, and the mountains and hills shout with joy.

# SECTION II
# THE EARTHLINGS

# HISTORICAL ROOTS

**WE BEGAN THIS STUDY** of Christianity and resource use by reviewing two contrasting visions of the future, and our emphasis thus far has been on the physical facts behind those predictions: what indeed is the state of this vast, but limited, system of water, rock, air, and life, which we call the earth? We have seen that although there is no reason now to think that our great planet will shortly become the *late* great planet, there is nevertheless reason for grave concern. Consider some of the problems we have touched on:

—The worldwide degradation of the life-supporting environment.

—The approaching depletion of mineral and energy resources.

—The approaching limits of the land and water's capacity to produce food and fiber for humanity.

—The problems which technology creates—even though it solves other problems.

—Population increases in nations already crowding the limits of their resources.

—The growing difference in wealth and resource use between the rich nations and the poor.

Whether one feels that these problems signal the doom of human civilization or that they are easily soluble through the great wealth of the human intellect, all would agree to the presence and the severity of the problems themselves.

All of these problems have to do with the physical, measurable world—those levels of minerals, energy, or biological life we have summarized in the last section. But the ultimate problem is a matter of human resources: that combination of intelligence, creativity, and ingenuity which enables us to *use* the physical creation. Thus, against the bleak backdrop of these problems of our physical resources, there have been, during the last decade or so, countless calls for people to change not simply their behavior, but their attitudes and beliefs. Calls for change have been directed not only toward the *actions* of people and nations, but also toward the springs of those actions. For without a change in those impelling sources of action, the action itself is not likely to change significantly (except through coercion, or the threat of it—and that implies a change in attitude on the part of the coercers).

The purpose of this next section is to determine what, in fact, those springs of action are. What views of nature have shaped our use of it in the Western world? But before sketching those complex and changing views which have shaped (and continue to shape) our use of nature, it will be helpful to clarify several things.

First of all, we are limiting our discussion to the "Western world." One obvious reason for that limitation is that we who write this book, and most of you who read it, are "Westerners." But there is another, and more important, reason. For better or for worse, the tools and techniques for the large-scale manipulation of the earth have been developed mainly in the West. Today, for example, when a nation in Africa or Indonesia is spoken of as "developing," that "development" is understood in terms of Western tools— tractors for cultivation, turbines for the generation of electricity, computers for the storage of information, contraceptives for the control of population, and so forth—all organized under a commitment to efficiency and progress, ideals which also were developed in the West. Though the roots of these developments are worldwide, for a variety of reasons (which we will shortly consider) they have flowered most spectacularly in the West; and the fruits of that westernization have been, for most of the world, all but irresistible. This is not to say that the only environmental problems are recent and Western in origin. As we saw in an earlier chapter, exploitive attitudes have, at many times throughout history, turned rich lands into deserts and wiped out whole species of wildlife. Certainly the same sort of event can be brought about by very different causes; these sins have by no means been limited to Westerners. Nor does our emphasis on predominantly Western views of nature mean that there are no uniquely Oriental sources of wisdom on which to draw for principles of care for the environment; later, for example, in our discussion of Christian principles, we will find some value in Eastern ways of interpreting the Christian gospel.

Another aspect needing clarification is what, in fact, we mean by "views of nature." And a word in that phrase requires further clarification: what do we mean by "nature" (and "natural")? "Nature" is, of course, a notoriously broad and complex term, as is clear when one thinks about common phrases which contain it. "Mother nature," "human nature," and "laws of nature" give good examples of the range of diverse and often contradictory meanings. In what follows, we mean by "nature" the earth and all it contains, excluding those objects and systems which have significantly been formed by humans. Thus spoons, tables, and concrete blocks are not part of nature, but animals, plowed fields, and landscapes not severely altered from their untouched state are. Obviously, these are not clear-cut categories; it could be argued that nothing on the earth's surface is completely unaffected by human activity, or that nothing on earth is completely transformed out of its natural state. But this definition gives us at least an instrument with which to examine "views of nature."

A good way of understanding what we mean by "views of nature" is to see them as collections of attitudes and beliefs where answers to important questions about the relationship between humanity and nature might be found. These are some of the most important of those questions:

—What characteristics of nature are most important for humanity?

—Is humanity itself a part of nature or distinct from it?

—Are there any normative relationships between persons and nature, anything which we ought to do (or not do)? If so, should we do these things because of qualities in nature which call for a certain action? Or should we do those things because they are *decreed*—by God or our common humanity?

—Is there any purpose in nature? If so, is this purpose inherent in nature, or set for it by its Creator? Or, is its purpose derived only from human needs, desires, and drives?

As we shall see, in the history of Western thought many answers have been given to these questions—or, if not to the questions directly, *actions* have implied an answer. That horizon of beliefs, information, and assumptions within which those actions or answers appear is what we mean by "views of nature."

## Christianity or Christendom?

One brief, but very influential, analysis of the relationship between "views of nature" and treatment of nature is an article by the historian Lynn White, called "The Historic Roots of Our Ecologic Crisis." His basic thesis (which is shared by many others) is that the dominant attitudes toward nature in the Western world are derived from Christianity, or at least from a certain pervasive version of it. What White says about the impact of Christianity on Western views of nature may be summarized briefly. Christians, says White, have maintained that:

—Humans are rightfully masters over nature, and may do with it what they please; this attitude of mastery is the consequence of the scriptural teaching on human "dominion."

—Just as God is transcendent over nature, humans are transcendent over nature; our body, which is clearly natural, is only a vehicle for our spirit, which is transnatural and made in the image of the transcendent God.

—Nature is not sacred, nor does it, in itself, deserve any respect which would limit our treatment of it.

—Science (the understanding of the workings of nature) and technology (the human-directed transformation of nature) are appropriate
expressions of our dominion over nature. In the scientific revolution,
science and technology were wedded in a union which Christianity
blesses.

—The idea of progress, as opposed to a cyclic view of history, is most
clearly expressed in Christianity, thus giving rise to a need to move
continually beyond nature.

All of these views, White maintains, are a legacy of Christianity to the
post-Christian world. If a change is to take place in our behavior toward the
environment, these views, and the arrogant attitudes which they express,
must change.

It is our thesis that White is, with a few important exceptions, correct
in his analysis of the effect of Christianity on views of nature. However, the
most important of those exceptions is a crucial one. It is not Christianity,
but *Christendom*, which has caused the ecological crisis of which White speaks.
That is, those who call themselves Christians have been guided at times by
principles other than Christian.

That distinction gives us our main approach to this discussion of "views
of nature." In the pages which follow we are first going to consider in some
detail that complex of ideas and beliefs which, apart from the Christian
gospel, has shaped the mind of Western people, and which the gospel is
intended to clarify or transform. That transformation has seldom been complete. What White and others have pointed to as the destructive influence of
Christianity is, in fact, the destructive influence of pre-Christian ideas, imperfectly transformed by the gospel, and too often mistaken for the gospel
itself. In Section III we will turn to an exposition of what, indeed, that
Christian teaching concerning the human use of nature is.

### CHAPTER 6

# THE CONTRIBUTION OF THE GREEKS

*Plato thought nature but a spume that plays
Upon a ghostly paradigm of things; . . .*

—**William Butler Yeats,
"AMONG SCHOOL CHILDREN"**

The Christian gospel was first proclaimed in a world permeated with Greek thought. The earliest, and at that time the most influential, Christian thinkers explained the gospel in terms of Greek philosophy. Thus it is to Greek ideas that we must first turn in determining the main influences on those "springs of action" which have motivated Christendom's treatment of nature.

Four more or less distinct views of nature emerged in that Hellenistic thought which, for many centuries, shaped the worldview of the peoples around the Mediterranean. We will refer to them henceforth as the Platonic, Aristotelian, Epicurean, and Stoic views of nature, with the warning, however, that this brief summary contains only the dominant themes, without much regard for the refinements and niceties of individual thinkers. However, since it is those dominant themes which have exerted the greatest influence on views of nature, these summaries should not be misleading.

## PLATONIC VIEWS OF NATURE

For the Platonists, the most obvious and important characteristic of nature is that it keeps changing. Things come into being and pass away, are subject to the everlasting cycles of birth, growth, decay, and death, move here and there, and constantly change their character. The world of nature is the world revealed through the senses; and what the senses sense is a world full of motion and change, a world in which nothing is stable, and nothing is eternal.

This ceaseless mutability of the sensible world is abhorrent to the Platonists. For them, change is a mark of imperfection; only that which is immutable, eternal, and wholly orderly is perfect. Thus, insofar as the world of nature is a changing world, it is an imperfect one.

But nature is not entirely imperfect. It does display *some* order and stability. Even the constant change, in itself a sign of imperfection, can be orderly and harmonious. Since some perfection may be found, even in this imperfect world, nature is both orderly and disorderly; not wholly perfect, but not wholly imperfect either.

To explain these contradictions, the Platonists maintain that the orderliness in nature results from its participation in the Forms of a transcendent, perfect world, one not apprehended by the senses at all. These eternal Forms are unchanging and perfect, and are the source of whatever beauty or stability nature has. This world is perceived only by the intellect, and is the only legitimate focus of a good person's attention, for it alone is the source of truth, beauty, and perfection.

Thus the Platonic world is dualistic—split between a changeable, transient world of matter known by the senses and an eternal world of ideal Forms known only by the intellect. We, however, belong to neither world. The soul, which is the seat of the intellect, is forced to reside in a body, and the body is a part of mutable nature. The soul is therefore distracted from its true end: communion with that transnatural world of the Forms. As a venerable Greek pun puts it, the body, *soma*, is the tomb, *sema*, of the soul.

In this Platonic doctrine of the body as the tomb of the soul we find the source of an influential element in the Western treatment of nature. It is sometimes referred to as *contemptus mundi*, contempt for the world, and it issues in an attitude of flight from any dealings with the world which are not absolutely necessary for bodily survival. The body, and all of nature, is seen as something foreign to the essence of a person, a distraction from the soul's proper task. Nature itself is but a pale shadow of what is truly good and beautiful; it is not worthy of our serious involvement. This is one important consequence of the Platonic view of nature. And it is clearly a negative one, so far as any positive human treatment of the natural world is concerned.

There is, however, a more positive and constructive Platonic view of the proper relationship between persons and nature, and it stands in some tension with the otherworldly Platonism we have just outlined. For some of the Platonists—including Plato himself—believed that humans have a task with regard to nature. That task is, so far as possible, to bring order into nature itself.

The first place where we are to bring order is the body; the pleasures, pains, drives, and yearnings that distract it from its true task are to be brought under control. But the duty to bring order extends beyond the self. All good human actions consist of bringing form to the formless: the woodcarver imposes order on wood; the shoemaker imposes order on leather; the politician imposes order on the state. It is thus that the artisan, the craftsman, and the politician fulfill their duty as embodied souls.

To impose order is to follow the example of the master craftsman who first formed nature, and who maintains its order. In the creation story in Plato's *Timaeus*, that master craftsman encounters a nature in complete disarray, and, because of his goodness, imposes order upon it. Said Plato:

> He was good; and in the good no jealousy in any matter can ever arise. So, being without jealousy, he desired that all things should come as near as possible to being like himself. . . . Desiring, then, that all things should be good and, so far as might be, nothing imperfect, the god took over all that is visible—not at rest, but in discordant and unordered motion—and brought it from disorder into order, since he judged that order was in every way the better.[1]

But it is clear that no one, not even the god, can completely overcome the recalcitrance of the material with which he has to work; nature is inherently disorderly, and neither god nor man can bring order past what is allowed by the material itself. Nature can never be perfect. Three aspects of significance for subsequent views of nature should be noted about this Platonic view of man as orderer.

First, it reverses the emphasis on flight from the world which is an inevitable consequence of seeing nature as an impediment to the soul's attainment of the ideal. Indeed, were it not for this ordering element in Platonic thought, we would expect the Hellenistic heritage to be solely one of inward-looking mysticism, rather than the glorious collection of shaped marble, metrical language, and symmetrical architecture that has been preserved.

Second, though such artifacts clearly show that there is in Platonism an impetus for working with nature, it is clear that the order is *imposed* on nature. It is not that the ordering craftsman, through his work, somehow allows nature to reveal itself. To the Platonist, a revealed nature is simply chaos. All the order comes from the intellect, which alone is capable of perceiving the transcendent and thoroughly nonnatural Forms. Thus the thinking behind the humans-as-orderer Platonism is not fundamentally different from that other kind of Platonism which can easily result in "contempt of the world."

Third, it is clear (even in the brief passage from the *Timaeus* quoted above) that the action of the ordering craftsman is admirable not because of any benefit which appears in nature itself, for it is order which is good, not nature.

One more feature of Platonism deserves mention. There is in it no room for the idea that nature is divine. Though the Olympian religion has a pantheon of gods who are clearly present in nature, Platonists take great care to disassociate themselves from that religion, at least in any form which would confuse God and nature. It was not the presence of the gods in the natural world which was the great Greek influence on Christian thought, but the separation of the *good* from the natural world. One cannot look to Platonic sources for nourishment of any kind of reverence for nature.

In reviewing these two aspects of Platonism, we see that though the idea of humans as craftsmen does encourage an involvement with nature, there is little concern for nature itself. The source of goodness and order is always beyond nature, which remains a chaos in need of shaping. Thus, though the otherworldly nature of Platonism does not explicitly encourage ruthlessness toward nature, there is in it no room for anything in nature which would discourage such ruthlessness; no equivalent, for example, of the repeated declaration in the biblical creation story that this physical world is good—very good. But there are other traditions in Greek thought.

## ARISTOTELIAN VIEWS OF NATURE

The most influential of those other traditions is the Aristotelian. Though Aristotle was a pupil of Plato, his thought in many ways opposes Platonism. Together, Plato and Aristotle represent two frequently encountered poles in the relationship between humans and nature. As one historian of philosophy put it:

> Like the Gilbert and Sullivan Englishman who is born either a Liberal or a Conservative, it has been remarked that everyone is born either a Platonist or an Aristotelian. Plato and Aristotle, that is, represent two different attitudes toward the world. Plato was a perfectionist whose inclination . . . was always toward a utopian solution that was impractical precisely because the perfect is never realized in this world. Where Plato was otherworldly and idealistic, Aristotle was practical and empirical.[2]

Whereas in Platonism the true form of a thing is beyond nature, in Aristotelianism it is *in* nature. One need not leave the world of the senses to learn what a thing in reality *is*. Likewise, where Platonism tends to stress the desirability for all things to be unified in one transcendent whole, a fundamental feature of the Aristotelian world picture is that it is composed of countless diverse things: stone:   es, animals, men, and so forth.

These "things" are substances; they are capable of existing independently of other things—at least to a degree. Thus a stone is a substance, but its grayish color is not, for the color of the stone is not sufficiently independent of the stone to qualify as a substance. Substances, in turn, are composed of two parts: matter and form. The form of a substance is the property (or properties) which makes the substance what it is—the form of a horse, for example, is what makes a horse a horse and not a chair. The *matter* of a substance, on the other hand, is what receives the form; it is that on which the form is impressed.

We may notice at this point at least an important similarity to Platonic thought: the distinction between the matter of which a thing is composed and the principle of intelligibility which makes it accessible to the mind.

What is "matter" to Aristotle is to Plato the unformed chaos of nature. And "form" in Aristotle's conception of substance is that ordering principle which, in Platonic thought, resides in the changeless and eternal realm, and can only be imperfectly imposed upon a recalcitrant nature. Though there is a superficial similarity between the two conceptions, there is an all-important difference: for Aristotle, there is no transcendent realm of the forms, no way of encountering in nature a form apart from matter. The way to knowledge is, therefore, not through insight into the ideal realm; it is through the senses. Thus there is in Aristotle more recognition of the ability of nature to be a vehicle for truth, and potentially a much higher view of nature itself.

In Aristotelian thought, the substances that make up the world can be grouped into natural kinds, depending upon the sort of essential form they share. For example, all individual horses share an essential form—what it is which makes them horses—and thus they form a kind. Within that kind, the *best* horse is the one which most thoroughly receives the imprint of what a horse is: the best horse is the horsiest horse. Every substance is a member of some natural kind; and these natural kinds are not the imposition of human categories on nature. Nature, in itself, is divided into kinds.

These natural kinds, in turn, form natural groups, or kingdoms of kinds. Agates are of a kind in the mineral kingdom; maples are of a kind in the vegetable kingdom; horses are of a kind in the animal kingdom; humans are of a kind in the rational kingdom.

These kinds and kingdoms are marvelously interrelated; indeed, they form a continuous hierarchy. Consider, for example, an agate. It is a member of the mineral kingdom. Accordingly, it has a certain form imposed upon its matter which makes it spatial, solid, and organized. Now consider a maple. In addition to all the qualities of the mineral kingdom (which it shares with stones) it has other characteristics: the ability to grow and to multiply itself. This additional form makes it a member of the vegetative kingdom. In the same way, a horse has the characteristics of the mineral kingdom and the vegetable kingdom, but also has other forms which make it a member of the animal kingdom: the ability to move, to sense things, and to work toward goals. Thus the horse, and any other animal, shares form with the vegetable and mineral kingdoms, but it is more than anything else in these kingdoms; it is a sensing, self-moving, "mineral-vegetable" substance.

In the same way, humans share form with the mineral, vegetable, and animal kingdoms, but have more: the ability to think things out prudentially and scientifically. This thinking ability means that humankind transcends the other kingdoms. But it also includes them; in addition to being rational, people are also fully animals, vegetables, and minerals. Thus humans are embedded in nature, and share completely in its character.

The familiar Aristotelian definition of humans as rational animals thus contains far more information than is commonly realized. For it tells us our place in the whole continuity and hierarchy of nature; indeed, in the Aristotelian scheme there is a place for everything, and everything is in its place. To understand man is to see his place in the unity and diversity of the world.

The contrast with Plato's view of nature could not be more extreme. For Plato, nature is intrinsically disordered, and receives order only through the imposition of ideal forms which are alien to it and can never be fully realized within its stubborn materiality. For Aristotle, nature is intricately and intrinsically ordered.

The place of humans in nature is likewise radically different in Aristotle. The soul, in Platonic thought, exists distinct from the body, and is always in some tension with the body. Humanity is thus, for Plato, essentially an alien presence in nature. Aristotle, however, though he speaks of a soul, does not mean by it something distinct from the mineral-vegetable-animal human body; rather, it is that which is unique about persons: the form which humans possess but which all things below humans lack. Accordingly, the Aristotelians also spoke of animal and vegetable souls, but they meant only that form which made vegetable substances different from mineral, or animal substances different from vegetable.

Another important aspect of the Aristotelian view of nature is the idea of purpose. Nature, said Aristotle in *De Caelo*, does nothing in vain, nothing superfluous. There is a purpose for every substance, every characteristic, every change. However, these purposes are not decreed by some craftsman-god, as in Plato; rather, they are to be found in the substances themselves. The purposes which we seek—and find—in nature are not the product of any mind; they are unpurposed purposes, undesigned designs. The universe, for Aristotle, appears to be a great work of craftsmanship—but with no craftsman.

Interestingly, however, in one passage in the *Politics* Aristotle seems to reverse this teaching on purpose by declaring that the purposes in nature are ultimately centered in humanity: plants are for animals, and animals are for humans. Says Aristotle (or perhaps, Aristotle's confused student, since the passage is so counter to the rest of Aristotelian teaching): "If nature makes nothing incomplete, and nothing in vain, the inference must be that she has made all animals for the sake of man" (*Politics*, I, 8).

In contrast to Plato, whose overriding suspicion of the physical world causes him to speak often of the need either of transcending or of imposing order on it, Aristotle gives no clear teaching on our duty with regard to nature. He states clearly, in the *Ethics* and elsewhere, that the duty of a good man is to fulfill his function in the scheme of things. For man, this would be to fully realize his distinctiveness from the animal kingdom: his being rational. However, given Aristotle's teaching on the human relationship to nature, that teaching could have two consequences. Since humans are in fact also mineral, vegetable, and animal, their rational capacity could be understood as simply the capacity to wonder about, study, and classify the other natural kingdoms. In such a view, humans would be the *consciousness* of nature, and thus would have the same attitude of respect and care toward it that a person would have toward his or her own body.

Another consequence of Aristotle's teaching on nature—concentrating especially on the idea that all things are for human use—is that since all things are to have a purpose, and since all purposes seem to be directed toward man the rational animal, then humans are justified in using all the rest of nature to fulfill their own purpose.

Actually, both ideas have shaped subsequent thought. For the most part, though, despite Aristotle's insistence that matter and form were inseparable, Christian and non-Christian interpreters of him have tended to emphasize the ideal rather than the empirical (sense knowledge), and have perpetuated a more idealistic, less empirical kind of Aristotelianism. This was particularly true in the time right before the downfall of Aristotelian science. Thus, we will further consider Aristotle's effect on views of nature when we look at the scientific revolution.

## STOIC VIEWS OF NATURE

Stoicism, which arose in Greece after the time of Plato and Aristotle, has not had the abiding philosophical influence of those two thinkers, but—perhaps because it became more of a religion than either Platonism or Aristotelianism, and because its greatest popularity corresponded with the greatest power and influence of the Roman Empire—a few Stoic ideas have nevertheless contributed substantially to subsequent views of nature.

The basic Stoic doctrine is that there is in the universe a dynamic ordering principle which is the source, pattern, and goal of all things, including humans. The Stoics called this ordering principle by a variety of names: God, Zeus, creative fire, ether, the law of nature, providence, soul of the world, Word, and so forth. For the Stoic, the universe was like an orderly, spherical animal, held together by the divine ordering *logos*. Though all things—plants, animals, stones—are shaped by the *logos*, it is particularly in rational creatures—humans and gods—that the "divine fire" of the world soul burns brightest.

The goal, then, of a good person's life is to bring that life into ever greater conformity with this pervasive cosmic order; one is to live "according to nature." The good person is one who is in complete harmony with the rest of the universe, for he or she is guided by the same "life-giving word" which animates all the universe, humanity and nature alike.

As we would expect from this Stoic picture of the world as a vast organism (whose "soul" is God), every part within that organism has a purpose. This concept of the purposiveness of all things, which plays only a small role in Aristotle's thought, is very important in Stoicism. The air is a medium for birds, the sea for fish. Clouds bring water to the land, rain is for plants and animals who need it for sustenance; plants and animals them-selves are fitted to eat different foods and to inhabit different regions. To the Stoics, this order was clearly divine, and it was an ethical and religious duty for good persons to find their place in it.

However, humanity has a unique place in this beautifully ordered world: it is for it (and the gods) that the world exists at all. Cicero, in *On the Nature of the Gods*, puts it this way:

> Here somebody will ask, for whose sake was all this vast system contrived? For the sake of the trees and plants, for these, though without sensation, have their sustenance from nature? But this at any rate is absurd. Then for the sake of the animals? It is no more likely that the gods took all this trouble for the sake of dumb, irrational creatures. For whose sake then shall one pronounce the world to have been created? Doubtless for the sake of those living beings which have the use of reason. . . . Thus we are led to believe that the world and all the things that it contains were made for the sake of gods and men.[3]

In these words we see that the Stoic idea of humanity in harmony with nature does not exclude the idea of nature being for humanity. Note that nature is not *evil* or imperfect; it simply reaches its greatest perfection in humanity.

That nature is for humanity does not, for the Stoic, mean that one can do whatever one likes with nature. In the same work, Cicero writes:

> Think of all the various species of animals, both tame and wild! think of the flights and songs of birds! of the pastures filled with cattle, and the teeming life of the woodlands! Then why need I speak of the race of men? who are as it were the appointed tillers of the soil, and who suffer it not to become a savage haunt of monstrous beasts of prey nor a barren waste of thickets and brambles, and whose industry diversifies and adorns the lands and islands and coasts with houses and cities.[4]

Thus we see that, for the Stoic, though nature may be designed for human purposes, man also has a purpose with respect to nature: he is to tend it, maintain its order, and beautify it with his industry.

Again, it is difficult to trace exactly the influence which Stoic thought has had on our own view of nature. One thing is certain, however: the generally negative attitude toward nature which is characteristic of Platonism was replaced in Stoicism by an understanding of nature as divine. Instead of imposing order on nature, the purpose of humankind was to live according to the divine order found in nature. Stoicism had a good deal in common with Aristotelian notions of "a place for everything and everything in its place," but gave that doctrine much more moral force. Not only were hu-mans to find their place, but they were to use their place in nature as a way of tending and embellishing its own order.

A number of Stoic conceptions were prominent in medieval thought, and at least one of these persists in our own time: the near-personification of the natural order, as when we speak of "Mother Nature," or "Nature's

Way" or even (in a very Stoic phrase) the "laws of nature." Moreover, the
Stoic doctrine of the indwelling *logos*, or order of things, contributes to and
is clarified by the Christian doctrine of Christ as *logos*.

## EPICUREAN VIEWS OF NATURE

It remains for us to speak briefly of yet one more Greek idea which
has had a strong influence on Western views of nature: Epicureanism. However, since its greatest influence was exerted after the Middle Ages, when the
unity of the Christian world view was disintegrating, it has never had much
influence on Christian thought. It is, nevertheless, an accurate prefiguring of
some aspects of modern scientific views of nature, and thus we should be
aware of it.

In the Epicurean view, all things are composed of atoms (an idea based
on the theories of an earlier Greek philosopher, Democritus). Atoms are
small, solid, indivisible, indestructible, and move about in empty space. They
cannot be perceived by humans, but their motions result in collections of
atoms, which are the bodies which humans perceive. All things, including
our thoughts and sensations, are the result of these atoms and their combinations. And although our senses are the only certain basis for knowledge
of the world, the qualities which we associate with the beauty of nature—
color, taste, tone—are not a characteristic of that ultimate reality, the atom,
but only an accident of the atoms' combinations.

Although the motions of atoms are regular and uniform, as is the
behavior of the larger bodies which the congregated atoms form, this regularity is the result neither of divine direction nor of the internal form of the
atoms themselves. There are no ends, purposes, or forms for nature, as
Platonists, Aristotelians, and Stoics alike agreed there must be.

Since humans themselves are just one more part of nature, and since
there is no divinity or order beyond it, they have no obligation with regard
to nature, either to control it or to care for it. There is no purpose to a
person's life—as there is no purpose to anything else in nature; the goal of
human action, then, since there are no transcendent values motivating it, is
to live as comfortably as possible.

As a giver of meaning to the individual's life, Epicureanism never had
much following, and thus had little effect on the treatment of nature. But
the basis of Epicureanism—a universe explicable only in physical terms, with
no value other than what is available to the senses, also underlies modern
scientific conceptions of nature. The potential effect of Epicureanism on our
thoughts and treatment of nature is very great.

The importance of reviewing the Greek views of nature becomes evident as we continue our study of historical attitudes. To summarize those Greek views we may begin by saying that nature is seen from two almost opposite viewpoints. In Platonism nature is presumed to be evil because of its mainly "chaotic" tendencies. Although there are signs of order in nature—there is some regularity in the change from day to night and in seasonal cycles, for instance—humans are the only beings in nature which can contribute, through their knowledge of the Forms, to that order. Epicureanism takes the idea of "chaos" even further, stressing that everything, including order, is the result of the random movements of atoms.

Nature is held in higher esteem, however, by the Aristotelians and Stoics. Again the focus is on the question of order, but unlike the Platonic and Epicurean view, this more positive attitude toward nature assumes that order is inherent in the universe. The goodness of humankind is thought to be rooted in the goodness of nature.

One thing that both the positive and negative views share is the idea that humankind is somehow the center of the universe. For Plato, this means that humankind is the source of order; for Aristotle (or his student) and the Stoics, this anthropocentrism is evident in the conviction that the purpose of nature rests in its relationship to humanity. We must not forget that Epicureanism is an exception to this rule—humans are just as much accidental as nature is—but, as we said earlier, Epicureanism had little effect on later attitudes toward nature, at least not until the scientific revolution.

When reading the following chapter on the medieval view of nature, it will be helpful to remember that Christendom was influenced by both the Platonic and the Aristotelian/Stoic viewpoints. At times nature appears to be evil; at other times it appears to be good. In either case, the belief in humanity as the center of the universe is rarely questioned.

### CHAPTER 7

# THE MEDIEVAL VIEW OF NATURE

> *The human imagination has seldom had before it an object so sublimely ordered as the medieval cosmos. If it has an aesthetic fault, it is perhaps, for us who have known romanticism, a shade too ordered. For all its vast spaces, it might in the end afflict us with a kind of claustrophobia.*
>
> **—C. S. Lewis, THE DISCARDED IMAGE**

> *It is well to remind ourselves that, apart from incidental inaccuracies of observation and measurement due to a lack of instruments of precision, the Ptolemaic view of the universe is neither more true nor more false than our own: it is merely another way of describing the same phenomena. Its truth, however, is of a different kind from ours. The difference is like that between a realistic perspective drawing and a map. In the one, all the geometrical facts are falsified; the lines which we know to be parallel are made to meet; it is a faithful presentation of what we actually see. In the other, all the geometrical facts are adhered to, but the view presented is one we can never see so long as we keep our feet on earth. The first picture corresponds to our observations; the second is reached by inference.*
>
> **—Dorothy Sayers, notes to Dante's DIVINE COMEDY: HELL**

ince the Greek ideas of nature we have been considering are from 2200 to 2400 years old, it may seem irrelevant to spend so much time on them in a work devoted primarily to the solution of late twentieth-century problems. But the distance between our own thinking and that of the ancient Greeks is not, in time, as great as it appears. In addition to their influence (largely debilitating) on the Christian view of nature, these Greek ideas were an important part of that thousand years of intellectual stability which we call "The Middle Ages." When in the sixteenth and seventeenth centuries the old

**115**

ways of looking at nature began to be seriously challenged, it was an amalgam of Greek ideas and biblical texts which gave way. On the popular level, many of these Greek views of nature (such as "Nature abhors a vacuum") are still a part of our understanding of the world. And, in the strata of fossil poetry which makes up our language, we may discover innumerable imprints of those ancient pictures of nature. But more important than these figments of an old world picture is the shape of what has been rejected: modern views of nature took shape *against* old views, and so they are incurably affected by them.

In either case, Greek influence is mediated to us through the Middle Ages. It was not, for the most part, transmitted deliberately and carefully, as from teacher to pupil; rather, it was the unplanned product of a whole culture. The basic stuff was the stones of Greek thought, held together by a common Christian mortar, and the result, erected over centuries and not yet entirely in ruins, is the great cathedral of the medieval picture of the universe. Those parts of the edifice that deal with the relationship between humankind and nature we can now consider briefly.

Above all, the medieval universe was ordered; not simple, by any means, but marvelously structured. There are many examples of this medieval intricacy. It may be glimpsed in the elaborate machinery of crystal spheres which carried the planets, one within the other, in a complex of movements explaining with near perfection the apparent motions of the skies at night. It may be glimpsed in another way in the *Summa Theologica* of Thomas Aquinas, which answers the basic questions about God, humanity, and the world with a calm sense of the accessibility of all information necessary to understanding the universe. It is evident in yet a different way in the *Divine Comedy* of Dante, which builds a marvelously symmetrical structure around hell, purgatory, and heaven, ordering the circles of Hell, the plateaus of Purgatory, and the spheres of Heaven with an intricacy and confidence which admits little doubt as to the structure of the moral or physical universe.

The sense of order owes a good deal to Stoic and Aristotelian conceptions, but it is baptized by the Christian doctrine of a creating and purposing God. The most dramatic form of the idea is in the "great chain of being" or in the "principle of Plenitude." The idea is circuitously derived from Platonism; in its Christian form it consists of the assumption that since God wills to share his goodness with all things, everything which can be *is*; there is a niche for everything, and, in the divine chain of possibilities, no niche is left unfilled. The idea contains not only a great image of the order of the universe—beast, human, and angel alike—but it expresses clearly a principle of hierarchy. For the order of the universe is not arbitrary: the more noble things are placed above the lesser. A modern manifestation of this image of ascending order is the idea of evolution. But it is as characteristic of the medieval view of nature to see that hierarchy frozen in the universe like an infinitely decorated arch, as it is for the moderns to see the creatures of nature flowing and changing toward an unimaginable and yet-to-be-attained perfection. For, despite all the intricacy of the medieval model, it is static.

But if things are unmoving, they are unmoving not as stagnant water, but as a waterfall is unmoving—or, more accurately, as a dance is unmoving, though its members move continually in their appointed places. This ordered, dancelike quality of medieval motion is nowhere clearer than in its explanation of rest and motion. The doctrine is well summed up in lines of Chaucer:

> . . . every kyndely thyng that is
> Hath a kyndely stede ther he
> May best in hit conserved be;
> Unto which place every thyng,
> Through his kyndely enclyning,
> Moveth for to come to. . . .[1]

Everything has its "kyndely stede" or proper place. Thus, when stones fall to the earth or when fires rise, they do so not out of a blind submission to forces acting from without, but from something very much like desire—a "kyndely enclyning" to find one's proper place. The medieval world picture was therefore much more like a dance than a machine.

It was also something like an organism. Owen Barfield describes this ordered and organic universe with great vividness when he tries to recreate for us the "feel" of the universe to a medieval "man in the street":

> To begin with, we will look at the sky. We do not see it as empty space, for we know very well that a vacuum is something that nature does not allow, any more than she allows bodies to fall upwards. If it is daytime, we see the air filled with light proceeding from a living sun, rather as our own flesh is filled with blood proceeding from a living heart. If it is night-time, we do not merely see a plain, homogenous vault pricked with separate points of light, but a regional, qualitative sky, from which first of all the different sections of the great zodiacal belt, and secondly the planets and the moon . . . are raying down their complex influences upon the earth, its metals, its plants, its animals, and its men and women, including ourselves. . . . we know very well that growing things are specially beholden to the moon, that gold and silver draw their virtue from sun and moon respectively, copper from Venus, iron from Mars, lead from Saturn. And that our own health and temperament are joined by invisible threads to these heavenly bodies we are looking at. . . .
> We turn our eyes on the sea—and at once we are aware that we are looking at one of the four elements, of which all things on earth are composed, including our own bodies. . . . Earth, Water, Air and Fire are part of ourselves, and we of them. . . .
> A stone falls to the ground—we see it seeking the centre of the earth, moved by something much more like desire than what we today call gravity.[2]

That passage describes several important features of medieval nature. One is the correspondence between the macrocosm and the microcosm—the great world of nature, and the small world of the individual human. The person was affected by the influences of that larger world, particularly by the planets. Indeed, the word "influenza" is a forgotten fragment of that old doctrine of human imbeddedness in the world of nature. Nor is it simply the physical person which is affected by the macrocosm. One's very personality is made up of elements which correspond to the four elements in nature: Phlegmatic, Sanguine, Choleric, and Melancholic temperaments, corresponding to Water, Fire, Air, and Earth, respectively.

We could go on characterizing that medieval model in great detail, but we wish here only to convey a little of its "feel" or flavor. The reader who wishes to explore it further may find a superb guide in C. S. Lewis' *The Discarded Image*. But out purpose here is not contemplation of that cathedral of ideas, however aesthetic an object of contemplation it may be (and Lewis suggests that it is the greatest of medieval works of art). We are interested rather in seeing how it affected the medieval treatment of nature and how our own attitude toward nature is shaped by it.

From the very character of the medieval model of the universe, we might accurately imagine what was, in fact, the primary feature of the medieval attitude toward nature. Since nature was characterized by an unchanging order, with everything in its place, and since people found their place within that order, they had no impetus to rearrange nature or to study it in order to determine its laws. The harmony of humankind with nature was such that there was no great effort to stand apart from it and analyze it. The universe was experienced more as a dancer experiences the dance, not as a sociologist might observe it. And, since the conviction of the order, rationality, and fundamental changelessness of the universe was so great, there was little interest in observing nature for its own sake; one could as well determine how a body fell by *thinking* about its fall, as by measuring its fall. Thus medieval science was primarily deductive rather than inductive.

We are, however, oversimplifying. For within this picture of a harmonious but static universe, there did slowly emerge a greater emphasis on the human ability to order and change it. The emergence of this idea of human power over nature was slow, and it was confined to the world of the craftsman and the artisan. For the most part, it was kept separate from the philosopher's and theologian's ideas about what the universe ultimately was. Indeed, when the world of the craftsman and the world of the philosopher came together, the medieval age ended, and the scientific revolution—and not long after it, the industrial revolution—began. But before turning to a consideration of that great change, we should consider briefly the uses medieval people made of nature—some details of medieval technology.

## MEDIEVAL USE OF NATURE

Since our own treatment of nature has as a backdrop those long centuries when the medieval view of the universe was taking shape, it will be helpful to consider what kind of actions resulted from that intricate medieval picture. We have sketched how medieval persons *saw* nature; it remains for us to consider briefly what they *did* to nature. A danger for most modern people, in considering those centuries which we call the "Middle Ages," is to assume that little of consequence went on in them. They are "middle," our language leads us to believe, because they are a transition (sometimes painfully slow) between the cultural vitality of the ancients and the progressive enlightenment of our own age. The less neutral phrase, "Dark Ages," even more vividly conveys the idea that those centuries were (at least in Europe) a slow purgatory, a painful, continentwide waiting for light.

It comes as a surprise then to learn that the Middle Ages were a time of considerable technological advance and a time of great impact on the natural environment. The great forests of Europe's plains were, in these centuries, largely reduced to fertile fields; marshes and estuaries were likewise drained and made habitable. All over Europe, rivers were harnessed in mills; in 1120, for example, there were over 5000 watermills in England. The popular image of a world sinking into savagery after the fall of the Roman Empire is not very accurate, as contemplation of any one of the great medieval cathedrals will show. Human powers to build, to use, to alter, and to destroy nature were certainly alive in the Middle Ages.

There is, however, some basis for that impression of quiescence which we associate with medieval life. Despite the changes which were made in agriculture, in milling, and in husbandry, there was still far more in common between the lives of a fourth-century and a fourteenth-century person than there is between the lives of a fourteenth-century and a twentieth-century person. Between the Middle Ages and our own time there occurred a great change in our way of viewing and using nature. The medieval world picture was of a fixed, hierarchical order, in which humans had a given place. The medieval concept of the relationship of humans to nature is summed up well by Clarence Glacken in his account of the thought of Gregory of Nyssa, a late Church Father on the threshold of the Middle Ages:

> Man is a master over nature which helps him on his way to God, nature itself being raised up and exalted in the process. God made an earth full of riches, including the gold, silver, stones, valued by man; he allowed men to appear on earth to witness these wonder works and to assume his role as master of them. Mastery over the lower beings was necessary to satisfy his needs: mastery over the horse because of the slowness and difficulty of human bodily movements; over the sheep because of our nakedness; over the oxen because humans are not grass eaters; over the dog because his jawbone is a living knife for men. His mastery of iron gives him the protection that horns and claws afford the animals.[3]

Gregory describes for humans a very high place with respect to the rest of nature, but there is no urge to move beyond that decreed place, which is furnished not only with deduced or inherited knowledge about the nature of plants, animals, and physical causes, but also with a kind of basic tool kit for using the world of nature. Though the medieval world was not a small one, it was enclosed. There was no "outside"—little concept of infinite space, or even of undiscovered and, therefore, beckoning lands. That absence of a sense of the unknown, that very *tidiness* of the medieval view of nature, discouraged both the search for a more basic knowledge of nature and the search for more effective techniques of using nature. It is hard for us to comprehend, for example, that a simple, but workable, steam engine was built in ancient Greece—but neither then, nor in the long centuries afterward, did it occur to anyone to apply those energies to work.

Certainly one reason for the great slowness in the growth of these abilities to manipulate nature is the distinction between what the philosophers thought about nature and what the workmen—the farmers, craftsmen, and artisans—did to (and with) nature. Today we would call it a split between science and technology.

The reason for this split is, in large part, the Platonic view of the relationship between humans and nature. It will be remembered that a dominant theme in Platonism was that nature was an impediment to the soul. A consequence of this attitude was that the good person should be occupied not with things of the body, but with things of the mind. Those who worked with animals, or stone, or even fire were, by their very involvement with such physical stuff, limiting their soul's ability to achieve the ideal.

This otherworldly attitude dominated medieval science. Inasmuch as speculation went on about the movements and the appearances of the physical world, that speculation was directed toward understanding the changeless and eternal principles, not in applying to practical work the knowledge thus gained. This general disdain of the learned person for involvement with the physical, together with the fact that the laborer was very likely unable to read, and thus was without access to the physical theories of the scholars (either to confirm or disprove them), produced a state of affairs in which the people who worked with nature had little knowledge of theories about nature, while the people who dealt with the theories did not apply them to working in the world. As the historian of science, Reijer Hooykaas, puts it, "In the Middle Ages, as in antiquity, reason led experience into captivity, art was judged incapable of successful competition with nature, and technology was separated from science. Head and hand were not encouraged to co-operate."[4]

The result was that, for most of the Middle Ages, the great wealth of human knowledge was not applied to human use of nature. The most significant technological inventions of the age—the horse-collar, the crossbow, the windmill—as well as the broadening application of older inventions, like the waterwheel and the sail, were made not by the "scientists"—the people concerned with knowledge—but by the workers: the people concerned with getting the job done. Thus the treatment of nature in medieval Europe was not, on the whole, much accelerated by the philosophical or theological thinking; it proceeded slowly, out of the trial-and-error, day-to-day work of nameless craftsmen.

There were exceptions to this general separation of head and hand, and out of some of them grew the modern conception of nature. One of the most prominent and earliest exceptions came from the abundant Benedictine monasteries. These were usually situated in remote places—in mountains, or forests—far away from the run of ordinary life. But the monks felt a kind of obligation, in such a setting, to recreate a kind of earthly paradise. Jean LeClerq, a historian of monasticism, sums up this idea of the monastery as a kind of "Jerusalem in anticipation":

> The cloister is a "true paradise," and the surrounding countryside shares in its dignity. Nature "in the raw," unembellished by work or art, inspires the learned man with a sort of horror: the abysses and peaks which we like to gaze at, are to him an occasion of fear. A wild spot, not hallowed by prayer and asceticism and which is not the scene of any spiritual life is, as it were, in the state of original sin. But once it has become fertile and purposeful, it takes on the utmost significance.[5]

A necessary part of this siting of monasteries in remote places was the conviction that the work necessary to transform the wilderness into a fruitful Eden was itself a kind of spiritual activity. Work, far from being the exercise of their base and un-soulish nature, was to the monks a kind of prayer. And, most significantly for the history of the development of the West, it was in the Benedictine monasteries that complex machines were first used on a large scale for the processing of nature. Humans were to use their hands to participate, with God, in the shaping of creation; and if their hands could be aided by river-powered mills, so much the better. Such large-scale physical work, coupled with the use and development of machines by men of the church, gave a kind of blessing to such machines, and began the breakdown of the barrier between mind and hand which had impeded medieval use of nature.

A further impetus to the study and (ultimately) the manipulation of the sensible world came about in connection with a mendicant order. Toward the end of the twelfth century, St. Francis of Assisi revolutionized medieval piety by living a life characterized by a joyous, self-giving poverty, and by a strong sense of kinship with the rest of creation. Though it is hard to distinguish fact from legend, it is clear that Francis possessed, for his time, a remarkable sensitivity to nature—indeed, to the whole material world. It was Francis, for example, who first placed animals in a churchyard at Christmas, saying, "Behold your God, a poor and helpless child, the ox and ass beside Him. Your God is of your flesh. . . ." And his Canticle of the Sun, in which he reaffirmed his ties with the rest of creation by speaking of

Brother Sun, Sister Moon, Brother Wind, and so forth, is famous even today.

In a short time, Francis had a tremendous following—the sheer success of which compromised his emphasis on extreme poverty. But the Franciscans kept alive the openness to the physical world; even when they did philosophy, they kept little of that aloofness of the mind from nature which was largely a Greek heritage. Thus Bonaventure, the greatest of the Franciscan philosophers, wrote eloquently of the Book of Nature and the Book of Revelation, and encouraged Christians to study nature in order to learn of God. It was within the Franciscan order that many of the greatest medieval scientists found a congenial home—men like Roger Bacon and Robert Grosseteste. Unlike the Greek and early medieval deductive science, this Franciscan science was based on *observation* of the world of nature; and that empiricism (which we now consider to be essential to science) was largely a result of Francis' openness to Sister Creation.

No immediate influential change in the treatment of nature came out of Franciscan science. But, just as the Benedictines broke down the barrier between hands and head, the Franciscans broke down the barrier between the senses and the head. The Benedictines encouraged technology, and the Franciscans encouraged an understanding of nature based on observation of nature itself, not on categories deduced from first principles and then imposed upon the world. This tendency culminated in the philosophy of a later Franciscan, William of Ockham, who maintained that "What can be done with fewer is done in vain with more." In other words, those explanations of nature are best which do not impose upon nature a variety of hypotheses derived from reason but irrelevant to the facts. And, as the fourteenth-century followers of Ockham discovered, such explanations are the ones most likely to result in usable knowledge of nature.

So, as the Middle Ages drew to a close, there were two tendencies at work which countered the generally otherworldly character of the medieval world picture and encouraged an increasing human involvement in nature. One was the accelerating control of the environment—through windmills, watermills, new kinds of harnesses, better ships, stronger metals, and so forth. These technological advances were still primarily the result of the work of common, uneducated people, though there was in the Benedictine monasteries a long tradition of learned, "spiritual" men, not ashamed of shaping nature with hand and tool.

The other tendency was a greater emphasis on the study of the world itself as a source of knowledge about it. Franciscans like Grosseteste and Roger Bacon founded their knowledge of nature in the divinely given book of nature, and Franciscan philosophers like Bonaventure, Duns Scotus, and Ockham developed good reasons, theological and logical, for thus basing knowledge in the impressions of particular things. The old separation of mind from the world, encouraged by the prevailing Platonism of medieval philosophy, was ending. When mind, hand, and sense came together in the scientific and industrial revolutions, the view of nature drastically changed, and the human capability to alter nature began an acceleration which has yet to slow down.

### CHAPTER 8

# THE SCIENTIFIC REVOLUTION

*Then felt I like some watcher of the skies*
  *When a new planet swims into his ken;*
*Or like stout Cortez when with eagle eyes*
  *He star'd at the Pacific—and all his men*
*Look'd at each other with a wild surmise—*
  *Silent, upon a peak in Darien.*

—**John Keats,**
**"ON FIRST LOOKING INTO CHAPMAN'S HOMER"**

*There is no question here of the old Model's being shattered by the inrush of new phenomena. The truth would seem to be the reverse; that when changes in the human mind produce a sufficient disrelish of the old Model and a sufficient hankering for some new one, phenomena to support that new one will obediently turn up. I do not at all mean that these new phenomena are illusory. Nature has all sorts of phenomena in stock and can suit many different tastes . . . nature gives most of her evidence in answer to the questions we ask her.*

—**C. S. Lewis, THE DISCARDED IMAGE**

cience and technology coalesced into a powerful tool at the same time as the discovery and initial exploitation of the New World. The physical new world became a kind of symbol of the rapidly emerging new world of human powers. The discovery of vast new lands across the oceans, and the growing tide of information brought back by the explorers and exploiters washed at the foundations of the splendid edifice of the medieval view of nature. Several consequences of the New World exploration need mentioning.

First, the discovery and the exploitation of the New World were far more the work of practical men, with practical goals, than they were the work of philosophers reasoning how the world should be. From the improved ships that carried the explorers such vast distances to the conquests and settlements in the New World itself, these mind-expanding changes in the size of the world were being wrought by people who advanced knowledge not by reflecting on first principles, but by applying clever hands to axe, adze, tiller, and sword. The New World opened up possibilities for men of action which had been unavailable in the Middle Ages. The results, whether they were new lands or Inca gold, were immediate and satisfying.

A second consequence of the New World for the old view of nature was that its very existence strained many old categories of what nature had been understood to be. For example, voyages into the southern hemisphere proved false the honored notion of medieval science that people could not live in the Antipodes, since a belt of fire would keep them from getting there. The discovery of a bewildering variety of new plants and animals, not to mention whole peoples of vastly different history, strained old conceptions of "a place for everything" to a disturbing—or exhilarating—breaking point.

A third consequence was more subtle, but it was perhaps the most important of all. The medieval world was self-contained. That physical "breaking out" of the bounds of previously known human endeavor became a symbol for a mental "breaking out" of old ways of thinking and old ways of action. The discovery of the New World was not only an effect, but also a cause, of a radically new attitude toward nature, the formulation of which we will attempt to trace briefly. For, with only slight changes, the understanding of the relationship between man and nature that emerged in the seventeenth century is the view of nature most commonly held today.

## THE ASTRONOMERS: COPERNICUS, KEPLER, GALILEO, NEWTON

The way man looked at nature in the seventeenth century was shaped as much by new theories in astronomy as it was by discoveries in the Americas. It had been accepted, throughout the Middle Ages, that the plain evidence of the senses was correct, and that the heavens moved around the earth. In order to account for these motions ancient and medieval astronomers—and especially a first-century Greek, Ptolemy—had devised an elaborate hypothesis of moving crystal spheres within spheres (or epicycles upon deferents) which accounted reasonably well for all the observed motions of the heavenly bodies, and which did not violate the ideal of uniform circular motion around an earthly center. Such motion, the philosophers felt, was the only motion suitable to the heavens, since they were unaffected by the corruption, mutability, and general imperfection of the earth. Early in the sixteenth century a Polish Canon, Nicholas Copernicus, developed a theory which explained the heavenly movements by placing the sun at the center of the system. Copernicus was timid, and delayed publishing his theory for nearly thirty years. He need not have feared: revolutionary as the theory was, it was nearly a hundred years before it attracted much attention. But the most revolutionary part of the theory was not that it described the sun as the center of the planetary motions; it was that it said this explanation of the planetary motions was not (as was the case with the old Ptolemaic astronomy) simply a convenient device for calculating the positions of the planets, but a description of reality.

A word or two of explanation is needed here. It will be remembered that the Platonic conception of reality maintained that truth is to be encountered not by the senses, in nature, but by the mind, in contemplation of that which is beyond nature. Thus observation of the movements of the heavenly bodies, though they provided good training for the mind, would not in itself yield truth, which was beyond any appearance. The movements of the planets were, in fact, only an appearance of an ultimately trans-sensible (and transnatural) reality. The Ptolemaic theory was not, then, supposed to describe how the heavens were in fact actually composed and impelled. Rather, it was a way of "saving the appearances." When Copernicus (timidly, to be sure) proposed that ". . . all that is beneath the moon, with the centre of the earth, describe among the planets a great orbit round the sun which is the centre of the world; and what appears to be a motion of the sun is in truth a motion of the earth . . . ,"[1] he signaled a radical change of the relationship of the mind to nature. He said, in effect, that the model which the mind makes of nature is a way of getting at the ultimate reality of a phenomenon, and that a hypothesis that saves all the appearances is not simply another hypothesis, but is equivalent with the truth.

It was nearly sixty years later that a fiery young Lutheran astronomer, Johannes Kepler, openly defended the neglected theory of Copernicus, and said more strongly what Copernicus had said: a hypothesis which did not aim at final truth was an inadequate instrument for understanding God's universe. Thus Kepler, throughout most of his life, worked laboriously at developing principles which would describe the *real* motions of the planets. He based his calculations on a great wealth of data compiled over many years by Tycho Brahe, a Danish astronomer. And, unlike earlier astronomers, Kepler was absolutely loyal to what the data said. Once, a small discrepancy of eight minutes of arc forced him to abandon the ancient idea of the circularity of the motions of heavenly bodies. That decision to accept the authority of observed nature over the authority of traditions *about* nature had far-reaching consequences. As Hooykaas put it, ". . . a lonely man submitted to facts and broke away from a tradition of two thousand years. With full justice he could declare: 'These eight minutes paved the way for the reformation of the whole of astronomy. . . .' "[2] They did more than that: they paved the way for the triumphal march of that attitude toward nature which says that the way to certain knowledge and control of it is through precise measurement, which increasingly becomes the only basis for the truth.

A third figure whose speculations on the movements of heavenly bodies prepared the way for a new relationship between mind and nature is

Galileo. Galileo is best known for being tried by the church for defending and teaching the Copernican system. It is important to note again, however, that the most significant issue was not the *idea* that the earth moved around the sun, but the conviction that this idea was equivalent with the truth. In any case, Galileo's greatest contributions to the changing view of nature are not in his defense of Copernicus, or even in his turning of the telescope onto the heavens and in the revelations of the size and complexity of the universe that resulted; they are rather in his theories of the movements of bodies and in the method that underlies them. Galileo sought to answer ancient questions about why falling or projected bodies move in the way they do. However, unlike earlier (predominantly Aristotelian) attempts to answer those questions, Galileo attempted to explain such movements not by philosophy— what the bodies *should* do—but by observation, by seeing what the bodies actually *did* do. He accurately recorded these movements of falling bodies under different conditions. Based on them, he arrived at principles of motion which, he asserted, encompassed the truth about such motions, even as he claimed that the Copernican theory got at the truth of the motions of the heavenly bodies. Much as Kepler did when he was forced, by the data of Tycho Brahe's observations (counter to all good philosophy about movements in the heavens), to declare that the orbit of Mars was not circular but elliptical, Galileo maintained that the precise measurement of falling bodies was the only way to knowledge about the laws that governed them. And his conviction that measurement and observation were the most certain way of knowing nature continues to our own times.

Another element of Galileo's thought is important for our modern view of nature. We have already encountered his distinction between "primary" and "secondary" qualities as part of that Epicurean explanation of the universe as the result of indestructible atoms falling forever in a void. Like Epicurus, Galileo maintained that such sensible qualities as color, smell, taste, and warmth were not a part of the fundamental particles, but "secondary," added by the mind. Said Galileo,

> . . . I think that tastes, odors, colors, and so on are no more than mere names so far as the object in which we place them is concerned, and that they reside only in the consciousness. Hence, if the living creature were removed, all these qualities would be wiped away and annihilated.[3]

The only thing that remains are the qualities which can be precisely measured and known not by the senses, but by the abstract mind: size, shape, and weight.

Galileo's dismissal of the world of the senses as unimportant in arriving at genuine knowledge of nature is so basic to contemporary science that it may not strike us today as very important. We have no difficulty in understanding that the real world is not what our senses show us, but is rather what can be measured precisely and reduced to numerical data. But consider for a moment what this idea does to the old medieval view of man embedded in the world of nature. If Galileo is correct, then nature is not the colored, textured, fragrant complexity which the senses encounter, but is instead a sized, shaped, weighed abstraction about which the more spectacular sense information is irrelevant. Knowledge of such a nature is achieved, rather, through the mind acting on data that have been reduced from sense knowledge to numerical certainties unavailable to the senses. That process of abstracting the mind from the world began with the Copernican theory, which presents the world not as we sense it, with sunrise and sunset, but as it would appear if we could be lifted out of the body, out of the planet, out of "nature" as we know it, and placed in a detached viewpoint far beyond the earth. It continues with Galileo's views, which reduced nature to the measurable "primary" qualities—those which underlie and are basic to the world which our senses show us. Though knowledge is, for Galileo, rooted in observation of nature, there is no room in this observation for anything which cannot be reduced to number. Increasingly, then, the vital cosmos of the medieval view—in which stones fell because they desired their place, and the microcosm of the person paralleled the macrocosm of the universe—is replaced by a kind of machine in which only the mind is alive.

It was left for Isaac Newton to make the final transformation from the medieval to the modern view of nature. His laws of gravitation explained the movements of the heavenly bodies as the result of the same forces which affect the movements of things near us—apples, stones, ourselves. All motions could be accounted for, in Newton's theory, by the same simple mathematical explanations. His was an elegant simplification of that complex picture of the universe which had prevailed through the Middle Ages. But it was also a rather cold and mechanical model. The important things were matter and motion, not the colors, tastes, or textures of the world as we sense them. As a result of the burgeoning availability of new and effective knowledge about nature, intricate machines (of which the clock was the most common) were being used and admired. And because Newton's universe seemed to work very much like a vast machine, nature, the heavens, and to some extent man himself came increasingly to be understood as a kind of elaborate clockwork. The old living world was dead; what had replaced it was a nature that could be explained in mechanical terms. The implications for the human use of nature, after such a transformation, are tremendous, as are the powers which became available to assist such use. But before considering those modern uses of nature, it will be helpful to consider two other seventeenth-century thinkers whose ideas about nature have shaped our own: René Descartes and Francis Bacon.

## DESCARTES' VIEW OF NATURE

The Frenchman René Descartes was a younger contemporary of Galileo. He was a devout and brilliant mathematician, and as he viewed the increasing certainty available to the physicists when they acted on the assumption that the universe could be explained by mathematical principles, he longed for the same kind of certainty in philosophy and theology. Thus he determined to rethink the nature of man according to the insights available from the new physics.

Kepler, as we have seen, was determined to show of the motions of the heavens ". . . how these physical causes are to be given numerical and geometric expression." He said of the motions of the heavens, "What else can the human mind hold besides numbers and magnitudes? These alone we apprehend correctly, and if piety permits to say so, our comprehension is in this case of the same kind as God's. . . ."[4] Likewise Galileo declared of the "book of nature" that, "This book is written in the mathematical language, and the symbols are triangles, circles, and other geometrical figures, without whose help it is impossible to comprehend a single word of it. . . ."[5] Descartes wished to place philosophy and theology—and indeed all knowledge—on similarly certain foundations.

But we must point out here a kind of paradox that is evident in Galileo, Kepler, and indeed all through the scientific revolution. We have stressed that the great strength of the work of these men was due to their insistence upon accurate observation of the created world: on seeing, measuring, and recording nature itself, rather than determining by reason how nature *should* behave. And certainly neither Kepler's laws of planetary motion nor Galileo's ballistics would be possible without such data. But the wealth of observed data is not a wealth at all until it is somehow transformed into mental models—those which Kepler and Galileo understood to be mathematical. These models are then imposed as a form of intelligibility on that blossoming world of sense particulars from which they were derived. Ultimately, then, the basis for certainty is not the sense world, but the mental, mathematical categories to which the sense world is reduced. Descartes, while recognizing the importance of empirical data, stressed the supreme importance of this mental world.

Descartes concluded that there were two sorts of things in the world: "thinking things" and "extended things." The mind was a "thinking thing" and the only source of absolute certainty, for it was the one thing which could not be doubted. Inasmuch as the world apart from the mind, the world of "extended things," could be known with certainty, it could (and must) be reduced into measurable things, a conclusion much like Galileo's distinction between primary and secondary qualities. To the mind, the whole world is a vast machine. Any explanation of anything in nature (including one's own body) is to be given only in terms of that which can be measured, and hence certain: extension, motion, and force.

The consequences of this view for the understanding of nature are far-reaching and extreme. One immediate consequence is a rigid distinction between body and soul (or mind). The body is a machine and the mind exists within it, but the mind is radically different. Sometimes the image of humans thus portrayed is characterized as "the ghost in the machine." Descartes had problems with this idea, for he could not determine clearly how the mind and the body affected each other. His half-hearted solution to the problem was to regard the pineal gland at the top of the brain (for which no other function was then known) as the organ of interaction between mind and body. But in this distinction of mind from body Descartes was only making explicit what was already implicit in physicists like Kepler and Galileo: knowledge is a function not of bodily participation in the world, but of the detached models which the mind builds out of that participation.

A further consequence of Descartes' view is that all of nature is a machine: it can be explained in terms of matter, extension, and motion, but not in terms of any purpose within it. That purpose is provided, rather, by the observing, thinking mind, which is detached from nature and is a different sort of substance altogether. Some of the destructive implications of this idea became immediately evident when Descartes said that, whereas a human was a machine with a mind conjoined, the body of an animal was simply a machine without a mind. There was no such thing as an "animal soul." Thus it was thought by Descartes (or at least, by Descartes' followers) to be impossible to be cruel to animals, since animals have no feelings. As one Cartesian put it, "An organ makes more noise when I play it than an animal when it cries out, yet we do not ascribe feelings to the organ." Nor was it long before some Cartesians began to apply this new view of nature. Lafontaine writes of Cartesian scientists of the seventeenth century who "administered beatings to dogs with perfect indifference and made fun of those who pitied the creatures as if they felt pain. . . . They nailed poor animals up on boards by their four paws to vivisect them and see the circulation of the blood which was a great subject of conversation."[6]

It is interesting to contrast this view of animals and humans with the Aristotelian view prevalent throughout the Middle Ages: that man shared a "soul" with rocks, plants, and animals, but in addition had a "rational soul, which was his distinctive." In Descartes' view, the mind shares nothing with the body and hence with the rest of nature; it is completely and categorically separate from stone, tree, and beast alike. Its knowledge of those things is colored by no feeling of kinship with the nonhuman world, but is instead a reduction of that world to the certain mathematical qualities which only the "thinking thing" can know.

Subsequent thought has not taken very seriously Descartes' radical distinction between the mind and the body; in fact, the modern philosopher Gilbert Ryle goes so far as to say that we have no need of the category "mind"; we need only speak of actions, for the behavior of individuals does not require us to speak of their mind, any more than it requires us to speak of "mind" or "soul" in animals. Contemporary behaviorist psychologists have effectively done the same thing, dispensing with concepts like purpose, value, and motivation, and approaching their study of humans and animals alike only in terms of measurable behavior.

Though such thinkers would disagree with Descartes' idea of the mind, they are following directly in the method he established: the attempt to understand nature not according to any internal purpose or intrinsic quality, but by reducing it to only the measurable, mathematical qualities which the separated transcendent mind can comprehend. In the interests of putting knowledge on a secure footing, Descartes effectively eliminated (theoretically, at least) the meaningful participation of humankind in the world. This sort of draining of significance from things is described vividly by C. S. Lewis.

> At the outset . . . the universe appears packed with will, intelligence, life and positive qualities; every tree is a nymph and every planet a god. Man himself is akin to the gods. The advance of knowledge gradually empties this rich and genial universe: first of its gods, then of its colours, smells, sounds and tastes, finally of solidity itself as solidity was originally imagined. As these items are taken from the world, they are transferred to the subjective side of the account: classified as our sensations, thoughts, images or emotions. The Subject becomes gorged, inflated, at the expense of the Object. But the matter does not end there. The same method which has emptied the world now proceeds to empty ourselves. The masters of the method soon announce that we were just as mistaken (and mistaken in much the same way) when we attributed "souls," or "selves" or "minds" to human organisms, as when we attributed Dryads to the trees. . . . We, who have personified all other things, turn out to be ourselves mere personifications. . . .[7]

This Cartesian process of reducing the world, the body, and ultimately, in twentieth-century thought, the mind, to matter and motion is one consequence of the curious two-sidedness of the method that emerges in the seventeenth century: that is, the simultaneous importance of both mental models and empirical data in order to know nature. The first stresses the distinction between man and nature, the other stresses the unity between man and nature. And if Descartes stresses the separation of the mind from nature, there is another side to modern views of nature which stress the practical, empirical origin of knowledge. There the goal is not certain knowledge (which can be experienced only in the separated mind); more and more it is *power* over the nature which we daily encounter and which, so often in human history, whether in storm, disease, or earthquake, has disastrously encountered *us*. That use of knowledge of the world in order to have power over the world was the great theme of another seventeenth-century thinker, Francis Bacon.

## FRANCIS BACON'S VIEW OF NATURE

"Nature to be commanded must be obeyed." These words occur near the beginning of Francis Bacon's most important work, the *Novum Organum*, and they summarize well not only Bacon's approach to nature and knowledge, but also the underlying attitude that emerged from the new science of the seventeenth century. First of all, Bacon's aphorism leaves little doubt that nature is to be controlled; to do so is man's rightful place. But nature is also to be *obeyed*. What does Bacon mean by this paradox? Some of the background of his thinking will be helpful here.

Bacon grew up in Elizabethan England, the same era which produced Shakespeare. It was an exciting time; England, in defeating the Spanish Armada, had become a world power. Her ships were exploring the world, and there was a pervasive sense of a "brave new world" to be conquered and used. It was also an era of statecraft and intricate politics. Queen Elizabeth showed that she knew how to use power, as did her successor, King James. Francis Bacon was close to that power; his father had an important position in the court of Queen Elizabeth, and he himself held various offices in the court of King James, including that of Lord Chancellor, the highest political post in the kingdom. Thus Bacon was intimately involved with the use of political power.

But from his youth on, Bacon saw that ultimately power is derived from knowledge. And he was disturbed that man's knowledge had, in the centuries of its accumulation, produced so little power over nature. Therefore he was bitterly critical of medieval science (which by then had been cast almost entirely in Aristotelian terms). Such knowledge had no offspring. And, declared Bacon, "knowledge that tendeth but to satisfaction is but as a courtesan which is for pleasure, and not for fruit or generation."[8]

Bacon's goal, then, was to establish a kind of knowledge which would bear fruit—or, to put it another way, a kind of knowledge which would give power. Such a task sounds ominous to us who are aware of the misuses of power over nature. But it is important to recall the problems of life in the Elizabethan age: infant mortality was very high; plague was a frequent and awful possibility; transportation and communication were slow and difficult; and the distribution of wealth was such that the great majority of Europeans were ill-clothed and ill-fed. To Bacon, who believed in the biblical commandment that humankind is to have dominion over nature, this seemed like very poor dominion indeed. So he proposed a "great instauration": that is, a restoration to humankind of the power over nature which was given at creation, but lost through the fall. He argued, in the preface to *The Great Instauration*:

> That the state of knowledge is not prosperous nor greatly advancing; and
> that a way must be opened for the human understanding entirely different
> from any hitherto known, and other helps provided, in order that the mind
> may exercise over the nature of things the authority which properly belongs
> to it.[9]

The old kind of knowledge, which "was not prosperous nor greatly advancing," Bacon compared to the work of a spider, who from his own innards spun forth webs: this was the deductive, rationalistic knowledge, which reasoned from first principles and had little room in it for learning directly from nature. The kind of knowledge which Bacon proposed would be, instead, of the sort produced by bees who went from flower to flower and penetrated deeply into them. Thus they produced sweetness (honey) and light (the wax which could produce candles). In other words, what Bacon proposed was a knowledge which would provide power over nature and which would proceed not by deduction from rationally derived first principles, but by the observation of nature. This is what Bacon meant when he said, "nature to be commanded must be obeyed": obedience to nature is becoming like a child before its facts, the information brought through the senses. That sense data, meticulously observed, would then issue in knowledge and power. This method was far preferable to the infertile, ancient method of proceeding from first principles, a method which Bacon felt all the ancients—with the possible exception of Democritus—were guilty of. Bacon himself summed up the relative benefits of this untried "inductive method":

> There are and can be only two ways of searching into and discovering truth. The one flies from the senses and particulars to the most general axioms, and from these principles, the truth of which it takes for settled and immoveable, proceeds to judgment and to the discovery of middle axioms. And this way is now in fashion. The other derives axioms from the senses and particulars, rising by a gradual and unbroken ascent, so that it arrives at the most general axioms last of all. This is the true way, but as yet untried.[10]

Thus Bacon proposed a "new organ" of knowledge, which would proceed with unfailing progression from nature to knowledge and from knowledge to power over nature, applied for the good of humankind who had too long been subject to nature's power.

Such an achievement would depend neither on genius nor on great discoveries, but rather on the systematic work of ordinary people applying the method to the study of nature. Thus Bacon anticipated the basic form of modern scientific research.

Equally important, Bacon recognized the time, money, and manpower which such an enterprise would require; indeed, in his dedication to the *Novum Organum*, Bacon asked King James to take it upon himself to furnish the means for carrying out such a plan. It was perhaps the first request for a government grant to fund research. "I have provided the machine," Francis concluded, "but the stuff must be gathered from nature."[11] And for such gathering, large resources of time, money, and personnel were needed—then, as they are now.

Francis himself was no scientist, but he saw clearly what science could be used for, and how it could proceed; thus he articulated more than anyone else the place of nature in modern science. Three things about his method that are important for our view of nature stand out very clearly. First, the goal of human knowledge is to have power over nature. Second, the way to attain that knowledge is by studying nature itself—not for nature's sake, but for humankind's. Third, knowledge is to be built up out of particulars; there is no overarching meaning to the knowledge thus inductively arrived at. It need have no coherence, so long as it yields *usable* knowledge.

Whether he prophetically described the course science was to take regardless of himself, or whether he actually shaped that course, Bacon nevertheless succeeded in setting forth with boldness and clarity the way in which twentieth-century knowledge and use of nature proceeds. The ancient and medieval goals of a harmonious world picture, which included human values and physical facts in the same framework, as well as Descartes' rationally, mathematically coherent universe, are eclipsed by the simple admission that the real value of what we know of nature is in the power it gives. And the way to that knowledge is not by looking at the meaning of larger and larger wholes, but rather by examining behavior of smaller and smaller parts.

Nowhere have the ambivalent fruits of such an approach to nature been more obvious than in the New World. Indeed, the New World may be seen as a kind of proving ground, a giant laboratory, for the testing of the emerging view of knowledge as power. The cover of the first edition of Bacon's *Novum Organum* suggests this, for it pictures two ships sailing westward into open sea, past two pillars which (Bacon tells us) are the pillars of Hercules— the ancient limits to the known. The ships of human endeavor are heading for a western frontier to prove themselves. It is one of the more significant coincidences of history that the date of publication of *Novum Organum* is 1620, the date of the first permanent settlement in North America. It is appropriate, then, that we consider the way in which our attitude toward nature has been shaped by the European presence on this vast, fertile American continent.

### CHAPTER 9

# THE NORTH AMERICAN EXPERIENCE

*. . . as the moon rose higher the inessential houses began to melt away until gradually I became aware of the old island here that flowered once for Dutch sailors' eyes—a fresh, green breast of the new world. . . . for a transitory enchanted moment man must have held his breath in the presence of this continent, compelled into an aesthetic contemplation he neither understood nor desired, face to face for the last time in history with something commensurate to his capacity for wonder.*

**—F. Scott Fitzgerald, THE GREAT GATSBY**

W e have already referred to the way in which the very knowledge of the New World served to open up medieval conceptions of nature to new possibilities in methods and content. What we are to consider now is the way the actual experience of living in the New World shaped conceptions of nature.

In the previous chapter, we outlined Francis Bacon's conviction that knowledge should give power over nature. Bacon was not a Puritan, but he was a Christian and quite sympathetic to the Puritan attitudes. His attitude toward nature is not at all unlike that of the first Puritan settlers in New England. In a very practical sense they were using knowledge to bring nature under the control of human power. Since the nature they found in North America had an extent and vitality that had not been encountered in Europe for more than a thousand years, the New World became a great proving ground for that ideal of knowledge as power which Bacon had so eloquently outlined.

Like Bacon, the first American Puritans saw the recalcitrance of nature

**135**

as a consequence of sin; indeed, the whole New World, with its tangled forests and untamed beasts, became a kind of metaphor for the human heart which, since the fall, was desperately wicked. To attempt to build a place to live, a commonwealth, in such an environment, was a fearsome task for the first settlers. William Bradford, in his account of the Plymouth Colony, described their situation in these words:

> Neither could they, as it were, go up to the top of Pisgah to view from this wilderness a more goodly country to feed their hopes; for which way soever they turned their eyes (save upward to the heavens) they could have little solace or content in respect of any outward objects. For summer being done, all things stand upon them with a weatherbeaten face; and the whole country, full of woods and thickets, represented a wild and savage hew. If they looked behind them, there was the mighty ocean which they had passed, and was now as a main bar and gulf to separate them from all the civil parts of the world [spelling modernized].[1]

Nor did the people which the Puritans encountered in this rugged world (full of "wild beasts and wild men," said Bradford) give them at first any reason to consider nature as anything other than an enemy.

Though it was not long before the first settlers had established comfortable farms and villages, the great western forest and its sometimes hostile inhabitants continually impressed upon them that nature was to be conquered. And that conquest was often understood in religious terms. Not only was the state of nature itself seen as a metaphor of the fallen condition, but the settlements were understood to be the first victories in a promised land. Indeed, place names such as "Salem" (Jerusalem), Massachusetts testify to the religious zeal with which the New World was transformed (as Bacon would have approved) into prosperous human communities where nature was tamed to serve man. Though the idea of "The Promised Land" was indeed present, the Puritans understood the promise to refer not to the land in its natural state, but to the land which, through human enterprise and divine blessing, it could become. To cut down the trees, to build cities and farms, was to bring order into chaos and to advance the kingdom of God.

Though the Puritan zeal and rigor of the early colonies did not last long, the practical Baconianism of that Puritan attitude toward nature has survived, in modified forms, even into the present. The 3,000-mile breadth of the continent provided nearly three centuries to perfect the skills needed to develop man's power over nature. And the great wealth of that nature— whether it was the lumber of the forests, the fertility of the plains, the coal of the hills, or the fish and game of the wilderness—confirmed Bacon's idea that knowledge equaled power. One of the fruits of that determination to apply knowledge to the task of making nature serve man was what has come to be known as "Yankee ingenuity": the ability to take a hard problem and solve it, whether it be in building a bridge, a reaper, or a cotton gin. On the frontier, at least, nature was an enemy to be turned into a servant. There is little recorded to prove that the early settlers ever saw it as much more than that; they were merely trying to find a place to live and a source of food and pasture. The result was a great deal of practical knowledge about how to use nature, but not much interest in nature for its own sake. The attitude is captured excellently in Alexis de Tocqueville's description of the pioneer, in contrast to the European, attitude toward nature.

> In Europe people talk a great deal of the wilds of America, but the Americans themselves never think about them: they are insensible to the wonders of inanimate Nature, and they may be said not to perceive the mighty forests which surround them till they fall beneath the hatchet. Their eyes are fixed upon another sight: the . . . march across these wilds—drying swamps, turning the course of rivers, peopling solitudes, and subduing Nature.[2]

This understanding of nature as primarily something to be conquered is a main subject of that most American of poets, Walt Whitman, who wrote many poems in celebration of "the New arriving, assuming, taking possession, a swarming and busy race settling and organizing everywhere." In "Song of the Broad-Axe," Whitman summed up this prevailing theme in the American treatment of nature:

> The axe leaps!
> The solid forest gives fluid utterances,
> They tumble forth, they rise and form,
> Hut, tent, landing, survey,
> Flail, plough, pick, crowbar, spade,
> Shingle, rail, prop, wainscot, jamb, lath, panel, gable, . . .
> Hoe, rake, pitchfork, pencil, wagon, staff, saw,
>     jack-plane, mallet, wedge, rounce,
> Chair, tub, hoop, table, wicket, vane, sash, floor. . . .

These, Whitman says, are the utterances of the forest: yet they are all man-made.

This Baconian (and Puritan) attitude toward nature as something to be used resulted in great prosperity. But it resulted, also, in some tragedies: the extinction of billions of passenger pigeons and the near-extinction of the bison are only two of the most moving examples. And yet few in North America have seriously questioned the beneficence of reducing the continent to human use. Many today still share that basic Puritan idea that uncontrolled nature is a failure of the divine commandment to have dominion.

But while regarding the North American continent as raw material to be subdued was certainly the prevailing attitude of the first settlers, and is perhaps the prevailing attitude today, it is by no means the only way of understanding nature. In Canada (where the haunting proximity of the vast and hostile North has been a continual pressure on both success and imagination) the idea of the hostility of nature has been prevalent until quite recent times; in the United States, however, there arose very early a gentler conception of nature, which was implicit in the Puritan metaphors of the New

World as the promised land. This is sometimes referred to as the pastoral or agrarian ideal, and it achieved its most eloquent description in the words of Thomas Jefferson. Nature and man should be in harmony, according to this attitude, and that harmony is most realized in the husbandry of agriculture, which has no need of cities for its support. Jefferson's ideal for America was a nation of independent farmers. He wrote:

> . . . we have an immensity of land courting the industry of the husbandman. Is it best then that all our citizens should be employed in its improvement, or that one half should be called off from that to exercise manufactures and handicraft arts for the other? Those who labour in the earth are the chosen people of God, if ever he had a chosen people. . . . Corruption of morals in the mass of cultivators is a phenomenon of which no age nor nation has furnished an example. . . . let our work-shops remain in Europe. . . . The mobs of great cities add just so much to the support of pure government, as sores do to the strength of the human body.[3]

Underlying Jefferson's remarkably strong defense of an agricultural way of life is an attitude toward nature significantly different from the ideal of subjection which seems to characterize Bacon and the Puritans. While nature is not personified or deified, by Jefferson's time there nevertheless had crept into American thought the possibility of nature as a source of strength: "Those who labour in the earth are the chosen people of God."

One source of this softening attitude toward nature is undoubtedly a sort of nostalgia. As the frontier moved further and further westward, those left in the comfortable (and increasingly crowded) East remembered with a kind of longing the nature which had given way for the cities, and the rewarding human endeavor which had made it give way. Indeed, a persuasive and influential theory of the American character, sometimes called the "frontier thesis," was developed near the turn of this century (shortly after the official disappearance of the American frontier in the census of 1890) by Frederick Jackson Turner. He maintained that the frontier had been a kind of safety valve for social discontent; the continual possibility for people to prove themselves by shaping nature to their ends had given rise to a kind of democratic greatness. Whether or not we accept Turner's thesis, it is clear that by the nineteenth century people regarded American nature—especially if it was safely in the West, or encountered under conditions which could be easily controlled—with a kind of fondness.

Americans also viewed nature with a kind of pride, as they cast about for ways of defending their young nation in the presence of the older and often snobbish European nations. The one thing that America had in greater abundance than the Europeans was undisturbed nature. Thus, in the nineteenth century, a kind of national pride in the American wilderness helped shape a kindlier attitude toward unhumanized nature—and probably gave considerable impetus to the uniquely American "National Parks" movement.

But by far the largest influence on this change of the American attitude from animosity to awe and affection is an amorphous and hard-to-define change in sensibility usually called by the unhelpful name of "Romanticism." And in order to understand Romanticism, it will be necessary to return to the Old World.

## THE ROMANTIC VIEW OF NATURE

In many ways, Romanticism (which emerged as a force in European thought at about the same time as the American and French Revolutions, and which was not entirely unconnected with those revolutions) may be seen, at least in its attitude toward nature, as a reaction. It was a reaction against the mechanization of nature, which came about as a consequence of the scientific revolution, and against the pervasive image of the universe as a machine. Toward the end of the eighteenth century, a few German and English poets began to believe that seeing the earth, animals, or their own selves as an elaborate machine and thinking mathematically in a way that excluded sights, smells, colors, and odors from importance was more than inaccurate: it was false and evil. Thus William Blake sang the praises of a "fourfold" vision of nature, and prayed, "May God us keep/From a Single vision & Newton's sleep!"[4] Accompanying this disgust at mechanistic portrayals of man and nature was a stress on the beauty and vitality of nature, strengthened by a kind of wonder and awe which some critics have mistaken for pantheism.

But it is quite misleading to see that changed Romantic attitude toward nature as simply a reaction against the new mechanistic ways of thinking and an attempt to go back to some sort of primitive nature worship. (It is, however, a mistake which is often made by both contemporary Romantics and critics of Romanticism alike.) Rather, the Romantics were vividly and painfully aware of that exclusion of man from the world which was a consequence of the new science. In every case, whether we speak of Kepler, Galileo, Descartes, or Bacon, the early theorists of science maintained that the aesthetic aspects of sense knowledge—the things delightful to the eye, the ear, the touch—were irrelevant or even misleading in getting at the real truth. There was no room for the feelings in such an attitude. Yet the Romantics agreed with the idea underlying this mechanistic distinction between primary and secondary qualities; that is, they too saw the primacy of the mind over nature and the dependence of nature on the mind for any beauty, meaning, or significance which it seems to have.

Samuel Taylor Coleridge (the deepest thinker of the English Romantics) expressed this in a poem:

> I may not hope from outward forms to win
> The passion and the life, whose fountains are within.
>
> O Lady! we receive but what we give,
> And in our life alone does Nature live.[5]

The philosopher who most systematically articulated the ideas underlying the Romantic view of the relation between mind and nature was Im-
manuel Kant. He maintained that the mind could know the world only
through the categories which it imposed upon the world; thus the very act
of knowing structured the world, so far as the perceiver was concerned. And
there was no way of getting outside these mentally constructed categories
to the experience of nature itself.

Though the pioneers of the scientific revolution, whose thought we
have briefly summarized, stressed the detachment of the mind from nature,
the goal of their detachment was measurable knowledge, resulting in accuracy of prediction, consistency of hypothesis, or efficiency in manipulation.
Not so with the Romantics. For them, the proper use of the mind's distinctness from nature was the creative revitalization of the natural world. Coleridge's lines, "in our life alone does nature live," should not be read "without
us nature is dead," but "with us nature *lives*." For the Romantics, the great
agent of this revitalization of nature was the imagination. Coleridge called
it "the repetition in the finite mind of the infinite I AM," and thus linked
human imaginative power over nature with the divine creative power itself.

Thus an unexpected consequence of the mind's detachment from nature
was an ability to experience nature with a great intensity of feeling. Indeed,
many of the contemporary appreciative attitudes toward nature which we
now take for granted—the motives for mountain-climbing, bird-watching,
or backpacking—have their origins in what we could call the "Romantic
Revolution." The imaginative synthesis of the mind with nature brought
both intense personal pleasure and an appreciation of the things in nature
which, in the light of the human imagination, now stood forth in a kind of
radiant worth never before noticed.

This Romantic attitude toward nature, when it crossed the Atlantic and
began to influence American thought, combined with those other tendencies
toward an appreciative view of nature which we have spoken of earlier, and
began to be a potent force in what Americans did with and to their land.
The most identifiable form of Romanticism in America is sometimes known
as "Transcendentalism," and its two main prophets were Ralph Waldo
Emerson and Henry David Thoreau. Both men exercised—and continue to
exercise—a tremendous influence on American thought in general and on
American attitudes toward nature in particular.

The label "Transcendentalist" is somewhat paradoxical, if we consider
that the ideas of Transcendentalism lead Thoreau to immerse himself in the
woods by Walden Pond for two years and John Muir (an ardent disciple of
Thoreau) to spend weeks at a time alone in the wilderness of the western
mountains. "Immanentalist" would at first glance seem a more accurate label.
But the word "transcendental" reveals that the origin of the new view of
nature is in the separateness of the mind from nature and in the consequent
access of the mind to a reality beyond nature. Said Emerson, "Nature is the

symbol of spirit. . . . The world is emblematic."[6] And Thoreau echoed this statement in his version of empiricism: "let us not underrate the value of a fact; it will one day flower in a truth."[7]

The philosophy behind Thoreau's thought may have stressed the transcendence of the mind. But in practice that awareness of the transcendent mind impelled Thoreau to a deep appreciation of the natural world and a fundamental critique of the manipulative attitude toward nature which seemed to motivate the "lives of quiet desperation" he observed in his contemporaries.

"In wilderness is the preservation of the world," said Thoreau, and his words sum up the change in attitude toward nature that took place in nineteenth-century America, and which continues unabated in our own time. Thoreau's was still a very lonely voice in his time, but by the last quarter of the nineteenth century he had come to be regarded by some as a prophet. Toward the close of that century the first official recognition of the new view of nature took place in the establishment of the Adirondack forest preserve, "forever wild" in upstate New York; in the creation of Yellowstone, the world's first National Park; and in the similar establishment by the state of California of Yosemite Park.

These token preserves of unutilized nature, and even the growing enthusiasm for the wild which swept America in the early twentieth century (resulting, for example, in such oddities as Roosevelt's "Boone and Crockett Club" or the establishment of the Boy Scouts) failed to significantly slow the rate at which America was channeling resources into human use. But the interest in "wilderness" reveals a peculiarly modern response to the relationship between man and nature. Instead of establishing a kind of harmony (as is evident in some European countries, and as is clearly called for in Jefferson's agrarian ideal), the American solution is to use most of nature intensively and even destructively, but to leave large tracts of land untouched as "wilderness areas." Such an attitude did not become official policy until the Wilderness Act of 1963, but it was already implicit in the nineteenth century. It shows a recognition, forced perhaps by the uniqueness of the North American experience, of both the priority of human use of the land and an equal priority to preserve and care for the land. It has been recognized by a few that the ideal solution is instead a kind of harmony; but this ideal of harmony has not been nearly so attractive as the polarization of city/nature which we now see in America.

---

In these past four chapters we have attempted to trace the main influences, apart from Christianity, on Western use of nature. It will be helpful at this point to sum up what those influences have been.

The Greeks were ambivalent in their attitude toward the natural world, and we have in the West inherited much of that ambivalence. On one extreme was a distrust of all that is natural—and hence, mutable and imperfect. The only thing worthy of our attention, in this view, was the eternal realm of ideal forms—the tradition embodied in Platonism. The other pole of Greek thought, however, affirmed the idea of nature as a vast organism, of which man, or mind, was the rationality. Human reason was not (as in Plato) in tension with the natural world, but was a self-conscious embodiment of its essence. The good person, then, was in tune with "nature"—and was nature's highest form. This tradition was expressed in the thought of Aristotle and, more religiously, in Stoicism.

During the Middle Ages, both aspects of these Greek views combined with Christianity. The Platonic distrust of nature appeared in the Middle Ages as the *contemptus mundi* attitude, resulting in attempts to deny the physical. But the affirmation of nature as organism is embodied in most of medieval cosmology, from the idea of the "great chain of being" to the macrocosm-microcosm correspondence which are the foundation of both alchemy and astrology.

The scientific revolution is an outgrowth of both the positive and the negative attitudes toward nature. It is rooted in an empiricism which comes from the more accepting pole of medieval thought: from the Franciscan scientists onward, the investigation of phenomena, not prior ideas about the phenomena, was seen as an important pathway to truth. On the other hand, the Platonic separation of the mind from nature increasingly worked its way into the investigative method, so that both Descartes and Galileo could affirm, in different ways, that a mathematical expression of the world was a higher form of truth than any sense experience of it. This increasing conflict between a mathematically consistent explanation and a sensuously experienced one was very evident in the Copernican controversy. The new science maintained that the fundamental truth was not the truth which man, embodied on solid earth, perceived, but was the truth perceived from a point in space which a person could experience only mentally.

Accompanying this detachment from nature was an increasing awareness that knowledge of nature could bring power over nature. This was the motivating force of Bacon's work and the practical attitude that was the basis for the exploration and settlement of the New World.

The Puritan settlers operated on the Baconian assumption that it was Christian duty to subdue a wild and heathen nature, and this model of dominance became the prevailing American attitude until quite recent times. By the beginning of the twentieth century the North American continent had already been, for nearly three centuries, a kind of laboratory for working out the ideas about the relationship between man and nature which had been developing for millennia in the Old World.

In America, though the prevailing idea was that nature was to be subjected to human purpose, there grew up a more preserving attitude. This concern was nurtured by the Romantic ideal of imaginatively reviving a world drained of its meaning. But it was aided also, in the New World, by a recognition of the beneficial role contact with wilderness had played in the nation's development. The result has been a uniquely modern polarity between wilderness preserves on the one hand and a completely humanized landscape on the other.

The twentieth century, with its spectacular increase in the power available to man, its rapidly expanding technology, its explosion of human population, and its spread of Western ideas about nature, has seen the blossoming of these historical roots into flowers both horrible (pollution and the atomic bomb) and beautiful (the elimination of many diseases, rapid communication, and human flight). Since a further consideration of the current relationship between man and nature involves some analysis of the social, political, and economic forces at work in this explosive century, we will postpone a consideration of contemporary views of nature in our own time until after we have considered some of the economic structures and motives underlying the human systems through which we process, shape, and control the world.

"Oh, the music of the songbird, sittin' in the trees,
The rustle of the meadow and its echo in the leaves,
The babble of the waters and the buzzin' of the bee,
Put them all together and they're Nature's sym-pho-ny."

"What's the difference? It was a man-made lake in the first place."

From *American Scientist Magazine.* © 1975 by Sidney Harris. Used by permission.

# OUR MIND TODAY ___

*. . . try to escape*
*From the darkness outside and within*
*By dreaming of systems so perfect*
*that no one will need to be good.*

*—T. S. Eliot*

**AS WE HAVE DONE** before in this study (and will do again) we turn first not to actual instances of human use of nature, but instead to discussions of the reasons and motives for such usage. We will concentrate on the philosophical discussion first for two reasons. To begin with, some philosophies tend to draw together the prevailing mood and underlying values of an age in precise and easily identifiable form. Thus, like a barometer, a philosophy registers the shifting weather of its time. On the other hand, the very precision and perceptiveness of some philosophies have themselves exerted a considerable pressure on the intellectual currents of a period. The most important philosophies thus partake of the characteristics of both barometers and weather fronts: that is, they both reflect human values and change them. But whether we look at a barometer or watch the line of advancing clouds, it is helpful to know something of a hurricane before we deal with its consequences.

The ethical idea which, since the eighteenth century, has blown with gale force through the institutions and attitudes which control our treatment of nature—and indeed, of each other—is what we will call, with some violence to established usage, "Utilitarianism."

We do not have to look far to find the origins of the utilitarian ethic in Western thought. It first appears in Epicurus; then, after a near total absence (at least as an explicit philosophy) through most of the Christian era, it reappears in force in the philosophy underlying the scientific revolution.

Epicurus maintained that the universe had no purpose, but was only the consequence of random combinations of atoms falling endlessly in a void. As far as personal ethics were concerned, what mattered was pleasure and pain—the subjective effect of all those purposeless atomic swervings.

Galileo, who was the first to revive Epicurus' view in modern times, adapted it, saying that what mattered was not the "inner" or Aristotelian cause of a particular action, but its outward, observable *consequences*. For the Epicurean, since there was no intrinsic right and wrong by which to judge action, the only valid standard of action was the more immediate one of avoidance of pain. Likewise, Galileo dismissed as unfounded those ideas of intrinsic purpose and desire which had informed Aristotelian physics—such as a stone falling to the ground because it "desired" the ground, accelerating out of inner jubilation at approaching the object of desire. He maintained that it was futile to speculate on the inner *causes* or "motives" of such action; true knowledge, and the only kind of any value, was knowledge of outer *effects*. Galileo, and others of his time, revolutionized physics by observing and measuring what things actually *did*. The irreducible truth about a thing, they believed, could be gained by obtaining an ever more precise record of *what* happened, not by reflecting on the Aristotelian *cause*. Truth was in the measurable effects, not in the working out of some intrinsic principle or purpose. Any "law" of nature which resulted from this method was thus rooted not in intrinsic reality, but in the observation of particular consequences.

Utilitarianism is an application to ethics of the same attitude—the divorce of values from anything intrinsic to the action, and a focus on the consequences of actions. It thus partakes of that general increase in the detachment of mind from nature whose development we have traced sketchily from Christian beginnings to the present. For in this viewpoint, only humans experience "intrinsic" qualities; to see such qualities outside of humankind is to postulate a false animism. In thus denying intrinsic meanings or values to everything but the human, these thinkers furthered that image of the mind as a detached presence in a lifeless, mechanical world. In the discussion which follows, we will concentrate on the manifestations of Utilitarianism in economic thought and in our presuppositions about technology. We will also discuss various modern reactions against narrowly utilitarian attitudes toward resource use.

But before turning to those considerations, we will discuss briefly the main outlines of Utilitarian thought. Briefly stated (to quote the *Encyclopedia of Philosophy*), Utilitarianism is that doctrine which states that "the rightness or wrongness of actions is determined solely by the goodness and badness of their consequences." Such an ethic is in sharp contrast to any ethical theory which maintains that the goodness or badness of an action is in the act itself. This had been the predominant ethic throughout the Middle Ages. Just as color, scent, and taste were seen to be qualities *in* a thing, rather than varying responses to it, so the moral quality of an action was, in earlier times, thought to inhere in the act itself.

In the Utilitarian view, not only is the moral value of an action independent of the act itself; it is independent of the motive. Thus greed is wrong not in itself, but only because it tends to produce actions with bad consequences. It is even conceivable that greed could produce actions with good consequences. This was, in effect, the argument of some defenders of capitalism who argued that the greatest good for society could be achieved by each person acting out of self-interest which is regarded as a virtue; an "invisible hand" would, in the long run, cause self-interest to produce the greatest good for everyone in society.

Value, for the classical Utilitarian, is determined by wants and desires. The satisfaction of desires is, by definition, good; the frustration of desires, evil. Ultimately, all desires are reduced to the avoidance of pain or the fulfillment of pleasure. Thus pleasure is the only good, and pain the only evil. The satisfaction of a desire is happiness; the frustration of a desire (and thus the consequent pain) is unhappiness.

It is important to note that we are speaking not only of basic *needs* such as food, clothing, and shelter (though they too may be desired). If a chocolate bar is desired more than an apple, then the chocolate bar has more value for the person, despite the fact that it could be shown on nutritional grounds that the eater has much more *need* of an apple. But Utilitarianism is not based on objective needs; it is based on subjective *wants*.

It is important to understand that the amount of satisfaction is the *total* satisfaction over a period of time. It is possible, for example, that our hypothetical eater would be more immediately happy with a chocolate bar than with an apple; but if he or she calculates the unhappiness which is likely to follow from the two, he or she may not choose the chocolate bar, for it will result in pimples, fat, and a bad conscience, the unpleasantness of which outweighs the immediate pleasure of the candy. Thus a person who carefully calculates the full results of pleasures and displeasures is likely to choose the apple. Jeremy Bentham, the eighteenth-century philosopher usually considered the founder of Utilitarian philosophy, developed a complex "hedonic calculus" for weighing happiness and unhappiness and coming up with guides for action.

It is obvious that Utilitarianism is subjective: one decides one wants a car because of the happiness it will bring, not because having cars is good, or good for society. It is also individualistic, in that the basis for the rightness or wrongness of an action is always in the individual, not in the consideration of the health and well-being of a community. The basis of value is still the satisfaction of *individual* wants and desires. A community is not an organic whole for which value is to be determined apart from the individual; rather, it is a collection of individuals. Effects of one's actions on a specific human community, on other species, or on the whole household of life are not the starting point; rather, the happiness of the individual is always primary.

The fact that the basis for value is the satisfaction of the individual's wants does not mean, however, that the welfare of the broader community is irrelevant. At least one form of Utilitarianism maintains that the goal is "the greatest good for the greatest number." And even if one stays with the more "egoistic" form of Utilitarianism, in which the individual's happiness is the only consideration, one may recognize that an immediate satisfaction of a desire (stealing a chocolate bar in a store, for example) will ultimately result in more unhappiness—such as a jail sentence for shoplifting. Thus a concern for individual happiness may work out for the total welfare of the whole society and even for the greatest good for the greatest number. Moreover, it is conceivable that a sufficiently enlightened awareness of the interrelationships of the ecosphere could, motivated purely by individual human satisfaction, lead to a wise use of resources. That has, in fact, been the implicit assumption in the past. But such deteriorations of the environment as have been outlined in earlier sections argue against such an optimistic outcome of egoistic Utilitarianism.

Before considering some specific workings out of this aspect of the modern mind in economics and technology, it will be helpful to point out a basic assumption behind Utilitarianism: freedom is an ideal to be sought. The freedom that the Utilitarian has in mind, however, is freedom from impediments to the satisfaction of individual desire. This is a far cry from the sort of freedom the Scriptures hold as ideal when, for example, they claim that Christ brings freedom from sin. The Christian ideal of freedom is freedom from impediments—and sin is an impediment—to being what God intended us to be. So the Utilitarian approves freedom from what stands in the way of satisfying our desires (however sinful), whereas the Scriptures approve freedom from what stands in the path of being what we are meant to be.

The consequences of these ideas for our use of resources may not be immediately obvious. However, they will become clearer when we consider the working-out of the Utilitarian ideal in two main areas of modern action: economics and technology. So crucial are these areas to our treatment of nature that both of them—usually in some combination—are frequently blamed, almost as though they were vast demons, for current misuses of creation. We are not arguing, however, that economics and technology are the demons of our age; rather, we are concerned to point out how both economic and technological activity have been thoroughly formed by the Utilitarian ethic. Therefore, until that Utilitarian center is transformed, it is unlikely that economics or technology will be likely to provide much positive direction for stewardship of the earth.

The Utilitarian presuppositions appear in different ways in economics and technology. As will become clear in the next chapter, contemporary economic thought is based very firmly on the premise that what drives economic activity is individual happiness, or utility. Indeed, a favorite idea of economic theory is that people are "rational utility maximizers."

In modern attitudes toward technique, on the other hand, the emphasis is not so much on the importance of individual happiness as it is on the fact that the consequences of an act, rather than the act itself, are important. This emphasis on ends (consequences) rather than means (acts) can produce a way of thinking in which there is no room for any thing, process, or person which fails to achieve the best end in the most efficient way. In different ways, then, the theory and practice of both economics and technology are permeated by the ethical individualism of Utilitarianism.

"Oh, for Pete's sake, let's just get some ozone and send it back up there!"

From *American Scientist Magazine*. © 1976 by Sidney Harris. Used by permission.

### CHAPTER 10

# ECONOMICS: MANAGING OUR HOUSEHOLD

*There's no such thing as a free lunch.*

—**Economist's maxim**

*Ho, every one who thirsts, come to the waters;*
*And he who has no money, come, buy and eat!*
*Come, buy wine and milk*
*Without money and without price.*

—**Isaiah 55:1**

"The final decisions are economic ones," or "Economics rules the day," or "You can't fight the economics of it"—these are the sorts of comments (usually delivered with a shrug or a frustrated sigh) one is likely to overhear in any conversation having to do with resource use. Whether one is speaking of turning a farm into a suburb, or of adding dyes to food, or of exploiting the products of a Third World country, the blame for behavior which wastes people and resources is likely to be laid on economics—if not on economists.

What do people mean when they speak of economics as a vaguely evil force? Is there a group of economic czars who sit somewhere in a back room and make the decisions which frustrate people and waste resources? Or is there some mysterious and disembodied set of principles which never seem entirely clear to ordinary people, but which nevertheless have the power to shape our lives, no matter how hard we try to resist?

There is a good deal of appeal to these ideas and to other explanations in which "economics" appears as a sort of villain. We all love a conspiracy, and it is comfortable to blame a distant and unseen enemy for our problems. But before we begin to discuss economics, economists, and the effect of economic principles on our use of the earth's resources, it will be helpful to point out a few things about the word "economics" and the concept it expresses (and has expressed).

The word "economics" comes from two Greek words, *oikos*, house, and *nomos*, order (or law). *Oikonomos*, then, is the ordering of a household: the principles by which it is managed. By a significant linguistic coincidence, the word "ecology" has a very similar origin: it comes from *oikos* and *logos*. The word *logos* in this usage means "knowledge," or "study of." *Oikonomos* is an ancient word (it occurs many times in the New Testament), but *oikologos*, "ecology," is a recent word, invented by a nineteenth-century biologist. "Economics," in its original sense, meant the management of one's own household, and thus was quite limited in scope. (Its meaning, as we shall see, has since broadened considerably.) But "ecology" has, from the first, denoted a recognition of humanity's extended household—the worldwide community of living things in all the intricacies of their coherence and exchange.

"Economics" could be roughly translated as "managing the household," and "ecology" as "studying the household." And the differences between "managing" and "studying" suggest why it is important to consider "ecology" and "economics" together. For, in order to maintain the narrow household of human enterprise, it has been necessary to "manage," and hence interfere with, that extended household of all the earth's life. Thus what the economists manage has interfered with what the ecologists study, and vice versa, so that the line between the two is no longer very distinct.

The fact that the management of our collective human household has interfered seriously with the earth's household of life is one of the main reasons for this book, and it leads us to another linguistic coincidence: the most common translation of the word *oikonomos* in the New Testament is "steward," and *oikonomia* is "stewardship." The concerns of ecology suggest that we broaden our stewardship to include not only monetary wealth and income, but also the great, living wealth of the planet. This involves "economics," for, as the word suggests, in one sense stewardship *is* economics.

Which brings us back to that more literal translation of *oikonomia*—economics. One thing this brief reflection on the word has shown is that we all are "economists," since we all have some responsibility for managing the affairs, financial and otherwise, of our household. Inasmuch as a million—or a billion—household managers determine that they require the indiscriminate use of an automobile, unlimited electrical appliances, and the convenience of disposability, then those "economists" require also a rapid and destructive depletion of our resources. In one sense, then, the theory of a conspiracy of economists dictating the destruction of the natural environment is true: we all "conspire" for the welfare of our little household, and do so with little regard for the welfare of the great house, the earth. As the comic strip character Pogo said, "We have met the enemy, and he is us." Or, as

Wendell Berry puts it, a protest meeting on environmental abuse is a convocation of the guilty.

But, of course, it is not as simple as that. A word means more than its origins, and though "economist" is a translation of a word that means steward, and thus applies to all of us, it also has come to have a more specialized and much more widely known meaning. In the more modern sense of the word, an "economist" is one who seeks to understand principles of economics not only for the purpose of understanding in itself, but also for the purposes of prediction, management, and control. Nevertheless, the basis of economics—the thing the economist studies—remains the behavior of individual "managers-of-the-house." Thus we should take great care before accusing economists: to do so would be somewhat like the legendary despot who killed the messenger bringing bad news. A better approach would be to learn from the economist the principles, held consciously or not, by which the various levels of our private and collective household are managed. When we understand those principles and the patterns that clarify them, we may be in a better position to change and direct our management, both of the small household and the great.

For the information on which we base our management of the household—and all the choices about resource use which management entails—may have been handed down largely as folklore. Individuals—or governments—may or may not be aware that they are seeing their economic activity from the viewpoint of one particular economist (be he Karl Marx, Adam Smith, or John Keynes). But ignorance of the origins or details of an economic theory does not relax the grip of that theory.

## HISTORICAL VIEWS OF "ECONOMIC REALITY"

Since there is a great deal more uniformity in contemporary Western economic views than there is in Western views of nature, this chapter will concentrate on the one economic principle which prevails in the West: free-market capitalism. But since such a system, guided by self-interest, is relatively recent, it will be helpful to set it against the background of other economic principles which have guided Westerners in the past.

### Economics in Plato and Aristotle

For Plato, the production of goods was not the result of any longing for wealth or propensity for trade. It was, rather, based on inherent differences among individuals: some were sculptors, some carpenters, some teachers. The purpose of society was to give each of them a field in which to work out his own nature. If the city needed to grow, it was only because more room was needed for another sculptor to work out his nature. In

Plato's economy, then, "division of labor" is dictated by the essence of the individual. The driving force is not the production of goods or the accumulation of wealth; it is the fulfillment of an individual's nature.

Aristotle's economic theory is similar. In his thought, property and goods have no value in themselves apart from the way a person uses them to attain happiness or well-being. Values are not determined by scarcity or demand, but by whether or not they enable a person to achieve true humanity. "It is impossible," said Aristotle, "or not easy, to do noble acts without the proper equipment."[1]

Included in this concept of "proper equipment" is the idea of "too much," for an excess of goods might well be as detrimental to noble action as a deficiency. Thus, says Aristotle:

> . . . whereas external goods have a limit, like any other instrument and all things useful [they] are of such a nature they must either do harm or at any rate be of no use to their possessors. . . .[2]

Clearly, for both Plato and Aristotle, economic activity is not an end in itself or even an important part of the human make-up. Instead, another ideal—the achievement of full human selfhood or the doing of noble acts— is the controlling value. In both cases, the resource-devouring spiral of economic growth for its own sake is avoided.

In setting forth an economics motivated by values of fulfillment and nobility, Plato and Aristotle are undeniably reflecting something of the Greek culture of their day. But the very fact that Aristotle, at least, speaks of the possibility of *too much* wealth indicates that the attitude of wealth-for-its-own-sake was already a problem. That some avariciousness was prevalent in the ancient world is evident in an anecdote related by Augustine, who told of the theater performer who promised he would reveal what was in the mind of each person in the audience. He made good on his promise by telling them that each of them wanted to "buy cheap and sell dear."

### Medieval Economics

Such an attitude would ultimately produce a "growth" economy. That it failed to do so during the Middle Ages is undoubtedly the consequence of a vigorous Christian doctrine of sin and an accompanying emphasis on the need for salvation. Throughout the Middle Ages, economic interests were subordinated to the real business of life, which was understood to be the salvation of one's soul. Economic activity was simply one element of personal conduct, over which the rules of morality were totally binding. Unlike our own time (at least in theory) a business transaction was much more likely to be called off because it was immoral than because it was uneconomic.

Certainly there were, in the Middle Ages, accumulations of wealth. Material wealth was even viewed as necessary—if not for everyone, then at least for feudal lords. But whereas material wealth was considered to be necessary, economic motives—in which an action was undertaken only to gain wealth—were suspect. As one medieval commentator put it, "To engage in economic activity is to have a wolf by the ears."

Toward the end of the Middle Ages, Thomas Aquinas combined the philosophical system of Aristotle with Christian theology, and worked out, as part of his monumental synthesis, a Christian economic theory. Like Aristotle's, it was pragmatic with regard to economics. Economic activity, and wealth itself, were important only as they led to improvement of the soul. But it was also Christian, in that the state of the soul was understood not in Greek terms of balance and order, but in Christian terms of salvation and righteousness.

Aquinas did, however, make one important distinction which Aristotle failed to make. He maintained that the acquisition and administration of wealth and property were legitimate private rights, which could result in greater care, order, and satisfaction within a society than if they were had in common. *Use* of resources, however, was understood, as it was with Aristotle, to be common: things were to be shared with the needy, in accordance with their purpose, as created by God. Implicit in this idea—private acquisition and administration, but public use—is a strong concept of stewardship. It is clear that in Aquinas' economics, the welfare of the whole community (which today we would extend to include the whole *oikos* or household of life) is to receive the benefit of a person's wealth. Aquinas strengthens this idea by citing Ambrose: "Let no one call his own that which is common," and again, "He who spends too much is a robber."

### Calvin's Economics

With the Reformation came a new emphasis on the salvation of the individual, and it was accompanied by a theology which ultimately gave greater validity to individual wealth. A strong element in John Calvin's teaching, for instance, was the appropriateness of material things as instruments of God's grace. And money was the symbol of these material things. As André Biéler, an interpreter of Calvin, puts it:

> Money is the means which God uses in granting to man what is necessary to the support of the existence of man and his companions. God puts wealth at the disposal of man so that he may organize his life and the life of society for which he is solidarily responsible as well.[3]

From this affirmation of money as a symbol of God's providence, Calvin derives two important ideas. By far the most influential (perhaps unfortunately) is the idea of money as a sign of the favor of God. Again, we quote Biéler's summary of Calvin:

Further, by dispensing all material goods and particularly money to his creature, the Creator makes himself known as a life-giving Father. Money therefore does not have a merely utilitarian function. It has really a spiritual mission. It is a sign of the grace of God who makes his children live. Moreover, money is a sign of the Kingdom of God.[4]

The fact that money can be a sign of the grace of God does not necessarily mean, however, that the more wealthy are the more blessed. Indeed, says Calvin, money can also be "a sign of condemnation of him who gets the goods of his living without discerning that they are a gift of God." For money is always, by both its absence and its presence, a way of testing both our trust in God and our readiness to love and obey him.

Which brings us to the second, and more neglected, of Calvin's important economic concepts: both rich and poor have a spiritual mission to fulfill through their wealth or poverty. The inequality of wealth is not arbitrary. It exists instead to provoke "a continuous distribution of goods." The poor person has a mission: to be the neighbor to whom the rich person can give. The rich person, obviously, has a complementary mission: to be the poor person's benefactor. The goal of this redistribution, however, is not the perpetuation of inequality, but a state of equality. In Calvin's words:

Thus the Lord recommends to us a proportion of this nature, that we may, in so far as every one's resources admit, afford help to the needy, so that there may not be some in affluence, and, others in need.[5]

The motive for this redistribution is love. Indeed, says Calvin, economic exchange is one of the ways God ordained that we demonstrate love or fellowship. Such fellowship, he said, is clearly evident in marital love and in the family. But it is also evident in the exchanges of work and of the marketplace. For the division of labor separates us from each other, but mutual exchange reunites: it is a concrete sign of fellowship, of the solidarity of human existence. Sin has ruined this harmonious picture; and restoration comes from Christ. To be born again is to be born into the body of Christ, and "the saints . . . are gathered into the society of Christ on the condition that they mutually exchange among themselves the gifts conferred to them by God."[6]

Ultimately, then, for Calvin the goal of economic activity is a harmonious society, bound together by love. Calvin declares this clearly in a sermon on Ephesians:

It is not enough when one can say, "Oh, I work, I have my trade, I set the pace." This is not enough; for one must be concerned whether it is good and profitable to the community and if it is able to serve our neighbors. . . . And this is why we are compared to members of a body. But now, if one's hand be employed to give some support to another member and that even to his damage, the whole body will by this means fall into ruin. . . . It is certain that no occupation will be approved by him which is not useful and that does not serve the common good and that also redounds to the profit of everyone.[7]

We have, in this summary of some important economic ideas preceding current free-market capitalism, dealt at somewhat greater length with Calvin's thought. The reason for this emphasis is that interpreters of Calvin, both from within and without the Calvinist tradition, have seen a basis for the industriousness and the exploitativeness of the capitalist countries in his teaching of money as a sign of God's blessing. The "Protestant Work Ethic," as it has sometimes been called, is seen by some as underlying and justifying the acquisition of private wealth. But whatever the connections might be between Calvin's teaching and the current market system, it is plain that Calvin saw economic activity as secondary to the goals of fellowship among people and profit to the whole community.

It is when interpreters of Calvin saw the pursuit of gain as a morally approvable act in itself that capitalism and Christendom began to be closely associated. Thus it was in the Christian West that our current economic system, dominated by the ideal of "scarcity," originated. And it is primarily through that system that we today make our major contact with natural resources.

For today we are as likely to encounter "nature" in the marketplace of economic activity as we are in the state of creation. We use lumber, not trees; steel, not rock; meat, not animals. In each case, some economic transaction has taken place. Objects in nature have become "property" or "goods" to be sold, bought, and used. Thus we turn now to a discussion of that contemporary mechanism which determines how, through economic activity, we encounter the world of creation.

### Scarcity as an Economic Force

Fairy tales and daydreams are filled with the notion of a genie in a bottle—the magic genie who can grant any wish. The fairy tales usually end in disillusionment: the wishes go mad as the lust for riches and power eat up the sanity of the wisher, and power and wealth corrupt so thoroughly that disaster or poverty, or occasionally a chastened life of wisdom and virtue, ensues. But the daydreams seldom end this way. They tend to dwell on the munificent acts that the dreamer will do with his newfound riches and on the great deeds of kindness that will abound as the ills of the world—or at least some small corner of it—are cured by the freedom from want that having all one wishes will provide.

Thus many fantasize about overcoming a basic reality in our lives: scarcity. However, the "moral of the story" as it is frequently told is that the pursuit of riches leads to disaster. It seems indeed that in trying to gain the whole world one can lose one's soul. The book of Proverbs recommends:

. . . give me neither poverty nor riches;
feed me with the food that is needful for me,
lest I be full, and deny thee,
and say, "Who is the Lord?"
or lest I be poor, and steal,
and profane the name of my God.

(Prov. 30:8, 9)

From the outset it would be wrong, then, to see economics or economic activity as being about the accumulation of riches. It ought instead to
be more like the ancient and medieval ideas about obtaining the "food that
is needful." It is usually by the faithful acts of humans, not divine fiat, that
the petition, "Give us this day our daily bread," is answered. Even manna
must be gathered; people must be busy earning their bread, not by their own
merit, but by being faithful in tending the garden, husbanding the flocks,
and receiving the fruits with gratitude. Such husbandry, such stewardship,
requires attention to what is demanded by the circumstances in which we
live and to the application of principles of love, justice, and stewardship.
This activity requires ingenuity, organization, coordination, and effort. In
a world where tasks are highly differentiated and the number of products
very large, economic activity is extremely complex indeed.

But we must speak of the circumstances of this world that form the
set of conditions under which economic activity goes on. The genie-in-a-
bottle dreams have in mind the overcoming of scarcity—the fact that for
most individuals, and for humanity as a whole, there seems to be not enough
of the things that they want. Such scarcity is not the same thing as rarity or
even the truth that we live in a finite world with finite resources. There are,
for example, some things which are rare but for which there is no scarcity.
The annual production of belly button lint, for example, comes to a very
few tons per year and yet there is no real scarcity of it. On the other hand,
the annual production of bread is a very high tonnage; yet there is a scarcity
of it, especially for some people. Some will die for want of bread before you
read to the end of this page. Here the large amount of bread, or of all
foodstuffs taken together, is still insufficient, either because total production
is not adequate for the need or because the distribution of bread is such that
some have too much and others have too little. Thus scarcity is *relative*—
relative to the need for the goods or, when wants and not needs drive economic acquisition, relative to the desire to have more of the goods. Lacking
a genie in a bottle, some needs or desires go unsatisfied, and we call the
goods needed for that satisfaction *scarce*.

Of course in most cases we could produce enough of a certain good
to meet the needs or perhaps even the desires of everyone. Take bread, for
example. There are enough resources in the world to produce a surfeit of
bread, but because there are other competing needs and desires, such a surfeit
is not produced. The demands placed upon the resources of the world are

not for bread alone, but for many other things. Without deciding whether or not these demands are legitimate, it is nevertheless true that if the actions of individuals and economic systems work to satisfy these demands, they compete for the use of the world's resources. Taken together, then, the quantity of goods demanded in any given time period exceeds the quantity that can be supplied: our economic activity always takes place in a world characterized by scarcity.

It is also true, however, that the needs of any one person can be satisfied by the resources of the world. It is probably even true that the desires (however extravagant) of almost any single person could be satisfied. If only one person were to be the recipient of the earth's bounty, that one person could have a great deal of goods and not experience any scarcity. But if all the desires of all the persons of the world are to be considered, scarcity once again is a problem.

Thus the basic questions for economics are: *What* is to be produced? At what *rate* is it to be produced? And *who* will get what is produced? In addition, the *method* of production—the relative use of capital and labor, for example—is also strongly influenced by economic considerations.

The answers to these questions will, on the one hand, determine the use to which resources are put and the rate at which they are used. On the other hand, they will determine the distribution of the fruits of production among users and uses. In the meantime, many of the factors which very strongly affect people's lives will also be determined: for example, the sort of work which people will have to do—the conditions of the workplace, the role of people versus machines, the degree of personal fulfillment that can be achieved through work, and the rewards for putting forth the effort of working. It is hardly any wonder, then, that we sometimes think of our lives as almost entirely economic in character.

Of course, as earlier thinkers from Plato to Calvin have stressed, our lives should not be exclusively economic in purpose or in conduct. One reason that our experience seems not to comport well with this obvious statement is that we have failed to keep economic aspects of our lives in their proper place. This can happen in at least two ways. First, we may overvalue the things that economics deals with: the material goods of this world. To ensure that we do indeed place inordinately high value on these goods, we have the help, complicity, and to some extent the manipulation of our society. Western society in particular has been unabashedly materialistic. Billboards, TV, radios, and magazines all implore us to have more wants and thus increase scarcity. This materialism has formed much of the driving force for the accumulation of things and for the rapid use of resources. In so doing, it has also affected deep-seated values about what is important in life—what constitutes "progress" and what can be relied upon to give meaning in life. Given such basic commitments, the activities of life have also been affected— the things we spend our time doing, the activities that we are willing to devote ourselves to, and in many cases, the things to which we believe we "must" devote ourselves.

A second instance in which the economic aspect gets misplaced in our lives occurs when we do not distinguish adequately between the economic and the noneconomic. We must recognize that while economic goods are a necessary part of our lives, not all goods are economic; not even all scarce goods are economic. While a loaf of bread is a reasonable candidate for an "economic good," a pleasing sunset (scarce enough in our lives) is not. A tube of toothpaste is likely to be an economic good, but a kiss is not, and should not be (despite the way in which toothpaste advertising sells toothpaste by promising kisses). Of course, the dividing line between what is or is not an "economic good" is not always clear.

Likewise, not all decisions are economic decisions, or at least not purely economic decisions. The decision whether to marry and whom to marry, for example, has economic implications, as does the decision by a married couple on whether or not to have children. But while there is clearly an economic aspect to marriage and the family, these decisions are not primarily economic in character. And it is abundantly clear that, if the logic of economic decision making is viewed as reducible to a cost-benefit calculation, it would be ludicrous to apply this logic to the decisions mentioned above. And yet this is precisely what has been done by a number of economists.

Having acknowledged the importance of knowing more about economic activity and its place in our lives, we will turn first to what is called in contemporary theorizing a "market system." We will then examine aspects of the theory and practice in that system as it relates to the problem of resource use and good stewardship.

### The Market View of "Economic Reality"

A basic assumption of the market system is that the title to every economic good is held by some individual. These individuals are also assumed to be free to dispose of their goods in any way they like, as long as it is legal. A main purpose of the market system is to help in transferring the ownership of goods from one person to another and, in so doing, committing resources to specific uses desired by their owners.

If one leaves aside the complexities of values and motivations which affect real people, the logic of the market system is simple—and even rather convincing. It maintains that people who want to have a particular good—say, a new car—and are limited in what they can pay for it will therefore engage in "economizing" behavior: that is, they will try to buy the car they want with the smallest possible expense. And what that smallest possible expenditure is going to be depends upon competition among the various agencies or individuals selling cars.

On the other hand, producers who manufacture cars wish to make the greatest possible profit; one of the ways in which they do so is by incurring the smallest possible cost. They force each other to do this, as they all seek to "maximize" their profits.

Thus "economizing" occurs at two levels: the buyers seek the best (or most satisfying) car possible for the least expense; and the producers seek to produce a car as cheaply as possible, in order to compete successfully with other producers and make the greatest possible profit.

Such a pattern has a predictable effect: in general, if the demand for a certain kind of car increases or if the cost of producing it increases, the price of the car will go up. In that case, people will either go without or find a cheaper substitute. Since price (theoretically, at least) increases as scarcity increases, scarce resources will be conserved and abundant ones used (assuming that the cheaper can be substituted for the more expensive). We are beginning to see something like this happening in the United States, as more and more users turn to coal in response to the high cost and relative scarcity of oil.

In this ideal market system, the opportunity cost must be paid for each use of a good. If a coal seam and a wooded mountain occupy the same space, then preserving the mountain must, in some way, pay the cost of the unused coal. If someone wants to use land for farming, he or she must pay the foregone profit from the houses which could have been built on that land, and so on.

Thus, in an open market, where people are outbidding each other whenever they value a resource more than others (assuming that they have the budget to do so), resources presumably will be used only for the highest-valued purpose. On this basis, its defenders claim that the market system effectively determines the best use for each resource.

It is of course true that some method of allocating resources is needed. The virtues of price allocation are said to be that it allows consumers to choose the things that they want from the array of economic goods that are available, at least up to the point that each consumer's budget allows; in addition, the choices that consumers make will in turn set in motion the process by which the decisions are made by producers about the kinds and quantities of goods to make. This latter point is usually called "consumer sovereignty" and may be contrasted to, for example, producer sovereignty or political sovereignty. The use of a price mechanism also avoids the use of relatively unpleasant alternatives such as standing in line. It also does something to assure that only those who intend to make use of the goods will get them, since buying goods implies giving up some portion of one's budget, something which would not be done if the goods were not thought to be useful to the buyer.

It is difficult, however, to justify the claim made by defenders of the market system that the market distributes goods justly. Though they can be made, arguments for such market-achieved justice are complex (and not very persuasive), so we will not go into them here. We should take note, however, that a distribution of wealth and income lies behind every market operation, and that most market operations in turn affect this distribution. It is absolutely essential to be able to claim a fair distribution of income and wealth in order to claim fair market allocation. Questions of such a just distribution and of an efficient allocation of resources are not really inseparable. For, as we have pointed out, those who are willing to pay for a resource determine its use. In order for that to be the "best" use, in fact, the values of the buyers must be correct; or, to put it another way, the people with the proper values must have enough money to communicate their values to the market—they must be able to outbid everybody else.

Thus if a person or a group wishes to preserve a mountain from a coal mine, they must have not only the insight into why the mountain should be preserved, but also enough money to outbid the coal company. Ultimately, no logic, nor wisdom, nor set of values can outbid cash in market competition. Thus income and resource use are intimately linked in a market economy.

As the fate of our hypothetical mountain makes clear, one of the problems of a market system is that there is no guarantee that the ability to give value to things (*market* value, that is) will be distributed in proportion to wisdom or virtue. For ultimately, valuation is a consequence of buying power, and buying power is itself a result not of the buyer's ethics, but of the market and other factors. In such a system, the valuation of things is entrusted only to those who have succeeded financially. We sacrifice or ignore, therefore, the wisdom of persons whose wealth is not proportionate to their wisdom. There is no room for the "village elder" who, on the basis of wisdom and experience, can speak with authority about the society's values. We say instead, "Put your money where your mouth is," or "If you think what we are doing with resources is stupid, buy us out."

We have been considering one consequence of a market system as a way of illustrating not only its consequences, but also the way in which it operates. Let us now consider briefly some of the other features of this system which seems to have such a pervasive effect on the economic worth of natural resources.

In a market system, all persons are (theoretically) free to make their own choices over resources that they own. Thus, in order for the system to work, people must have some incentive to buy and sell; there must be a motivation for them to produce and transfer goods. The basic theory about what motivates people in a market system is relatively simple: people are believed to seek the highest level of their own happiness. Both the content of that happiness and the means of achieving it are (so the theory goes) arrived at through rational thought. In economists' jargon, people in the market system are understood to be "rational utility maximizers." It is this urge to increase their own happiness (or "utility") which enables them to overcome their natural preference for leisure and to engage in productive activities.

Since the basic motivation in the market system is not related to what people *need* to live, but to what they *think* they need to be *happy*, what keeps the market going is not real human needs, but individually perceived wants and appetites backed by purchasing power. For the market economist, the distinction between needs and wants is irrelevant—the important thing is *demand*.

Demand in a market system (more precisely, "economic demand" or "effective demand," but in either case the only demand which counts) is, put simply, the ability and willingness to pay. It is only the ability to pay which puts pressure on resources. Whether the wants are legitimate or whether the ability to pay is properly distributed or ethically arrived at is not of concern. In this view, a want backed by a dollar is (illegal goods excepted) equal to any other want backed by a dollar. A dollar-want for milk to feed one's cat is equal to a dollar-want for milk to feed someone else's baby, and the market makes no distinction as to the relative merits of those demands. Most important: if a mother lacks a dollar to buy milk for her baby, she has no *effective* demand. The milk goes to the cat. A man may be starving, but unless his demand for food is backed up by an ability to pay, the market does not recognize his demand; in market terms, it is not a demand at all.

The supply of goods in a market is a result not only of the various limitations discussed earlier (the factors which produce scarcity), but also of the decisions made by the owners of the means of production. An assumption of the market system, therefore, is that all factors of production, including natural resources, are owned by someone. The legitimacy of this ownership is rarely called into question, and is usually accepted as part of the status quo. We simply begin with the fact that the resources are owned by someone, and work from there. Historical acts leading to ownership are usually not called into question. War, conquest, deception, and coercion are all ways of obtaining ownership, but the market is concerned with none of these; its concern is only with the *transfer* of ownership or use. And not only is the legal title owned by individuals, but all rights and obligations for the use of goods are viewed as an individual matter. Goods are legally and morally (within the market view) private property.

In such a system, all appeals for coordination of economic activities to meet the real needs of all people must be addressed only to the self-interest of those who own the resources. As "maximizers" of their own happiness, they will produce and sell what is needed by others only if they see it is to their advantage to do so. With ownership of resources as the basis for exchange, any exchange that is mutually agreed upon is considered to be a fair exchange. The assumptions of equal knowledge and equal bargaining power are also minimally necessary.

The result of all this buying and selling—the sum total of all transactions throughout the economic system—is said to be the efficient and proper allocation of all resources. That is, resources will be used to produce not only as much output as possible, but also as much of the right sort of output as possible. Since this is a remarkable claim, it is worthwhile to review its basis.

The "right" sort of output is understood as that which is most valuable. But how could a group of persons who pay no attention to each other's needs, and who presumably have no interest in what others regard as valuable, arrive at any agreement as to the most valuable use of resources? The genius of the market system, reply its defenders, is that no such agreement is necessary. As long as free bargains are conducted, the higher-valued uses will outbid the lower-valued ones, and therefore will get the resources. Thus, the proper amount of every resource will be directed to every use for which there is a market demand.

It is obvious that many familiar terms are being used here in a specialized way, according to definitions which make sense only within the market theory. "Production" is limited to those things which are "goods" by the market definition—that is, those things for which people will pay. Correspondingly, "value" means those things upon which the *market* places value, in direct proportion to the market valuation, or price. Further, the "effective demand" for a good is not only determined by wants (rather than needs), but is recognized as legitimate by the market only if it is backed by an ability to pay. But the ability to pay—that is, income (with the exception of inheritance, gifts, or some other noneconomic source of wealth)—is itself determined by the market.

We see then that any claim for optimal use of resources is based, among other things, on the initial distribution of power, especially wealth and income. We see also that such claims are somewhat circular in that the means of resource allocation and the means of income distribution are interrelated, and thus affect each other. The claim for economic efficiency in the allocation of resources finally comes down to something like this: the market is an efficient mechanism for seeing to it that the claims put forth by those with wealth and income are honored and in most cases perpetuated. Within such a framework, the movement of relative prices serves to reallocate resources in response to changing conditions of demand and supply.

## RESOURCES AND THE MARKET SYSTEM: SOME PROBLEMS

We have outlined at least the main theory of the system within which most of our economic activity is carried out. Since almost all of our own use of resources is within the framework of this market system (whether we buy a car, or use electricity, or go camping in a wilderness area that could be producing lumber), it will be helpful to consider in more detail some features of the market system which affect the way in which we use resources.

## The Problem of Individualism

In a previous chapter, when we discussed the development of various Western views of the relationship between humanity and nature, we noted that the period following the Middle Ages has, in a variety of ways, been characterized by an increasing *individualism*. Our sense of participation in a community of other people and other life is much less than it was for the medieval person. Today, our conviction of what is true is more a private, inward thing than an assent to traditional beliefs. These convictions were strengthened by certain historical circumstances. The Protestant Reformation stressed individual salvation, based on individual interpretation of Scripture. The discovery of the New World, and especially the long North American adventure of settling it, developed rapidly the picture of the individual pitted against nature, with the desired outcome being his or her own survival and success. Economically and politically, the breakdown of the ties of mutual responsibility between a feudal lord and his serfs, as well as the growing possibilities for trade and amassing wealth, brought about heightened possibilities for the individual. In such a milieu the market system was born. And, as we might expect, it rests squarely on the idea that natural resources, and the means of producing marketable goods from them, are owned by individuals. Likewise, individuals purchase the goods and thus keep the economic system going.

Market economy has at its base the ideas that human existence is basically *individual* in character and that the relationship between individuals can be (so far as scarce material goods are concerned) reduced to economic transactions.

In economic activity, the individual is almost always a buying and selling abstraction, separated in theory from indissoluble links with other people, with nature, and even with God. Yet our lives are obviously not so severely isolated as this. In fact, the more our lives are intertwined with other people and with nature, the less adequate the market system is for dealing with abuses of both man and nature.

One reason this is so is that public policy—whereby the conflicting claims and wishes of individuals are reconciled—is likely to concentrate on the one thing everyone agrees it should: protecting the sanctity of individual ownership and individual contracts. For the purpose of government is widely understood to be the guarantee of one's freedom to do whatever one likes with the resources placed under one's control. Such an assumption naturally gives great weight to decisions by individual owners, since anything else would require agreement among individuals on the interests of society and on the meaning of society itself. Of particular importance in resource usage is the question of whether society consists of only the living members of a political unit or whether it involves future members. For until the present members of a society decide that future members have some share in their resources, there is little hope for a use that will conserve them. The same is true for recognizing the links to people of other political units and to the diverse life of the natural world. The assumption of individual ownership leaves little room for such possibilities.

One of the impacts of economic individualism is that the entire system acts accordingly. It is hard for anyone to rise above the operation of the economic system, to transcend the calculation of prices and profits. The primary objective in life becomes working for a wage, earning a profit, achieving a higher "standard of living." To serve God, to work for the good of neighbor, or to be a good steward over nature appears secondary, if it enters the consciousness at all. The variables of economic decisions become the biggest thing in our lives: the response to price movements, the max-imization of money incomes, the pursuit of never-ending economic growth. Meanwhile the larger and overarching bases for decisions are forgotten, dis-missed as irrelevant to the "real" world, or rejected as inconsistent with the pursuit of economic gain. To so reverse the ordering of things is a trick not solely of the wickedness of each individual, but also of societies' possessive tendencies to enlarge economic activity to proportions which are inconsistent with a healthy life. Such enlargement could be called cancerous.

Of course, economic activity and even some aspects of the scarcity that so frequently cause the unhealthy concentration on economic activity are not in themselves bad. For example, the existence of some degree of scarcity can mean the opportunity (as Calvin maintained) for community, for fellowship, for sharing. The self-interested, individualistic approach to the economic problem is not necessary. Economic activity could bring people together in concrete manifestation of the meaning of human society. It is the evil in the hearts of human beings and the continual intellectual reinforcement of the idea that self-interest is, after all, the right way to behave that leads to the rejection of this possibility and the cancerous growth of selfish tendencies.

In the recent past we have seen dramatic illustrations of the two options. A case in point is the gasoline shortages caused by the Arab oil embargo. A similar case was the canning lid shortage of a few years ago. In response to the reduced availability of these materials two possible actions could have been taken: sharing or hoarding. The first response regards the needs of others as being important—as important as the needs of self. When there is less to go around than was planned, each person can try to insure that what is available is used for the most critical needs, whether they are one's own needs or those of others. There is a second possibility for sharing which such situations can stimulate. This is the case in which the material in short supply is not itself transferred to the ownership of others, but is shared in order to use the material more efficiently. So when gasoline was in short supply, neighbors rode to the store or to work together, and in some cases stayed home together and found new meanings to human fellowship.

The hoarding option is exercised when people are only self-interested. The strategy is to get there before your neighbor does in order to grab first. Large quantities of the material already in short supply are taken off the market and kept for the future potential use of the hoarder, thus worsening the shortage problem for others.

Some of each kind of behavior went on during the situations mentioned, though it would be difficult to maintain that sharing predominated. If it is indeed the case that hoarding was the dominant behavior, then two kinds of costs were incurred. First, opportunities for human fellowship were rejected in favor of self-convenience. Second, resources were wasted as the garden crops of many home canners rotted for want of the lids in their neighbors' closet, or hoarders of gasoline discovered how dangerous it is to try to store quantities of a volatile, flammable liquid. Of the two costs, the waste of resources may be less damaging than the rejection of the possibility of community. Yet it seems likely, apart from some change in human nature, that the inevitable resource shortages of the future will bring about waste— not only that caused by hoarding (on both national and individual levels), but also waste of human fellowship and community.

## The Problem of Common Property

One of the most dramatic ways to point out the problems of individual ownership in a market economy is to consider the problem of common property, or what the biologist Garett Hardin has called "The Tragedy of the Commons."

In its simplest form, the problem may be seen in what happened repeatedly to preindustrial English villages which had a common grazing ground, or simply, a "commons." Everyone in the village knew that the commons would support only a limited number of cattle; everyone knew, too, approximately what that number was and how many cattle each individual could graze. Beyond that number, the commons would be overgrazed, there would not be enough forage, and all the cattle (and their owners) would suffer. Thus, for the welfare of the whole group, it was clearly better to stay within the carrying capacity of the commons. For the individual, however, the problem was complicated by the fact that if he would (for example) increase the number of his cattle by one, or two, or several, he would receive *all* the benefits from those cattle—but the consequences of the common's decline in productivity would be distributed among all of the other owners. As long as the individual regarded himself as independent of the other cattle owners (and of the health of the commons itself), he would, at least for a little while, profit by exceeding the carrying capacity of the commons. If (as often happened) the carrying capacity were exceeded too much for too long, it was, for grazing purposes, destroyed entirely, and everyone would lose.

This "tragedy of the commons" is helpful in understanding what happens when individual ownership and common ownership come in conflict— as they almost invariably do. Air, water, the ocean, and certain parts of the land (such as national parks and forests) are examples of "common property resources" which are being pressured by individual ownership abstracted from its ties with humanity or nature. This problem is compounded by the difficulty in communicating, harmonizing, and mobilizing the opinions of a large group of people, in contrast with the efficiency and speed with which an individual assesses and acts in his or her own interests.

There are other, more complex problems of common property. Take, for example, the case of building a flood-control dam for the purpose of protecting the lives and property in a river valley. If, after all the costs and all the benefits of the dam are calculated, the project is considered worthwhile (that is, the benefits exceed the cost), it is nevertheless unlikely that any private individual will want to build the dam. Why? First of all, he must identify those who will benefit from the dam, convince them to pay their share, and collect that money. And he will have to avoid "free riders." A "free rider" is one who (as good market behavior dictates) gains benefits at the lowest possible cost. If he can enjoy a benefit (freedom from flooding) at no cost, the principle of "maximizing" benefits requires him to do so. Only those who are motivated not by self-interest, but by some sense of fairness and justice, will thus contribute to the building of the dam. The rest will be "free riders," hoping that their neighbors will build the dam.

Yet even if all the people would pay their share, it would still be unlikely for an individual to take it upon himself to build the dam. The transaction costs would be high: there would be many doors to knock on and many calculations necessary to determine the benefit of the dam. In addition, the private dam builder would consider only the costs that he had to pay. If the construction of the dam ruined some natural area, or if the impounded water destroyed wildlife habitats, made travel difficult, or caused earthquakes, the dam builder would not pay the costs (nor would it be at all clear to whom he should pay them, if he did). Thus, in a system which is based on the hypothesis of individual interests, detached from ties with nature, humanity, or God, it is almost inevitable that resources held in common will be misused—or that common actions which need to be taken will not be taken unless someone can speak for the whole interconnected system, not just for one individual's interests.

### The Problem of "Economic Externalities"

Another premise of the market system with negative consequences for resource use is that people are willing to pay for a good only when the satisfaction received exceeds the satisfaction given up. This presumes, in turn, that all the costs are paid and all the benefits received by the participants in the transaction. All goods are presumed to be privately, individually owned and transferable from one owner to another without any appreciable external or "spill-over" effect. But such "clean" transactions rarely take place. If, for example, someone wants steel—perhaps in the form of a car—then ideally the costs of producing the car will all be borne by the car buyer. But the mining of the iron ore and the smelting of the steel may destroy part of the environment in which the mining and smelting takes place, and the workers may have to take uncompensated risks to produce the steel and the car; yet neither the producers nor the buyer of the car will pay for these costs. They spill over, or are "externalized," from market operations, and are paid by others who derive no benefit from the car. Just as the other cattle owners on the commons pay for the extra animal of their ambitious neighbor by decreased forage for their own, so those who breathe the air near a smelter or who live in the ruined landscape near a mine pay some of the costs of the steel in the car. These are "economic externalities," but the externality is only to that abstraction, the market system; the effects of such "externalities" are often very near the heart of an ecosystem or a human environment. In such complex ways, the market system and the abstraction of individual ownership and "clean" transaction negatively affect the way in which we use resources.

## HOW FAST TO USE IT UP:
## THE OPTIMAL DEPLETION RATE

All economies depend to some degree upon the consumption of resources. If we are concerned with maintaining those resources, for the use of future generations or the health of nonhuman life, the *rate* at which they are depleted is an important consideration. This concern for the rate of depletion applies not only to reserves with a fixed stock (such as a deposit of coal), but also to "flow resources." Soil, for example, is a "flow resource," since it can be gradually replenished. But if intensive agriculture diminishes it too rapidly, its fertility falls below the point at which it can replenish itself. Schools of fish and herds of game are other examples of "flow resources" which nevertheless can be effectively destroyed by too rapid depletion.

In a market economy, the best rate of depletion of a resource is usually established not by considering what the resource itself will bear or how long we want it to last, but rather by the interest rate. This is so because to forgo the use of a resource is to forgo the income which could be gained from its use. It is thus a form of wealth, a kind of investment, and the owner requires from it interest, as he or she would from other investments. Since the interest rate in a society is usually determined by what will be profitable to an individual within a lifetime (to take the broadest possible horizon), the effective interest rate—and hence, the pressure to deplete the resource—often requires a much more rapid depletion than is good for either the maintenance of a healthy environment or the preservation of the stock for future users.

Society is likely to prefer a different depletion rate for its resources than are individuals for several reasons. The most obvious one is that a society is expected to have a longer lifespan than an individual. Thus society would prefer to conserve a resource, while an individual, with no reason to be concerned for posterity (other than for existing children or grandchildren), would prefer to use it rapidly, reaping its benefits during his or her lifetime. Also, it is assumed that society is more likely than an individual to feel an ethical obligation to future generations. Society regards itself as continuing, whereas individuals, while concerned perhaps for their own progeny, lack interest in providing for the future of society as a whole. Both these reasons argue that if the rate of depletion is left to individuals, resources will be used more rapidly than is desirable for both human society and the whole community of life. However, since title to resources is usually held by individuals, rather than by society, there is little motivation today to slow the rate of depletion.

Many other economic factors—uncertainty, the irreversibility of decisions, one's motivation for risk taking, and one's vision of the future—affect the rate of resource use. These factors are too complex to examine here, but as this discussion has shown, there are a number of principles which work against wise resource use, and which are built into the framework of economic axioms in general and into the market system in particular. It is thus appropriate that we close this discussion of the economic dimension of our use of nature with a statement of some doubts about these widely held economic presuppositions.

## DOUBTS ABOUT OUR ECONOMIC SYSTEM

Disturbed by technical and moral doubts, our modern mind has not been able to find the peace it might feel with our economic system. Technically, it is not at all obvious—in fact, it is increasingly *less* obvious—that *laissez-faire* market views and systems or even government "intervention," based on all available knowledge, will solve the problems we have alluded to above and lead us to economic stability and a policy of wise and sustainable resource use.

Morally, there is a growing doubt that it is *right* to go about economic life in the way briefly described in these pages. In addition to the rapid and wasteful use of resources which such an economy encourages, there are other problems even more immediate. The loneliness, the lack of enduring purpose and fulfillment, the absence of happiness (whose pursuit, at many points, is said to be the main motive in the economic system), the pain of treating others and being treated in an "economic" way, and basic questions about the justice of economic relationships—all of these contribute to doubts about the moral acceptability of our present way of economic life. Someone has suggested that the only problem with capitalism is that no one loves it. Perhaps a more basic problem is that it is not part of the ethos of capitalism that anyone should love *in* it, or *through* it—at least, all find it very hard to do so.

Fifty years ago, the most influential economist of this century, John Maynard Keynes, predicted that the time when virtue would rule in men's lives was yet a hundred years off. He counseled that the path to this blissful day, the day of "principles of religion and traditional virtue," was one upon which we must invert these moral principles and "pretend to ourselves and to every one that fair is foul and foul is fair; for foul is useful," he said, "and fair is not."[8] "Foul"—in the particular form of avarice—is viewed as useful in overcoming economic necessity and bringing the day when people will be free from the drive to accumulate more, the day (as Keynes put it) of "the lilies of the field who toil not, neither do they spin."

More recently, Robert Heilbroner, another widely published economist, lamented that this day promised by Keynes does not seem to be dawning, and that the limits to economic growth and (more important) people's reaction to those limits threaten its ever coming. In *An Inquiry into the Human Prospect*, Heilbroner writes:

> . . . whatever its economic strengths, the social ethos of capitalism is ultimately unsatisfying for the individual and unstable for the community. The stress on personal achievement, the relentless pressure for advancement, the acquisitive drive that is touted as the Good Life—all this may be, in the end, the critical weakness of capitalist society, although providing so much of the motor force of its economy.
>
> The lesson of the past may then only confirm what both radicals and conservatives have often said but have not always really believed—that man does not live by bread alone.[9]

One important reason for that continual dissatisfaction which, says Heilbroner, saps the moral strength from our capitalist society is the pervasiveness of the idea that growth in all areas is good. We have seen what happens to the natural environment when this doctrine of human growth affects it; it is clearly a main cause of our current problems with resource use. And the problem of unquestioned growth is itself an outgrowth of certain ideas about happiness and wealth.

Two concepts of the relationship between wealth and happiness have been presented in Western history. One, articulated by Plato and Aristotle, is that wealth consists of only such things as are necessary to live a good life, and that happiness—economically speaking, at least—is the reduction of wants, not the increase in wealth. A second view holds that happiness consists of the pursuit of wealth—a wealth which, in practice, can never be completely attained. This view seems to proceed out of the assumption that scarcity, and the problems of choice which it presents, is only a temporary condition of human existence. This condition is to be overcome, particularly through economic growth. Through growth, the poor will presumably have a better chance to overcome their poverty. The rich will also expand their wealth, since in this view there is no such thing as *enough* of economic goods. A situation in which choice is curtailed by a limited availability of economic goods is viewed as unsatisfactory. The ideal situation would be one of free choice, unencumbered by any scarcity in material goods. An economic growth which widens the possibility of choice is viewed as progress.

In general, growth in economic output, particularly the output associated with an industrial society, has been thought to produce such a widening of choice. Relatively recently, however, doubt has been cast on the desirability of unlimited growth: the depletion of resources, the pollution of earth, air, and water, the general frenzy of attempts to increase production, and the recognition that such increases in production might ultimately mean the reduction of meaningful choice, not its widening—all these have begun to temper the growth mentality and even to raise some questions about the market system as it now exists.

In general, however, continual growth is largely understood as desirable, and frequently is looked to as the only way to solve such problems as poverty, unemployment, and inflation. But for such growth to continue, several problems must be solved: more resources found and pollution controlled, for example. The older idea—that happiness may consist not in the increase of wealth, but in the decrease of wants—has yet to attract many followers. Until it does, it is unlikely that the demands which drive a market economy—and place such great burdens on the resources of our planet—will significantly diminish.

---

We have seen that the "econ     ic" appears to play a very large role in our lives. This is not only because we all have our individual houses to manage and thus are all "economists"; it is also because the logic of one particular form of decision making has pervaded our thinking to an unwarranted and dangerous extent. This skewing of our own economy, or stewardship, has occurred for two reasons.

The first is that economic activity—buying and selling, not just economizing—has become such a large part of our lives. The pursuit of more goods, the work devoted to that pursuit (which usually requires even more equipment), and the frantic play in an attempt to escape the drudgery of the work have all impressed upon our collective minds that life is a scramble, and that one needs to be hardheaded, calculating, and scheming in order to succeed or even to survive. One can never let one's guard down or an opportunity will get away, someone will "ace us out," the chance of a life-time will be gone. So economic actions and a certain economic mentality pervade all our waking, and some of our sleeping, hours.

The second reason for the pervasiveness of the economic in our lives is that the line between what is an economic decision and what is not is not easy to maintain. It is tempting to try to simplify all decisions by some sort of cost-benefit analysis. But to really be done correctly, such analysis would have to deal with large and difficult questions: What are we really trying to accomplish? What is life about? Does nature have any value in itself? What is the value of clean air or of a sparkling stream?

But such considerations are difficult, and we are likely to bypass them. Instead we compute costs and benefits and make our decisions based on the best payoff. In so doing, we will have on our side not only the irrefutable efficiency of cost-benefit analysis, but we can also turn over most of the drudgery of decision making to a computer. Of course, in order to make a decision on the basis of such analysis, we must do what Galileo proposed to do to the universe: reduce everything to a numerical variable, namely, the measuring rod of money.

Some variables, such as the cost of human life and health, will resist this reduction more than others. Others will raise the question of what weight to give certain factors: should we assign any weight—any negative value—to the destruction of species, the loss of habitat, the disappearance of a valley under the waters held back by a power-producing dam? If so, how much? Could it compete with the benefit of hydroelectric power, the new apartment building, the new freeway? It could be simpler and more precise to compute these things numerically, for anyone who presumes to speak for the trees (or the species, or the valley) is likely to be only an environmentalist who doesn't understand economics anyway.

How, indeed, are we to put a value on things? How can we compare the value of an animal species with the benefits of industrial production or the comforts of air-conditioning? How can we weigh the presence of a forest against a factory full of jobs? The answer, given over and over, is "put a price on them." But what if no price can be given, and the whole market system in which prices have been set in the past is flawed? What do we do when some things are left out of the price-setting mechanism? What do we do when an economic system neglects to give a price to clean air because that crucial link between an object and a valuation—an *owner*—is missing?

These are hard questions, and they force us to reevaluate basic premises of our whole economic system. But the answer is certainly not to declare economic analysis—or economists—as the villain and try to make decisions without reference to economic principles, many of which have great value in our thinking about "managing the household."

The difficulty, however, is the lack of a larger matrix in which the elements of economic principles may be applied to wise decisions on resource use. If the market system does not provide such a matrix, what does? What would such a system look like? How would it accord with Christian principles? And then, how could it be achieved? But before suggesting answers to those questions, we must explore other problems and consider also the great wealth of biblical teaching on the principles which govern our *oikonomos* —our economics, or stewardship of the household of life.

"Remember—it's better to light just one little thermonuclear power station than to curse the darkness."

From *American Scientist Magazine*. © 1974 by Sidney Harris. Used by permission.

### CHAPTER 11

# THE APPROPRIATENESS OF TECHNOLOGY

*And lastly, since all Heaven was not enough*
*To share that triumph, He made His Masterpiece,*
*Man, that like God can call beauty from dust,*
*Order from chaos, and create new worlds*
*To praise their maker. Oh, but in making man*
*God over-reached Himself and gave away*
*His Godhead. He must now depend on man*
*For what man's brain, creative and divine*
*Can give Him. Man stands equal with Him now,*
*Partner and rival. . . .*

—**architect's speech in Dorothy Sayers,**
**THE ZEAL OF THY HOUSE**

In the previous chapter, we pointed out the widespread tendency to blame economics (and economists) for all sorts of problems, including the misuse and destruction of natural resources. Such an accusation certainly cannot be entirely true, for at its basic level "economics" is simply what we do when we manage the everyday affairs of a household, however large that household may be. We cannot escape economic activity.

Similar, and even more violent, accusations have been made against technology. It is not uncommon to hear a person blaming technology for suburban sprawl, the breakdown of the family, pollution, waste, and the atomic bomb. And, as is the case with economics, such an unqualified condemnation of technology cannot be true. For, like economics, technology is something people *do*; it is not an independent force. Just as we are all "economists" in that we carry on the orderings and exchanges which nourish our households, so are we "technologists." The word *techne* means craft, or

**175**

skill, or art (indeed, it is the basic Greek word for art). It describes the general human ability to shape the world to new ends. *Techne* is "know-how": knowledge of how to make things. Thus all humans, almost by definition, are technologists, whether they are interested in making a fondue, a fountain, or a factory.

However, just as we noted dangerous tendencies in certain theories and assumptions about economic activity, we can point out dangers in the theories and assumptions about technology, some of which have been made eloquently and frequently in recent years. Then we will consider some of the defenses of technology. Finally, we will suggest a kind of reconciliation of the two opinions, sketching a Christian view of technology, the basis for which will be more thoroughly developed in Sections III and IV.

## THE CRITIQUE OF TECHNOLOGY

When contemporary critics speak of technology they do not mean simple "know-how" of the sort needed to cook a meal or light a fire. They are speaking of the particular, and recent, combination of know-how and empirically based, utilitarian science—the sort of knowledge-as-power described clearly in the work of Francis Bacon. Before considering the distinctive features of such a technology, however, it will be good to start where the critics start: with some of the *consequences* of technology. Both the substance of those consequences and the attitudes behind them can best be understood by quoting directly from some recent critiques of technology. Charles Reich, whose book *The Greening of America* (1970) became a popular and widely read exegesis of the "counterculture," linked technology with free-market capitalism and declared that:

> Modern society makes war on nature. A competitive market uses nature as a commodity to be exploited—turned into profit. Technology sees nature as an element to be conquered, regulated, controlled. . . . When the forces seized the once beautiful eastern states of America, they left forests denuded; rivers, harbors, and seacoasts polluted; the cities sterile; the land ripped by highways, high tension wires and suburban swaths. They left little of the country unblighted, not even the miraculous and seemingly limitless beauty of California where today the devastation seems most wanton and cruel of all.[1]

Thus, according to Reich, technology (together with our economic system) is to blame for those vast disruptions of our environment discussed earlier in this book. He considers urban sprawl, air and water pollution, and the disappearance of agricultural land to be direct consequences of technology.

The biologist Barry Commoner, with more statistics and fewer emotions, makes the same basic point. First, he points out that the greatest increase in damage to the natural environment has come in the years since World War II. Whereas between 1945 and 1970 population in the United States increased only a modest 42 percent, the increase in most kinds of

"How should I refer to you in my chronicle, as the discoverer of fire, or as the first man to pollute the atmosphere?"

From *Audubon*. Used by permission of Vahan Shirvanian.

pollution was many times greater. Also greater were the increases in production of a number of manufactured goods.

> The winner of this economic sweepstakes, with the highest postwar growth rate, is the production of non-returnable soda bottles, which has increased about 53,000 percent in that time. . . . In second place is the production of synthetic fibers, up 5,980 percent; third is mercury used for chlorine production, up 3,930 percent; succeeding places are held as follows: mercury used in mildew resistant paint, up 3,120 percent; air conditioner compressor units, up 2,850 percent; plastics up 1,960 per cent; fertilizer nitrogen, up 1,050 percent; electric housewares (such as can-openers and corn-poppers) up 1,040 percent. . . .[2]

And so on. From such statistics, Commoner concludes that the primary change, the change which has brought about such damage, is not increase in population. Instead, says Commoner,

> The over-all evidence seems clear. The chief reason for the environmental crisis that has engulfed the United States is the sweeping transformation of productive technology since World War II. The economy has grown enough to give the United States population about the same amount of basic goods, per capita, as it did in 1946. However, productive technologies with intense impacts on the environment have replaced less destructive ones. The environmental crisis is the inevitable result of this counterecological pattern of growth.[3]

Ultimately then, the problem (according to Commoner) is technology—more precisely, "the sweeping transformation of productive technology since World War II."

Theodore Roszak, in his book *Where the Wasteland Ends* (1973), catalogues the further effect on contemporary living conditions of what he calls our "technological imperialism":

> Already in the western world and Japan millions of city-dwellers and suburbanites have grown accustomed to an almost hermetically-sealed and sanitized pattern of living in which very little of their experience ever impinges on non-human phenomena. For those of us born to such an existence, it is all but impossible to believe that anything is any longer beyond human adjustment, domination, and improvement. That is the lesson in vanity the city teaches us every moment of every day. For on all sides we see, hear, and smell the evidence of human supremacy over nature—right down to the noise and odor and irritants that foul the air around us. Like Narcissus, modern men and women take pride in seeing themselves—their product, their planning—reflected in all they behold. The more artifice, the more progress; the more progress, the more security.[4]

Technology not only affects the whole biological environment and the immediate environment of humankind; it affects the very nature of the individual. This is the major point of Jacques Ellul, whose book *The Technological Society* (1955) remains by far the most thorough and thoughtful of the critiques of technology. In order for man to survive in an increasingly technical society, says Ellul, he must change—or be changed; Ellul calls this remaking of man *reintegration*.

> What yet remains of private life must be forced into line by invisible techniques, which are also implacable because they are derived from personal conviction. Reintegration involves man's covert spiritual activities as well as his overt actions. Amusements, friendship, art—*all* must be compelled toward the new integration, thanks to which there is to be no more social maladjustment or neurosis. Man is to be smoothed out, like a pair of pants under a steam iron. . . .
>
> The human being must be completely subjected to an omnipotent technique, and all his acts and thoughts must be the object of the human techniques.[5]

The consequences of such a technical reshaping of man extend from his preferences in food, to his attitude toward authority, to his use of leisure time. Thus Ellul mocks "the modern passion for nature. When it is not stockbrokers out after moose, it is a crowd of brainless conformists camping out on order and as they are told. Nowhere is there any initiative or eccentricity."[6]

There are many such critiques of technology; we have quoted from only a few of the more influential of them. What these passages have described is the effect of technology, or "technique," on nature, on man's environment, on man himself. But what *is* the technique of which they speak? Before going on to a defense of technology, it will be helpful to outline in a little more detail the nature of the force which, say the critics, is causing such damage.

Ellul's analysis is the most thorough. For that reason, and because the relatively early date of his work makes it a background for much subsequent discussion of technique, we will limit our analysis of technology as the critics see it to his arguments in *The Technological Society*.

First of all, Ellul distinguishes between "Technical Operation" and "Technical Phenomenon." "Technical Operation" is simply the ordinary choices made by a person in getting a job done.

> Every operation obviously entails a certain technique, even the gathering of fruit among primitive peoples—climbing the tree, picking the fruit as quickly and with as little effort as possible, distinguishing between the ripe and the unripe fruit, and so on.[7]

Thus all humans, in all times, in doing any task, have used technique. The "Technical Phenomenon," on the other hand, begins when "consciousness and judgment" enter in. This intervention "takes what was previously tentative, unconscious, and spontaneous and brings it into the realm of clear, voluntary, and reasoned concepts."[8] The result, says Ellul, is "a rapid and far-flung expansion of technique."[8a] It is, in short, the "technology" whose negative effects we have just summarized. But why should the mere use of reason and judgment have such dire consequences when applied to technique? Because, says Ellul,

> The twofold intervention of reason and consciousness in the technical world, which produces the technical phenomenon, can be described as the quest of the one best means in every field. And this "one best means" is, in fact, the technical means. It is the aggregate of these means that produces technical civilization.[9]

The fact that reason and judgment point to "the one best means" ultimately eliminates the individual's freedom of choice, for

> The choice is less and less a subjective one among several means which are potentially applicable. It is really a question of finding the best means in the absolute sense, on the basis of numerical calculation.[10]

The consequence of this narrowing of choice to the one absolute best way is not only the effective elimination of freedom of choice, says Ellul; it is "the creation of a science of means." All things are henceforth done according to the best means: friendship, swimming, war, industrial organization, economic activity. "Today," says Ellul, "no human activity escapes this technical imperative."[11]

The society thus governed irresistibly by the choice of the best means is a technocracy. And it is very difficult—if not impossible—to resist. As Ellul puts it:

> If a desired result is stipulated, there is no choice possible between technical means and nontechnical means based on imagination, individual qualities, or tradition. Nothing can compete with the technical means. The choice is made *a priori*. It is not in the power of the individual or of the group to decide to follow some method other than the technical.[12]

Nor is there, in this autonomy of technique, any room for hesitation or resistance on moral grounds—"a principal characteristic of technique . . . is its refusal to tolerate moral judgments. It is absolutely independent of them and eliminates them from its domain."[13]

Whether or not Ellul is correct in his analysis of the overarching tyranny of means, his view at least gets at an important aspect of modern life. Ellul's analysis appears most powerfully correct when it is combined with an economic argument. A simple example will illustrate the general accuracy of his analysis. In the Pacific Northwest there has been a good deal of fear (based on disastrous oil spills elsewhere) that supertanker transport (mainly from the Alaska pipeline terminus in Valdez) to refineries in the fertile and sheltered waters of Puget Sound will result, sooner or later, in a major oil spill. Since maneuverability for large ships in the restricted waters of the area is a particular worry, a representative of a large refinery depending on the tankers was asked why smaller ships did not bring the oil. "Oh, there's a formula for that," he answered—and proceeded to explain that for a completely efficient operation, oil transport distances of a certain length must be covered by tankers of a certain size—that is the efficient means, and no other factor can counter it. The same sort of thinking has dictated the placement of shopping centers, the design of buildings, the siting of power plants, and the safety of cars. Given the desired end, one means emerges, and there seems little one can do to counter the decision.

Before considering a criticism of Ellul's position, it will be helpful to trace some points of contact between modern technology and earlier ideas. First of all, the affinity with Bacon is strong. Bacon argued that a method for knowledge must be designed which could, almost like a machine and without depending on human genius, arrive at the proper end. And that end was always power over nature. That image of a method which unerringly points to the right conclusion is distressingly like the "autonomous" and irresistible technique described by Ellul. It should be clear, too, that the very application of consciousness and reason to the problem is a manifestation of those abilities to abstract oneself from a problem and regard it not as a participant, but as an observer. Thus technology, in Ellul's analysis, has a good deal in common with that detachment of the mind from participation in the body and in the sensuous universe—which idea appeared about the time of the scientific revolution and which we have seen in Galileo and Descartes.

Another point of contact between "technology" in Ellul's analysis and ideas we have discussed earlier in this book is the link with Utilitarianism. We have noted how Utilitarianism judges an action not by its intrinsic value, but by the end it produces. This might look like a tyranny of ends; actually, it is a tyranny of means much like that which Ellul outlines. In a technological society, according to Ellul, it is the end which determines the means. Once an end is chosen, the means which most efficiently bring that end about are dictated; not to follow them would be irrational. Another similarity between Utilitarianism and Ellul's analysis of technology is in Jeremy Bentham's "hedonic calculus." In such a method one weighs different alternatives according to the amount of pleasure or pain they will produce. And, presumably, since we are rational, we will necessarily choose the correct alternative. The same is true with technology, according to Ellul: if one rationally and consciously chooses among particular means, one will always choose the best means, thus producing the greatest degree of "happiness." But it is a truncated sort of happiness, fundamentally without freedom and leaving no room for the individuality of either man or nature.

## TOWARD AN "APPROPRIATE" TECHNOLOGY

In sketching a Christian view of technology, we shall begin with a critique of the arguments which we have just encountered. From there we shall go on to discuss the idea of "appropriate" technology, especially as it has been presented by E. F. Schumacher. In the process of reading the next few pages, we may begin to gain an understanding of the place which technology ought to occupy in talk of Christian stewardship.

Ellul's argument is that reason and consciousness *require* a person to choose the best means. Ultimately there is no freedom of choice, for efficiency will always dictate the best means, with no room for alternatives. Such a view seems to split the individual up into reason and will, and vastly oversimplifies the decision-making process. It is quite common, in fact, for people to choose to do something counter to reason, or even to their self-interest and pleasure. Reason does not necessarily dictate to a person what he or she must do: it is a complex human being who chooses a particular course of action, not detached "reason" or "technique." Thus it cannot be said that technology itself is a force requiring us to do various dehumanizing and destructive things. Such things are indeed done, but it is the whole person who does them, not technology. Daniel Callahan makes this point very clearly:

> At the very outset we have to do away with a false and misleading dualism, one which abstracts man on the one hand and technology on the other, as if the two were quite separate kinds of realities. I believe that there is no dualism inherent here. Man is by nature a technological animal; to be human is to be technological. If I am correct in that judgment, then there is no room for a dualism at all. Instead, we should recognize that when we speak of technology, this is another way of speaking about man himself in one of his manifestations.[14]

It is through this idea, that "to be human is to be technological," that we must disagree in one important way with the critics of technology. We do not disagree with their analysis of the deplorable things which have been done to the earth and its inhabitants. But it is we ourselves who have done these things, not technology. It is not technology, for example, which forces us to invent the automobile, then (because of increased mobility) to spread out from our cities in suburbs and shopping centers which cover good farmland. It is rather that we humans like to be mobile. And we like to live outside the city, on a plot of ground big enough to have grass and trees around us; the mobility makes that goal possible. And having chosen to live outside the city, we prefer also to have our shopping areas and even our places of work close by. We could choose otherwise, but we usually do not. The mobility of the automobile makes it possible for us to make such choices, but they are still our choices, not those of technology.

The same sort of response could be made for any of the things which "technology" has supposedly done. The tides of oil that increasingly wash up on miles of beaches near shipping lanes are not the product of technology: they are the result of a complex of decisions which begins with an individual's desire for cars, fuel, and plastics and which ends with an oil company's decision to ship the oil in the cheapest way possible. Cars, furnaces, oil wells, and supertankers are tools which we choose to make or use in certain ways. We often choose wrongly or unwisely, but it is we who choose, and not technology.

However, this recognition of the flaw in the arguments of those who blame technology for our social and environmental problems should not diminish our concern for the problems. The increasing power available to us through technology means that the consequences of our choices continually become greater. Neither should we overlook the subtle ways in which a concern for efficiency and the end product is likely to affect our very thinking. It is important, then, that we consider the truth in Ellul's (and others') contention that technology becomes a force in itself, taking away our freedom of choice.

As we have pointed out, it is dangerously misleading to blame technology: the problem lies rather in individual choices. But our choice can be so warped or obscured that technology effectively *does* become an independent force.

For we might succumb to that tendency to separate mind from nature, and proceed to reduce nature, man, indeed the whole of reality, to numerical values only. That tendency to disembody the mind we saw emerging in the scientific revolution. If, indeed, our thoughts become thoroughly guided by the Cartesian view of the transcendent mind manipulating a nature which is quite alien to itself, then we are likely to be persuaded by the inexorable logic of a way of thinking which rationally establishes the "best means" for every task. But to do so would be to forsake a part of our humanity—we are not only minds. To rigidly distinguish the mind from the body, and both from nature, is to abandon a part of one's humanity. For whole people, technology is a tool. But for people who have given in to the illusion that their mind is totally apart from nature, technology is indeed likely to become a master. A person genuinely sensitive to the task and joy of growing crops in rich but fragile soil is not likely to give in to the logic which determines that the fertile soil of a flood plain is the best place for a shopping center. The person who maintains a barefoot, wet-skinned wonder at the life of the tidal pools is not so likely to let efficiency convince him to risk those starfish, crabs, and urchins for Alaskan (or Kuwaiti) crude oil. As long as people remember that the mind that makes technical decisions is part of the much more complex whole of a flesh and blood person embedded in the natural world, they need not fear an autonomous technology. Unfortunately, such a whole vision of the human person is not easy to maintain.

One of the fruits of this deep rooting of the whole people in the natural world is the ability to use technology wisely. Much has been written in the past few years about "appropriate" or "intermediate" or "soft" technologies. One of the most influential of such works is *Small is Beautiful*, by E. F. Schumacher. In it, Schumacher repeats Gandhi's distinction between "mass production" and "production by the masses," and argues eloquently for the latter, what he calls "technology with a human face, which, instead of making human hands and brains redundant, helps them to become far more productive than they have ever been before."[15]

Schumacher's description of such a technology is worth quoting at some length:

> The system of *production by the masses* mobilises the priceless resources which are possessed by all human beings, their clever brains and skilful hands, *and supports them with first-class tools*. The technology of *mass production* is inherently violent, ecologically damaging, self-defeating in terms of non-renewable resources, and stultifying for the human person. The technology of *production by the masses*, making use of the best of modern knowledge and experience, is conducive to decentralisation, compatible with the laws of ecology, gentle in its use of scarce resources, and designed to serve the human person instead of making him the servant of machines. I have named it *intermediate technology* to signify that it is vastly superior to the primitive technology of bygone ages but at the same time much simpler, cheaper, and freer than the super-technology of the rich. . . . a technology to which everybody can gain admittance and which is not reserved to those already rich and powerful.[16]

We are only groping toward what such a technology might be. But we may say that it certainly does not involve a curtailment of human ingenuity or invention. Indeed, it requires this more than ever, as anyone who has tried to repair a factory-produced machine can witness. In Schumacher's words, "Any third-rate engineer or researcher can increase complexity; but it takes a certain flair of real insight to make things simple again."[17] Such a technology might include a much greater involvement of individuals in producing their own food, in private or communal gardens; it might involve small-scale use of the sun for home and water heating. What is certain, however, is that it would place people more in touch with the physical sustenance of their life in the bounty of the earth and the sun. To do so would increase not only our need as individuals to become capable and ingenious stewards of the earth, but also our awareness of being master of the earth and fellow creature with it.

Given that firm and living rootage in the realities of nature and one's own body, the exercise of human *techne*—skill, craft, the management of matter—can be a delightful and positive thing. Indeed, it is a way of reminding the artist or "technician" of the necessary human rootedness in matter. The desire to *do* something with the world is basic. Says Samuel Florman (himself an engineer) in defending the activity of the engineer, the artist, the "technologist":

> What is it precisely that we might be doing? It is all very well for Aristotle to maintain that God is happy immersed in contemplation, because nothing else is worthy of Him. But we are human beings, not gods. Most of us are not constituted to become yogis. We take another look into the depths of our being, a clear, hard, earnest, passionate look. We recognize that we cannot survive on meditation, poems and sunsets. We are restless. We have an irresistible urge to dip our hands into the stuff of the earth and do something with it.[18]

Of course, the very capability to "do something with" the earth—or even with fellow humans—suggests the darker possibilities of this technical delight. In the third section of this book we will look in detail at both the biblical confirmation of that delight in the world and the principles which direct its wise use. Both are centered in the Incarnate God who was "a master workman with God in the creation of the universe"—and who dipped his hands into the stuff of the earth so thoroughly and lovingly that they were spiked bleeding onto a cross.

### CHAPTER 12

# MODELS:
# OUR HIDDEN MIND __

*No Model is a catalogue of ultimate realities, and none is a mere fantasy. Each is a serious attempt to get in all the phenomena known at a given period, and each succeeds in getting in a great many. But also, no less surely, each reflects the prevalent psychology of an age almost as much as it reflects the state of that age's knowledge.*

**—C. S. Lewis, THE DISCARDED IMAGE**

One way of summing up much of the material in this long discussion of the sources of our modern mind is through the concept of *models*. People have treated the earth differently in different periods, in part because they have used different models to help them understand it. Sometimes these have been conscious and deliberate models, especially in recent times. More often, they have not been consciously developed by anyone, but stand, like folklore or mythology, as a sort of backdrop to all thought about the world and human action in it. These various world models have in turn shaped models of the person, and thus have provided different motives for acting toward the earth and its creatures. Before we look at the more influential of these models of the earth, however, we should consider briefly what a model is, and how it affects our thinking.

Currently, we use the word "model" to mean many things. It can mean a miniature replica as in "model airplane." It can mean a kind of design, as in a "1980 model car." It can refer to an ideal, as in "model home." "Mathematical models" represent a system or a process by means of formulae and relationships. Finally, ideas that have been used since the scientific revolution have come, in recent times, to be spoken of as "theoretical models."

The purpose of such models is to sum up or represent a complex reality, including the main features of the system one is seeking to explain, but omitting details which will not contribute to the basic idea. The model of the solar system, with the sun at the center circled by tiny planets (a model which most of us carry unconsciously in our head) neglects the relative size of the sun and the planets, the mass distribution of the individual planets, the rotation of the sun around the center of the system, and so forth.

The danger of such models is that they can be mistaken for reality. This is particularly the case in the Utilitarian marriage of science and technology discussed earlier in this section. As long as we understand knowledge to be power, we are likely to take very seriously those models of the universe which give us power over it. Thus our era—particularly among those who do not make the models, but experience the beneficial consequences of manipulations based on them—is particularly prone to forget that its models are only abstractions. The relationship of models to reality is not, however, as C. S. Lewis puts it, a matter of saying,

> "The medievals thought the universe to be like that, but we now know it to be like this." Part of what we know is that we cannot, in the old sense, "know what the universe is like" and that no model we can build will be, in that old sense, "like" it.[1]

In any case, whether we are dealing with a tenth-century-B.C. Egyptian or a modern scientist's model of the universe, the following principles about models, and their effect on our motives, hold true:

1. Our behavior is strongly affected by internal models; they develop a type of hidden mind which helps us structure the world in our thought and directs the specific use we make of it.

2. The predominant models of a given period (and of preceding eras) have a strong effect on the private and internal models constructed by an individual. To quote Lewis again, ". . . in every age the human mind is deeply influenced by the accepted Model of the universe."[2]

3. We are often careless in recognizing the tentative nature of the models we deal with, and that carelessness is likely to lead to unwise actions toward the natural world. This has been particularly crucial in recent times, when the very utility of the model urges its acceptance as reality.

4. World models can, and perhaps *should*, be changed. That change can come about when we learn that the accuracy, scope, or simplicity of another model makes it more valid. And one of the ways in which we learn that our old model needs changing is through the problems which result when we try to apply that model to action in the world.

So much for models in general. What then are some of the models that have shaped—or continue to shape—our treatment of the world?

The ancient model of the earth seems to have been that of the earth as a god. This was not a model which any one person developed, but it was present in the origins of nearly all mythologies. The American Indian attitude toward nature often included much of this kind of reverence for the divinity of the earth and its creatures. Such an attitude was also in the background of Greek thought, but was largely replaced by another model by the time of those Greek philosophers who have most influenced Western attitudes. But so appealing is the attitude of reverence which this model of the earth as god encourages, that more than a few people in our own age have attempted—unsuccessfully—to revive it.

The model of the earth that emerged in Aristotelian and Stoic thought, and which was very influential in medieval times, was that of the earth as an *organism*—a vast animal whose behavior could be understood by analogy with the human body. Earth, air, fire, and water were like the "humours" of human bodies. Objects fell to the earth or rose to the air out of a longing to seek their proper place. This view also suggested harmony, but not reverence, since the consciousness of the organism was in man, who was a master of the whole.

Both the organic and the divine models of the world had as a kind of backdrop a similar model of space and time. Space was limited (though very large); it was something one could come to the end of. Though the limits of the earth were not yet clearly known, there was no picture of an infinite universe or earth to encourage wasteful use. It was a limited world, where everything had its place and proper use.

Time, in both views, was cyclic: all things would grow old and be renewed after the manner of the cycles of the moon, day and night, and the progression of the seasons. If one had to choose a figure to illustrate time, it would be the circle.

With the scientific revolution, a very different model of the universe entered human thought, and was accompanied by different ways of picturing space and time. Although parts of the new model had been implicit in Judeo-Christian beliefs, this new model did not begin to much affect popular views of the world until the sixteenth or seventeenth century. The universe came to be understood as a mechanical artifact—a created object, constructed by the great artificer, God. Its laws could, with diligence and skill, be learned, controlled, and applied to other machines. Space came to be viewed as infinite. And time came increasingly to be modeled by the arrow of progress: it was going somewhere, and humankind was going somewhere with it, eager to hasten the journey.

There were several consequences of this model for the way in which people used the earth. Seeing nature as a machine, rather than as a god or an organism, drew forth neither reverence nor respect; the world was instead something to be changed and used. The view of space as infinite (an idea which was supported by the practically unlimited resources being discovered in the New World) encouraged the accelerated use of nature, as did the triumph of linear time, which gave man a justification for regarding things as means to a beckoning, but always elusive, end.

In many ways, our current use of the earth has been shaped primarily by this model of the earth—or the universe—as a machine. Without the restrictions on its use imposed by the models of deity or organism, creation could be used more totally. This thorough use was supported by the idea of progress suggested by linear time, and by the idea of limitless resources suggested by infinite space (and made concrete by the New World).

A particular form of this model of the universe, especially related to the use of resources in North America, can be called the "frontier" model. Nature, in this model, is there for man to use. When he uses it up, he can move on, for there is always a further-on—a *West* to move into. This attitude was exemplified by the American doctrine of "Manifest Destiny." Obviously, the vastness and the fertility of the North American landscape encouraged this model, one which was in force for at least three centuries. It still affects many of our policies—in land use, in mining, in logging, and so forth.

Thinking of resources by means of the model provided by one's own finances is another way of understanding the frontier model. A person is likely to have two sources of wealth: income—from wages or a salary—and capital—as in a savings account. It is a truism of personal economics that one must live within one's income. But the frontier model of resources, which implies that there is always *more*—land, timber, game, iron, oil—encourages one to regard *capital*—all finite and limited resources—as *income*. As we saw in an earlier chapter, solar energy is the only real income the earth has on which to operate. Yet we have ignored that fact in North America, drawing on the "capital" of fossil fuels and mineral deposits as though they could be used forever. Only very recently have there been minor attempts to "live within our income."

Those penny-pinching attempts have led to another, yet more recent model of the earth: that is, of the earth as a spaceship. Such a model was not even possible until we had at least some imaginative experience of what it would be like to be out in empty space in a limited, but life-supporting, environment. Shortly after that possibility entered our imagination, it became a reality in early space flight. Thus phrases like "life-support system" entered our vocabulary, pointing to our basic need for food, air, and water. More dramatically, those early space flights gave us images of the earth which immediately began forcing us to restructure the old models—especially the model of the earth as a machine and the frontier model of resources as infinite. For, as those photographs continue to remind us, the earth is clearly somewhat like a spaceship: finite and vulnerable, with a cargo of life.

On our trip through space we have limited resources, both of energy and material, just as do those who travel to the moon in contemporary spaceships. Astronauts going to the moon, however, have the advantage of knowing how long the trip will last, and thus they know at what rate they must use their resources. On "spaceship earth" we have no knowledge of the length of the trip. Therefore, the only way to be fair to future generations is to assume that the journey will go on a long time—effectively, forever. Thus the "spaceship earth" model indicates that we must recycle our material resources (our "capital") and live within our income resources of energy.

Some have objected to the spaceship model of the earth, for it still pictures the earth as a machine. Real spaceships are machines, but they are designed to recreate an environment for human organisms. As the pictures of earth from space suggest, the earth is far more like a vast living organism than a machine. To use the model of the spaceship to speak of the earth neglects the fact that the real machines—individual spaceships—are very imperfect attempts to reproduce the stability of the earth itself, which has far more complexity, stability—and intrinsic worth and beauty—than any machine.

So, by informing the insights gained by the "spaceship" model with the insights provided by ecological knowledge, some have suggested that we ought to think again, as did medieval man, of the earth as an organism. But now our understanding of how that organism lives is much more precise and thorough. As we have learned more about ecosystems, about energy flow in a food chain, about the way living things are adapted to each other and their nonliving environment, it has been possible to see the earth as an "ecosphere." Or, as one modern biologist has suggested, it is like a living cell: separate parts working in symbiotic relationship, surrounded by an information- and energy-exchanging membrane, the atmosphere.

The advantage of seeing the earth as a living thing, rather than as a spaceship, is that it does not encourage us to manipulate the earth as though it were entirely different from ourselves. But whether one views the earth as a living organism—a vast "cell" in space—or as a spaceship, the pattern suggested for use of nature is much different from that suggested by the frontier model. Ultimately, as in a living cell, the goal should be to live on incoming energy, using that flow to use and re-use the materials which cannot be replaced. There is no room in either the spaceship or the cell model for seeing the earth as an infinite source of raw materials for human use, the waste of which can be poured indiscriminately back into the earth; in such a model the earth becomes an infinite storehouse and an infinite garbage pail. The contrast between the two views—the frontier model and the spaceship model—is shown accurately in the following diagram.

The two models we have just outlined—the frontier model and the spaceship model—are helpful in understanding twentieth-century attitudes toward the use of natural resources. At the beginning of the last century, the frontier model was almost totally dominant. Though there was, as we noted,

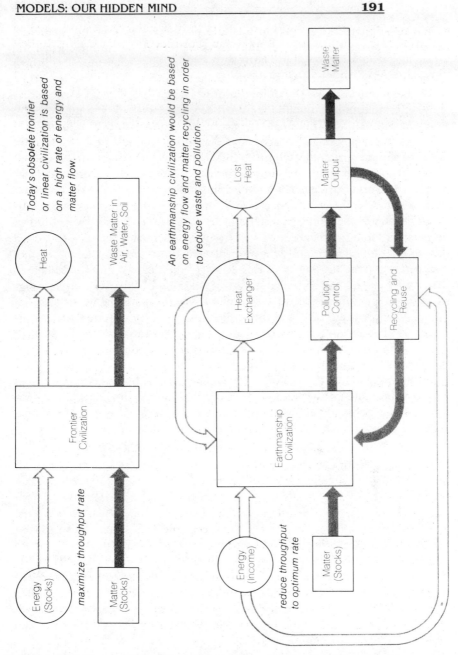

Figure 12:1  The frontier model of our world assumes an infinite supply of resources and a pass-through process of resource utilization. The spaceship-earth model assumes limited stocks of resources and an income of energy, along with recycling of material resources.[3]

© 1975 by Wadsworth Publishing Company. Reprinted by permission of the publisher.

a growing interest in preserving bits and pieces of scenic beauty and wild nature (as places for experiencing aesthetic pleasure or for practicing the pioneer arts of hunting and pathfinding), the model that controlled North American use of the land was still the frontier model. Land was there to be used, to be transformed into human profit. These were also days when free-market capitalism was the unquestioned economic system, and guidance by the government was minimal. It was a day, too, of rapid technological change—the beginning, in fact, of a period of technological acceleration which continues into our own time. But there was little suggestion then that some technologies might be "inappropriate." Conquests and tamings of nature were everywhere evident and exciting: the crossing of the continent by railroads and highways; the decrease of distance by the automobile and the airplane; the application of machine technology to agriculture, resulting in intensive farming and increased yields—these were all seen as unqualified blessings, despite their growing dependence on a massive use of natural resources. By the beginning of this century, the deforestation of Michigan had nearly ended, and a similar large-scale logging of Oregon and Washington was just getting underway. The plow was breaking the Plains states at an increasingly rapid rate, and the virgin soil was still producing rich crops. Settlers were spreading into the western states, and there was still room for them; immigrants were still streaming into the port cities of the East Coast, in search of the opportunities of the last frontier.

There was little to modify that frontier model eighty years ago—except the disappearance of the frontier itself. That disappearance took place officially in the national census of 1890, and it signaled the beginning of that slow recognition of limitations on resources which, in the last third of this century, has brought a model based on limits—the spaceship-earth model—into public consciousness.

These limits were first recognized by the artists, the writers, and the historians—not by the loggers, miners, and farmers. We have already referred to Turner's "frontier thesis" which explained the distinctiveness of American character in terms of the frontier, and speculated what the disappearance of that frontier would do to the American psyche. Toward the end of the first quarter of the century a disillusioned group of writers and artists emerged, many of whom, in reaction to a kind of loss and bewilderment which they felt in America, lived abroad. "The Lost Generation" was a label applied to these writers, and the most famous of them, Ernest Hemingway, set forth clearly his perception of what had gone wrong with America. In *The Green Hills of Africa* he wrote:

> A continent ages quickly once we come. The natives live in harmony with it. But the foreigner destroys, cuts down the trees, drains the water, so that the water supply is altered and in a short time the soil, once the sod is turned under, is cropped out and, next, it starts to blow away as it has blown away in every old country and as I had seen it start to blow in Canada. The earth

gets tired of being exploited. A country wears out quickly unless man puts
back in it all his residue and that of all his beasts. When he quits using beasts
and uses machines, the earth defeats him quickly. The machine can't reproduce, nor does it fertilize the soil, and it eats what he cannot raise. A country
was made to be as we found it.[4]

This is a remarkably contemporary-sounding insight for 1935. But
drought, the Dust Bowl, and the Depression had struck America, and its
people were learning, on a number of fronts, the consequences of the frontier
model. The remarkable thing about the Hemingway passage is neither the
accuracy of its insights into the health of a landscape nor his recognition of
the dangers of a frontier mentality; rather, it is his continued longing for a
frontier, and his reluctance to give up the idea. For he follows this eloquent
passage with these words:

> Our people went to America because that was the place to go then. It had
> been a good country and we had made a bloody mess of it and I would go,
> now, somewhere else as we had always had the right to go somewhere else
> and as we had always gone. You could always come back. Let the others
> come to America who did not know that they had come too late. Our people
> had seen it at its best and fought for it when it was well worth fighting for.
> Now I would go somewhere else. We always went in the old days and there
> were still good places to go.[5]

Hemingway clearly recognized, in 1935, the dangers of the frontier model.
But his solution was to search for another frontier, not to recognize the limits
of the earth. The full lesson of the twentieth century, the lesson made so
vivid by space flight and the photographs of the earth it has given us, is that
we can no longer say, with Hemingway, that we will "go, now, somewhere
else as we had always had the right to go somewhere else and as we had
always gone." For, unlike Hemingway, we now realize that there are no
more "good places to go."

The Dust Bowl years and the years of the Great Depression were times
for Americans to take stock of the nation. And, out of the necessity for
survival, they caused some of the earlier Romantic and Transcendentalist
notions to come together with a scientific and utilitarian concern for the land
itself. "Conservation" became a common word in the thirties, referring
mainly to the conservation of soil which, to the horror of farmers and of a
whole nation, blew away in the dry years following several decades of farming for quick profit. The American people, heretofore optimistic pioneers,
were forced by the limitations of the land and of the planet to reflect on the
consequences of pioneering when the frontier disappeared. Though the change
toward the spaceship-earth model proceeded slowly, it drew considerable
force from these years of agonized introspection. In some people, it took the
form of a kind of detached despair about man's ability to ever live wholly
on the land. The poet Robinson Jeffers wrote:

> . . . however ugly the parts appear the
> whole remains beautiful. A severed hand
> Is an ugly thing, and man dissevered from the earth and stars
> and his history . . . for contemplation or in fact . . .
> Often appears atrociously ugly. Integrity is wholeness, the greatest beauty
> is
> Organic wholeness, the wholeness of life and things, the divine beauty of
> the universe. Love that, not man
> Apart from that, or else you will share man's pitiful confusions, or drown
> in despair when his days darken.[6]

Nevertheless, there were some in those times who did not despair at the painful lesson of limitations, but worked toward enabling Americans to adopt a different model of the earth and their use of it. The most important of those persons was Aldo Leopold. Trained as a forester, and with a deep appreciation for both the beauty and the complexity of what he called "healthy land," he did more than anyone to bring the precise knowledge of the scientist together with the aesthetic sensibility of a Thoreau or a Muir. As a forester in the Southwest, as a teacher at the University of Wisconsin, and especially as the author of many powerful essays and articles, brought together and published posthumously in *A Sand County Almanac*, Leopold was primarily responsible for replacing the frontier model with that of spaceship earth. That insight is expressed clearly in the following passage:

> We know now what was unknown to all the preceding caravan of generations: that men are only fellow-voyagers with other creatures in the odyssey of evolution. This new knowledge should have given us, by this time, a sense of kinship with fellow-creatures; a wish to live and let live; a sense of wonder over the magnitude and duration of the biotic enterprise. . . .
> These things, I say, should have come to us. I fear they have not come to many.[7]

The image of the long voyage and the fragile cargo of irreplaceable life is clearly implicit in Leopold's words. Based on his understanding of the interrelationships of creatures, he proposed the necessity of a "land ethic." Humanity, wrote Leopold, once felt it proper for slaveholders to treat slaves without concern for ethical principles. Hanging slaves at the mere suspicion of misbehavior was not regarded as wrong; it was simply what one did with property. Today we have extended our concept of right and wrong to include all of humanity. No civilized person is likely to defend the idea that other persons are to be treated as property; but land is a different story. Writes Leopold:

> There is as yet no ethic dealing with man's relation to land and to the animals and plants which grow upon it. Land, like Odysseus' slave-girls, is still property. The land-relation is still strictly economic, entailing privileges but not obligations.[8]

So, based on his recognition that man is not "conqueror of the land community," but "plain member and citizen of it," Leopold observes that,

The extension of ethics to this third element in human environment [the land and its non-human life] is, if I read the evidence correctly, an evolutionary possibility and an ecological necessity. It is the third step in a sequence. The first two [affirming relationships to individual and to society] have already been taken. Individual thinkers since the days of Ezekiel and Isaiah have asserted that the despoliation of land is not only inexpedient but wrong. Society, however, has not yet affirmed their belief. I regard the present conservation movement as the embryo of such an affirmation.[9]

That embryonic conservation movement has since reached a kind of maturity (or at least a late adolescence) in America, largely thanks to Leopold's influence.

The influence of what was yet beginning in Leopold's time—the "environmentalist" movement—began to be exerted in the early fifties, contemporaneous with that post-war enthusiasm for convenience and development whose technological consequences we have noted earlier. It is hard to say how much the movement on the part of many people toward something like a "land ethic" is a reaction against the negative aspects of that growth (from smog to shopping centers on farmland) or the result of the ideas put forth by Leopold and others. Certainly many factors contributed to the growth of the idea of the earth as a fragile, limited ecosphere, a "spaceship." One was the threat of worldwide destruction that came from the development of atomic weapons. Another was the dramatic increase in certain kinds of pollution, chronicled most dramatically in Rachel Carson's *Silent Spring*. The space flights themselves have tremendously increased our appreciation for the finitude and beauty of the planet. In America, the incident of the Arab oil embargo taught us our dependence on limited supplies of fuel—and so on.

Whatever the combination of reasons, we find in North America today two strongly developed models by which we understand our relationship to natural resources: the model of the frontier, which would encourage us to go on using resources indiscriminately, and the model of the spaceship, which encourages restraint, recycling, and restoration. The frontier model is certainly giving way; yet there are many forces in our society, and many forces within individuals, which make it hard to abandon. Nor is it clear just what consequences the spaceship-earth model might have.

Which of the two models should Christians use? Or does Christianity suggest a third? What is the biblical teaching about resource use? We have, for the most part, only hinted at it in this long summary of the other forces shaping our attitudes toward nature. It is now time to consider in some detail biblical principles which can guide us.

That such a study will be neither brief nor simple is suggested by the conflicting use which Leopold makes of Scripture. In the same chapter in which he quotes approvingly the warnings of Ezekiel and Isaiah against land abuse, he also speaks disapprovingly of what he calls "the Abrahamic concept of land":

Abraham knew exactly what the land was for: it was to drip milk and honey into Abraham's mouth. At the present moment, the assurance with which we regard this assumption is inverse to the degree of our education.[10]

If Christians do not believe that the land is only to drip milk and honey into their mouths, what do they believe? What *is* the Christian teaching about the human use of the richness of the earth?

"Then we're all agreed. As it has always done with its difficulties in the past, America will *somehow* find a way to solve its energy problems."

From *The New Yorker*, June 18, 1979. Drawing by Dana Fradon; © 1979 The New Yorker Magazine, Inc. Used by permission.

# CALLED TO BE ISAIAHS

**IN THE PREVIOUS INTERLUDE,** we spoke of causes for both joy and despair. We saw how humans can delight in the life God gives to them and to all creation, but we also saw that the same intelligence and creativity that leads to delight can also yield despair—and there are abundant reasons for despair at the contemporary state of the earth. Yet we ended that discussion of the problems with joy at the challenge of caring for the earth as Christ cares for it.

We have just concluded a long discussion of the spiritual and intellectual forces which have produced the problem, and there has been as much despair as joy in that analysis. We are left with the cacophony of the modern world ringing in our ears. But despite all our reasons for despair, we can continue to delight in the earth and in our redemptive task. Such an attitude rises not out of a blind optimism, but is rooted in our being in Christ, who is the life of the world.

As Christians, we say that we place our trust in him who can change world views and value structures. Yet we often look too long at the dark. We are like Peter who let the waves frighten him into forgetting the Christ who was holding him up. Sometimes, indeed, when we look at the extent of environmental problems, we sink like Peter. We too are overwhelmed— by a sea of hungry people, eroding fields, dwindling fuel, and manipulative attitudes.

But our despair would be dispelled if we took more seriously our task as prophets. For we are messengers of the Good News that the redemption of this world has begun, often in ways of which we are unaware. The night in Bethlehem culminated in the morning at Joseph's tomb—and so Christ's power is manifest in this world. Christians are the agents of that redemptive power. And a part of their task is to speak out against the forces which rob creation of its life.

We are not saying that Christians ought to stand apart to judge what goes on in the world. They are called instead to obey God in all the work they do, for nothing falls outside the realm of that redemptive work. We are saying, however, that Christians cannot hope to place their faith in their own work. First of all, such misplaced confidence would soon fade away—all our

**197**

efforts at changing attitudes and restructuring governments, economics, and technology would soon appear futile. But we must reject such confidence for another reason: we place our trust in Christ, not only because we wish to avoid despair, but also, and more importantly, because he commands us to do so.

As Christians, we go about our tasks in this world not because we hope for world-changing results—although God could use us to produce them—but because we know that we are setting up signs along the road, pointing to the transformation of this world into the kingdom of God. We are much like Noah, a hero in other ways, who continued about his work despite the laughs and jeers of those around him.

In another way, we are much like the prophets of the Old Testament: as we do our work in obedience to God's commands we wear the sackcloth of Isaiah. For in effect, our feeble attempts at restoring creation are ways of saying,

> Their land is filled with silver and gold,
>     and there is no end to their treasures;
> their land is filled with horses,
>     and there is no end to their chariots.
> Their land is filled with idols;
>     they bow down to the work of their hands,
>     to what their own fingers have made.
> So man is humbled,
>     and men are brought low—
>     forgive them not!
>
> (Isa. 2:7–9)

The mad gropings for ever more growth and wealth, the scrabblings at the earth's surface for greater treasures, the trampling of the creature who gets in the way of our pursuit of happiness: all these are like the treasures, chariots, and idols of the people of Israel.

But this disgust and hatred, this righteous anger against the things humans have done—is this joy? Surely such feelings cannot remain pure; we are not yet like Christ the whip-handler, the drover of money merchants. A continual hatred of the obscenities arising from the hearts of evil people would certainly drive out all thoughts of Christian love and forgiveness. Thus we may look again to the prophet Isaiah for a model of Christian prophecy. For despite his anger, the righteous anger of God, Isaiah is also the prophet whom we remember for his messages of God's love and forgiveness. To those on whom he lays God's judgment, Isaiah says,

> The people who walked in darkness have seen a great light;
> those who dealt in a land of deep darkness,
> on them has light shined.
>
> (Isa. 9:2)

Our joy in creation, and at our own redemptive and recreative task, rises out of the despair of a hard look at the world. Guided by the Word of God—Incarnate and in Scripture—we must arm ourselves to the task of being new Isaiahs, witnessing to God's judgment and mercy in our own times—and above all, to his ability to redeem and transform the values and structures of the world. And our armor consists no longer of sackcloth and ashes, but of a redeemed wonder at, knowledge of, and power over God's creation.

"Eve, this place is so vast we couldn't pollute it if we tried."

From *Christianity Today*, February 27, 1970. © 1970 by John Lawing. Used by permission.

# THE EARTH
# IS THE LORD'S

"But pastor, why can't the church stick to its own business instead of med-
dling into people's beliefs?"

From *Christianity Today*, May 24, 1974. © 1974 by John Lawing. Used by permission.

### CHAPTER 13

# WHO'S IN CHARGE?

*He, therefore, who is not illumined by such great splendor of created things is blind; he who is not awakened by such great clamour is deaf; he who does not praise God because of all these effects is dumb; he who does not note the first principle from such great signs is foolish. Open your eyes, therefore, prick up your spiritual ears, open your lips and apply your heart, that you may see our God in all creatures.*

—St. Bonaventure, THE MIND'S ROAD TO GOD

*It was the divinely appointed function of the first man . . . to unite in himself the whole of created being; and at the same time to reach his perfect union with God and thus grant the state of deification to the whole creation. . . . Since this task was not fulfilled by Adam, it is in the work of Christ, the second Adam, that we can see what it was meant to be.*

—Vladimir Lossky,
THE MYSTICAL THEOLOGY OF THE EASTERN CHURCH

One of the wisest books to come out of our time of increased environmental awareness is *Design with Nature* by the land planner, Ian McHarg. It is a beautiful book, one which is beginning to exert a good deal of influence on the way in which new human uses of the land are actually being conducted. McHarg's basic thesis is that although human beings have the capability of imposing their structures on the land without any concern for the land itself, they also have the ability, and the responsibility, to build out of an awareness of natural processes. Such design can maintain and enhance both the diversity of the natural communities and the livability of the structures for humans. The book is full of both good and bad examples of "designing with nature." And McHarg leaves no doubt as to the ultimate source of the kind of design which destroys nature. That source is, he says, the biblical, Christian elements of our civilization. He maintains:

Our failure is that of the Western World and lies in prevailing values. Show me a man-oriented society in which it is believed that reality exists only

**203**

because man can perceive it, that the cosmos is a structure erected to support man on its pinnacle, that man exclusively is divine and given dominion over all things, indeed that God is made in the image of man, and I will predict the nature of its cities and their landscapes. I need not look far for we have seen them—the hot-dog stands, the neon shill, the ticky-tacky houses, dysgenic city and mined landscapes. This is the image of the anthropomorphic, anthropocentric man; he seeks not unity with nature but conquest.[1]

McHarg's words have a familiar sound: we encountered similar accusations in the critique of Lynn White when he said that "Christianity is the most anthropocentric religion the world has ever seen," and linked much of the current environmental degradation to that anthropocentricity. But McHarg is much more forceful in his critique than White. Thus the very vigor of his attack makes his analysis a good starting point for an exposition of biblical attitudes toward nature. For the biblical story, McHarg says,

> . . . in its insistence upon dominion and subjugation of nature, encourages the most exploitative and destructive instincts in man rather than those that are deferential and creative. Indeed, if one seeks license for those who would increase radioactivity, create canals and harbors with atomic bombs, employ poisons without constraint, or give consent to the bulldozer mentality, there could be no better injunction than this text. Here can be found the sanction and injunction to conquer nature—the enemy, the threat to Jehovah.[2]

At the beginning of our brief history of views of nature in Western thought, we asserted that, with some important exceptions, White's critique of Christianity is justified: Christians *have* interpreted the biblical teaching on human dominion over nature—and divine transcendence over the world—as a license for the ruthlessly exploitative subjugation of nature. But, as we have already pointed out, the most important exception to our agreement with those accusations of White—or McHarg—is that this ruthlessness results from Christians *misunderstanding* and *misusing* Scripture, rather than the actual teaching of Scripture itself.

The origin then is not so much Christianity as it is Christendom—a Christendom which has, in many cases, failed to redeem fully the various attitudes toward nature which it encountered. We have, in the previous section of this book, discussed in some detail those various attitudes. In these next chapters, we will consider what the biblical teaching about the use of nature indeed is when considered in the light of the central Christian claim: that "God is in Christ, redeeming the world to Himself." And the principles that emerge from that discussion point to a use of nature much more like the careful stewardship of life, beauty, and diversity advocated by McHarg, than the blind, human-centered destructiveness which he describes as the Christian teaching.

## CREATION

It is not unusual for those who speak of the negative effects of Christianity on nature to speak also, rather nostalgically, of the harmony between humanity and nature evident in pagan, pantheist, or animistic religions. In such religions, ranging from the early Greek belief in the Olympic pantheon to the various earthy animisms of the American Indians, there is always some degree of identity between nature and the god or gods. All Christians immediately disassociate themselves from such views of the relationship between God and nature, for if there is one thing about biblical religion which is abundantly clear, it is that God is the maker of the world, and thus he is completely apart from it. He does not depend on it, but it depends utterly and completely on him.

This dependence of the world on God is the clearest teaching of the creation account in Genesis. "In the beginning, God created the heavens and the earth." Creation is his, and he is not to be confused with it. The confusion of creation and Creator is the sin against which the Hebrews are repeatedly warned and which they repeatedly commit. In those days it appears to have been a very easy sin to commit—almost an inevitable one. To "kiss one's hand to the sun" (a gesture of reverence for creation which Job declares himself to be innocent of) or to build a temple in a grove on a hilltop and there to merge ecstatically with the divine forces of nature—that was what came naturally. Now, though such paganism is probably irretrievable to people who, like ourselves, are intensely aware of their separateness from nature, more than a few environmentalist crusaders have called for a return to such a paganism. It is clear, though, that this confusion of creation and Creator is as much a sin for the contemporary Christian as it was for the biblical Hebrew.

However, though Genesis teaches that God is utterly outside the world, it does not teach that he is utterly uninterested in it, any more than we would expect the composition of a symphony to indicate a composer's disinterest in its performance. This divine concern for creation is abundantly evident, not only in the intricate ordering of the created world, but also in the repeated statement of its goodness.

There are two ways of reading the phrase, "and God saw that it was good," which appears six times in Genesis 1. The first is that the goodness of creation is a reflection of the goodness of God: a way of saying "I am good." This meaning is evident in such declarations of the Psalmist as "the heavens declare the glory of God." Unquestionably, then, one purpose of creation is to give God glory.

The other dimension to the phrase does not contradict the first, but it is often overlooked, particularly by those who persist in seeing in Genesis divine license for the misuse of nature. The statement is not just a reflection of the goodness of God; it is a declaration of the goodness of creation. More precisely, it is a *recognition* of the goodness of creation. The phrase is often misquoted as "God *said* that it was good," implying that the goodness of creation is the result of divine fiat. But in the wording "God saw" there is a recognition of the independence of creation. Though its origin is clearly

from God, the very fact of creation gives creatures an independence, a goodness, and a freedom of their own. "God *saw* that it was good" is thus not
so much a declaration as it is a *response* to creation. Implicit here is not only
the possible independence and waywardness of a creature separated from the
Creator, but also that ultimate response to a wayward creation, the crucifixion of Christ, "the Lamb slain before the foundation of the world."

It is clear, then, that in creation God creates something other than
himself; he upholds it, but is not present in it. It is clear also that he gives
that creation both goodness and freedom. Creatures are not God's slaves, as
his delight in their goodness makes plain.

We have yet to consider the creation of humans and their relationship
to the rest of creation. But these indications of a divine *response* to creation,
in which God allows freedom for the individual creature to be, already
counters the claim of those who maintain that the doctrine of creation gives
people license to exploit. These verses in Genesis 1 make clear that the goodness of creation is a goodness in the things themselves, not in their usefulness
to humans—who are not even mentioned until the end of the chapter. To
say that the goodness of creation is only a goodness of utility, because it can
be used by the one creature made in God's image, is to miss most of the
force of the boisterous and blossoming complexity of life which Genesis 1
suggests.

A number of other passages in Scripture make clear that "nature" is
good for its own sake, not just because it can be used for humans. One of
the most striking of such passages is Psalm 104. Though in this remarkable
hymn some of the bounties of creation are clearly described as being for
people ("plants for man to cultivate," "wine to gladden the heart of man,"
"bread to strengthen man's heart"), they are all general things which humans
may adapt to their use. In the same Psalm the more specific descriptions are
of a detailed, lovingly perceived world where humanity does not figure in
at all, and yet which God cares for just as much:

> The trees of the Lord are watered abundantly,
>   the cedars of Lebanon which he planted.
> In them the birds build their nests;
>   the stork has her home in the fir trees.
> The high mountains are for the wild goats;
>   the rocks are a refuge for the badgers.
>
> (Ps. 104:16–18)

There is no suggestion that cedars, storks, goats, or badgers are there for the
sake of humans; yet, the Psalmist says, God cares for them and exults in
their individuality.

This is not an isolated passage; there are many like it throughout the
Old Testament. But perhaps the most striking is in the book of Job, where
God answers Job's complaint by referring to various works of creation. And
the point of the answer is precisely that these things in creation are outside

human understanding and control. Humans have neither use nor understanding of them, yet they are God's, and good. God's answer to Job spans several chapters, but a brief sampling makes the point: creation is not just for human benefit. It is good in the very strength of its strangeness and diversity.

> Then the Lord answered Job out of the whirlwind:
> "Who is this that darkens counsel by words without knowledge?
> . . . Where were you when I laid the foundations of the earth? . . .
> when the morning stars sang together,
>     and all the sons of God shouted for joy?
> . . . Have you entered into the springs of the sea?
>     or walked in the recesses of the deep?
> . . . Have you entered the storehouses of the snow,
>     or have you seen the storehouses of the hail. . . .
> Do you know when the mountain goats give forth?
> Do you observe the calving of the hinds?
> . . . Is the wild ox willing to serve you?
> Will he spend the night at your crib?
> . . . Is it by your wisdom that the hawk soars,
>     and spreads his wings toward the south?
> Is it at your command that the eagle mounts up
>     and makes his nest on high?
>
> (Job 38–39, passim)

The message is clear: not all stars are to provide light for humans; not all snowflakes are for human appreciation; there are oxen we should not tame, deer whose freedom is to be preserved, hawks and eagles which fly far above us.

As we are to see, humans do have a unique place in creation and a unique responsibility to all of it. But such passages as these make plain that the goodness of creation does not depend on people. Its purpose is not merely to fuel the engines of human progress; it is also to provide water for the thirsty trees, crags for the goats, and open sky for the south-flying hawks.


## MAN AND DOMINION

We may now consider the explicit teaching in Genesis about the relationship of humanity to nature. That inexhaustibly rich account of the creation of humans and nature, may (for the purposes of this study) be considered under two categories: what humans *are* and what humans *do* (or rather, what they are told to do, since the two are, unfortunately, rarely the same). As a preliminary, it is helpful to point out what many biblical scholars have noticed and speculated upon (with varying degrees of insight): the Genesis record of the origin of humanity is divided into two accounts, or at least two perspectives on the same event. One common explanation for this division is that two revelations of different age and origin, welded together with the seam still showing, are recorded here in Scripture. Whether or not this is the case, it is as one story that the account made its historical impact. So, in the discussion which follows, we will ignore the break which most commentators agree occurs in Genesis 2:4, and discuss the account as though it were one story.

When we consider what is said or implied in Genesis 1 and 2 about what humans are, two sorts of images emerge. First of all, humans, like stars, seas, whales, fish, and birds, are simply a part of creation. They are made on the sixth day and are the final act of creation, but they share a day of creation with other animals, and they are clearly made in the same way the animals are. Thus they are embedded in creation. This image of human relatedness to the rest of nature is made even more vivid when they are described as being made "from the dust of the earth." The Hebrew word used here for "earth" is *adamah*, and the Hebrew word for man is *Adam*. What the words and the whole account suggest, then, is what contemporary biologists and ecologists have been trying hard to tell us: whatever else they are, humans are also *earth*; they share their nature with its soil, its plants, its animals.

Yet this earthiness of humanity—its commonality with the rest of creation—is only half of the Genesis picture. (It is, however, a half that needs more recognition, especially by Christians.) It is balanced by another aspect of humanity, and it is this aspect that writers like McHarg and White are speaking to when they speak of human separation from nature. For humans are also described as being very special in creation: they are made "in the image of God." Leaving aside for a moment what that image consists of, it is important to acknowledge its uniqueness in humanity. Humans share with God something which the rest of creation does not share. In this sense they are above creation. And, in support of this unique relationship to God, humans are given a unique position in creation. The "Garden of Eden" (which has been understood variously as either a specific and limited place or as a now-destroyed relationship to the whole earth) is planted for humans, and everything (with, of course, the important exception of the two trees) is given for their use. Thus Genesis pictures humanity as being both *in* nature and *over* it. Christians and critics alike, unfortunately, have stressed human transcendence over nature at the expense of human immanence in it. But before seeing how these two poles of the humanity/nature relationship are to be understood and acted upon, we must move beyond what humans *are* according to Genesis, and examine what they are told to *do*.

When we consider the tasks given to humans, we notice a polarity similar to the extremes of what humans are. They are told to do two sorts of things, which are, at first glance, as contradictory as saying that humans are both *in* nature and *over* it.

The first sort of thing humans are told to do is contained in Genesis 1:28. It is a notorious verse, for, more than any other passage of Scripture, it has been understood as giving humans license, even a command, to exploit the earth.

> And God blessed them; and God said to them, "Be fruitful and multiply, and fill the earth, and subdue it; and rule over the fish of the sea and over the birds of the sky and over every living thing that moves on the earth." (NASB)

"Be fruitful" and "multiply" are commands given to other creatures. But in this divine command to humanity are two commands which are given to no other creatures: "subdue" and "rule." Any softening of these forceful words would not be an adequate translation; in fact, this translation of the Hebrew words (*kabash* and *radah*) is already considerably milder than the Hebrew terms. *Kabash* is drawn from a Hebrew word meaning to tread down or bring into bondage, and conveys the image of a conqueror placing his foot on the neck of the conquered; in one passage the word even means "rape." The other verb, *radah*, comes from a word meaning to trample or to prevail against and conveys the image of one treading grapes in a wine-press. Thus there is no doubt at all that man is placed *over* the rest of creation. These verses express that superiority in the strongest possible terms.

Certainly if these commands were the only directive given to humanity, it would be correct to look to the Hebrew-Christian tradition as the source of the Western exploitative attitudes toward nature. But the image of forceful dominion which this verse conveys is balanced (and, in some sense, reversed) by the rest of Scripture. That balance first appears in the next chapter, where Adam is given tasks which seem quite different from the kind of dominion decreed earlier: "The Lord God took the man and put him in the garden of Eden to till it and keep it." Again, human responsibility is described by two verbs, *abad* and *shamar*, here translated "till" and "keep." The first of these verbs, *abad*, is often translated "till," but it is sometimes translated "work" or "serve." And in fact, *abad* is the basic Hebrew word for "serve" or even "be a slave to." The other word, *shamar*, is translated variously "keep," "watch," or "preserve." The significant thing about both words is that they describe actions undertaken not primarily for the sake of the doer, but for the sake of the object of the action. The kind of tilling which is to be done is a *service* of the earth. The keeping of the garden is not just for human comfort, but is a kind of *preservation*. Both verbs severely restrict the way the other two verbs—subdue and rule—are to be applied. Human ruling, then, should be exercised in such a way as to *serve* and *preserve* the beasts, the trees, the earth itself—all of which is being ruled.

The original command to subdue and rule is not withdrawn, but the *type* of ruling is explicitly directed. There is never any doubt that humans are masters; but the concept of mastery itself here begins to be clarified in a process which will culminate only in the crucifixion of Christ.

Some further direction to this uniquely human subduing-which-is-service is indicated in yet another, more specific, task which God gives Adam.

So out of the ground the Lord God formed every beast of the field and every
bird of the air, and brought them to the man to see what he would call them;
and whatever the man called every living creature, that was its name. (Gen.
2:19)

We can understand this task in the superficial modern sense of naming,
in which the mystery of a thing is reduced to a label and applied to the object
named. In modern thought, however, naming tends to become one more
way of imposing on a nameless world the categories of our mind. In terms
of that Cartesian caricature we referred to in an earlier chapter, it is the man-
ghost's way of running the great machine nature.

On the other hand, naming in the biblical sense is not "labeling," but
is a recognition of the innermost being of a thing. When Abram makes a
covenant with God, and acknowledges God's full purpose for him, that
change is expressed by his new name, Abraham. A similar use of naming
occurs in the change from Jacob to Israel. Ideally, names are not imposed
labels, but recognitions of what one *is*. True naming thus involves a thorough,
sympathetic *knowing*.

This high view of naming survives in some contemporary "primitive"
cultures. Among the Kwakiutl of the Pacific Northwest, for example, the
name of a thing is the sum total of all its relationships, and to name something
is to place oneself in relationship with it. (Curiously, the name of God in
such a language is a very long word indeed, requiring two years of preparation and a month for pronunciation, after which the namer himself receives
a new name.) Such anthropological curiosities suggest that there is a good
deal more in Adam's task of naming than we normally acknowledge: they
suggest, in short, that naming involves a deep knowledge of the subject and
a sympathetic relationship with it.

Another feature of the naming task refers back beyond what humans
*do* to what they *are*. Naming involves a separation from the thing named
and a kind of superiority. As far as we know, no other creature gives names
to things. The task and the ability seem to be marks of what it means to be
made "in the image of God."

Further, this naming ability links man the namer with God the maker,
clarifying human uniqueness from the rest of creation. This human potential
to share in the creative act is suggested by the curious wording of the verse:
God brings the creatures to Adam "to see what he would call them." The
clear impression is that God *waits* for Adam's perception and for the creative
(and responsive) act of his naming, as though it is in humanity that God's
creation is made complete. We noted a similar wording in God's blessing of
creation. God does not simply declare that things are good; he *sees* that they
are good. Likewise, God waits to *see* what Adam will see in the creature—
and as a result of that seeing, what he will utter.

Thus in Genesis 1 and 2 humans are described as *being* two different
kinds of things: *a part of* nature and *apart from* nature; likewise, they are

described as *doing* two different things: *ruling* nature and *serving* nature. We have suggested further that an indication of the form which both that dominion and that service should take is provided by the descriptions of Adam's *naming* the animals.

How are these contraries (or at least, polarities) to be resolved? Which is the human: the ruthless ruler, or the caring servant? The answer, of course, is both—and the key to understanding what humans *do* in nature lies in first seeing clearly what humans *are*. They are, as we saw, over nature—apart from it. It is this superiority which enables them to subdue and rule it. Yet they are also in nature—a part of it. And it is this presence with the rest of creation which enables them to share, to understand, to sympathize: the kinds of actions which underlie naming, serving, and preserving.

It has become commonplace to associate the exploitative aspect of the human relationship to nature with Genesis 1, in which those harsh verbs are used to describe the human task, and the more careful relationship with nature with Genesis 2, where the gentler verbs are used. But, as we have seen, a consideration of what humans *are* shows that in the first chapter they are most closely linked with nature, and in the second chapter they are most clearly placed above nature, all of Eden being made for them. Certainly, then, one way to harmonize this apparent paradox is to recognize that it is only by virtue of human separation from nature that they can serve, and that it is the ability to be consciously a part of nature which enables them to be its legitimate master.

That, at least, is the pattern suggested by Genesis, particularly when we regard this account as one coherent story and not a poorly patched amalgam. But that pattern has not been one which has been used as a basis for human action; both biblical history and our own observation of the past show that we departed very early from the ability to use superiority as a basis for service.

### THE LONG LESSON:
### DOMINION IN THE OLD TESTAMENT

The whole of biblical history, and even of church history, can helpfully be understood as a long lesson in how humans are to use their ability to manipulate, dominate, and rule. We are accustomed to considering that story mainly in connection with our relationship with God and with other people, but a third dimension of that relationship concerns our attitude toward "nature"—nonhuman creation.

The lesson begins with human sin. In the biblical story, the tempter's appeal is to the human desire for illegitimate authority: to eat of the tree of knowledge, and thus become, in human terms and time, like God. It is the first time in history that humans have longed for the power of gods, but certainly not the last. The consequence of their action is, as is often pointed out, alienation between God and humans, between man and woman, and between humanity and nature. But the verses describing the "curse on nature" need a closer look, for they have often been appealed to as a justification of the harsh measures people must take toward their natural environment:

> . . . cursed is the ground because of you;
> in toil you shall eat of it all the days of your life;
> thorns and thistles it shall bring forth to you;
> and you shall eat the plants of the field.
> In the sweat of your face you shall eat bread
> till you return to the ground,
> for out of it you were taken;
> you are dust,
> and to dust you shall return.
>
> (Gen. 3:17–19)

This passage is often read in such a way as to suggest that "thorns and thistles"—that is, weeds in general, all plants which "get in the way"—are not a part of the created order, but are a consequence of human sin. In the Middle Ages this doctrine was expanded from biology into geology, and the very ruggedness of the earth, which so often was a burden for human attempts to move about on it, was seen as a result of the fall. But, as our own time has shown us painfully, there are very few plants, animals, hills, or valleys which we are not capable of regarding as weeds. The ground is cursed because we are set against it. Significantly, the word here for "ground" is also *adamah*, suggesting that the curse pronounced on Adam is in fact describing a division within himself.

That division is his own inability to be at harmony with the earth—his tendency to regard his difference from nature as enmity with nature. In short, the curse describes not a quality in the earth itself, but human misuse of his dominion. An accurate reading of the Hebrew would be, "Cursed is the ground *to you*."

Because of this attitude of enmity between people and nature, humanity has lost its ability to be the "preserver" of the garden in which it was placed. This loss is poignantly implied in the statement that God "placed the cherubim, and a flaming sword which turned every way, to guard the way to the tree of life." The word "guard" is the same word, *shamar,* used to describe humanity's failed task in the garden. Their misunderstanding of dominion, a dominion that issues in enmity, makes them unable to "guard" or "preserve" the life of the garden. It is an inability we still see manifested today.

An early indication of this human failure to understand dominion is the murder of Cain. Not only is the killing a clear misuse of divinely given strength, but when Cain defends himself against God's questioning, he does so by asking, "Am I my brother's keeper?" The verb again is *shamar,* the same used to define human care for nature. Here Cain reveals the human reluctance to use strength for service, whether it be toward people or toward nature.

Such misuse of human dominion occurs throughout the Bible. It climaxes early in an earth filled with violence, which God determines to wipe clean by flood. Yet in this climax of evil in which the misused strength of humans is nearly responsible for the destruction of life on earth, there is also a divinely given indication of how humans can use their dominion for the sake of the rest of creation. The story of Noah still stands, for Christians, as a kind of metaphor for how humanity should use its capacities for dominion; the benefit of human tool-wielding is the ark, a means of salvation to creatures which humans consider useless.

Another misuse of dominion is the tower of Babel—an early manifestation of "that old dream of man as God." If Noah's ark is a primeval example of *appropriate* technology, used to hold life up in a flood, Babel is an excellent emblem of *inappropriate* technology, for its only purpose is to lift its builders up for their own glory. The ark uses human creativity to identify with and preserve nature; the tower of Babel uses those same powers to lift humans out of nature.

From Abraham (who is asked to sacrifice his son, his one link with dominion) on through the prophets (who continually proclaim to the people God's message that their strength is not in their chariots, but rather in their giving up of their strength to God), the Old Testament is a record of this painful lesson which God must teach his people: whether we speak of humanity or nature, dominion does not mean simply imposing one's will on the weaker.

A passage in Ezekiel will serve to show clearly the typical sorts of reminders, given to the Hebrews, of the legitimate uses of dominion. Ezekiel is told to say to the "shepherds," the spiritual and political leaders of Israel:

> Ho, shepherds of Israel who have been feeding yourselves! Should not shepherds feed the sheep? You eat the fat, you clothe yourselves with the wool, you slaughter the fatlings; but you do not feed the sheep. The weak you have not strengthened, the sick you have not healed, the crippled you have not bound up, the strayed you have not brought back, the lost you have not sought, and with force and harshness you have ruled them. (Ezek. 34:2–4)

The passage is directed against the "shepherds of Israel," and it is clear that the shepherd/sheep relationship is a metaphor used to speak of the leaders' treatment of their people; it is a parable about the use of dominion, not primarily a tract on livestock management. But what Ezekiel is saying about the leaders of Israel will only be meaningful if the principles from which he draws are valid guides for shepherding sheep. Since shepherding is a particularly good example of the exercise of human dominion over the natural world, we are justified in treating the passage also on its literal level of meaning—that is, as telling us something about the way dominion may properly be exercised over any of the creatures which, the Psalmist says, were put "under our feet."

It is immediately obvious that the primary duty of the shepherd is to maintain the welfare of the flock. Though there is in the passage some suggestion that the ultimate purpose of the flock is to provide wool and food for human use, the fact that the shepherds are chastised for taking these things without "feeding the flock" suggests strongly that the welfare of the sheep *for the sheep's own sake* is an important use which the shepherd is to make of his position of superiority. This is made very clear when the writer accuses, "With force and with severity you have dominated them" (NASB). The word "dominated" is from *kabas*, the same word used in Genesis 1 to describe the general human stance toward nature. The lesson about dominion is clear: unless such dominion is used for the benefit of the dominated, it is misused.

Isaiah 53, one of the most powerful passages in the Old Testament, also teaches that the divine model for dominion is a radical kind of servitude. Christians have understood this portrait of the "suffering servant" to speak of the supreme demonstration of the character of dominion manifest in Jesus. But whatever prophetic or messianic content we might see in this description of one "despised and rejected by men," the increasingly familiar pattern is evident: dominion is servitude. That such a use of authority is counter to human expectation, which normally equates dominion with *lording*, not serving, is evident in the question at the opening of the chapter: "Who has believed what we have heard? And to whom has the arm of the Lord been revealed?" That the *arm* of the Lord—his strength, his authority, in short, his dominion—could be revealed in meekness and servitude is so contrary to the warped human expectation for the uses of dominion that the implicit answer to the question is, "No one will believe this." Yet the whole chapter—indeed, one might say the whole of biblical history—is a demonstration of this link between dominion and vulnerability.

We have only sampled briefly the abundant Old Testament teaching that the dominion that humans are to exercise is not a kind of exploitation, but a kind of service. Though most of the passages we have considered do not speak exclusively of the human relationship to nature, they nevertheless outline the *concept* of dominion. And what they point to is what we noticed in the Genesis account: though the words describing human authority are very strong, that authority over nature is to be applied in the ways indicated by such other-directed verbs as "serve" and "guard." Such use of strength goes counter to most of what seems to come naturally to us as humans—so much so that many would say it is simply not possible. But Christians say such a transformation of dominion *is* possible because of the sacrifice of Christ, which is both a pattern for action and a power enabling us to carry it out. The whole long lesson of Old Testament history points to this supreme example of God's use of dominion, which henceforth must be the model for all who would, in the name and service of God, exercise stewardship over his creation.

## CHRIST AND DOMINION

It is, perhaps, an indication of our fallen condition that we humans have not only seized the Genesis commandment to rule as a permit to use nature only for *human* comfort, but have interpreted the sacrificial death of Christ as being only for *human* salvation. Thus the most compelling argument in favor of any degradation of the environment, whether it be strip-mining a hill, clear-cutting a mountain, or butchering a whale, is always the contribution such an action will make to *human* survival—if not the actual survival of individuals, at least the survival of a certain kind of comfort or security.

The unique message of the Christian gospel, however, is not only the proclamation of the infinite worth of human life (for God, in Christ, died to redeem it); it also is the importance of being willing to give up that life—or at least to forgo one's comfort and material security—for the sake of another. We have tended to interpret that sacrificial Christian *caritas* as directed only toward other humans. Yet our record—particularly in North America—of forgoing some wealth and comfort even for other suffering people is a dismal one. Despite the remarkably explicit teaching of Christ on sharing one's wealth, we still find it very difficult to do anything other than multiply our own comforts and securities.

The case for doing otherwise, for using one's wealth and power for the sake of others, has been made convincingly in a number of recent books, perhaps most notably in Ron Sider's *Rich Christians in an Age of Hunger*. That book, and others like it, have shown that biblical teaching leaves no room for the kind of self-centered dominion condemned (for example) in Ezekiel's criticism of "the shepherds of Israel." The abuses of wealth and power criticized in such works are clearly a misuse of our power over other humans, to be continually judged by the gospel of Christ. Such selfish domination of resources is discussed elsewhere in the book. But, as the foregoing discussion should make clear, it is just as possible to misuse dominion toward nature as it is to misuse it toward humans. And if the pattern for our use of power is established in Christ, then it is a pattern for our treatment of nature, as well as of humanity. This is not to say that one should treat nature and humanity in the same way, though such corrective confusions of priorities are hard to avoid. Such an error in proportion was made not long ago by a well-known biologist, who argued that since there were far more humans than redwoods, if he had to choose between preserving a mature redwood and an infant human, he would choose the redwood.

But to acknowledge a greater worth to the human than to the natural does not mean that the human is of infinite value and the natural of no value. Since it is clear from Scripture that God values all of creation, and that we are placed in it to care for it, we must work out the difficult choices of nature *or* humanity with care and wisdom, and one case at a time. All our actions should be guided by the *example* of the use of dominion provided by Christ.

The central statement of that divine use of power is in Philippians 2. There Christians are told to have the "mind of Christ." And the verses which follow leave little doubt as to the sort of actions the mind of Christ should impel us to. For Christ was he who,

> . . . though he was in the form of God, did not count equality with God a thing to be grasped, but emptied himself, taking the form of a servant, being born in the likeness of men. And being found in human form he humbled himself and became obedient unto death, even death on a cross. (Phil. 2:6–8)

In the words of Ian McHarg, with which we began this chapter, the misuse of nature is attributed to the damaging consequences of the idea of humans as divine: "Show me a man-oriented society in which it is believed . . . that the cosmos is a structure erected to support man on its pinnacle, that man exclusively is divine and given dominion over all things, . . . and I will predict the nature of its cities and their landscapes." Yet Christians place at the center of their faith the example of one who, "in the form of God" and thus on the "pinnacle of the cosmos," gave up the dominion which was a consequence of that position, "did not regard it as a thing to be grasped," and became a servant. The implication is clear: what God became for us, we are to become for nature. But that McHarg (and others) should make such accurate criticisms of what a Christian civilization has done to nature suggests that we have almost totally ignored the application of "the mind of Christ" to our treatment of the natural world.

Christians have not only neglected to apply "the mind of Christ" to their use of nature, but they have also rarely reflected enough on the involvement of Christ in nature. It is easy to neglect care for nature if we see it only as a backdrop for the drama of human salvation. But the Bible is quite clear in affirming that Christ's involvement with creation is not an involvement with humans only.

It is true, as Christians and their critics alike have affirmed, that God the Creator is utterly beyond nature. Thus it is idolatrous to worship nature as divine—whatever the environmental benefits of such nature worship may be thought to be. But it is equally true that Scripture teaches a continual, creative, and sustaining presence of God with his creation. And that creative and sustaining presence is understood as the second person of the Trinity, Christ Jesus of Nazareth, who is the Word without which nothing was made. In choosing to speak of Jesus as the Word, Logos, the apostle John brilliantly clarifies those half understood gropings of the Stoics to comprehend the ordering presence of God in nature.

Another source for this idea of the presence of the Word of God in nature is the Jewish Wisdom literature, in which a passage from Proverbs is the most striking. There the personified figure of Wisdom speaks:

The Lord created me at the beginning of his work,
　　the first of his acts of old.
Ages ago I was set up,
　　at the first, before the beginning of the earth.
　. . . then I was beside him, like a master workman;
and I was daily his delight,
　　rejoicing before him always,
　rejoicing in his inhabited world
　　and delighting in the sons of men.
　　　　　　　　　　　　　　　(Prov. 8:22–23, 30–31)

Christians have usually seen this figure of God's master workman, "rejoicing in his inhabited world," as a prefiguring of Christ. And there is abundant Scripture in the New Testament which, in a similar way, describes the involvement of Christ with nature. It will be enough to simply enumerate these passages, emphasizing the lines which speak of Christ's involvement with nature. The author of Hebrews writes that God

. . . has spoken to us by a Son, whom he appointed the heir of all things, *through whom also he created the world*. He reflects the glory of God and bears the very stamp of his nature, *upholding the universe by his word of power*. (Italics added.) (Heb. 1:2–3)

Paul writes in I Corinthians:

Yet for us there is one God, the Father, from whom are all things and for whom we exist, and one Lord, Jesus Christ, *through whom are all things* and through whom we exist. (Italics added.) (I Cor. 8:6)

Likewise Paul declares in Colossians 1:

He is the image of the invisible God, the first-born of all creation; *for in him all things were created*, in heaven and on earth, visible and invisible, whether thrones or dominions or principalities or authorities—*all things were created through him and for him*. He is before all things, and *in him all things hold together*. (Italics added.) (Col. 1:15–17)

The best known of these many passages that speak of Christ's involvement with nature is the Prologue to the Gospel of John:

In the beginning was the Word, and the Word was with God, and the Word was God. He was in the beginning with God; *all things were made through him, and without him was not anything made that was made*. (Italics added.) (John 3:1–3)

In the face of these clear statements of God's involvement in the created order, it is necessary to revise somewhat our understanding of the Christian doctrine of transcendence with a doctrine of immanence. Though God, the Creator, is indeed beyond the world, he is also in it. The historical Incarnation is the center, the exemplification in time, of God's willingness in Christ to create, sustain, delight in, and (if necessary) sacrificially *redeem* creation. Robert Farrar Capon put this mystery of the sustaining presence of Christ superbly:

> Christ wins in every triumph and loses in every loss. Christ dies when a chicken dies, and rises when an egg hatches. He lies slain in the wreckage of all Aprils. He weeps in the ruins of all springs. This strange, savage, gorgeous world is the way it is because, incomprehensibly, that is his style. The Gospel of the Incarnation is preached, not so that we can tell men that the world now means something it didn't mean before, but so they may finally learn what it has been about all along.[3]

This may sound superficially like Pantheism, but it is the opposite of Pantheism. It is because God stands apart from the world that he creates and sustains it. Likewise, it is because of the specific, historic entrance of Christ into nature that we are able to understand the continual involvement of Christ, the upholding Word, in all of nature.

If we grant that Scripture teaches an involvement of Christ in all of nature, what does this imply for *human* involvement in nature? Without yet considering the pertinent Scripture, we can notice a kind of symmetry between God's relationship to nature and the human relationship to nature. We noticed it first in Genesis, but when we come to the gospel of the Incarnation, its significance for contemporary Christians becomes much more practical. God is transcendent over nature. That is a fact of Christian faith, but it has been scorned, in recent years, because of the supposed indifference to nature which that divine transcendence produces in people. For we have seen also, in the doctrine of the "image of God" and the accompanying task to have dominion over creation, that Scripture speaks of a kind of *human* transcendence.

What a consideration of the Incarnation shows, however, is that in Christ, both as Creator and Redeemer, God is immanent in creation. The "equality with God" enables the creating Word to share the flesh of his creation in an immanence which grasps neither at glory nor survival, but which leads ultimately to death. Likewise, though Christians transcend the world, they also are directed to become a redemptive part of what they transcend. Humans are to become saviors of nature, as Christ is the savior of humanity (and hence, through humans, of nature).

This idea of humans as the saviors of nature is not simply theological speculation. It is implied in all of those many Scripture passages which speak of redeemed humans as "joint-heirs" with Christ. As Christ is Ruler, Creator, and Sustainer of the world, so also is man to be. Being heirs with Christ involves (as Paul saw) being crucified with Christ; it also involves sharing in the sustaining activity in nature of Christ the Creator.

Most specifically, this startling, but orthodox, idea of man as sharing in the redemption of nature is taught in several verses in Romans 8. After a passage which speaks of Christians as fellow heirs with Christ, there follow these verses:

> For the creation waits with eager longing for the revealing of the sons of
> God; for the creation was subjected to futility, not of its own will but by the
> will of him who subjected it in hope; because the creation itself will be set
> free from its bondage to decay and obtain the glorious liberty of the children
> of God. We know that the whole creation has been groaning in travail to-
> gether until now. . . . (Rom. 8:19–22)

In this suggestively cryptic passage, it is clear that the fate of creation is
bound up with the fate of humanity and that whatever glory comes to humans as a result of their participation in divine redemption will come also
to creation. Is this a promise in reference only to some far future millennial
kingdom, or are we *now* to be redemptively involved in that groaning and
suffering creation? Scripture does not generally put tasks off into some es-
chatological future, a fact which would point to the present as the occasion
for our work with nature. So also does the wording of the final sentence:
the "until now" suggests that the childbirth is over and that humans, who
have been shown the pattern of their dominion as stewards of the earth, can
begin to exercise it wisely, according to the mind of Christ. It remains for
us to see how Christians have understood and acted on that stewardship in
the centuries since the Incarnation.

## THE LONG LESSON CONTINUED:
## DOMINION IN CHURCH HISTORY

We have already pointed out in an earlier chapter that the idea of human
redemptive involvement in nature has not played a very important part in
the development of Western thought. The brief biblical analysis in this chapter has shown us one reason why: there is a valid biblical teaching of human
separateness from nature. This idea of human transcendence became joined,
in the early years of the church, with the prevailing Platonic idea of physical
nature as a source of ignorance and evil and a snare to the soul. The result
was a theology which laid most stress on the salvation of the soul, and tended
to ignore the body and the nature of which it was a part. Perhaps the most
influential of those who taught that Christians should turn away from the
world and devote their attention solely to the spiritual and the eternal was
St. Augustine. Augustine arrived at Christianity after a long pilgrimage
through the religions of the day, including Neo-Platonism, which held a
strong doctrine of the evil of matter. Augustine never quite ceased to be
influenced by this idea; his Platonic attitude is clearly evident in these words
from his *Soliloquies:* "These things of the senses are to be utterly shunned
and the utmost care must be used lest while we bear this body our wings be
impeded by their snare. . . ."[4]

Augustine was also an important source of a related idea which we
traced in some detail through Western thought: the superiority of the mind
over nature. Augustine was acutely aware of his own consciousness, and this

emphasis on self-consciousness grew in the West—slowly, to be sure—until it appeared in a powerful form in those ideas of the detached mind (as in Descartes, or Bacon, or Galileo) which were so important in the scientific revolution. Notice how, in this passage from the *Confessions* (which is for its day a remarkably mind-centered book), the emphasis is on the importance of the separateness of the mind from nature:

> Men go forth to marvel at the heights of mountains and the huge waves of the sea, the broad flow of the rivers, the vastness of the ocean, the orbits of the stars, and yet they neglect to marvel at themselves. Nor do they wonder how it is that, when I spoke of all these things, I was not looking at them with my eyes. . . .[5]

Thus both in his ethics—his understanding of what is good—and in his epistemology—his understanding of what and how we know—Augustine tends to stress the transcendent human mind, or soul, above nature. Nature, for all its beauty (which Augustine readily responds to), is counted of no worth on the soul's journey to God. With some exceptions, this has been typical of the Western approach to nature. Humans—their minds, their souls, their eternal destinies—are placed as the central object for salvation. There is little concern for—or even awareness of—nature itself. The *contemptus mundi* tradition, with a few exceptions, keeps Christendom from recognizing an essential part of Christianity. That is, to the same extent that man's mind, soul, creativity, and destiny elevate him over nature, he is to use those gifts for the lifting, the nourishing, the *husbanding* of the creation for whose care he is responsible.

However, the idea of the Christian's responsibility to nature was not entirely ignored by Christendom. It formed, for example, an important part of the theology of the second-century Church Father Irenaeus. Irenaeus emphasized the New Testament doctrine of Christ as the "Second Adam." But he did not, as did so many subsequent theologians, forget that Adam was given responsibility for nature. Christ succeeds, said Irenaeus, in doing what Adam was to do. And that success amounts not only to a victory over Satan, but to a redemption of nature as well. In Christ, nature has the kind of human master God intended for it. And through both his example and our adoption into him, we share in that redemption of nature. Says Irenaeus, "It is right, therefore, for this created order to be restored to its pristine state."[6]

Unfortunately, with the Platonically inclined influence of Augustine on Western Christian thought, this idea of human involvement in the redemption of nature played very little part. It does appear sporadically—for example, in the tradition of the Benedictine monastery discussed in an earlier chapter, in which work becomes a kind of prayer, and human presence is directed toward transforming nature into a kind of New Eden or "Jerusalem in waiting."

It appears again in Francis and his followers, who demonstrated a remarkable ability to love and care for the glowing, irreducible realities of wolf, bird, lamb, cicada—even grass. The Franciscan attitude toward nature is captured well in these words by Thomas Celano, an early biographer of St. Francis:

> When the brothers were cutting wood, he would forbid them to cut down the whole tree so that it might grow up again. He also ordered the gardeners not to dig up the edges of gardens so that wild flowers and green grasses could grow and glorify the Father of all things. . . . He picked up worms so they would not be trampled on and had honey and wine set out for the bees in the winter season. He called by the name of brother all animals. . . .[7]

Yet even this insight of Francis (as we traced in an earlier chapter), though it begins to direct people's attention to close observation of nature, does not succeed in substantially changing Christendom's view of nature. Its greatest influence (somewhat ironically) is on the empiricism at the roots of modern science. The nature-centered attitudes of St. Francis are, through time and the Western milieu, mutated into a mind-centered, and ultimately manipulative, *observation* of nature.

Thus in the West—with such important exceptions as the Franciscans and the Benedictines—Christian theology and action have stressed not man's involvement with nature, but his separation from nature and particularly the individual, conscious separation of the mind from nature. And as we saw in our discussion of Genesis, that distinctness of humanity from nature is an important part of the created order—including the *power* over nature which goes with it. Unmodified, however, the sheer human difference from nature, that naked human power over nature, is a horrible thing. Some of the monstrosities of that unredeemed human transcendence have been spoken of in previous chapters, and in itself it is clearly not a reflection of the mind of Christ, however much it validly affirms the human distinctiveness.

But Christendom has not been without a consistent, coherent, and ancient tradition of the involvement of man in the redemption of creation. That idea has been maintained as an important part of Eastern Orthodox theology.

Because Eastern Orthodoxy has not stressed the very thing which has been at the center of Western theology—that is, the experience of personal, individual salvation—it has tended to appear stagnant to critics from Western Christendom. Beards, black robes, and a vague impression of Byzantine complexity is all that has filtered through to most Western Christians. This sense that Eastern Orthodoxy is a kind of theological and cultural dead end is the prevailing attitude even among Western historians of the church. Kenneth Scott Latourette, for example, observes that "there was in this Byzantine Christianity less of activism and more of other-worldliness than in its Latin counterpart." This dynamic activism appeared not just in theology, but in the working-out of culture. It was in the West, not in the Byzantine East, that the great changes in outlook and technology which shaped the scientific revolution took place. Lynn White, whose opinions on Christendom we have already referred to, records the astonishment of a visitor from Greece to Italy in the fifteenth century who "is amazed by the superiority of Western ships, arms, textiles, glass. But above all he is astonished by the spectacle of waterwheels sawing timbers and pumping the bellows of the blast furnaces. Clearly, he had seen nothing of the sort in the Near East."[8] But the very fact that it is this technological dynamism which has produced so many of our environmental problems, combined with the fact that its theological basis is the thoroughgoing separation in Western thought between mind and body or humanity and nature, makes it essential to consider Eastern Orthodoxy's embodiment of the truth of the gospel.

When we turn to a consideration of the theology of the East, we discover that its strength is precisely in the area where Western thought is weakest: in its inclusion of the whole of creation, and not humans only, in redemption. Instead of that general suspicion of creation which dominates Western Christianity, there is a strong affirmation of the goodness of matter, its redeemability, and its dependence upon humans for its access to that divine redemption. In such a view humans are not so much pilgrims, leaving the world behind, as they are priests, lifting it all, through their priestly actions, into a kind of divine life. A contemporary Eastern Orthodox theologian puts it this way:

> The first, the basic definition of man is that he is *the priest*. He stands in the center of the world and unifies it in his act of blessing God, of both receiving the world from God and offering it to God—and by filling the world with this eucharist, he transforms his life, the one that he receives from the world, into life in God, into communion with Him. The world was created as the "matter," the material of one all-embracing eucharist, and man was created as the priest of this cosmic sacrament.[9]

Thus in Eastern thought humans are the agent for the "deification" of nature and the lifting of all of creation up into Godhead. This does not imply consciousless union, but rather is a development of that idea of humans as "heirs" with Christ, the second Adam of the fully redeemed creation.

Vladimir Lossky, another contemporary Orthodox theologian, confirms this idea of man as priest of nature: "In his way to union with God, man in no way leaves creatures aside, but gathers together in his love the whole cosmos disordered by sin, that it may at last be transfigured by grace."[10]

One of the results of this idea—or perhaps one of its causes—is a healthier view of matter than has prevailed throughout much of Western Christendom. Instead of considering matter (and nature in general) a snare to drag down the soul, for example, John of Damascus states its value by linking it with the Incarnation: "I do not venerate matter, but I venerate the creator of matter, who became matter for my sake, who assumed life in the flesh, and who, through matter, accomplished my salvation."[11]

Out of this high view of matter, and out of the idea of humans as the agents for extending redemption to all of creation, there comes an attitude toward creatures much different from that which has often prevailed in the West. St. Isaac the Syrian declares, for example:

> What is a charitable heart? . . . It is a heart which is burning with charity for the whole of creation, for men, for the birds, for the beasts . . . for all creatures. . . . This is why such a man never ceases to pray also for the animals. . . . He will pray even for the reptiles, moved by the infinite pity which reigns in the hearts of those who are becoming united to God.[12]

The purpose of this brief consideration of Eastern Orthodox attitudes toward nature is not to imply that Western Christianity is wrong and Eastern is correct. But it does suggest that in Eastern Christianity there has been a fuller development of those Scriptural teachings which speak of human responsibility to nature, and even (in the case of the passage in Romans about the eager longing of creation) of the human role as a mediator for nature of the cosmic redemption centered in Christ.

And yet it is in the West, and especially since the Reformation, that the doctrine of the worth of the individual human person has reached its fullest potential. It is likely that the dramatic development of Western technology is an accompanying feature of this individualism—just as a negative feature of stressing the individual separateness from nature is the regarding of nature as raw material to be manipulated.

These considerations indicate that in the unfolding of the meaning for creation of the gospel of Incarnation, there is room both for the benign Eastern concept of humans as nature's saviors and the more manipulative concept of humans as radically apart from nature. Certainly, as we have seen in our consideration of Scripture, there is basis for both tendencies in the biblical revelation. A fuller understanding of the Incarnation, an event which combines both dominion and servitude, is the key, perhaps, to the way in which the manipulative subjectivity of the West might be directed by the meditative, sacramental, and other-directed *caritas* of the East. At any rate, some such union seems necessary if Christendom is to apply with power the teaching of Christianity regarding human use of nature.

### CHAPTER 14

# STEWARDSHIP

> *. . . the rule of no realm is mine, neither of Gondor nor any other, great or small. But all worthy things that are in peril as the world now stands, those are my care. And for my part, I shall not wholly fail of my task, though Gondor should perish, if anything passes through this night that can still grow fair or bear fruit and flower again in days to come. For I also am a steward.*

> —Gandalf in J. R. R. Tolkien,
> **THE LORD OF THE RINGS**

> *The Lord God took man and put him in the garden of Eden to till it and keep it.*

> —GENESIS 2:15

W e have concluded, based on Scripture, that humans have been given dominion over nature and that they are to use that dominion to serve nature and humanity. Such service is the will of him who charged us with dominion; its purpose is to preserve, enhance, and glorify the creation, and in so doing, to glorify the Creator. In short, we are *stewards* of God, managers of this particular part of his household (to recall the *oikonomos* root of the word "steward").

If stewardship is indeed dominion as service—as the whole Christian gospel affirms—then stewardship (used or misused) is an inescapable condition of human existence. All humans exercise dominion over things and over people. Most often, that dominion increases only their own glory, and does not seem like "stewardly" behavior. But the basic question is not *whether* we are stewards; the fact of dominion, and the possibility of using it for service, decides that. The question is *how* we are to exercise our stewardship.

In claiming that humans are stewards appointed by God, we have suggested answers to some of the basic questions about what being human means. Some of those questions are these:

—What is the essential nature of the human?

—What is the composition of humans? Are they mind (or soul) and body? Mind only? Body only? Or none of these?

—What tasks (if any) should humans perform?

—Are we responsible for those tasks as individuals, or as part of a community?

—What, finally, is the destiny of humanity?

To call stewardship the exercise of delegated dominion in the service of creation is to say something about human nature and the human task. It also is to imply a good deal about our composition—about what we humans are. But to clarify these implications of calling people stewards, it will be necessary to look in some greater detail at traditional ways of answering such questions about human nature. The result will be a more thorough understanding of what sort of creature God has charged with care of his creation.

## THE NATURE OF THE HUMAN

The question concerning the essential nature of humanity needs to be clarified. It expresses our concern to know what is distinctively human: what is it that distinguishes humanity from all other creatures in the universe? The question also attempts to get at the important distinguishing marks of humanity. To say that humans are furless and featherless bipeds may distinguish them from everything else, but the distinction is trivial and unimportant. We are concerned with the *important* distinctive of humanity.

Perhaps the question can be framed more precisely this way: what characteristic (or characteristics) do *all* humans possess, *only* humans possess, and humans possess *necessarily*? If there are any such characteristics, they would constitute the essential nature of the species. All three parts of the question are important. The first part requires that the characteristic be possessed by everyone. The second requires that the characteristic be possessed by nothing else than humans. The third requires that possession of these characteristics be necessary for being human—that is, when one lacks such a characteristic, one is not human.

Furthermore, all parts of the question are important in conjunction. It may be that all humans are featherless, furless, and bipedal, to the exclusion of everything else. But our humanity does not depend upon that fact. Had God given us feathers and four feet, while leaving the rest of our makeup the same, we would still be human. To be an *essentially* human trait, the characteristic must meet all the criteria: all humans, and only humans, must have it, and they must have it necessarily.

In discussing the origins of human attitudes about nature, we already have encountered several answers to this question about what makes the human distinct. For Plato and Aristotle, the ability to reason constitutes the human essence; for Descartes, it is sheer consciousness; for Francis Bacon, it is the ability to manipulate the world for human ends. And there are many other theories of human uniqueness we have not considered. Some say humans are symbol-making animals; others, that they are the only creatures able to step outside the deterministic cause-and-effect chain; still others, that they are the only organisms capable of love, and so on.

Within the last century or so, all of these traditional ideas of human uniqueness have come under attack. Tool-making was once thought to be a uniquely human trait, but chimpanzees make sponges of leaves to drink water from inaccessible cracks, and finches have been observed to use a twig to extricate ants from holes. So our uniqueness is not in the ability to use tools. Humans were long thought to be the only beings capable of reason, but many of the great apes, as well as dolphins and killer whales, have solved problems by a process that cannot be distinguished from "rationality." Again, chimps have been taught the use of symbols, and have been able not only to recognize them, but to combine them in order to "say" new words. There seems little left to distinguish humanity from nature; indeed, recent studies in human psychology have led many to question whether people are significantly free from the push and pull of cause and effect, and to conclude that we are "beyond freedom and dignity."

Because of this rapid erosion at the pedestal of human uniqueness, many today have answered the question, "What is the essential nature of the human?" with a simple reply: nothing. The differences between humans and animals, according to this modern view, are either trivial or are different in degree, not kind. Humans can undoubtedly use tools, symbols, or intelligence *better* than the animals. But they seem to have no capacity that at least some animals don't have. The differences are those of degree; humans have no essential uniqueness.

This is an interesting debate, but it is not directly related to our study. We should point out, though, that it is increased care in observing other creatures—particularly in their natural settings—which has enabled us to understand what we share with the animals and with the natural world in general. Thus the very knowledge of our community with nature is an expression of a stewardship rooted in looking at the natural world, not just thinking about it. It seems to have been humans who discovered the rationality of chimps, not vice versa. But in any case, we are not at this point attempting to declare that there is, or is not, an "essence of humanity" which distinguishes humans from the rest of nature.

What we do wish to point out, however, is that to call humans "stewards of God" is to claim implicitly that humans are accountable, that is, *responsible* to God. In giving humans dominion over the earth, God has made them answerable for the way in which they use that dominion. And, as far as we know, accountability is unique to humanity.

And being held accountable is no trivial characteristic. For to be accountable to the very Creator of heaven and earth is to be endowed with dignity and honor. It is this wonder at the high place God has given humans that the Psalmist expresses when he exclaims, "Thou hast made him [man] a little lower than God, and dost crown him with glory and majesty" (NASB). And in the same Psalm, that place of honor is explicitly linked with human dominion over nature:

> Thou hast given him dominion over the works of thy hands;
>    thou hast put all things under his feet,
> all sheep and oxen,
>    and also the beasts of the field,
> the birds of the air, and the fish of the sea,
>    whatever passes along the paths of the sea.
>
> (Ps. 8:6–8)

But (as we discussed in the previous chapter) the Christian's exemplar of this dominion is Christ. Though God has given him "a name above every name," his greatest glory is in "taking the form of a bondservant"; Christ's Lordship is most clearly exemplified in his stewardship. And it is a similar kind of lordship—and stewardship—as well as a similar kind of dignity and honor for which we are accountable to the Lord of the universe. This accountability is the distinctive of our dominion—and our humanity.

We are accountable, of course, not only for the way in which we exercise our dominion, but also for a variety of other tasks: to love and cherish others, to seek justice, to develop our own abilities, and so on. Accountability permeates our existence.

To be declared accountable by the Creator implies, furthermore, that he has given humanity what it needs for actually *being* accountable. Rationality, no doubt, is required for the planning, imagining, and knowing necessary to exercise dominion, love, and justice. No doubt the ability to manipulate the natural world is required. No doubt, too, we must be able to act freely and independently of causes working upon us, for one cannot be held accountable for that which one does not do freely. Likewise, the human symbol-making capacity—and the language, the mathematics, the art which come from it—is doubtless necessary if we are to know, name, and celebrate creation successfully.

## THE COMPOSITION OF THE HUMAN

Thus far we have been dealing with the essential nature of humanity—what it *is*. And we have determined that, as far as stewardship is concerned, the human distinctiveness is *accountability* to the Creator. We have now to consider what sort of creature it is who is thus accountable to the Creator. For, as we shall see, different theories about how we are composed can produce very different theories about how we are to act toward creation. Is there, then, a clearly Christian teaching on the composition of man?

It is difficult to discuss human "composition" with much precision. For the very language of the question, "What is the composition of the human?" betrays traces of a time-honored, but troubling, premise of the question, namely, that humans are composed of parts, or aspects. In different discussions and times the two main parts have different names. But most often the division has been made this way: on the one hand is that part of humans which is clearly like the rest of nature—the material component: body, flesh; on the other hand is that which seems unlike anything in nature—the mind, or soul, or spirit. And, without exception and whatever terms are used, it is the spiritual, mental, "un-natural" part of man which is considered to be of primary importance, while the material, bodily, "natural" part is considered to be of secondary and derivative value.

Perhaps we can better see the importance of the question by returning to the views of Plato and Aristotle, whose contrasting visions of what it means to be human continue to exert an enormous effect on our way of regarding ourselves and the world. As we have noted before, Plato believed that the essential nature of the human was rationality. This rationality, however, is not a characteristic of anything in the shifting, mutable, and imperfect world of nature. Rather, says Plato, it resides in a unique sort of entity, the soul. Essentially, humans are souls. To be sure, for an unfortunate part of their existence humans are embodied (or en-*natured*) souls: that is, their souls are joined, in an uneasy union, with something within nature—a human body. It is to the soul that the body owes its life; it is the body which keeps the soul from fully realizing its rationality. For rationality is a characteristic only of the soul, not of the body.

This Platonic view of human composition has, of course, been profoundly influential in the history of Western thought. In some Christian circles it has even been accepted as the straightforward teaching of Scripture. Descartes' view of man as "the ghost in the machine" is only one example of this.

Aristotle's understanding of the relation of soul to body was quite different, and his ideas will help us understand the composition of human beings. As we have seen, Aristotle thought of humans not as apart from nature, but as a part of it. He agreed with Plato that rationality was the essential part of human nature. But, in contrast to Plato (who believed that rationality was imposed from a transcendent realm onto a recalcitrant physical body), Aristotle understood rationality to be the distinguishing and "natural" characteristic of one sort of thing within nature, namely, the human. Humans are things within nature with a special capacity, not things from outside of nature saddled with an alien body. Rationality is uniquely human, but the rationality is rooted within nature, not imposed from without.

One of the ways to bring the difference between Plato and Aristotle into sharp relief is to ask this question: "Can one exist apart from one's body?" For Plato, the answer is a relieved "yes." For Aristotle, the answer is flatly "no." For Plato, humans are not a part of nature, and hence not fundamentally joined to their bodies. For Aristotle, humans are a part of nature, and hence inseparable from their bodies.

And how does the Christian answer this question? What do the Scriptures say about the composition of humans, these creatures who have been given dominion, yet are accountable before their Lord? The Scriptures speak of humans in a multitude of ways, implying a variety of ideas about their makeup. Consider just a few:

> You shall love the Lord your God with all your heart, and with all your soul, and with all your mind. (Mt. 22:37)

> For the word of God is living and active, sharper than any two-edged sword, piercing to the division of soul and spirit, of joints and marrow, and discerning the thoughts and intentions of the heart. (Heb. 4:12)

> . . . do not be anxious about your life, what you shall eat, nor about your body, what you shall put on. (Luke 12:22)

Here, in three passages, are found six names for humans or aspects of them: "heart," "soul," "mind," "spirit," "body," and "life." Other passages use yet other terms to speak of humans: "flesh," "conscience," "innermost part," and "reins."

One approach to this plethora of components is the Platonic, and Cartesian, one—understanding these names as descriptions of distinct parts of humans, then choosing one of them as the "true" human, and determining the relationship between this "true" human and the other parts. Thus Descartes decided that the uniquely human is the mind, and speculated on its relationship with the body through the pineal gland. But as G. C. Berkouwer has convincingly argued in *Man: The Image of God* (chapter six, "The Whole Man"), the biblical writers did not use these terms to designate distinct parts of humans, nor did they intend any sort of Platonic mind-body dualism. Rather, the writers focused on the whole person, calling attention by these terms to a variety of characteristics possessed by that wholeness.

Of course, the fact that the biblical writers did not, for example, use the term "soul" *(psyche)* to designate the "true" human does not necessarily mean that humans cannot exist apart from their bodies. The biblical writers had no intention of presenting a philosophical anthropology—an abstract, technical discussion of human composition. They were concerned with more important things, and they speak the language of everyday life. Says Berkouwer:

> The general judgment of theologians has been that the Bible gives us no scientific teaching on man, no anthropology, which should or could concur with scientific anthropological research on man in the many aspects of his existence or with philosophic anthropology.[1]

The Bible is not a handbook of either science or philosophy.

In distinction from this Platonic attempt to choose one part of humans and subordinate the rest to it, there is another approach to the multitude of biblical terms for the composition of humans—one which agrees better with the biblical writer's emphasis on the whole person, and parallels Aristotle's. In this view, one's "body," one's "mind," and one's "soul" all designate only one whole person, but they all call attention to different functions and characteristics of that person. Thus to speak of the "body" of a person is to speak about humans insofar as they have physical, chemical, and biotic characteristics. To speak about the "mind" of a person is to speak of humans in their psychical, rational, language-using capacities. And to speak of the "soul" of a person is to refer to human aesthetic, moral, and religious capacities.

We may also think of these characteristics of the human as together forming a unity: *one* person, to have aesthetic, moral, and religious capacities, requires psychical, rational, and language-using capacities; to have these qualities of "mind" depends upon possession of physical, chemical, and biological characteristics. Put another way, having a soul depends upon having a mind, and having a mind depends upon having a body. The person *is* body, mind, and soul. But this is not to say (as a Platonist would) that the human is a collection of separate entities, only one of which is the truly human; rather, the human is a unity displaying a remarkable variety of interdependent characteristics.

The implications of such a view for the human relationship to the natural world are profound. For, if it is correct, we see that the human is embedded in nature, and shares characteristics with stones, trees, fish, and dogs. But humans also transcend nature: they have capacities which all else lacks. Humans are fully dust, and fully soul; they are soulish dust.

The Christian, however, must raise one powerful objection to the integrity and unity of humans which this view attempts to capture: such an understanding implies that persons cannot exist apart from their bodies. Yet it seems to be the clear teaching of the New Testament that those who have died, and whose bodies decay, nevertheless continue to exist until the day of resurrection, when they will be clothed with "spiritual bodies." Thus this portrayal of mind and soul as dependent upon the body would seem to be incorrect.

Yet something of the basic unity of body, mind, and soul must be preserved. Scripture is also clear that humans were *meant* to have a body, meant to be a part of the physical world of creation. To allow some sort of interim existence apart from the body (and thus apart from "nature") does not eliminate the idea that there is an intimate connection between humanity and nature. Nor does it suggest, as the Platonists did, any devaluation of the human body or of nature in general. The Christian's hope, therefore, is not for disembodied existence, but for bodily existence on the day of resurrection and in the unimaginable hereafter.

Gerard Manley Hopkins, a Christian poet with a deep sensitivity to the ambivalence of the relationship between man and nature, sums up well this discussion of man's composition. Hopkins wrote a sonnet called "The Caged Skylark," in which he straightforwardly compares the human spirit (or soul) in its body to a skylark in a cage. At first, the prison imagery suggests the Platonic deprecation of body and nature:

> As a dare-gale skylark scanted in a dull cage
>   Man's mounting spirit in his bone-house, mean house, dwells—

Both man and lark, says Hopkins, feel a kind of restriction, a limitation. But that restriction does not imply, in the case of the skylark, that he has no natural home:

> Not that the sweet-fowl, song-fowl, needs no rest—
> Why, hear him, hear him babble and drop down to his nest,
>   But his own nest, wild nest, no prison.

Hopkins concludes, then, with an affirmation of that essential unity between body and soul—and thus, between man and nature:

> Man's spirit will be flesh-bound when found at best,
> But unencumberèd: meadow-down is not distressed
>   For a rainbow footing it nor he for his bónes rísen.[2]

*Man's spirit will be flesh-bound when found at best*: though accountable to God, nature is the human's home. Thus, in exercising our God-given dominion over it, we are not to think of ourselves as kings conquering aliens. Nature is not something alien to us. We bear a most intimate relationship to it: it is the same creation which God, in Genesis, recognized as good and which he entered in Christ.

## THE HUMAN TASK

Accountability to God and embeddedness in nature make the human perfectly constituted to carry out the task of stewardship. We have, in the course of talking about the sort of creature who is called to be a steward, already implied a good deal about the *task* of stewardship. Let us now consider that task explicitly.

First of all, the task of stewardship is a *general* task. It is ours simply because of our humanity, and it overarches our entire life. Unlike our more specific tasks and obligations, it does not arise from any particular circumstance in which we find ourselves. The specific task of providing for children, for example, normally arises from the particular circumstances of being a parent. Those who are not parents do not normally have that task. This is not the case with stewardship: we are called to that task whatever our life situation might be.

Stewardship is a general task in another sense: it is *contextual*—that is, it forms the context within which more specific obligations are understood and the horizon within which they are performed and given meaning. The general task of stewardship, for example, gives rise to the more specific obligation not to mistreat animals, or let cropland erode. Thus stewardship is, in a sense, a general axiom from which more specific principles, relating to the situations we encounter in day-to-day life, can be drawn. (We will consider some of these more specific principles in Section IV of this book.)

Our concentration on stewardship may have given the impression that it is our *only* general task. This is not the case. Clearly, we also have the task of love, *agape*. We are to love our Creator and our fellow creatures. In addition, we have the task of doing and seeking justice. These tasks are also general tasks; they too are a part of our humanity, overarch our lives, and form the context within which more specific tasks are carried out. But the focus of our study leads us, at this point, to concentrate on stewardship; later, we will consider our obligation to seek justice.

Before we attempt to clarify the meaning of the task of stewardship, let us first recall three points already discussed. First, our authority over nature is derived from its Creator and Sustainer: *our dominion is a delegated dominion*. Second, our use and treatment of nature must be of service to God, to our fellow humans, and to nature: *the steward is a servant*. Third, as stewards we are responsible to God for the way we treat nature and for the ends we choose in using it: *the steward is accountable*.

Another feature of stewardship, closely related to the fact that our dominion is a delegated dominion, is that God is *owner of all*. As stewards, we are not the owners of that over which we have authority. Thus our authority is more characteristic of a trustee than an owner—the use and care of nature is entrusted to us. The Creator retains ownership. This is the clear and repeated testimony of the Scriptures. Over and over again the Old Testament writers record divine declarations like, "all the earth is mine" (Exod. 19:5) or "the land is mine" (Lev. 25:23). A Psalm of David declares, "The earth is the Lord's and all it contains, the world and those who dwell in it" (Ps. 24:1, NASB). And a prayer of David makes it plain that any dominion humans have is a delegated dominion:

> Thine, O Lord, is the greatness and the power and the glory and the victory and the majesty, indeed, everything that is in the heavens and the earth; Thine is the dominion, O Lord, and Thou dost exalt Thyself as head over all. (I Chron. 29:11, NASB)

Nor are such affirmations of God's ownership of all things limited to the Old Testament; in the New, all wealth, gifts, and even our own bodies are understood as gifts from God, the owner of all things. In I Corinthians 6, Paul declares, ". . . do you not know that your body is a temple of the Holy Spirit who is in you, whom you have from God, and that you are not your own?" And in John's Revelation, all dominion is declared to belong to Christ, whose sacrifice provides our own great example of dominion:

> Worthy is the Lamb that was slain to receive power and riches and wisdom
> and might and honor and glory and blessing. . . . To Him who sits on the
> throne, and to the Lamb, be blessing and honor and glory and dominion
> forever and ever. (Rev. 5:12–13, NASB)

If God is owner of all and human dominion is clearly delegated, then
it is also clear that the steward is both a servant and a *manager*. The Greek
term for steward, as we discussed earlier, is *oiko-nomos*, manager of the
household. Thus God's steward over nature is to be a manager of the earth's
household: rock, water, air, tree, bird, and beast, in the infinite complexity
of their interrelationships. This human management or stewardship must be
directed to benefit the household of the earth and the creatures who depend
on it for life, health, and fulfillment. Thus the manager of the earth, even
in the most ideal conditions, is often called upon to balance conflicting needs.
For the richness of nature is given, in part, to provide for the human necessities of food, clothing, shelter, health, delight, work, and joy. But that
richness is there also to provide similar needs for nonhuman creatures: food,
shelter, health, procreation, delight—and perhaps other needs we have not
yet learned. The stewards of nature must balance these needs, establish priorities, smooth out conflict. In short, they must *manage* for the welfare of the
creation and the glory of God.

The earth's managers must also balance present needs with future ones:
the needs of present humans and nonhumans with the needs of future humans
and nonhumans. Their balancing ought not to be of the sort proposed by
Winston Churchill, when he said:

> . . . I would like to make the people who live in this world at the same time
> as I do better fed and happier generally. If incidentally I benefit posterity—
> so much the better—but I would not sacrifice my own generation to a prin-
> ciple however high or a truth however great.[3]

In short, the steward will treat nature sparingly, sharingly, and caringly.

In order to manage correctly—with all the intricate decisions which
such managing requires—the stewards must have "ecological knowledge."
As we noted earlier, the same Greek word which has given us "steward"
and "economic" has given us also "ecology." A century ago the German
biologist Ernst Haeckel defined *ecology* as follows:

> The ecology of organisms, the knowledge of the sum of the relations of
> organisms to the surrounding outer world, to organic and inorganic condi-
> tions of existence; the so-called "economy of nature," the correlations be-
> tween all organisms living together in one and the same locality, their
> adaptation to their surroundings, their modification in the struggle for exis-
> tence, especially the circumstances of parasitism, etc.[4]

As stewards, we should have such a rudimentary knowledge of *ecology*.
We cannot adequately "manage the household" without knowing something

about that great household of life which we are to manage. In order to manage and to balance (or maintain a balance), we must become acquainted with at least the general features of the interrelationships of God's living creatures and of their relationship with the inorganic. Otherwise, we shall be ignorant of the effects on nature of our own use of it, and will not be able to act responsibly in the sustaining, renewing, and preserving of the rich diversity of that creation.

Finally, as stewards we are not hedged in on every side by exact rules concerning the proper use of nature. God has not given us a handbook for deciding precisely how we are to manage, how to balance, how to set priorities; rather, he has set general guidelines, and within those guidelines he holds us responsible for our decisions. Stewards have a *range of freedom* in their managing. Different stewards might make different decisions, but, as long as the goal is the care of the whole household, both decisions might be correct. The freedom given us as stewards of creation is suggested in the description of Adam's naming the animals: not only does such naming require deep knowledge, but God "waits to see" what the naming will be. It is like this with our managing. As long as we draw our principles for management from the Creator and his creation, we are given the freedom to be cocreators with God, adopted into the sonship of him in whom all things consist.


## SHARED STEWARDSHIP

We have spoken thus far as though stewardship were only an individual matter. But it is not the case, of course, that each person is delegated to be responsible for *all* of nature. It is often to humanity corporately that God has given stewardly responsibility. We have divided among ourselves that responsibility, and thus we have limited the scope of any one person's actual exercise of stewardship.

To divide in this way our stewardly responsibility is, in many cases, right and proper. Just as, for example, some portions of nature were given to Abraham and others to Lot, so too some responsibility is given to us and some to others. Of course, the actual divisions that have taken place historically may not have expressed the will of God; some people may have received too much, others too little, still others the wrong sorts of things. But there is nothing intrinsically wrong in dividing stewardship possibilities.

The Scriptures certainly condone private property—and private property implies a division of stewardship. In forbidding stealing and coveting, for example, the sixth and tenth commandments imply rights of ownership. Even in the early Jerusalem church, which Luke characterizes as possessing "everything in common," Christians apparently held some private property. As Ron Sider points out, the fact that Christians are, in Acts 2 and 4, described as periodically selling their possessions in order to help each other suggests that they did divide stewardship possibilities among them.[5] Clearly, then, division of stewardship among people is not wrong according to the Bible.

And yet, since our stewardship possibilities are delegated, clear directives in Scripture show that private ownership is to be exercised for the benefit of the whole community. In the formation of the nation of Israel, limitations on acquisition and use of the land were embodied in divine legislation. The Law of Jubilee required that after a certain length of time the land be redistributed among families. The laws of the Sabbath, the tithe, and gleaning required that a portion of the harvest be left for the poor, the sojourner, the fatherless, and the widow.

These divine directives concerning the acquisition and use of private property in early Israel show God's concern that our stewardship profit not only ourselves, but our neighbor and the land itself as well. Of course, such directives were issued to an agrarian people and are not always applicable to our industrialized societies. The fact is, though, we are quite accustomed to having ordinances limit what property we may acquire and how we are to use it; the exercise of our stewardship is restricted by government. Cities, townships, counties, and other governmental units severely limit what we may do on and with our houses and the lands they occupy, our farms and the fields they contain.

We said at the outset that opportunities for stewardship are divided among *people*. Left unqualified, that is misleading. To be sure, one important type of division is that which occurs among individuals (or families). The division into things which are mine and yours is only one sort of division, however. We must consider other sorts and the challenges of stewardship which they entail.

Often stewardship is exercised by entities other than individual persons or families. Consider just a few: governments are stewards of roadways, parks, forest lands, waterways, wilderness areas, buildings, and so forth; corporations, businesses, and banks exercise stewardship over lands of various sorts, raw materials, manufacturing plants, distribution centers, and the like; institutions such as churches and denominations, private schools, and service clubs are stewards of lands and buildings. All of these are in a position to exercise stewardship over nature, and the portion of nature over which they are stewards is vast.

But individuals are not unrelated to these entities. We are citizens of states in which governments act and, in some nations, the authority (theoretically) behind governments. We are often stockholders in corporations or partners in a business. We are members of churches and denominations, of associations which control private schools, or of service clubs. And some of us are in direct positions of authority: besides being citizens, some hold political office; besides being members of a church, some are also ruling elders. Individuals are related to these stewardship-exercising entities in a variety of ways, and some of us are more directly connected with these entities than others.

The fact is, though, that with respect to many of the entities mentioned above, there is no one individual (or even small group of individuals) who exercises stewardship—no one person is directly responsible for the actions of the entity. Take, for example, the actions of governments such as those of North America. Decisions are made by a *body* of people—the legislature. But no individual is directly responsible for the decisions; the body as a whole and, to a more limited degree, the citizens, as a body which elects that legislating body, are responsible.

In instances when entities other than individuals exercise stewardship over nature—and our influence as individuals to the decision-making bodies of these entities can vary from being quite strong to very weak—our stewardship is always less than fully direct, and is shared with others.

But what is our individual duty toward these entities and their decision-making bodies? Given that we are called to be stewards, our task of stewardship with respect to the actions of these entities involves at least the following: if we are part of a group (whether a church, a business, or a government) which allows us a degree of influence upon its decisions, we must use that influence (or perhaps seek it if we do not have it now) in order to make the entities' decisions and actions conform to the norms of stewardship. Clearly, the politician bears greater responsibility for the actions of government than the citizen; the member of the board of trustees more than the association member; the chairman of the board more than the stockholder. But all have some degree of responsibility.

So far we have discussed the division of humankind's corporate stewardship over nature. With respect to some of nature, however, we have not seen fit to make a division. Consider the air we breathe, the oceans—their fish and their mineral deposits—    navigable rivers, and the like. In an important sense, these have remained "ours together." They do not belong to any individual; neither do they belong to a government or any other human institution. They are a common heritage. They are, as we spoke of it earlier, the "commons."

The trouble is that these commons—at least a large number of them—face despoiling, if they are not already spoiled. Perhaps, therefore, the call to stewardship of the "commons" translates into a call to establish appropriate governing bodies, capable of restricting the use of the commons in ways which nevertheless respect everyone's right to them. If so, the efforts at various levels of government to establish and enforce reasonable pollution levels should be encouraged. And likewise, we should support international efforts to establish and enforce standards for proper use of the ocean, as well as just standards for the exploitation of its common resources, such as fish and minerals. This kind of encouragement and approval, manifested in our political lives, may be what stewardship demands of the individual today. Perhaps the days of the commons should be over. To remove areas from the commons is not to strike out in totally unexplored areas; we have models for change. The national, state, and county parks and forests are "ours together," but the use of them is severely restricted.

Our intent, however, is not to solve the complicated problems which surround the questions of a division of stewardship or (as in these last examples) the lack of such division. Rather, we wish to create an awareness of the complexities which divisions of stewardship introduce and of the varying degrees and types of stewardship responsibilities which these divisions create. Translation of the overarching task of stewardship into concrete tasks must take into account these realities of *shared* stewardship. For it is clear that we exercise stewardship over nature not only as individuals but as members of various groups to which are entrusted the care of vast quantities of the earth's resources.

## THE DESTINY OF NATURE AND HUMANITY

The Old Testament writers spoke repeatedly of a time when peace, *shalom*, would, as in Eden, reign again. Once and for all, the awful alienation between God and man, between man and man, and between man and nature would be healed; no longer would dominion be understood as tyranny. In the place of hostility would come harmony; in the place of enmity, tranquility.

The Old Testament writers saw, however dimly, that the Lord would usher in the reign of *shalom* through the Anointed One, the Christ, the Prince of Peace:

> For to us a child is born,
>     to us a son is given;
> and the government will be upon his shoulder,
>     and his name will be called
> "Wonderful Counselor, Mighty God,
>     Everlasting Father, Prince of Peace."
> Of the increase of his government and of peace
>     there will be no end,
> upon the throne of David, and over his kingdom,
>     to establish it, and to uphold it
> with justice and with righteousness
>     from this time forth and for evermore.
> The zeal of the Lord of hosts will do this.
>
> (Isa. 9:6–7)

The zeal of the Lord will bring *shalom*—and not only to man, but to man living in nature:

The wolf shall dwell with the lamb,
  and the leopard shall lie down with the kid,
and the calf and the lion and the fatling together,
  and a little child shall lead them.
The cow and the bear shall feed;
  their young shall lie down together;
  and the lion shall eat straw like the ox.
The sucking child shall play over the hole of the asp,
  and the weaned child shall put his hand on the adder's den.
They shall not hurt or destroy in all my holy mountain;
for the earth shall be full of the knowledge of the Lord
  as the waters cover the sea.

(Isa. 11:6–10)

The prophet's vision is one of harmony between humanity and the rest of creation, not of enmity, nor of a creation forced cruelly into doing human tasks. It is important to note that these apocalyptic visions do not diminish the diversity of creation, or speak of it as something to be destroyed. The evil is not in the cobra, the viper, or the lion; rather, it is in the alienation between those things and man—and between those things and each other. How such a noncarnivorous world could in fact be sustained is a mystery to us, but certainly it is no greater than the mystery of the creation itself. The image of a rich, complex nature in harmony with man, with itself, and with God is clear.

The New Testament writers proclaim Jesus of Nazareth as the prince of that peace. It is he who is calling the world to himself, redeeming it to himself. And it is he who calls us to partnership in his glorious work: "The anxious longing of the creation waits eagerly for the revealing of the sons of God."

His kingdom of peace shall come. The king has already come, and is reigning. In Galilee he has already shown his power over water, wind, plant, beast—and over death itself. He reigns, and his peace shall reign with him: "The zeal of the Lord of hosts will accomplish this."

Throughout the Scriptures, the visions of the kingdom of God are visions of man in harmony with nature. Ralph Smith expresses this well in "Old Testament Concepts of Stewardship" when he observes, "If biblical man did not ever foresee a time when man would have no need of nature, perhaps modern man should begin to make his peace with it now."[6]

### CHAPTER 15

# INHERITING THE LAND: RESOURCES AND JUSTICE

> *Justice is the first virtue of social institutions, as truth is of systems of thought.*
>
> **—Reinhold Niebuhr**
>
> *You shall not pervert justice. . . . Justice, and only justice, you shall follow, that you may live and inherit the land which the Lord your God gives you.*
>
> **—DEUTERONOMY 16:19–20**

Our central claim is this: we are stewards called to exercise our dominion in accord with the standard evident in the life and death of Christ. The rights of lordship are to be exercised for the benefit of others, not simply for ourselves. The example and the power for such a stewarding is the sacrificial death of Christ.

To be stewards at all, however, we must have something over which we can exercise control. If we are called to be God's managers, there must be something sufficiently within our control to manage. Otherwise, the call to be proper stewards would be hollow indeed. Of course, no one is without at least something over which stewardship can be exercised. All people can exercise stewardship over their time and talents—at least to some degree. The fact is, though, that literally millions of people around the world have insufficient control over the earth's resources to prevent their own and their children's starvation. They lack, as it were, "stewardship possibilities" over the earth's resources.

In an earlier chapter we mentioned some of the reasons for this terrible state of affairs and shall not rehearse them here. Rather, we wish to raise a very general question concerning the distribution of the earth's resources among people: What would be a just and fair distribution of those resources? Who should get and control how much? It is the goal of this chapter to outline some basic principles of justice, ones which are consistent with the principles of stewardship.

There are, of course, many types of justice. We are not concerned here with *commercial* justice (which involves faithfulness to agreements), nor with *retributive* justice (which deals with the punishment of those who have violated laws), nor yet with *procedural* justice (which deals with the fair application of rules, principles, or policies). Rather, our concern here is with *distributive* justice. Given a world in which life proceeds through the use of things—whether it be a fox "using" rabbits, a tree "using" light, air, soil, and water, a person "using" food for his or her dinner or fuel for his or her car, or even a nation "using" the mineral resources that lie beneath its soil— we are concerned with the fair sharing of the use of those various things. Who should use how much of what? Who "owns" what? How, in short, may the goods of the world and the opportunities to use them be distributed justly?

It is common to speak of the just distribution of a wide range of goods, services, opportunities, burdens, and benefits: chores in a family, food at a meal, police protection in a city, educational opportunities within a nation, or the use of the seas among the nations. Policies, laws, and courts are set up to insure that each person gets a "fair share" of such things. But what is a fair share?

## THE GENERAL PRINCIPLE OF JUSTICE

The general principle governing the distribution of anything among people is that parties which are alike ought to be treated alike, and those which are different ought to be treated differently and in proportion to their relevant differences. In a nation, therefore, this principle requires that the benefits (and burdens) be distributed so that everyone receives the same degree of benefit and bears the same degree of burden, unless there are differences among the members which would justify different treatment. If there are such differences, they demand that (if justice is to be done) the benefits and burdens be shared in proportion to them. Thus the basic principle of justice allows for discrimination, but not arbitrary discrimination.

Clearly, however, before such a principle of justice can work it must be supplemented by a principle specifying *which differences are indeed relevant*. And here we find enormous disagreements, for there is little agreement in the world on what makes up "relevant" differences. Many opinions differ so violently that they issue in wars and revolutions. Yet these same disagreements are appealed to in order to perpetuate the inequities in resource distribution which many find to be unjust. Here are some of those differing views:

1. *To each according to social status.* Those in one class of society, by virtue simply of the fact that they are in that class, are thought (by some) to deserve more. An extreme form of such a "relevant difference" is slavery. Slaveholders saw nothing wrong with their using resources on a much grander scale than did their slaves; it seemed to them to be "what they deserved." Similarly, the caste system in India apportions resources in accord with class. And perhaps something of this "relevant difference principle" can be heard in the cries of "unjust" when Americans react to the rising cost of Arabian oil or Brazilian coffee—as though we somehow *deserve* to have such goods at a price which perpetuates inequities among nations. In all of these cases the "relevant difference" governing the "justice" of the distribution is national, social, or racial status. The accident of being born into a particular society, in a certain class within the society, is seen as justification for receiving a greater or lesser share of the earth's resources.

2. *To each according to contribution.* In this view, if one actually accomplishes more in the business of processing the world's goods into what humans can use, or actually provides more of the desired services, he or she is entitled to a greater share of the earth's resources. In short, the more one contributes to total wealth, the more one should receive.

Labor unions and profit-sharing movements in business and industry which consider *actual work accomplished* to be the major "relevant difference" in determining the just distribution of wealth are examples of entities which work with this definition of justice.

3. *To each according to effort.* The actual contribution to total wealth, some say, is not nearly as relevant as the amount of effort actually expended. For the environment a person is born into, as well as the physical and mental "equipment" he or she is born with, are outside that person's control. According to this principle, to those who expend no effort, no income is due; to those who expend much, much is due. Anyone who has gone to school has reflected on, and perhaps been angered or pleased by, a teacher's decision to grade on the basis of effort rather than performance. And in terms of just distribution of the world's resources, who deserves more? A Third World worker who toils sixteen hours a day to produce a hundred bushels of grain, or an American farmer who might work fewer hours but produces a million bushels?

4. *To each according to need.* According to this view, differences in need are far more relevant than differences in contribution. Needs, of course, can be variously defined. But once one has determined what a person needs, then (in this view) it is unjust to deprive a person of it. Certainly it is this view which motivates people when they deplore the "injustice" of poverty, starvation, or illiteracy. They feel that if justice is to be done, those with great need should receive more than those with little need.

5. *To each the same.* Some thinkers have despaired of finding any certain "relevant difference" among people, and have consequently decided that each person should have an equal share of the world's wealth. On this view, in effect, there are no relevant differences among people which would justify some in having more than others.

6. *To each the same unless an inequality benefits the poorest in society.* This position, articulated by John Rawls,[1] has exerted a good deal of influence in American thought in recent years. Those who hold this view (and it has been the philosophical mainstay of much "liberal" thinking in America) say that the only relevant difference in determining a person's income is his or her ability (though not necessarily his or her intention) to make the poor richer through his or her own greater wealth. Thus a person who opens a mine or builds a factory may become disproportionately wealthy, but if in so doing jobs are provided for others who without this wealth would have no such opportunity, then that person's greater wealth is considered justified.

This bewildering variety of views makes at least one thing clear: different people mean quite different things when they claim to be seeking justice. As Christians, we ought to ask whether there is any biblical principle which can cut through this maze of conflicting positions.

And, indeed, the Bible does imply a solution—or, at least, the beginnings of one. The Old Testament record of God's intention to build a nation of Israel, which deals most explicitly with the laws and principles by which a people are governed, serves as a guide for determining how, in today's more vastly complicated world economy, the earth's resources are to be used and distributed.

## A BIBLICAL PRINCIPLE OF RESOURCE DISTRIBUTION

The biblical record of the establishment of Israel following her delivery from Egyptian bondage relates God's concern that the unfortunate of the society share in the "milk and honey" of the nation—at least to the extent that their basic food needs are met. This concern was manifested in a series of laws.

The Law of Jubilee required that every fifty years, regardless of whatever buying and selling of land had taken place, and whatever the reasons for those transactions, the original distribution of land among families was to be restored:

> And you shall hallow the fiftieth year, and proclaim liberty throughout the land to all its inhabitants; it shall be a jubilee for you, when each of you shall return to his property and each of you shall return to his family. (Lev. 25:10)

Had it been enacted, this law—strikingly impractical by today's standards—would have perpetuated the original, just distribution of land decreed by

God at the beginning of the nation's establishment. Thus it was a guard against the inevitable, and unjust, accumulation of the means of sustenance—the land—in the hands of one person.

The law of the Sabbath year required that every seventh year the land was to "rest" and lie fallow—but that anything which grew in that seventh year was to be for the poor:

> For six years you shall sow your land and gather in its yield; but the seventh year you shall let it rest and lie fallow, that the poor of your people may eat. (Exod. 23:10–11)

This practice met the needs of both humans and the land.

To further guarantee the needs of the poor, the law of the tithe required that a tenth of all the yield of the land be reserved for the landless Levites and for the travelers, the widows, and the fatherless:

> At the end of every three years you shall bring forth all the tithe of your produce in the same year, and lay it up within your towns; and the Levite, because he has no portion or inheritance with you, and the sojourner, the fatherless, and the widow, who are within your towns, shall come and eat and be filled; that the Lord your God may bless you in all the work of your hands that you do. (Deut. 14:28–29)

For the same purpose, the law on gleaning required that a portion of the harvest be left for the poor, the sojourner, the fatherless, and the widow.

> When you reap the harvest of your land, you shall not reap your field to its very border, neither shall you gather the gleanings after your harvest. And you shall not strip your vineyard bare, neither shall you gather the fallen grapes of your vineyard; you shall leave them for the poor and for the sojourner: I am the Lord your God. (Lev. 19:9–10)

The purpose of all these laws is clear: to guarantee that the food needs of the poor are met. And there is a hint of an even broader application of justice: in the law of the Sabbath year there is demonstrated a concern that even the land lie fallow and "rest." Clearly, God expected the people of this largely agrarian society to share access to the land's resources with its unfortunates.

Note that many of the laws require some labor on the part of the unfortunates to meet their food needs. Strictly speaking, what is to be guaranteed by these laws is not the food itself, but the *opportunity to obtain food*, and that opportunity often involves work: gleaning the corners of a field, reharvesting a vineyard, or working land returned to the family. Of course, for those who cannot work, the only way the opportunity to obtain food can be satisfied is by a handout. But, apart from these cases, work is required. In this way, not only the productivity of the land is to be shared, but also the *burden* of creating that productivity—for the poor are to work also.

For our purposes, in seeking to find a principle which we may use to determine what is a just distribution of the earth's resources, one thing is clear: access to a country's resources is not to be determined in the first instance by social status, contribution, or effort. It is determined by *need*—for the concern is always for the poor.

Some people have noted that there is little evidence that the divine legislation mentioned above was ever obeyed by the people of Israel, and hint broadly that the sort of attention which we have paid to it is misplaced. But the fact that the Israelites did not obey these commands does not cast any doubt upon the validity of the laws or the principles which undergird them. Israel habitually violated or ignored God's norms—and was punished for doing so by captivity.

## THE APPLICATION OF BIBLICAL JUSTICE

The Old Testament legislation implies that basic human needs must affect the distribution of a nation's wealth and, by extension to today's interrelated world, of the world's wealth. The "milk and honey" is fairly shared only if each person has sufficient opportunity to meet basic needs. Of course, once everyone's basic needs are met, the surplus must be distributed according to some other criterion. Minimally, however, biblical justice demands that basic needs be met.

But a further difficult question needs answering: "What are basic needs?" As we see it, basic needs are subsistence needs. People have a subsistence need for something if the lack of it will harm or deprive them in some fundamental way—by suffering psychological or physical injury, ill health, malnutrition, early death, extreme discomfort, and so forth. And to satisfy many of these needs, we must draw upon the earth's energy and material resources; they cannot be met apart from the earth itself. Of course, the extent to which a person must draw upon such needs can vary a great deal; the manual laborer and the nursing mother normally must have more food than the small child and the office worker. Those who live in colder climates must draw more heavily from the earth for clothing, warmth, and shelter than those in warmer climates. The application must be flexible enough to permit such variation. But the main principle, one we might call the principle of *minimal* justice, is inflexible: *a nation—or a world—will have a just economic system only if it provides opportunity for all the people to have sufficient income to draw enough from the earth's resources to meet basic needs.* This is clearly the biblical teaching regarding a just society. Of course, the gospel asks Christians to do much more—to "go the second mile," even to lay down one's life. But inasmuch as any society can and must seek justice, the Bible suggests that it seek a world in which all "subsistence needs" are met.

But with the concept of "subsistence needs" there is another difficulty. Christians, who know that a person is more than a mouth to be fed or a body to be warmed, must go further in their definition of human needs. They would want to consider as needs all those capabilities which are part of the *imago Dei* in humans: the ability to create, to relate lovingly and deeply to friends, parents, and children, and to serve God and care for creation. Since all these abilities deal either with the development of human selfhood or the use of that selfhood to enhance creation, they amount in fact to our ability to be stewards. Ultimately, then, the Christian would say that these are basic human needs.

Nevertheless, there is clearly a sense in which "subsistence needs" are more basic than "development needs." If subsistence needs are not met first, then most development needs cannot be met at all. A starving man is not likely to care greatly about the well-being of a tree or an animal—or even for the expression of his own creativity. Though some Christians may choose, rightly or wrongly, to punish their bodies for the kingdom of God, we should not make that choice for other people. Thus subsistence needs—for everyone—should be met first, even, it would seem, before the fulfillment of some development needs which we in the wealthy West have taken for granted.

Therefore, important as development needs are, there is a great potential for injustice in considering them before subsistence needs. This raises particular difficulty for those of us who consume far more of the earth's resources than is necessary for subsistence. To understand the difficulty more clearly, we must distinguish between our subsistence needs and development needs, on the one hand, and the way we satisfy those needs, on the other.

If we habitually satisfy a certain subsistence or development need in a certain way or with a certain thing, we often think of that way or that thing as being one of our *needs* also. Most of us satisfy our subsistence need for warmth by burning gas, oil, or wood. We then say that we *need* gas, oil, or wood. And that is right; given the *way* we satisfy our more basic subsistence need, we have created a second-order need.

Now we in the developed world do in fact have more second-order needs for the earth's resources than do those in many less developed countries. For the *ways* in which we meet subsistence and development needs involve complicated, resource-hungry structures and systems. Nor can these structures and systems simply be abolished. Imagine, for example, what would happen—particularly in our cities—if supplies of oil, gas, coal, and electricity were completely cut off. There would almost certainly be massive starvation, for, in quest of an ease which permits development and subsistence needs to be met, we have made the meeting of those needs dependent on a massive foundation of resource-using activities. We *do* in fact need more—at a second level—to meet our subsistence and development needs than, for example, do people in India. But recognizing that fact should also impel us to meet those needs more efficiently.

Which brings us to another matter: "wants." We have become accustomed to demanding many things in our diet, in our homes, in our transportation, and in our communication, which we declare are necessary for our full development as humans or even for our very subsistence. This confusion of wants with needs has, in large part, occasioned the much greater demand on the earth's resources. Since in many cases our resource-expensive ways of meeting development and subsistence needs already divert resources from meeting the much more modest needs of billions of humans, it would seem that the path of justice would be to learn to want less, to consume less, to use fewer resources in meeting all of our needs.

Which brings us to another consideration regarding "needs." Many of the most important ones—education, friendship, self-expression—can be fulfilled using a minimum of resources. Perhaps we ought to place much more emphasis on such resource-cheap development, and avoid the sumptuously consumptive meeting of needs urged on us by most television and magazine advertising.

## FURTHER DIMENSIONS OF JUSTICE

Before considering this dimension of the just distribution of resources, it is necessary to consider a few other justice-related concerns which have not been a part of our main argument.

The first of these, referred to in an earlier chapter, is the scope of our concern for justice. Justice is done within a recognized community: family, city, state, nation, or world. We seek to do justice to those with whom we are bound in some sort of community. We have learned, in recent decades, that the community to which we belong is vaster and more complex than we had ever imagined. One dimension of this expanded community is becoming quite familiar to us, and we have mentioned it frequently in this chapter; that is, our relationship not simply to those within our own nation, but to all the peoples of the world. The more we become aware of how widely spread the net is that gathers in our resources—oil from Iran, ships from Japan, coffee from Brazil, bananas from Central America—the more we ought to realize that our resource-using decisions affect the capabilities of those in other nations to meet their own subsistence and development needs. Thus, we need first of all to be sure our concern for justice extends into all the world, to all humans. It is not just a cliché that we live in a world community—a "global village."

The second—and much more radical—enlargement on our concept of community is the inclusion of nothing less than all of creation. The ecologists have conclusively demonstrated in recent years that we affect, and are affected by, what goes on anywhere in this vast organism of a planet. Likewise, it was the burden of a previous chapter to show that we are portrayed biblically as part of the physical creation, and are directed to care for it. Thus, when we speak of a "just distribution" of the earth's resources, we cannot exclude other species. A society which meets all the subsistence and development needs of its people but which destroys or tortures all living things under its

control is not a just society. This is not, of course, to say that the needs of
a tree, a wolf, or a cow are to be equated with the needs of a human. But
neither are they to be ignored. It is in the difficult business of doing justice
to the creation placed under our care that our stewardship—our husbanding—is most clearly demonstrated.

Finally, our concern for justice should include recognition of future
life. It is true that, as one with tainted ethics puts it, "posterity has done
nothing for me." It is also true that the demands of flesh-and-blood beings
in the present should touch us more deeply than the increasingly hypothetical
demands of future beings. Nevertheless, a simple recognition of what we
owe to our own ancestors—the simple, bewildering gift of *being* is the greatest of these debts—suggests that we must extend to *our* descendents the
similar privilege of tending a rich and living earth. And even as our present
concern for justice ought to extend beyond the human to include all of
creation, so also our concern for a just distribution of resources in the future
should allow for the needs of nonhuman creatures.

There is also a sense in which our concern for justice involves the past.
In Chapter 10 we discussed the way in which our current use of resources
(at least in the free world) is determined largely by the operations of the
market system. We may or may not consider the market system as a just
way of determining who gets what in the world, but whether or not we
agree with those who say that the market will automatically allocate resources
to their highest-valued ends in the most efficient way possible, we must
recognize one inescapable fact of the market system: it must start somewhere.
It does not begin with a pristine set of resources to be distributed to buyers
who never have owned anything before. Rather, the market system—and
any consideration of it—begins with resources already allocated. Those allocations all took place in the past, some by processes we know about—as,
for example, in the gradual displacement of the North American Indian on
this continent—or by processes about which we can only conjecture—such
as the even slower dispersal of North American Indians to various regions
on this continent over thousands of years in the past. The point is that the
market system fails to reckon with the justice of those allocations. As one
economist put it, "We start from here, not from somewhere else." Without
arguing the irrefutable logic of this statement, a concern for justice requires
that we add, "But *ought* we to start from here?"

Certainly a little reflection on how present property rights came to
be—for example, with regard to the natural resource wealth of the United
States—would not lead us to believe intuitively that such an allocation is
just. In the history of humankind, "grabbing it," either before someone else
gets to it or because someone else is weaker, has been the main means of
obtaining property. We would not want to argue for the justice of such an
allocation of resources, yet it is precisely such an allocation which lies at the

roots of the distribution resulting from the market system. Again, that is where we begin—but *ought* we to begin there?

Perhaps because the primary offenders in such a distribution are all (or mostly) in the distant past, such speculation is fruitless. But if the idea of redistributing the wealth of the world seems too radical, we might reflect on a more workable problem. For example, take the case of the resources of the deep seabed, or outer space, or of the moon. Here a prior distribution does not stand in the way of just distribution. To whom does the wealth of the deep seabed belong? Why? Is it to the powerful, either militarily or technologically? Is it right that they use their power in this way? Do they even have a right to such power?

Distribution of the wealth of the deep seabed is a good example of the possibility of distributive justice, but while some debate the just distribution of this wealth, at least one country—the United States—is preparing to proceed with mining operations, guaranteeing military protection to the property of corporations doing the mining. The reasons given for this move are an impatience with the debate itself and a desire to develop the technology. But it seems obvious that these arguments do not justify another "grab" of resource wealth, just as it seems obvious that this wealth does not "belong" only to those powerful enough to take it.

Yet the distribution of wealth of the seabed is only a small example— and one within our power to change—of the vast *de facto* distributions which are assumed without question as the basis for doing business in the world today. Those concerned with justice ought to ponder such distributions and, at least, question their justice.

## DOING JUSTICE OUT OF GUILT OR RIGHT?

This chapter (indeed, this whole book, along with many books on the use of the earth's resources) is likely to make many of us feel somewhat guilty, for it is obvious that we are in a privileged position with regard to the wealth of the earth—one which we do not necessarily deserve. Thus, one motive for seeking to do justice in the distribution of resources is likely to be a sense of guilt. Such a desire to right wrongs to which we may unwittingly have contributed is commendable. But in many of the cases we have considered, our own direct culpability—however deeply we might sense it—is very difficult to prove. How does a home, two cars, and steak dinner deprive a child in Bangladesh of food? While it is possible to show, with a good deal of validity, that there are links between our way of life and the suffering of those in resource-poor countries, these links are not always convincing. Nor is it easy to show how a change in our way of life can directly help the poor, especially in faraway places. Because of the complicated, indirect, and uncertain connections between our actions and the unjust distribution of resources in other parts of the world, some people have argued that there is no need for any change in our own way of life, that a vague sense of guilt is an inadequate reason for living differently.

And we would agree to the extent that guilt alone is not a good reason for action in this case. We may in fact bear no guilt for the suffering of much of the world. But that we are not directly to blame for injustice does not mean that we should have no concern for justice. There is a more important reason to do and seek justice than our own sense of guilt: we are commanded by God to do so. The primary motivation for our trying to right the wrongs of resource distribution is that it is a working-out of our calling to be stewards. It is the command of the King—an obligation and a challenge placed on all Christians.

The commandment given to the Israelites, with which we opened this chapter, is certainly a commandment binding on all Christians:

> You shall not distort justice. . . . Justice, and only justice, you shall pursue, that you may live and possess the land which the Lord your God is giving you. (NASB)

But in our case, "the land" is not just one country—Israel, Canada, or the United States. It is rather the whole earth, the earth in which we are placed as stewards—servants of the land and of its king, seeking justice for all its creatures.

From *Audubon*. Used by permission of Dan Leavitt.

# A CHALLENGE
# TO WOULD-BE
# STEWARDS

**WE KNOW NOW THAT** we are "in charge" of God's creation, that we are to serve the earth, and that we are to do so justly. Those who attempt to obey the will of God and to follow the mind of Christ are those who are to speak out, to be the new Isaiahs; they are also to act, to be the new Noahs.

But guidance is needed. How are we to be the new prophets and doers? We in the present age do not receive the Word of God as directly as the Isaiah and Noah of Old Testament times did. We must depend on the Word of God as it speaks to us through the Holy Spirit and as it has been set down in Scripture.

But the Bible is not a textbook. It does not tell us how we in the twentieth century are to conduct our land use, energy, and trade policies. It does, however, give us certain principles, relevant to all times, which we must seek to understand and apply to our own situations. Some of those principles have been presented in Section III of this book.

We are now moving toward a discussion of the application of those principles to the situations outlined in Sections I and II. Here problems immediately arise. Proposing applications of biblical principles is difficult because we cannot see fully where they lead: they are like roads whose beginning we see, but whose course we have no way of knowing beyond the first bend. Suggestions about new economic orders are like this. Similarly, the proposed actions may be simple, like diving off a cliff into deep water, but it is that first leap which is difficult to take. Reducing our levels of food and resource consumption can be viewed in this way—most difficult to begin, though that it should be done is quite obvious. We may also stall in our attempts to apply biblical principles to our lifestyles and institutional structures when we contrast the trickle of individual impact with the ocean of public apathy. Most attempts to recycle waste are difficult in this way. Finally, it is always hard—and potentially embarrassing—to take a definite stand, and declare that we ought (or ought not) to do one thing rather than another. It is easier to remain anonymous and uncommitted.

**251**

Nevertheless, we offer the following "guideposts," proposals which the new Isaiahs and Noahs ought to keep in mind as they continue "down the road." Caution is needed, for guideposts are not permanent; they change the farther one gets along. Nor do guideposts hold any absolute authority; they are merely markers, pointing the direction to a full human stewardship. It is up to each of us to actually pick a way across the terrain of our times— and even, perhaps, to discover that some guideposts are wrong, and to come back and set them right for other travelers. Yet knowing that they are imperfect and incomplete should not keep us from following them; at this point they seem to represent the best directions our actions might take as we read the map of our times in the light of biblical principles.

This concluding section of the book is divided into two chapters. The first is the longest and most important. In it we attempt to review the ground we covered in Section I, the "State of the Planet," from the perspective provided by Section II of this book, the description of how our attitudes toward nature and each other have been shaped. We will try to evaluate the modern mindset and modern activities in the light of the biblical principles discussed in Section III. Those principles place many of our actions and attitudes under judgment, revealing the flawed humanity from which they have sprung. But they also show how the actions and attitudes of humans may be redeemed. Thus the first part of this chapter of guidelines provides a way of understanding, in the light of the gospel, who we humans are and why we act as we do toward creation and each other.

Having established clearly some overarching principles for our stewardship of creation and for justice, we turn in the second part of Chapter 16 to more specific guiding principles for our use of energy, minerals, land, plants, and animals, as well as our collective actions toward other nations. In short, we seek through these specific guideposts to point out a path through the bewildering tangle of problems which affect the home of God's creatures and relations among them.

In the concluding chapter, recognizing the variety of ways in which these guidelines might be followed, we change our focus and speculate on what life on this planet might be like if a serious attempt were made to live out our Christian principles. Our purpose here is not to design a utopia, but to sketch some features of a world which might plausibly result from the principles we have arrived at in this book. For those who wish even more practical suggestions, we include in Appendix A a list of specific areas requiring consideration and action on the part of Christian stewards. Together the guideposts, the sketchbook of a future world, and the specfic suggestions of the appendix constitute the challenge to all who would be true stewards of the King.

# WHAT SHALL WE DO?

"We heat with wood. What do you heat with?"

### CHAPTER 16

# GUIDEPOSTS

*And the Lord God took the man and put him into the garden of Eden to dress it and keep it. Look, Adam, he says, Look closely. This in no jungle, this is a park. It is not random, but shaped. I have laid it out for you this year, but you are its Lord from now on. The leaves will fall after the summer, and the bulbs will have to be split. You may want to put a hedge over there, and you might think about a gazebo down by the river— but do what you like; it's yours. Only look at its real shape, love it for itself, and lift it into the exchanges you and I shall have. You will make a garden the envy of the angels.*

—Robert Farrar Capon,
**HUNTING THE DIVINE FOX**

*Mankind cannot afford to wait for change to occur spontaneously and fortuitously. Rather, man must initiate on his own changes of necessary but tolerable magnitude in time to avert intolerably massive and externally generated change.*

—Mesarovic and Pestel,
**MANKIND AT THE TURNING POINT**

The guidelines which modern humanity follows in its use of creation are tangled and contradictory, for they are the result of centuries of conflicting philosophical and religious ideas. It has been our purpose in the second section of this book to explore those springs of action in some depth, for no one in the modern world is entirely free from their influence. Christians, however, as we have maintained in Section III, have a more certain guide for action, rooted in the Christian revelation. Thus it is our initial purpose in this chapter to evaluate those aspects of Western thought which have exercised the greatest influence on our use of the earth by measuring them against the principles implicit in Scripture. The principles which remain will then become the source for the more specific guidelines which make up the second part of this chapter.

## FLASHBACK: COMMON VIEWS OF THE EARTH

The tangle of ideas about human treatment of the earth can conveniently be summed up in twelve precepts. Drawn from ancient religions, from modern philosophies, from the presuppositions of Renaissance science, and from current economic convention, these ideas have had, or continue to have, an enormous influence on human treatment of the earth. We can summarize these often contradictory ideas as follows:

1. Man reverences nature, which is divine.

2. Man shuns nature, which is imperfect.

3. Man is the consciousness of nature, which is like a great organism.

4. Man is a self-conscious but accidental occurrence in nature, which is nothing but matter in motion.

These four ideas are a part of the legacy of Greek philosophy, though all of them continue to have influence today. They correspond roughly to animistic, Platonic, Aristotelian, and Epicurean views of nature. The next four, though they have their roots in these Greek ideas, came to prominence during and after the scientific revolution:

5. Nature is like a great machine, whose laws of operation can be discovered and applied.

6. Nature is to be used entirely for the purposes of humans, who are the part of the world's mechanism which can think.

7. Nature provides an inexhaustible supply of raw material for the needs of human activity.

8. Nature is limited, fragile, intricate, and valuable, comparable to a spaceship or a cell.

The last of these attitudes toward nature is clearly in tension with the previous three; yet all are a legacy of, or a condition for, the "scientific" view of nature. They are related in turn to four specific principles for human action:

9. The rightness of an action is to be judged solely by the utility of its consequences upon humans.

10. Maximizing individual happiness (which means satisfying individual wants) is the driving force of human activity.

11. Wealth and power are to be used for the benefit of whoever holds them.

12. Technology and resources are to be used sparingly and appropriately, their use determined by considering the total welfare of the ecosphere.

The first three of these four principles for acting in the world result from the three attitudes listed above. The fourth principle is again in tension with the first three, but like them it springs from a certain attitude toward nature which was fostered by the scientific revolution.

## CHRISTIAN CRITIQUE OF THE COMMON VIEWS

These twelve influential guidelines for human thought and activity must be evaluated in terms of the Christian principles which were discussed

at some length in Section III. These we summarize, at greater length than
those listed above, as follows:

a. God is creator and lord of the universe. He is thus both utterly
separated from it, as any maker is lord over his or her work, and he is utterly
involved in it through Christ, the Incarnate Word, in whom all things are
made, sustained, and redeemed.

b. The creation, in all its intricacy and diversity, is good. This goodness is not simply a declaration by God, but a recognition. And in the very
independence of creation implied by that fact, we see the possibility that the
goodness of creation might, in its freedom, come to be flawed.

c. Through both their nature and their task, humans are made to share
in the care and sustaining of creation. Like the rest of creation, humans are
made by God, and depend on creation for their sustenance as surely as beasts
or trees. But unlike the rest of creation, they are made responsible to God.
Thus they share in God's separateness from creation.

d. The human relationship to God, to creation, and to other humans
has become flawed. Through the fall, it has become self-centered and destructive, a grotesque caricature of divine lordship. Instead of understanding
their unique abilities as a means to love and obey God, honor other humans,
and care for creation, humans have understood their dominion to be the
occasion for increasing their own comfort and power at the expense of everything and everyone else.

e. Both the model and the means for a restoration of the right human
relationship to God, nature, and fellow humans are in Christ. The Incarnation
demonstrates the Creator's willingness to forsake what humans wrongly take
to be the rights of lordship and dominion for the redemption of his creation.

f. Redeemed humanity is directed to exercise dominion, stewardship,
and justice, guided by the mind of Christ. Redeemed humans are not to shun
their powers of intellect, creativity, and technique. Rather, they are to use
them for the wise and loving management of creation, developing the full
potential of stone, beast, and human, and lifting all of that creation to share
in their own "sonship" with Christ, the Creator.

These biblical principles should underlie and direct any use we make
of the earth, whether for the praise of God, the benefit of other humans, or
the care of the earth itself. And they also form a standard by which we can
measure the twists and turns of human attitudes toward creation—both past
and present. Thus, before we suggest more specific ways in which these
biblical principles apply to environmental problems and problems of justice,
we must clarify those twelve tenets of resource use from which many of the
problems have sprung in the first place. Briefly, then, let us consider the
implications of these biblical principles for those twelve pervasive tenets of
the modern mind. We consider first those four ideas with Hellenic origins:

1. Man reverences nature, which is divine.

2. Man shuns nature, which is imperfect.

3. Man is the consciousness of nature, which is like a great organism.

4. Man is a random occurrence in nature, which is nothing but matter in motion.

Although a long tradition of casting Christian thought in the terms of Greek philosophy has confused the issue somewhat, it is not difficult, from the perspective provided by biblical teaching, to evaluate these ideas of the relationship between nature and humanity. First of all, biblical religion leaves no room for the animistic notion that nature is divine. The doctrine of creation by a transcendent God precludes that. But secondly, that same doctrine of creation also precludes the Platonic idea that nature is evil and to be avoided in preference to a transnatural realm. Such an idea is contrary to the whole tone of biblical revelation, from the recognition of the goodness of creation, through the Incarnation, to the doctrine of the resurrection of the body. Though the created world apart from humanity is indeed included in the consequences of the fall (as we discussed in Chapter 14), the biblical emphasis is far more on human evil than on nature's. And the imperfection of nature is always linked to the human failure to be human, rather than to nature's excess of gross materiality, as the Platonists would have it.

The biblical teaching seems to have most in common with the third, the Aristotelian, view of man as the intelligence or consciousness of nature. For according to the creation account, humans are both in nature and apart from it. They share (as in Aristotelian thought) the thingly, lively, and sentient nature of (respectively) stones, trees, and beasts, but they also transcend those parts of creation. However, the biblical view diverges from the Aristotelian as to the main component of that difference: it is not reason so much as it is *accountability* to the Creator which sets humanity off from the rest of creation. Likewise, the biblical view of the universe is quite different from Aristotle's. For him, it is like a great organism; there is no God in Aristotle's thought who makes and sustains, who *cares for* his creation.

Finally, the doctrine of creation precludes the Epicurean idea (dominant in modern thought, but under different names) which explains reality as only the result of random combinations of moving atoms. Rather, according to biblical teaching, all things are made by God, and work according to the divine purpose.

The next three tenets of contemporary resource use, though they are an important part of modern thought, share with Platonism a distrust for the world in itself, resulting in a kind of apotheosis of "mind over matter" which has resulted in much of the harsh usage contemporary humans have made of the earth.

5. Nature is like a great machine, whose laws of operation can be discovered and applied.

6. Nature is to be used entirely for the purposes of humans, the only part of the world's mechanism which can think.

7. Nature provides an inexhaustible supply of raw material for the needs of human activity.

Insofar as these precepts stress the distinction between physical nature and mental man, and use this distinction as the justification of a total human exploitation of nature, they are drawing on the Platonic distaste for the material. And again, the Christian doctrine of the goodness of creation must modify any attitude toward nature which says it is "merely" material and of no value apart from human use. The eighth idea is more in keeping with the Christian doctrine of creation:

8. Nature is limited, fragile, intricate, and valuable, comparable to a spaceship or a cell.

This tenet developed partly as the result of observation of creation, partly as a necessary premise for such observation, and partly as a reaction against a coldly reductionistic dissection of nature. And though it parallels the respect which biblical teaching says we should have toward creation, it is subject to one serious error: the idea that nature is sacred in itself, with its corollary that any human manipulation is a kind of profanation of a temple perfect apart from man.

Ideas 5 through 7 do contain a strong Christian element, though it has often been misunderstood and misused. Humans are, in the Christian view, not only *in* nature but *over* it. They not only can, but should use it. Inasmuch as we too are creators, we have the right and responsibility to shape nature, to continue in the process of creation. But our manipulation of creation must not be careless and self-centered; rather, it is tempered by the recognition that as stewards we are responsible to God. And it is tempered also by that divine model for all uses of dominion: the redemptive sacrifice of God Incarnate.

Considering the Christ-centered nature of all Christian behavior brings us to the need for evaluating the last four of the twelve views motivating current uses of nature.

9. The rightness of an action is to be judged solely by the utility of its consequences upon humans.

Such an idea follows from the view of the world as a machine, with man the mind a detached observer and operator. If, indeed, the world were simply a mechanism, of significance only to the detached human observer, then this principle would be valid. But, as we have seen, the biblical view of man in nature, though it directs man to shape and structure creation, nevertheless gives creation a worth of its own apart from man. Therefore, even in treatment of nature, the means must matter: we cannot look only at the ends of an action. Sheer efficiency in satisfying human want (though not bad in itself) cannot be the primary guideline for our treatment of the earth. Even less can it be our guideline for the treatment of people. So effective has been our mechanistic manipulation of nature that we have developed, in recent times, ways of treating humanity as though humans too were things with no value in themselves. But the Christian principle is clear. Though both things and people are *made* by God, they have a worth in themselves, and cannot be merely *manipulated*. Nothing in the universe is mere raw material.

10. Maximizing individual happiness (which means satisfying individual wants) is the driving force of human activity.

It is true that the Creator intends for humans not only happiness, but joy. Yet humans are flawed creatures, and thus the mere seeking of their own happiness ultimately brings misery and destruction to themselves, to their fellow humans, and to the rest of creation. Again, the model for human action here must be Christ, who gave himself for the life of the world. The principle was stated succinctly by St. Antony: "Your life and your death are with your neighbour."[1] Indeed, though the fundamental economic principle that each person seeks his or her own happiness may be *descriptive* of reality, the *normative* principle for the Christian is still the "Golden Rule": "Do unto others as you would have them do unto you." Despite the catastrophic effects which the practice of such a principle might have on the present world economy, there seems to be little doubt that Christians are to move toward the embodiment of such a principle in economic and political activity. And though it mainly describes relationships between persons, the same basic principle should apply to our use even of nonhuman parts of creation. Nothing exists *only* to be consumed for our happiness; again, there is no such thing, in the Christian viewpoint, as *mere* raw material.

11. Wealth and power are to be used for the benefit of whoever holds them.

Again, though this is the operating principle of all nations and of almost all individuals, it is not the principle demonstrated by Christ. Christians say that Christ gave up equality with God—which is infinite wealth and power— to die for the life of the world. Yet, despite the fact that Christians are told in the passage which describes that sacrifice to "have this mind in you, which was also in Christ Jesus," most find it exceedingly difficult to surrender even a little of their wealth and power. The unmistakable biblical teaching is that wealth is God's, and when it is given to humans, it is to be used not for their own glorification, but for the welfare of less fortunate creatures.

12. Technology and resources are to be used sparingly and appropriately, their use determined by considering the total welfare of the ecosphere.

This principle runs counter to the first three, but it is not entirely apart from them. For it recognizes that humans are to act: they are to use, manage, even consume resources, but out of a concern for the whole household of life. The idea has gained a good deal of impetus in recent years, and though it rarely acknowledges the fact, it recognizes the biblical truth that we are both in the ecosphere and outside it. And those who hold this view advocate the carrying out of Adam's task. That is, they see humans as a harmonious part of nature, persons who are able to use their gifts of intellect and technique to manage that nature. And it is a nature thoroughly understood and respected for what it is, not merely for what it is made of or what it can be used for. As Noah used his manipulative superiority over the animals to build a means for their preservation, so humans are to use their knowledge and technique to preserve, and to fulfill, the creation which "waits in eager anticipation" for those stewards who will use wisely their gifts for the sake of creation, out of accountability to God.

## GUIDELINES FOR CHRISTIAN STEWARDSHIP

We have, briefly, applied the insights of the Christian gospel to the values and attitudes which shape modern use of nature. What emerges from this redemptive restructuring of human tendencies are principles which can be applied to specific situations. Let us apply them then to the major problems described in the first part of this book, that report on "the state of the planet." We are not yet concerned with the level of specific actions, except as needed to illustrate a general principle. In most cases, we will leave those specific actions up to the responsible stewardly exercise of the individual's or community's gifts of wisdom, creativity, and technique. But the application of these principles to sample problems should go far toward suggesting specific individual and community actions.

Most of modern man's treatment of the world, from strip-mining to large-scale agriculture, is carried out on the assumption that man is apart from the earth and master over it. Underlying destructive agricultural processes (catalogued in Chapter 1), which have removed nearly half of America's topsoil, is the idea that the earth is raw material for human use. But, as we have repeatedly stressed, Christian stewardship allows us to treat nothing as mere raw material. Likewise, when forests come within the horizon of economic planning, they are generally considered for their value as lumber or fuel. Rivers are seen as unspun kilowatts, oceans and the atmosphere as sinks for human waste, and so forth. These uses are not necessarily illegitimate. But insofar as creation is seen only as a way of meeting human needs, the planner has not applied the gospel of Christ to the use of resources, for that gospel says that we can view nothing as merely a means to some human end. The concept of the ecosystem and the ecosphere—the discovery of the marvelous interrelatedness of life—is an aspect of modern thought which is more in keeping with biblical principles and which tends to control the rampant human-centeredness of our activity. We have referred often in this book to the symbolic power of that view of the earth from space. Insofar as such an understanding of the whole planet makes us plan and act out of a concern for the ecosphere, it is moving us toward the Christian principle of responsible stewardship of the household of life. From this understanding of ourselves as stewards of the ecosphere, a vast number of guiding principles may be drawn. We offer thirty such principles for your consideration.

---

*1. The exercise of power inherent in our dominion must be rooted in knowledge, wisdom, and wonder.* In most cases, our knowledge of the creation is compartmentalized into a host of specialized disciplines such as botany, zoology, or geology. Too often we ignore the *unity* of the creation, the fact that all that which is studied in the various disciplines forms a coherent, complex, integrated whole. We have much knowledge of *aspects* of the creation, but little knowledge of how these aspects form a whole. We have much knowledge, but little wisdom.

Knowledge, as Francis Bacon pointed out, creates opportunities for power. But the exercise of power based solely on knowledge and unaccompanied by wisdom—by a sense of the coherence and unity of all things—is often the exercise of destructive power. When the interrelationships and complexities of the whole are neglected, unforeseen or ignored side effects of our exercise of power create situations not worthy of God's stewards.

Just as importantly, the failure to cultivate wisdom along with our knowledge cuts us off from the tempering, internal force of wonder and awe. For wisdom instills awe and wonder at the beautiful, complex whole which the Lord of Lords has given to us to till and keep. And awe and wonder put brakes on our exercise of power.

Of course, we should have and exercise power over nature. But knowledge, wisdom, and wonder should precede the exercise of power. Such a sequence would alter much of our education about nature; it might alter many of our habits of recreation. Ultimately, it might change our industry and economics. Says Aldo Leopold, "Recreational development [and he might have spoken of other kinds of development] is a job not of building roads into lovely country, but of building receptivity into the still unlovely human mind."[2] Both formally and informally, ecology (the study of the full, complex interrelationship of the ecosphere) should be an important part of every person's education—and especially a part of the education of every Christian. Only out of such wonder and knowledge, and the loving care that comes from it, may the mute groanings of an unfulfilled creation be uttered.

*2. The demands placed on stewards by both the human population and the ecosphere are complementary.* The goal of Christian stewardship is to fulfill our own needs and those of the ecosphere in a harmonious fashion, thus glorifying the God who created us and the creation of which we are a part. Too often, however, our own needs are given supreme importance; we are willing to care for the environment only as long as such care does not require us to alter substantially our lifestyles, our patterns of consumption and production.

"Environmentalists" are often accused of caring for nature only, not for people. They are thought to serve a "special interest," ignoring the interests of the poor, the unemployed, and those trying to make an "honest buck." Stewards ought to avoid such a dichotomy by emphasizing that the needs of both ourselves as human beings and the ecosphere must be recognized and balanced. The needs of those millions suffering from hunger and malnutrition, for example, cannot be met without regard for the ecosphere. If the ecosphere is injured fatefully in some way, it can no longer support *any* life. But also, the ecosphere cannot be tended to while the needs of the hungry are ignored—we must find ways of action which will fulfill the commands of justice and stewardship without placing different parts of creation in tension with each other.

Ian McHarg, whose scathing critique of Christendom's lack of a land ethic we have had occasion to quote earlier, describes a large-scale achievement of the ideal ecosystem which is managed so as to satisfy both natural processes and human necessities. It is all the more remarkable because it is over 200 years old. He describes the achievement of eighteenth-century English landscape architecture:

> Starting with a denuded landscape, a backward agriculture and a medieval pattern of attenuated land holdings, this landscape tradition rehabilitated an entire countryside, allowing that fair image to persist to today. . . . lacking a science of ecology, they [the landscapers] used native plant materials to create communities that so well reflected natural processes that their creations have endured and are self-perpetuating.

> The functional objective was a productive, working landscape. Hilltops and hillsides were planted to forest, great meadows occupied the valley bottoms in which lakes were constructed and streams meandered. The product of this new landscape was the extensive meadow supporting cattle, horses and sheep. The forests provided valuable timber . . . and supported game, while free-standing copses in the meadows provided shade and shelter for grazing animals.

> The planting reflected the necessities of shipbuilding. The preferred trees— oak and beech—were climax species but they were planted *de novo*. On sites where these were inappropriate—northern slopes, thin soils, elevations—pine and birch were planted. Watercourses were graced with willows, alders and osiers, while the meadows supported grasses and meadow flowers.[3]

Admittedly this remarkable achievement, though large in scale for its time and place, is puny by world standards and needs. Nevertheless, given our much greater knowledge of ecology and our vastly increased power and technology, there is no reason why the whole earth could not be turned into such a garden, harmonizing both natural processes and human needs.

*3. We have the responsibility to work toward a just distribution of all energy and mineral resources.* The consumption of 40 percent of the earth's energy and mineral resources by 6 percent of the population is unjust. There are several forms which the righting of this injustice could take. We could develop vast new sources of energy and make them available to all people. But, as we have seen, our record of using energy carefully is not good. It is more likely that the best way of creating a just distribution of energy and mineral resources is to cut back on our own use of them. This would have a doubly beneficial effect. First of all, it would free more of those resources for use by other nations which need them. Secondly, it would cease to hold up before those nations a model of profligate and increasing consumption, but would instead present a model of restraint and self-denial, consistent not only with the demands of living on a finite planet, but with the demands of Christian ethics.

------

As our previous guideline suggests, our application of justice must in some ways be expanded to include the nonhuman parts of creation. The question of the rights of other life is therefore pertinent in discussing energy and mineral use—not because redwoods, whales, and snail darters need coal, oil, and electricity, but because our use of those resources inevitably has an impact—almost always a destructive one—on their life. Thus the demands of justice might require that we wait to mine a coal field until we can do it without damage to the nonhuman life of the "overburden." Or justice might determine that we not use microwaves to beam solar energy from collecting satellites back to earth if we cannot do so without injuring birds flying through the microwave beam, and so on.

------

*4. We have the responsibility to provide for future generations at least the same opportunities for resource use that we inherited from earlier generations. And we should not impose on future generations any responsibilities greater than those which prior generations have left for us.* An obvious implication of this principle is that we cannot simply use up fossil fuel "savings" as though there will be no more need for them when they (and we) are gone. In fact, the only way in which we can really justify drawing on the fund of ancient sunlight is if (to maintain the financial metaphor) we "reinvest" it to yield an equal or greater return. That is, it might be appropriate to use large amounts of mineral and fossil fuel resources to establish a means, such as building solar collectors, for sustained delivery of other forms of energy.

Obviously, another implication of this responsibility to future generations is that we cannot use energy today in such a way as to create problems for the future. Certainly the way in which we dispose of radioactive waste from nuclear fission (and fusion) processes involves future generations, for such material must be isolated from life forms for thousands of years. This responsibility does not necessarily mean that we should never create radioactive waste, but it places upon us the responsibility to do so only if we are sure of a safe method of very long-term storage.

Finally, what this guideline suggests most strongly is that we ought to limit, as much as possible, our consumption of irreplaceable materials. That specifically means phasing out fossil fuel use in favor of solar income sources. And it means using our inheritance of mineral wealth in such a way that it can be recycled.

*5. The time horizon for our long-term planning must be very broad.* As Christians, we believe there will be an end to this world as we know it, but we "know not the day nor the hour" of that end. And since we have no way of knowing when it will be, we must proceed as though there will not be a time when we no longer need minerals, land, water, energy, and the like. In the past, the "frontier" model of the earth encouraged a use of resources which did not consider the future at all. The "spaceship earth" model, on the other hand, encourages a planning horizon at least as long as the ten-billion-year life of the sun. Clearly it is better to err in the direction of the latter.

*6. In exploring alternatives to our present pattern of resource use, we must be sure that we reckon properly with all of the costs involved.* We have discovered that in many cases we have not properly included the costs that must be paid. This is because we have used the notion of *private* costs instead of social or total costs. Thus if a steel plant could get away with pollution of the air and water and not bear these costs, they would do so as they tried to maximize their private benefits and minimize their costs. But the costs must be paid, and if not by the producers and consumers of steel, then by others who derive no direct benefit from steel production. This is not fair. Further, some of the costs, once incurred, cannot ever be settled—or at least not for a very long time. If ecosystems are damaged, for example, they may never be able to recover. It is also the case that we have failed to reckon with the full costs of generating energy.

*7. We should seek to know, as fully as possible, the origin and production method of the things which sustain us and the processes by which they are brought to us.* What is the source of the food we eat, the fuel we burn, the materials we use for shelter, clothing, transportation? All are products of the earth and human ingenuity, and it is important that we not simply take such things for granted. To know the forest that grew the beams in our house, the soil that grew the vegetables in our salad, the ore which was the origin of our automobile is to increase our knowledge and participation in the production of what we use—to grow or pick our own food, for example. Even a little of such an activity is a valuable reminder that we are participants in a wide community of life. There is probably no stronger, more immediate, and more rewarding reminder of such participation than the cultivation of a small garden, even a kitchen garden.

---

So far our guidelines are very general ones. Each enjoins us, as it were, to develop habits of thought which will stand as contexts for our decisions concerning what we ought to do or not do. The next six guidelines are less general; they focus on production processes, nonhuman life, land use, and the like.

---

**8.** *No process of agriculture, mining, transportation, energy generation, waste disposal, recreation, and so forth should take place until its consequences for the household of life have been established.* To quote Aldo Leopold again, "A thing is right when it tends to preserve the integrity, stability, and beauty of the biotic community. It is wrong when it tends otherwise."[4] This does not mean that ecosystem-disturbing activities should be abandoned, but that they should continually be redesigned toward the ideal of a biota which can meet human needs without being diminished in intricacy, vigor, and diversity. That we are, in most cases, unable even to conceive of such a use of resources need not keep us from maintaining it as an ideal toward which we can devote all the efforts of our reasoning, manipulating, and creative powers. It is enough that in almost all cases of resource use we can imagine a way in which the process can be done better—not necessarily more cheaply in dollars, but with less cost to the ecosystem. Thus an agriculture in which crops are grown in a rotation which preserves and increases the fertile soil is closer to this ideal than the repeated single cropping of a soil-depleting plant like corn. A backyard in which the urge for pristine lawns and weedless shrubs is modified in favor of a remnant of native plants is another move in the right direction. Likewise, a housing development planned around existing trees, contours, and watercourses is better than one imposed with maximum efficiency on a shaved-off, leveled-down site. And so forth. The Environmental Protection Act, with its requirement for an environmental impact statement for most ecosystem-altering activities, is an encouraging legislation of this stewardly guideline. Thus Christians should encourage its wise application and discourage its abuse.

**9.** *A concern for the consequences our actions have on the ecosphere must include consideration of the other creatures with whom we share the earth and its resources.* We must remember that when we promote an agricultural or housing development which depletes the soil of its nutrients and the landscape of its trees, contours, and watercourses, and which pollutes the air and water, we are depriving both the animals and ourselves of habitats.

Woodlots, hedges, and fencerows, which provide homes for small birds and wildlife, are means of preserving the creatures under our care which must not be eliminated. Wilderness areas are also necessary for maintaining the habitats of bears, cougars, and wolves—it is unlikely that we will learn to coexist with these creatures in the near future.

Pesticides which enter into the foodchain—or more correctly, the food web—have done more damage than was originally expected. When we deal with ecosystems we must know how the animals are interrelated with each other as well as with their environment. In some cases, we have already interfered with ecosystems to such an extent that we can no longer pull out without further modifying or damaging the ecosystem. To abolish deer hunting, for instance, would be no kindness. Having long since eliminated their natural predators—cougars and wolves—we cannot allow the deer to increase to starvation levels.

Caring for animals extends also to domesticated ones. The suggestion is not that we stop butchering cows or keeping chickens, but that we recognize their worth as God's creatures, and that when we make use of them we do so with as little pain as possible. In effect, this means we ought not to regard domesticated creatures only as resources. Each creature within our care, whether wild or domesticated, must be given room to develop its created nature.

**10.** *In establishing new habits of land use, population growth, and energy and mineral resource use, we must learn, and live within, the natural patterns, processes, and cycles of the ecosphere.* A stewardship which promotes a creation in which all of God's creatures may coexist harmoniously must learn of and establish the limits for human growth and consumption. This does not constitute a suggestion that we all "return to the earth," that we all grow our own food, build our own homes, and so on. However, we must recognize that our goals as human beings cannot be projected outside the limits imposed on us by the ecosphere and by our obligation as stewards to care for it.

---

This general principle takes on more specific character when applied to the areas of land use, population growth, and energy and mineral resource use. The following guidelines, then, are attempts to apply this guideline, with its implications, to these specific aspects of human action in the world.

---

**11.** *We should work at and support policies that allow and encourage preservation of topsoil.* Land use in modern agriculture can and should conserve topsoil, both in the interest of preserving the food-producing function of the land and protecting the quality of the wetlands, rivers, and lakes which receive water runoff. This might involve the rotation of crops, including selection of plantings which build the topsoil. And it might also include soil conservation measures such as minimum tillage agriculture, contour cropping, and the use of grassy drainage ways. To the extent that economic and policy incentives foster poor stewardship, it is *everyone's* responsibility (not just the farmer's) to remove such adverse incentives, thus allowing both good stewardship of the land and a *just return* for the efforts of the farmer.

**12.** *The lands which produce our food and provide important natural functions must be protected from destruction.* We should develop policies which prevent the urbanization of the very lands upon which we and all life ultimately depend for our well-being. Urban development should be directed away from the land that feeds us; it should be directed away from the wetlands that naturally cleanse the water running into our lakes and rivers; and it should be directed away from the flood plains which protect our homes from destruction. New residential and industrial development should not be held solely responsible for the reduction of our food production potential, our fisheries, and the protection of our homes and business against flooding and pollution. As both individuals and a society we must increasingly recognize our dependence upon the land and its natural processes, and therefore increasingly behave in ways which reflect this dependence by protecting the land upon which we depend for our food, health, and well-being.

**13.** *Both the finiteness of the planet and the command to be stewards of all its life place restrictions on population growth.* Christian stewardship demands that we limit human population to a level which can be sustained within a healthy and diverse ecosphere. It takes little reflection to realize that only in theory does exponential growth expand to infinity. In the real world, some leveling-off point is always reached. Human ingenuity and the harnessing of fossil fuels have made it possible to continue geometric population increase for a surprisingly long time, although not, of course, without widespread malnutrition and starvation. No one ca    edict with certainty when the absolute limits of a technologized earth's human carrying capacity may be reached.

But there is more than one kind of limit. There is the limit which could be achieved if all nonhuman life were regarded only as a resource, a raw material. If sufficient supplies of energy become available, vast amounts of food could be grown under artificially controlled conditions, and many more billions of people could be supported. Some predictions of the earth's theoretical ability to contain human life have ranged into the trillions. But such levels could only be reached if the distinctiveness, the selfhood, of other creatures were denied. The other population limit, then, is one which provides sustenance not only for the human population, but for the full range of created life. Unless we decide now that we will leave room for "unnecessary" life and learn to exercise that decision in small ways, we may embark upon a course which leaves no option but a completely humanized ecosphere. But to Christian stewards, the choice for humans and against nonhumans is not open. Thus human population must be kept within a level which permits other life. Some indications show that we are already near that level, and that we may even need to reduce world population somewhat below present levels, despite the inevitable increases of the next half century.

---

The next six guidelines, unlike the previous six, all focus on a single and, at present, headline-grabbing topic: energy.

---

**14.** *In planning for future energy needs, it is essential to consider the end use of energy and to determine an appropriate source for it.* Too often our energy planning has been done by considering all energy needs to be of the same sort, delivered in the same form. This assumption is carried out, in fact, in the increasing tendency to electrify our energy use, since electricity is the most easily transportable and transferable form of energy. But in order to achieve this ease, we often create great waste. In a house, for example, it is desirable to have an air temperature near 70 degrees Fahrenheit. To produce that temperature, it may be necessary to have a medium somewhat warmer— perhaps a 120-degree radiator. Yet to produce that low temperature heat (and as much as 35 percent of the energy used in heating in America goes to producing such low heat) we must burn coal, oil, or gas in a furnace at temperatures up to 2,500 degrees. In the process of transferring it to water or air, much heat is wasted before it gets back to the desired temperature. Thermal electricity is the worst case: high temperature steam is used (at only 40 percent efficiency) to spin turbines to generate the electricity which is then transported to homes and run through resistance coils (a very inefficient means of heating) to heat the air, again to a temperature of near 70 degrees. Such a complicated process naturally incurs great energy loss.

Solar energy, on the other hand, delivers low temperature heat—somewhat below the boiling point of water—and is thus ideally suited for one of the main needs of such heat: space and water heating in homes. Such matching of end-use needs to energy source requires some flexibility in the design of both homes and utilities, but the potential for saving, both economically and ecologically, is very great.

**15.** *In exploring energy alternatives, the net energy balance of any proposed source of energy must be examined.* Proposals for new energy production must include calculations of the net energy balance. For example, a suggestion that liquified natural gas be transported in giant planes from remote Arctic islands to ports on the Canadian mainland was rejected because half the energy gained would be needed to fuel the planes. To plan on using nuclear fusion in the near future is similarly absurd, for the process presently uses more energy than it produces. There are less obvious situations in which the net energy concept should be considered. For instance, when one analyzes the net energy balance in nuclear fission reactors, including the energy to mine the ore, separate the uranium-235, construct the power plant, dispose of radioactive wastes, decommission the reactor at the end of its life, and so forth, the net energy balance for nuclear reactors looks far less favorable than a superficial analysis would suggest.

**16.** *Given the finitude of the earth and our stewardly obligation to model our use of it after the design of the ecosphere, it is important that we understand the distinction among income, savings, and inheritance resources, and seek to live within our income as much as possible, using savings and inheritance resources only in special cases.*

We have previously pointed out (in Chapter 4) that all resources may be categorized by analogy with personal financial resources. The most important distinction to be made is among income, savings, and inheritance resources. Examples of income resources are the various forms of solar energy: direct heat or light energy; wood; wind; ocean temperature differential; and so forth. Since these resources cannot run out as long as the sun burns, we should, in keeping with the planning horizon guideline, work toward the ideal situation in which all our energy is from this income source. Similarly, the minor amount of income energy available from the moon through taming of the tides should also be tapped where feasible and environmentally acceptable.

Aside from this constant *flow* of energy, there are also *stocks* of energy available in the earth. Because of the long time needed for solar savings resources (such as the fossil fuels) to accumulate, we can effectively consider them a "given," a stock, just as is the inheritance of geothermal and nuclear energy resources as well as mineral resources. Since these stocks of resources are finite and thus subject to depletion, we should use them sparingly. The fossil fuel and nuclear resources should be used only in those special cases where that particular type of energy source is best suited for a specific purpose, and our income sources of energy cannot effectively meet that need. Geothermal energy, because it tends to be radiated into space in any event, is less in need of conservation. Thus we can use it more freely where it is accessible from the surface of the earth and can be used without environmental harm.

As we pointed out earlier, all mineral resources are inheritance resources; there is no income of them. Thus it is imperative that we recycle all mineral resources whenever and wherever possible.

**17.** *The fossil "fuels"—coal, oil, and natural gas—are a unique chemical treasure and, as much as feasible, should not be burned as fuels but rather used as* *sources of synthetic material*. Oil, coal, and natural gas are our primary source of plastics. Yet currently we burn 95 percent of these hydrocarbons for fuel and use only 5 percent for synthetic materials, including medicines. Since there are many other potential sources for heat, but no comparable source for the chemical properties of these fossil materials, a stewardly use of resources would be to stop using them for fuel as much as possible, and as soon as possible. But instead, we operate as though we have a right to use up the hydrocarbons in only a few generations. Future generations are not likely to call us blessed, nor would we be exercising good stewardship of the earth's wealth, if we use this great chemical wealth merely as fuel. As good as sunlight is, we cannot make plastics from it.

**18.** *Energy conservation is the single most important part of any energy program.* It has been shown conclusively that a determined and concerted effort to conserve energy can, at much less expense, have a greater impact on the energy problem than the development of any new energy source—including solar energy. Again, conservation is not just a stop-gap measure until other sources are discovered; it is a way of developing permanent habits of stewardship of this most basic resource. Energy conservation is not just an economic or patriotic act; it is an application of concern for the human and nonhuman life of the world. For the alternative to conservation is waste; and waste not only destroys some creatures directly (through various forms of pollution), but it keeps others from the benefits of the resource as well.

**19.** *Since it is clear that we must rapidly shift from use of "savings" resources (fossil fuels) to use of "income" resources, we should give our greatest attention to the development and widespread use of solar energy conversion devices. Furthermore, the order in which we must attempt to use energy resources, as well as our research and development priorities, must be:*

I. Income (and Short-Term Savings) Resources
   A. Solar—passive
   B. Solar—active
      1. Hydroelectric
      2. Solar thermal
      3. Biomass—e.g., wood, methane from wastes, alcohol or petroleum from plants or plant products
      4. Wind
      5. Solar electric
      6. Ocean temperature differential
   C. Tidal

II. Inheritance Resources
   A. Geothermal
   B. Nuclear fusion
   C. Nuclear fission

III. Savings Resources (Long-Term)
     Fossil fuels

It is a dismal comment on our foresight that the least stewardly energy source—fossil fuels—is the one we now draw on the most heavily, simply because it is the most convenient and least expensive.

Development of efficient, compact energy storage devices is of great importance if solar energy is to become a widespread and flexible energy source. As long as solar energy is a minor part of our total energy picture—adapted, as suggested above, toward low temperature heat needs—energy storage is not a great problem. But good stewardship of the earth seems to indicate much greater dependence on solar energy. Thus the development of storage devices becomes the single most important piece of energy-related research.

---

"This is how I like my energy. *Straight!*"

From *The New Yorker*, June 19, 1978. Drawing by Ross; © 1978 The New Yorker Magazine, Inc. Used by permission.

We end our guidelines on energy with one more. This one, like the first seven, is very general in nature, enjoining us to adopt new patterns of thought. It also serves as a transition to a guideline which bears on the whole pattern of our lives—actions as well as thought.

---

**20.** *Since the change from our present pattern of energy use and production to one largely dependent on energy income is a major transition, people should be educated in the different values and attitudes which it will require.* Obviously, we cannot switch immediately from burning fossil fuels to using solar energy. But we must move in that direction as rapidly as possible, though there will be, for a time, conflicting patterns of resource use. The application of rigid conservation measures, the adaptation of energy sources to end-use needs, and some decentralization of energy generation are changes which must be accomplished rapidly, but with a minimum of disruption.

Short of being forced to make such changes through scarcity, these changes will take place only if the attitudes and values which lead to our resource-use profligacy are replaced with those which undergird the guidelines. The teaching of these new attitudes and values must be a major commitment of our educational institutions. The living-out of these new attitudes and values must be a major commitment of each of us.

**21.** *Our lives as stewards must give testimony to the fact that the achievement of the central purposes of life is not directly proportional to the level of consumption.* Our lifestyles, as well as our educational institutions, must convince others that the lack of restraint in consumption and production typical of the Western nations does not lead to increased happiness. It is not only our records of divorce, suicide, and drug and alcohol abuse which must point to the fact that, if anything, having everything—or the illusion of it—decreases happiness. Given the consequences of that persistent affluence, the basic guideline is biblical: the principle is clearly stated by Jesus at the beginning of the parable of the rich fool: ". . . be on your guard against every form of greed; for not even when one has an abundance does his life consist of his possessions" (Luke 12:15, NASB).

---

For Christians who take seriously the responsibility to be good stewards of the earth the reason for the changes mentioned above should be obvious, and the change required in their way of life should not be difficult. Yet large-scale changes can only be effected through large-scale transformation of societal systems and structures. The remaining eight guidelines concern such transformations.

---

**22.** *Christians should seek to reform those societal structures which damage the ecosphere and produce injustice among humans.* We referred earlier to our tendency to blame structures or processes for many of the problems mentioned in this book. We sidestep responsibility every time we begin a sentence with: "Technology forces us to . . ." or "The economics of it require. . . ." It is important to realize that structures and institutions are the creations of humans. Not only are we responsible for them, but we can, if we wish, change them. We participate in these larger structures in many different ways. As citizens, we are part of city, county, state or province, and nation. Obviously, we have an obligation to participate in those governments, even if our participation seems distant and peripheral. One kind of participation, of course, is to vote. Most candidates still say little about the issues discussed in this book, and Christian voters can perform a real service by bringing into public consciousness issues about land use, ecosystem preservation, solar energy, and so forth. We have an obligation, too, when the opportunity and need arises, to participate more actively in government. If, indeed, the Christian gospel shows how power may be exercised, Christians should temper the widespread misuses of power—over nature and over humanity—by their presence in the "power structure."

There is yet another important way in which persons can affect the power structure. Many of us own stock in corporations, and are, therefore, part of that corporate "body" which often treads so heavily on the earth and on human needs. We thus have an obligation to exercise whatever influence we have—financial and otherwise—to direct the action of that body to more stewardly practices.

**23.** *The self-interest which underlies the unrestricted free-market system needs to be tempered by a recognition that we share the planet and its life with other humans and other creatures.* The fact that something lies outside of market activity does not mean that it should be ignored.

The driving force behind economic activity (at least according to the most prevalent theories of economics) is the individual quest for happiness. But it goes counter to ordinary experience, and certainly to the biblical picture of ethics, to assume that happiness can or should be *isolated* happiness. The "Golden Rule" of Christian behavior recognizes both a legitimate self-interest and an all-important interest in others: "Do unto others as you would have them do unto you." It is the failure to recognize relationships—among fellow humans and fellow creatures—that leads inexorably to disastrous environmental consequences. The myth that there is such a thing as an "economic externality"—a consequence beyond the realm of responsible economic behavior—becomes less and less tenable the more we understand relationships to, and responsibility for, other life. Certainly the life of a bird is worth less than that of a man or woman, but the extinction of a whole species of birds is not worth the tiny increments of happiness which might result from human encroachment on the species' habitat. We simply cannot afford to say that some consequences of our activity are "external" to our concern. The more we learn, both of the relatedness of the ecosystem and the demands of Christianity, the less we can act as though there were "economic externalities."

**24.** *We must maintain a clear distinction between price and value.* Price is set by the market system, and is a result of the available supply and of demands made on the basis of wants. Value, on the other hand, depends not on someone's cash-backed yearnings, but on a quality intrinsic to the thing or to its function. To dispose of an object on the basis of price alone is to continue in that misunderstanding of dominion which says that humans are the only source of value and meaning on earth. Resources that are treated on the basis of *price* are dominated forcefully: their own selfhood is denied. Stewardship, on the other hand, recognizes *value*; it seeks to enhance that value. It may even be that to recognize and steward properly the value of a thing will demand considerable sacrifice on the part of the steward. We may have to answer such questions as: What is the *value* of clean air, or a sparkling mountain stream? And what then are their prices?

This is not to say that the market system is an illegitimate or un-Christian means of using resources. But certainly the human-centered concept of price needs to be moderated by the more creature-centered concept of God-given value. And that value ought to be understood not only in terms of human utility, but also in terms of the thing itself—though again, human utility is one important value of things.

**25.** *Stewards should exercise their managing and technological abilities, but the purpose of those dominating abilities is not only the welfare of the self: it is primarily the care and enhancement of other people and of the rest of creation.*

We are technological creatures: we are makers, and we have abilities to do things efficiently and well. These abilities enable us to have dominion, to exercise stewardship. Always, then, technology (which has so often been used for destructive dominion) should be the tool of stewardship. It should be genuinely "appropriate" technology. Practically, this means using all the devices and skills of science in order to understand the workings and the welfare of the earth's creatures and our fellow humans. But it also means a restraint on the use of those powers, if the integrity of a thing is wrongly interfered with. There are difficult issues here. The painful dissection of a living creature, out of curiosity, would seem to be an illegitimate use of technology; a careful program of medical research on animals, clearly directed for the solving of genuine problems and conducted with a maximum of care for the animals, is not. Again, the question is one of proportion. The human ability to manipulate, despite its misuses, is a God-given trait. Always, however, we should recognize that the most efficient means for doing something may not be the best. Again, efficiency must be moderated by the dominion-as-service whose pattern is made clear in Christ.

**26.** *All people should be free to exercise stewardship over a fair share of creation.* The commandment to exercise dominion was given to "the Adam": all humankind. Yet, because of the present inequities of the distribution of power over the earth's resources, vast numbers of people lack not only the basic means for sustenance, but also the very privilege to exercise stewardship. What this means is that we should regard "development" in Third World nations not simply as giving, as feeding, and as clothing, but rather as making it possible for people to use—and misuse—their abilities as stewards. In a sense, the position of the wealthy, technologized nations in the West makes them "stewards of stewards." They do have power over the peoples and their resources, but they should use that power as a means of helping those people attain their own independent selfhood and their own exercise of power.

**27.** *We should strive for justice, not selfish gain, in the distribution of the wealth of minerals found in the floor of the seabed.* The United States, as well as most other nations of the world, has agreed that the seabed minerals represent a "common heritage of mankind." To most people, this implies that the benefits of these minerals should be equitably shared with all of the nations of the world. But there has been a movement in the United States, led by the mining companies, to interpret "common heritage" as meaning that the seabed is common property, and whoever gets there first may keep its resources. Such a practice would be sure to exclude the poor nations who have no hope of developing the techniques of harvesting the seabed on their own. This approach to using our power to grab resources before others can get there is not consistent with justice and stewardship, and should be resisted and defeated by the citizens of the United States.

**28.** *Our aid to developing nations should work to encourage and enhance the cultural uniqueness of the nation and not to impose Western ideas on it.* The Christian view of humanity, it could be said, combines both that active manipulation in which the West has excelled and that selfless passivity with which the East has been preoccupied. Thus, the Christian gospel has within it the ability to let both aspects of humanity develop together in their uniqueness, balancing each other rather than conflicting with each other. We must avoid the arrogance of aid, and learn in stewardship and lifestyle practices from other peoples in their own integrity.

Westerners in general, and we North Americans in particular, must not encourage those in poorer nations to model their development on features of our own development. In many countries, pollution and labor-eliminating agriculture are encouraged as signs of progress. In order to convince these nations that the Western version of progress is not the best one, we must put into practice ideas of progress which are revised according to the principles of stewardship and justice.

Whenever we have dealings with developing nations, we ought to avoid the *arrogance* of aid that forgets that many of the problems currently experienced by those countries have resulted from their wish to attain the standards of overconsumption and overproduction which are exhibited in our lifestyles and institutions.

*29. We should remove trade practices which prevent self-development, and encourage countries to process their own raw materials.* The industrialized nations, following patterns established in colonial times, have tended to regard the poorer nations as storehouses of raw materials to be drawn on for their own industry. We perpetuate this destructive practice when we discourage the import of manufactured goods from developing countries, but give favorable entry to raw materials. Though this does not mean that trade itself is damaging, we do need to move away from that thinking which sees only one sort of thing—usually raw materials—as coming from the developing countries. We also need to be willing to ship raw materials to the labor-rich countries. In both cases, we need to be willing to bear the increased costs which such transitions might cause. Ultimately, however, because of diminishing need for transportation and handling, and because of the overall improvement in the state of the world community coming from such diversification of processing, costs are likely to diminish. We need also to be flexible enough to recognize that in some cases there may be advantages to some concentration of production.

*30. We should cease activities which increase destructive urbanization.* In many cases, the massive migration from agricultural areas into the cities is a recognition of defeat in the endeavor to live by farming. Often this is because aid has been directed only toward increasing the amount of food produced by means of Western techniques. The social values of labor-intensive agriculture need to be encouraged. Likewise, the increased manufacturing in Third World nations should be located in smaller communities, instead of in the swollen metropolises. Such vast cities not only impose new needs—for transportation, sewage disposal, and so forth—on the people, but they pose correspondingly new needs on resources—building materials, agricultural land, and fuel, among others. The goal should be a more even distribution of population, with the people near the sources of food and with the increased manufacturing located in smaller communities which are, in terms of food production, nearly self-supporting. Efforts should be made—not only in the developing nations, but in our own—to encourage small farms and the diversity of both wild and domestic life which those farms provide.

---

This concludes our attempt to develop new guidelines for carrying out our stewardly tasks. We recognize that our results are both incomplete and flawed, partly because humankind is still attempting to work out the implications of modern ecological knowledge, partly because Christians have barely begun the task of relating this new knowledge to God's work as it pertains to our responsibility toward this planet, and partly because many of the guidelines stand in need of qualification. We also recognize that there will not be unanimity of opinion regarding these proposed guidelines. Yet we hope that these modest proposals may serve as a fruitful basis for both discussion and action in the years ahead. Therefore, in spite of the incompleteness of these guidelines, we hope that they are more biblical and more useful than the tangled and contradictory ones which have historically guided humankind.

Our task as Christians, then, is to refine and add to these guidelines, and apply them as caretakers in the beautiful garden the Lord has entrusted to us. But how are they to be interpreted and put into action in the myriad situations we encounter daily? And, if applied, what type of world would they lead to? We will next address these questions.

### CHAPTER 17

# SKETCHBOOK: A POSSIBLE FUTURE

*In this time of reassessment, in this age of questioning as intense as any since the great debates of the millennium before the Birth of Christ, there is promise of an extraordinary and almost wholly unforeseen fusion of ideas which, separated and even hostile for many centuries, now seem capable of that mutual interpenetration which, in the nuclear as in the intellectual world, can release floods of new energy, new directions, new possibilities, new beings, new forms.*

—Barbara Ward, THE HOME OF MAN

*And the Lord will guide you continually,*
*and satisfy your desire with good things,*
*and make your bones strong;*
*and you shall be like a watered garden,*
*like a spring of water,*
*whose waters fail not.*
*And your ancient ruins shall be rebuilt;*
*you shall raise up the foundations of many generations;*
*you shall be called the repairer of the breach,*
*the restorer of streets to dwell in.*

—ISAIAH 58:11–12

ne of the best ways to understand the consequences of the guidelines of Chapter 16, short of printing long lists of do's and don'ts, is to sketch a world where they have been put into practice. For there are dangers in do's and don'ts. When we sense the weight of theology behind a set of principles, Christians are likely to turn those principles into a new decalogue, which, if not to be obeyed, at least makes us feel guilty about disobeying: "Thou shalt not drive a gas guzzler, neither shalt thou own two cars; Thou shalt discard neither can, bottle, paper nor slop, but recycle all.

. . ." There may well be good reasons for such commandments, but we are all too prone to take such lists and use them to stake out the perimeters of a new fundamentalism.

Indeed, it is to avoid the danger of such an "environmental fundamentalism" that we refrain from concluding this book with a long list of what we ought to do. Such a list would, of course, have to be inordinately long, for the problems we have outlined, and the principles which bear upon them, touch on practically everything we do.*

But such a list would be misleading as well, for two reasons (quite apart from its tendency to ossify into orthodoxy). First of all, it would necessarily fail to encompass the enormous range of variation in our situations, appetites, needs, and capabilities. For they are as diverse as the creation itself. To say that all paper should be recycled is good advice, and in keeping with what we are learning about the cyclical nature of the ecosphere. But given the water pollution problems of leaching ink from paper, it might be better to burn the paper for heat or use it for insulation. Or, given the spectacular damage caused by forest fires, we might declare that putting out forest fires should be an important priority. But in many cases, forest fires promote the diversity of species, provide space and browse for wild animals, and provide the heat necessary to release the seeds of certain cones. In some cases, then, putting out forest fires might be *poor* stewardship. No list of rules can ever be complete enough to make up an adequate operating manual for this planet.

The second reason why inflexible lists of environmental "oughts" are misleading is that they obscure one of our greatest gifts and greatest challenges: that of *responsible stewardship*. We have asserted repeatedly in this book that we do indeed share, both because of how we are made and because of what we are told to do, in the Creator's lordship over creation. Our challenge is to use well those gifts of dominion and stewardship. Therefore, walling up the legitimately creative and ingenious capabilities of redeemed humanity by specific—and necessarily short-sighted—advice is like placing light under a basket.

Some guidelines, some applications of the gospel to our use of the earth and its inhabitants are quite clear; we have tried to list such guiding principles in the previous chapter. But we simply do not know how all those guidelines should be applied in particular situations. For the answers, then and now, depend upon human creativity. To begin to let the gospel of Christ renew that stewardly ingenuity is the goal of this book. And to say precisely how each difficult decision should be made would defeat that goal.

A more helpful approach might be to sketch some features of a world,

---

*A brief list of what we can do is included as an appendix, primarily to provide some examples of how we may translate principles into action.

a nation, a home of "responsible stewards." So it is with a few glimpses of such a world of stewardly care that we end this book.

We began by looking back, with a sense of nostalgia and discovery, at our green and living planet as it was shown to us, from seven million miles out, by Voyager I. The contrast with the bone white sterility of the moon should have made us both uneasy at the earth's vulnerability and exultant at its beauty and life.

Suppose that we had gone on such a perspective-giving voyage in a ship—named, let's say, Enterprise II—to the outer planets and returned in about the year 2025 to an earth in which all or some of the guideposts of Chapter 16 had been followed. What might we see on such a voyage? Let's take a look—half-whimsical, half-serious. . . .

---

As Enterprise II continued out, past the red maelstrom of Jupiter, the volcanic violence of Io, the strangeness of the Galilean moons, and swung around past Saturn, we were confirmed, in what we saw of our own star's family, of the comfortable humanity of our own home, Earth.

We hoped that humans might have a destiny on Io, Callisto, Titan, and beyond, but we agreed that such a destiny would be far in the future, and only to be considered after we had learned to live at home. We were homesick for that beloved, beaten Eden in which we had failed to learn so many lessons of stewardship. And as we continued, extending our Adam's eyes to Uranus and beyond, we searched the far reaches of our solar system eagerly, but became more convinced that we ought not to abandon the world Christ died in, but try instead to learn what that death teaches for our life in that world. So, at the very fringes of the solar system, we turned Enterprise II around and began the long journey home.

As we got nearer to Earth, we saw that sphere of blues, browns, and whites, set against the black of space, and we were reminded of the fragile beauty of such a living object placed in a vastly hostile environment. And, as we got closer yet, we were able to make out with telescopes a thin, almost transparent shell surrounding the earth—the life-giving "biosphere" which was the only home (so far as we had found) for all the life forms in the entire universe. We were to see much that was new back on earth. But the wonder of that whole, living planet beckoning us home after a sterile voyage never left us.

Nevertheless, we landed fearfully. For when we left, Earth had been full of hard problems and dire prophecies. Would we find the prophecies fulfilled, and step out onto a world desolated by nuclear war, pollution, or roving hordes of hungry people? So on our long descent (which took us two times around the planet), we were relieved to see that the greens of forests, the blues of lakes and seas, and the browns of cultivated land were pure—

even purer than they had been when we left. And lower, we saw the patch-work of fields, the lights of cities on the nightside, and finally, the wake of a ship. But above all we saw green. The worst prophecies had not come true: at least Earth was still a living planet.

After landing safely, we were greeted by a crowd of healthy, happy looking people—much excited at our having set down in their area. And after we had rested and had been fed, the leader of that welcoming group began to describe to us the changes that had taken place since our departure forty-five years ago. She was a middle-aged woman, and she had (it seemed to us) an unusual insight into the world's affairs. Later, we learned that such "planetary consciousness" was typical in this world of stewards. We sat all morning in a sunny room (it seemed to be heated by the sun) and looked across a clean and tree-filled city, while she sketched for us the state of the planet.

---

*I must tell you from the start*, she said, that the general attitudes of people have changed tremendously since you left Earth. The concept of stewardship, and the ideal of justice it entails, have been incorporated into the general mentality of twenty-first-century people. Our attitudes toward nature have been tempered by our acceptance of the responsibility which we as stewards have; we act in light of that planetary vision—which you say struck you so forcefully as you neared Earth—a sense of the delicate balance of the inter-relating parts of Earth and the wish to care for all of creation. Some ideas promoted by what were called in your days "environmentalists" have now become common to all of us; we speak regularly of the "biosphere," "eco-systems," and the like.

One result of this change in heart probably struck you as you entered Earth's atmosphere: the air is clearer, the water purer, and the landscape less cluttered than when you left. The awareness of the planet as a biosphere—a dance of water, air, minerals, and living things, turning daily through a shower of life-giving radiance—has, for instance, led manufacturing cor-porations to set an example in recycling and conserving. They have made great efforts at treating their wastes. And they do so without seeing their actions simply as being forced by "government red-tape" or "environmental extremism." Instead, they recognize their careful actions to be acts promoting planetary, corporate, and individual health.

Concern for applying the principles of stewardship implied a concern for justice as well. The "planetary vision" made people more aware that life, resources, and the future of this planet were vastly more important than any short-lived political boundary or dispute. Such an attitude encouraged a con-cern for justice.

So we began to share resources among all the peoples of Earth, distributing according to needs, not desires. Tariff regulations and trade agreements now allow all nations to enjoy the bounty of Earth. They make it possible for the poorer nations to process their own raw materials. And with less demand of luxury goods—such as coffee, tea, bananas, chocolate, and sugar—those nations can devote more of their land to small-scale agriculture. I should add that although the demand for luxury goods is down, those who still want them are willing to pay higher prices for them, thus increasing the benefits to the poorer nations and enabling them to develop small-scale industries and, most important, to feed and house themselves adequately. The way deep seabed resources are distributed is an example of our new trade policies in a nutshell: like all of Earth's resources, they are seen as the common property of the inhabitants of Earth, to be used in stewarding Earth; they are not simply the property of those who have the most immediate access and sophisticated means to exploit them.

---

At this point some of us asked the woman who was leading us into this unfamiliar world of 2025 about changes in patterns of energy use. How had those patterns changed, and what effects did such changes have on the daily lives of Earth's inhabitants? She began her careful answer in a way which reminded us of our fearful anticipation as we had neared the earth.

---

In the late twentieth century, she said, profound possibilities for disaster were imminent because of the world's exponential increase in the use of energy—its most basic natural resource. If those trends had continued, you would have found on your return a strip-mined planet with a carbon-dioxide-laden atmosphere, mountains of waste left from processing oil from shale and sand, higher ambient radioactivity (fed by numerous reactors and heavily guarded pockets of intense and long-lived radiation), as well as a steadily growing world temperature caused by waste heat. Your fears before landing were well-founded, for in the early 80s, when you left, this was a reasonable future to expect, particularly if the growing populations of developing countries had continued to hold up the consumptiveness of the West as a model for their own development.

But because of that new planetary vision and, even more fundamentally, because of the prevalence of principles of good stewardship, you will find now very different patterns of energy use and, consequently, a much more habitable planet. For instance, giant central power plants have in most places been rendered unnecessary by a growing skill in tapping the torrent of solar energy in which Earth turns. Nearly all heat for dwellings now comes from the sun's rays, trapped and stored—even in northern climates— by improved house design and a redirected technology. We do not plan a building, large or small, without first planning the best way to use the energy of that place—usually solar, but also wind, sea, and geothermal—any more than in earlier times you planned a building without foundations or roof. Also, electricity now powers most vehicles—a much cleaner and more efficient method than the gasoline system you used for your cars and trucks. Mass production of cells which turn sunlight directly into electricity—though not cheap—has finally given us a large, clean supply of electrical energy.

Transportation—of both goods and people—has been most affected by the changes in energy use. When people became aware that the shortage of gas was not a temporary or contrived phenomenon, daily commuting from suburbs to cities grew much less appealing. Two changes then took place rather rapidly: first, cities became livable again, and people rediscovered such simple and practical pleasures as walking or tending small gardens. Instead of moving ever further and further out from their place of work in search of some elusive pastoral paradise, more people moved back into the cities, amplifying a trend which also had begun before you left. In thousands of towns and cities, this centripetal movement has resulted in a pooling of resources and the creation of that sense of community which had dwindled disastrously with the proliferation of the automobile and the lengthening distances between people.

The other change was the moving of various centers of business, entertainment, and work out to where the people lived. Again, this siting of work near people continued a trend that had begun much earlier—but with a significant difference. Business and industry now moved to the suburbs in a conscious, planned effort to contribute to self-contained communities and thus to minimize energy demands and environmental impact. Such moves have had several beneficial side effects. They not only have reduced much of the energy used in transportation—since it has now become possible for Westerners to walk or bicycle to work, or to use a workable public transit system—but they also have made possible a great deal more "cogeneration," in which the waste heat from nearby industrial processes is made available for home heating. Similarly, the vast rooftop space of factories, office buildings, and shopping centers has become the platform for collectors of the sun's energy in both the cities and the suburbs, further reducing demands on depletable resources.

You might say the optimistic pronouncements of a thinker of your time—Buckminster Fuller—have been largely vindicated: human ingenuity, properly applied, has enabled humans to do more and more with less and less. This is especially evident in the application of computers to problems of small-scale energy supply and generation. Populations now draw their energy from the sea, the sun, the wind, falling water, or from the conversion of organic matter—all in a complex system made workable by computers. These tools continue to decrease in cost and increase in capacity and availability. The computer has thus become one of the most valuable of human tools: like the axe or the bulldozer, potentially capable of great misuse; like them also, capable of becoming an extension of the human mind and will.

The world change in energy use accompanied a change in agricultural practices. No longer are the poorer nations of the world hideously crippled by increases in the cost and decreases in the supply of fossil fuels. Indeed, such a dependence drove even the wealthy nations close to bankruptcy and starvation by the close of the twentieth century. The old-fashioned "futuristic" dream of one person pushing buttons in a control tower in order to drive robot tractors, feed cattle and clean their waste in ten-story feedlots, or to pump nutrients through miles of hydroponic greenhouses never materialized. Such an agriculture not only would have required enormous amounts of energy, but those who proposed it in the energy-rich decades of the twentieth century failed to recognize both the abundance of human energy to husband the land and its creatures and the deep appropriateness of such husbandry.

In the "developing" countries, as you called them, agriculture has indeed improved, but (in the words of another of your thinkers, E. F. Schumacher) it has assumed a much more "human face." The same exercise of geneticists' ingenuity and persistence which produced the improved plants of the "green revolution" has continued. But it is now directed more toward the realities of a world unable to depend on fossil fuels; thus the emphasis is on producing plants which do not require huge amounts of chemical fertilizers, herbicides, and pesticides. And the research of plant geneticists has broadened to include not simply the familiar foods—rice, wheat, corn— but the immense range of hundreds of wild plants as well. Much more attention has been paid to agricultural methods and traditions in what you called "primitive" countries, where the people long ago learned to take advantage of plant symbioses—farming in a way quite unlike the cultivated rows of our tradition, but producing food for human consumption for many centuries.

Our measure of efficiency is much more subtle today. The need to provide jobs and the people's desire to husband the land are taken into account, resulting in the shift to smaller-scale tools, which use less energy and produce less food per person, but which lead to a better care of the land and which ultimately produce more food per acre from a soil that is well-nurtured, not single-cropped into dusty oblivion.

Further, a greater availability of land for people who want to work it—particularly in those countries where massive Westernization of agriculture had taken place—has resulted in a gradual redistribution of people back onto a newly nurtured land. A renewed "agriculture with a human face" has thus reversed the disastrous effects of rapid and massive urbanization.

A rather major change in our use of resources came from progressive disenchantment with nuclear energy. Two things brought about this about-face, though it had been building since Hiroshima. One was a series of small, but chilling nuclear accidents—the first major incident occurring at Three-Mile Island in 1979—which made Westerners aware of the potential disaster of commercial nuclear power. The other was the troubling ease with which other nations were able to turn nuclear power plant technology into nuclear warfare technology, reversing with a kind of perverse logic the "Atoms for Peace" program of the 1950s, which had shunted most energy research away from other viable energy options and into the development of large commercial nuclear electric plants.

The decision to discontinue support of nuclear energy—though it raised cries of Utopianism, fanaticism, and "You're sending us back into the Dark Ages" from some sectors—soon led to a reevaluation of nuclear technology in general. By happy coincidence, this reevaluation took place simultaneously with attempts to reduce the spread of nuclear weapons, and hence, the threat of nuclear war. It may be the greatest accomplishment of our time that such a threat has genuinely receded.

Although there was some attempt to fill the gap left by the demise of nuclear energy with a drastic increase in massive coal-fired plants, the "softer" technologies ultimately won out, even over the chimerical promise of nuclear fusion power. Increasingly, toward the end of the century, coal and oil were saved for their great wealth as bases for synthetic materials, and energy needs in this country and abroad were met through a complex combination of solar and geothermal energy and a significant reduction in energy demand. Once the decision had been made, and the full range of Western technological enthusiasm had been directed to the possibility of living within those forms of energy, the appropriate technologies were rapidly developed and adopted. And since the Western way of life continued to be a kind of world model for developing nations, the West's move to conserve, to use the energy of the sun, and to live in harmony with Earth's processes was more easily accepted by those who earlier had scorned practical devices such as "solar ovens" because they seemed to be condescendingly and specifically designed for poorer nations. By placing themselves in the same boat with the developing nations in their use of energy, the Western nations convinced the developing nations that they need not necessarily follow the same energy-addictive course that Westerners had taken in their development.

---

The woman's report of the changes in resource use and in the life-styles of Earth's inhabitants overwhelmed us. She paused for a while, giving us time to reflect on what she had told us. As we thought about this strange new world, it occurred to some of us that we had not yet heard a description of the social structures of this new society. Had a dictatorial government been necessary to put these principles of stewardship and justice into effect? She laughed at the puzzlement in our voices, and began to describe the way the society of 2025 was organized.

---

*Despite predictions and some hopes to the contrary,* she said, the family remains the center for the complex enterprise of human culture; it still makes up the circle within which the most basic and influential decisions about resource use are made. These family decisions about the use of Earth and its creatures include all of those specific choices by which we directly consume resources: choosing the locations we live in, the vacations we take, the jobs we have, and so forth—all that we require or desire. These important choices are made in most cases not simply by isolated individuals, but by people within the matrix of the family.

The most basic family decision is the decision to bear children—and how many children to bear. Given the pressures of human population, our societies, governed by the ideals of stewardship, choose their family sizes according to those ideals.

Some people, recognizing the inexorable tragedy of exponential population increase, had called (in your times) population increase the most significant human problem, and had gone so far as to say that involuntary solutions, such as forced sterilization, should be considered. Others had proposed legal and financial constraints, such as "child permits" or an income tax penalty, rather than an exemption, for each child. Others had said that under no circumstance should any couple bear more than two children, thus assuring an eventual "ZPG," or Zero Population Growth.

Our societies have taken none of these approaches, but have placed great emphasis on the individual's ability to make responsible decisions out of an awareness of his or her place on a finite and interrelated planet. Such an awareness has reduced the number of children born, though it has not necessarily restricted each couple to having two children. An awareness of the limitations of the planet—a part of that planetary vision described earlier—now makes each couple think very seriously about the environmental consequences of having not just three children or more, but any children at all. Again, the guiding principle is *responsible* stewardship.

For it is under the category of "responsibility" that the greatest effects of family decisions are felt. Just as no family of responsible stewards brings children into the world without thoughtful consideration of the impact on the household of life, so no family makes a resource-using decision or establishes any pattern of consumption without considering its full impact on that extended household.

---

The woman went on to depict the life of such a family. She began in a way which at first surprised us, until she reminded us that our attitudes toward women were only beginning to change when we had left Earth forty-five years ago.

---

*It has frequently been observed*, she said, that men in North America's formative years tended to treat their women much as they treated the land: as inexhaustible sources of fertility. With such an attitude, pioneer men wore out both farms and wives on a continent-wide scale.

In our society a different attitude toward women accompanies a different attitude toward the land. But there is also a different attitude toward *men* and their role in society. Traditionally, women stayed at home and reared the family; men went out and "won the bread," whether through conquering the land or through conquering the competition.

Already in the 1960s and 1970s, women and men alike were questioning that old division of labor. But the alternative to it which was usually proposed was for a woman to assume the same sort of competitive roles that men had held, struggling for the same kind of benefits, powers, and success, and measuring that success through the same levels of consumption. And one cost of this kind of equality was an increasing dependence on resource consumption: an increase in instant foods, more than one car in the family, labor-saving (and energy-using) devices, and so forth. Many of the techniques for stewarding resources at the home level—recycling, preparing food from basic materials, even taking the time to walk instead of to drive—were impossible in a family where both husband and wife were employed full time. And, of course, little convincing modeling of a stewardly life was conveyed to children whose parents were drawing heavily on Earth's resources to permit them both to keep a job—and, perhaps, make payments on their labor-efficient (and energy-*deficient*) house.

Many people concerned with women's rights argued that the availability of such time-saving and energy-consuming appliances such as a dishwasher, a second car, a microwave oven, a freezer, and so forth opened up women's worlds. Whereas their grandmothers had had to work 12 hours a day to manage the elaborate tasks of housekeeping, the same tasks could be accomplished in one-tenth the time, with the help of fossil-fuel servants. Yet that same energy-intensive technology was part of a very wasteful pattern in Western consumption.

Women's complaints were legitimate: women ought to have the freedom to pursue a career, to do all that men can do in society, just as men ought to have the freedom to be "home-makers." But once that freedom was granted, and once the crucial role of tending to Earth's resources through the home was recognized, the importance of such stewardship removed the stigma from, and made more crucial, the homemaker's role—whether it was filled by women, by men, or (in what is perhaps the most ideal solution) by women and men together, each spending some time at home and some time at work away from the home. The details of homemaking have now resumed an importance they have not had since the first part of the twentieth century. An awareness of the dimensions of the *oikos* or the household of all Earth has led to a husbandry of the home-household which is seen as a part of the vaster husbandry of the Earth-household. The economy that keeps a family running is linked to the economy of the larger *oikos* of Earth. Such husbanding is a complex and stewardly task which both men and women feel free to pursue without embarrassment.

Specifically, the management of the household involves an awareness of the impact which the smaller household has on the larger. The food that typical families eat does not consist nearly so much as it once did of things prepackaged, precooked, and preserved, thus making the preparation of meals a process which saved time but wasted energy. Fewer acres of the land are devoted to lawns, and more are devoted to gardens. The old tradition of the kitchen garden has been revived, even—and especially—in the cities. The lessons learned there—in tending the soil so as to produce food, in using the composted waste of our leavings—make those gardens a training ground for Earth stewardship. As more and more homes are designed or redesigned to take advantage of the sun, solar greenhouses capable of producing food most of the year are becoming increasingly common—not simply as avocations, but as basic parts of each family's living on Earth. The nurturing of small ecosystems of edible plants does much to link individuals back to the cycles of Earth and the sun which support them, but which the last century of frantic urbanization had obscured.

Such an agricultural center to the household makes the recycling of wastes an obvious and natural part of living, not some strange and disagreeable duty. And the very satisfaction of self-sufficiency—as old crafts of gardening, cooking, woodworking, and so forth have come to be appreciated not only as hobbies, but as ways of life—has reduced the massive search for entertainment that previously sent millions of Westerners restlessly out on the highway looking for some meaningful experience. Meaningful experiences increasingly are to be found in the maintaining of a home—in which the stewardship of plants, animals, and materials is harmonious with a careful stewardship of each other: the result is a caring for the whole planet and its life.

So ends our imaginary picture of what a society in 2025 *might* be like. Our imagined flight to the distant planets and our return to Earth are now over; we are back in our own time. And perhaps now discouragement will replace the gladness pervasive during the flight and landing of Enterprise II. Compared to the world as we now know it, and as most think it will continue, our imagined flight may seem only a Utopian dream.

In a sense that was the intended purpose of this chapter—not to provide a blueprint for a Utopia, but to imagine what it might mean to implement the guidelines (the "guideposts") of Chapter 16. At one level, such ideas seem indeed to be clearly unworkable. To assume that a nation would take upon itself the military vulnerability of disarmament or the economic vulnerability of trade agreements which allow other nations to process their raw materials runs counter to the perversity of the human character. So does assuming that men and women might willingly give up some of their "freedom"—even some of the success in their careers—in exchange for the stewarding of their own household and the household of all Earth's life.

Yet Christians, of all people, have the power in Christ to redeem the human character from its perversity and lead it into a new life in which stewardship, husbandry, and a nurturing vulnerability is "natural." We ought not, then, to object that a world such as we have imagined is unworkable, unreasonable, or uneconomical. Rather, we ought to take the lead in working toward it—in changing the institutions of our society and in changing our lives. Despair in such a task can only be overcome when, above all else, obedience to the gospel of Christ motivates our treatment of the earth and all of its creatures. Only then can we hope to become good and just stewards of the creation which God has placed under our care.

# A HYMN OF JOY

**OUR BOOK HAS DRAWN** to its close. We have completed a long journey—one fraught with both joy and despair.

We began by standing back from the earth, almost as if we were ourselves in the Voyager I space probe. From that vantage point we examined the wonderful complexity of God's creation and saw how all his creatures, both living and nonliving, seem to have their place in his intricate design.

But when we examined that design more closely, we were made aware of some disturbance in the design. Stitches here and there were dropped, in some places the colors were marred, in other areas were signs of further destruction. Storms, floods, and forest fires were disturbances which ecosystems could handle, but the damage wrought by humankind was harder to combat. Indeed, the closer we looked at the details of the design, the more we saw of irreparable destruction.

Ironically, we saw that the power wielded by humankind is itself threatened. Without their energy resources, human beings are threatened by visions of their mechanistic world grinding to a halt. No more destruction, perhaps, but no more benefits either.

We have also been made to realize that the human species is facing grave problems within its ranks. Its population is growing to such an extent that it is crowding out not only nonhuman populations, but, in some areas, its own as well. And yet not all humans participate in this wide-scale destruction of the ecosphere. Some are treated no better than other species nearing extinction, the only difference being that the poor people of the world do not seem to be decreasing in numbers.

Then we took a journey back in time. From the Greeks to the moderns, the roots we examined appeared, with a few exceptions, to be putting forth shoots which have been destructive to creation. We saw that attitudes toward nature, and the structures through which we used nature, appeared to be shot through with malignant designs.

But in our examination of biblical principles we began to see more clearly how things ought to be. We found that our attitudes toward nature must reflect God's response to what he had made: creation is good. From that understanding we have studied our own place in creation. We have seen that humans occupy a most unique place: we alone of God's creatures are

**291**

given dominion, and told to exercise that dominion by fulfilling the role of steward and by guaranteeing justice for all of God's creatures.

When sin entered the world through human beings, all this was changed. A reflection on the problems outlined in the first parts of the book illustrates the effects of our sinful misuse of dominion. Yet, through the redemption of Jesus Christ, this world may be restored. Christians, as the instruments of that redemption on earth, are called once again to take up the task of responsible stewardship.

Finally, we attempted to show what these principles look like when applied to our present situations. We saw that we must begin to use our God-given status in wonder, knowledge, and power. We must seek to find our place within the marvelous design of this creation; we do not have to destroy the ecosphere in order to live in it. From recycling cans to building solar energy units, we found that life in God's world can be a joyous thing, for there is joy in challenge and happiness in responsible stewardship.

Our journey, then, started off on a somber note, but as we progressed, we began to sense a lighter, though still serious, tone. Now that we have reached the crescendo, it is appropriate to end with a hymn of joy. Here, then, is the ending of our book, our "parting hymn of praise."

# A STEWARD'S HYMN

TALLIS' CANON

Calvin De Witt, b. 1935

1. Cre- a- tor Word by whose great power The
2. O Word of God Who Earth did frame, Who

o- ceans roar and plants do flower, Cre- ate in us a
gives to man all things to name; Grant us the know- ledge

love for Thee, the Earth, all life, the sky, the sea.
of Thy ways to care for Earth, to bring Thee praise.

3. Redeemer Lord who Earth did save,
Who lifted mankind from the grave;
Imbue us with redeeming grace
To heal the Earth, its blighted face.

4. Creator Word, by whose great power
The oceans roar and plants do flower,
May we, thine heirs, Thee emulate,
Our lives as stewards consecrate.

# NOTES

### Prelude
1. Lewis Thomas, *The Lives of a Cell: Notes of a Biology Watcher* (New York: Viking Press, 1974), p. 4.
2. Eric Hoffer, cited in Roderick Nash, *Wilderness and the American Mind*, rev. ed. (New Haven/London: Yale University Press, 1973), p. 240.
3. Lynn White, "Continuing the Conversation," in *Western Man and Environmental Ethics*, ed. Ian Barbour (Reading, MA: Addison-Wesley Publishing Company, 1973), p. 63.
4. Pierre Teilhard de Chardin, *The Phenomenon of Man*, trans. Bernard Wall, intro. Julian Huxley (New York: Harper and Row, 1959), pp. 182–183.

### Chapter One
1. Loren Eiseley, *The Firmament of Time* (New York: Atheneum Publishers, 1971), pp. 123–124.
2. G. Tyler Miller, Jr., *Living in the Environment: Concepts, Problems, and Alternatives* (Belmont, CA: Wadsworth Publishing Company, 1975); National Academy of Sciences, *Resources and Man* (San Francisco: W. H. Freeman & Co., 1969).
3. David Pimental et al., "Land Degradation: Effects on Food and Energy Resources," *Science*, 194 (1976), pp. 149–155.
4. Ibid.

### Chapter Two
1. See Erik Eckholm, *Disappearing Species: The Social Challenge* (Washington, D.C.: Worldwatch Institute, 1978). This book decries the alarming losses that result from continued human expansion.
2. Marvin W. Mikesell, "The Deforestation of Mount Lebanon," *Geographical Review*, 59 (1969), pp. 1–28.

### Chapter Three
1. T. Frejka, *The Future of Population Growth* (New York: John Wiley & Sons, 1973); A. M. Carr-Saunders, *World Population; Past Growth and Present Trends* (London: Frank Cass & Co., 1964).

### Chapter Four
1. Adapted from Earl Cook, "The Flow of Energy in an Industrial Society," *Scientific American*, 224, No. 3 (Sept. 1971), p. 136, with additional data from *EBASCO: 1977 Business and Economic Charts* (New York: Ebasco Services, Inc., 1978).
2. Adapted from M. K. Hubbert, "The Energy Resources of the Earth," *Scientific American*, 224, No. 3 (Sept. 1971), p. 69.
3. Based on information in Roger F. Naill, *Managing the Energy Transition* (Cambridge, MA: Ballinger Publishing Company, 1977), p. 54, and from Samuel M. Dix, *Energy: A Critical Decision for the United States Economy* (Grand Rapids, MI: Energy Education Publishers [Dix and Associates], 1977), p. 24.
4. Adapted from Hubbert, op. cit., p. 69.

5. Adapted from M. K. Hubbert, "Energy Resources" in *Resources and Man*, National Academy of Sciences—National Research Council (San Francisco: W. H. Freeman & Co., 1969), p. 206.

6. Alvin Weinberg, cited in Allen L. Hammond, William D. Metz, and Thomas H. Maugh III, *Energy and the Future* (Washington, D.C.: American Association for the Advancement of Science, 1973), p. 30.

7. Adapted from G. Tyler Miller, Jr., *Living in the Environment: Concepts, Problems, and Alternatives* (Belmont, CA: Wadsworth Publishing Company, 1975), p. 212.

### Chapter Five

1. Arthur Simon, *Bread for the World* (Grand Rapids, MI: Wm. B. Eerdmans Publishing Company, 1974), pp. 47–48.

2. Ibid., p. 40.

3. Julius K. Nyerere, in *Christian Science Monitor*, 12 April 1978, p. 8.

4. The first five points are an interpretation of remarks made by J. P. Tiemstra to the Fellows of the Calvin Center for Christian Scholarship, 27 April 1978. Of course, John bears no responsibility for these points.

5. Julius K. Nyerere, *Man and Development* (London/New York: Oxford University Press, 1974), p. 82.

6. Dudley Seers, "The Meaning of Development," *International Development Review*, 19, No. 2, p. 3.

7. Denis Goulet, "Development . . . or Liberation?" *International Development Review*, 13, No. 3, p. 8.

8. Ibid., p. 10.

9. Piero Gheddo, *Why is the Third World Poor?*, trans. Kathryn Sullivan (Maryknoll, NY: Orbis Books, 1973).

10. Simon, op. cit., pp. 62–63.

11. Gunnar Myrdal, *Rich Lands and Poor*, ed. Ruth Nanda Anshen (New York: Harper and Brothers, 1957).

12. Mahbub ul Haq, cited in Gerald M. Meier, *Leading Issues in Economic Development*, 3rd ed. (New York: Oxford University Press, 1976), p. 9.

13. United Nations, General Assembly, Resolution 2574D (XXIV), 15 December 1969.

14. United Nations, Resolution 2749 (XXV), 17 December 1970.

15. United States House of Representatives, House Committee on International Organization, "1978 Deep Seabed Minerals: Resources, Diplomacy, and Strategic Interest" (Washington, D.C.: U. S. Government Printing Office, 1978).

### Interlude—Joy or Despair?

1. C. S. Lewis, *That Hideous Strength* (New York: The Macmillan Company, 1947), pp. 234–235.

### Chapter Six

1. Plato, *Timaeus* (29E–30A), trans. F. M. Cornford, in *Plato's Cosmology* (Atlantic Highlands, NJ: Humanities Press, Inc., and London: Routledge & Kegan Paul Ltd., 1952).

2. W. T. Jones, "The Classical Mind," *A History of Western Philosophy*, 2nd ed. (New York: Harcourt Brace Jovanovich, Inc., 1970), pp. 217–218.

3. From Cicero, *On the Nature of the Gods*, cited in Clarence J. Glacken, *Traces on the Rhodian Shore* (Berkeley: University of California Press, 1967), p. 57.

4. Ibid., p. 59.

### Chapter Seven

1. Geoffrey Chaucer, *Hous of Fame*, II, 730 sq., cited in C. S. Lewis, *The Discarded Image* (Cambridge: Cambridge University Press, 1964), p. 92.
2. Owen Barfield, *Saving the Appearances* (London: Faber & Faber, 1957), pp. 76–77.
3. Gregory of Nyssa, cited in Clarence J. Glacken, *Traces on the Rhodian Shore* (Berkeley: University of California Press, 1967), p. 298.
4. Reijer Hooykaas, *Religion and the Rise of Modern Science* (Grand Rapids, MI: Wm. B. Eerdmans Publishing Company, 1972), p. 88.
5. Jean Leclerq, cited in Glacken, op. cit., p. 303.

### Chapter Eight

1. Copernicus, cited in Edward Grant, "Late Medieval Thought, Copernicus, and the Scientific Revolution," in *Journal of the History of Ideas*, 23, No. 2 (1962), p. 213.
2. Reijer Hooykaas, *Religion and the Rise of Modern Science* (Grand Rapids, MI: Wm. B. Eerdmans Publishing Company, 1972), p. 36.
3. Galileo, "The Assayer," in *Discoveries and Opinions of Galileo*, trans. Stillman Drake (Garden City, NY: Doubleday & Company, 1957), p. 274.
4. Kepler, cited in Arthur Koestler, *The Sleepwalkers* (New York: Grosset & Dunlap, 1959), p. 524.
5. Galileo, cited in E. A. Burtt, *The Metaphysical Foundations of Modern Physical Science*, rev. ed. (Garden City, NY: Doubleday & Company, 1932), p. 64.
6. Lafontaine, cited in Loren Eiseley, *The Firmament of Time* (New York: Atheneum Publishers, 1971), pp. 28–29.
7. C. S. Lewis, cited in Clyde S. Kilby, *The Christian World of C. S. Lewis* (Grand Rapids, MI: Wm. B. Eerdmans Publishing Company, 1964), p. 103.
8. Francis Bacon, cited in Max Horkheimer and Theodor W. Adorno, *Dialectic of Enlightenment* (New York: The Seabury Press, 1972), p. 5.
9. Bacon, in the preface to *The Great Instauration*, in *The Works of Francis Bacon*, ed. Spedding, Ellis, and Heath, popular edition (New York: Hurd and Houghton, 1878), Vol. I, Part II, p. 25.
10. Bacon, Book II, Aphorism XIX, *Novum Organum*, in *The Works of Francis Bacon*, p. 71.
11. Bacon, "Letter to King James I," in *The Works of Francis Bacon*, p. 24.

### Chapter Nine

1. William Bradford, *Bradford's History of Plymouth Plantation: 1606–1646*, ed. William T. Davis (New York: Charles Scribner's Sons, 1908), p. 96.
2. Alexis de Tocqueville, *Democracy in America*, trans. Henry Reeve (1835, 1840; reprint, London: Oxford University Press, 1952), pp. 343–344.
3. Thomas Jefferson, *Notes on the State of Virginia*, ed. William Peden (Chapel Hill, NC: University of North Carolina Press, 1955), pp. 164–165.
4. William Blake, "To Thomas Butts," in *The Letters of William Blake*, ed. Geoffrey Keynes (London: Rupert Hart-Davis, 1968), p. 62.
5. Samuel Taylor Coleridge, "Dejection: An Ode," in *The Complete Poetical Works of Samuel Taylor Coleridge*, ed. Ernest Hartley Coleridge (Oxford: The Clarendon Press, 1912), Vol. I, p. 365.
6. Ralph Waldo Emerson, "Nature," in *Nature, Addresses and Lectures: The Works of Ralph Waldo Emerson* (Boston: Standard Library, 1883), Vol. I, pp. 28, 35.
7. Henry David Thoreau, cited in Roderick Nash, *Wilderness and the American Mind*, rev. ed. (New Haven/London: Yale University Press, 1973), p. 85.

### Chapter Ten

1. Aristotle, *Politics*, trans. Benjamin Jowett (London: Oxford University Press, 1905), 1323a–b.
2. Ibid., 1323a–b.
3. André Biéler, *The Social Humanism of Calvin*, trans. Paul T. Fuhrmann (Richmond, VA: John Knox Press, 1964), pp. 30–31.
4. Ibid., p. 31.
5. From John Calvin, *Commentary on II Corinthians*, cited in W. Fred Graham, *The Constructive Revolutionary* (Richmond, VA: John Knox Press, 1971), p. 70.
6. Biéler, op. cit., p. 22.
7. From Calvin, "Sermon XXXI on the Epistle to the Ephesians," cited in Graham, op. cit., pp. 80–81.
8. John Maynard Keynes, *Essays in Persuasion* (New York: Harcourt, Brace and Company, 1932), p. 372.
9. Robert L. Heilbroner, *An Inquiry into the Human Prospect* (New York: W. W. Norton & Company, 1975), p. 70.

### Chapter Eleven

1. Charles A. Reich, *The Greening of America* (New York: Random House, 1970), pp. 28–29.
2. Barry Commoner, *The Closing Circle* (New York: Bantam Books, 1972), pp. 140–141.
3. Ibid., p. 175.
4. Theodore Roszak, *Where the Wasteland Ends* (Garden City, NY: Doubleday & Company, 1973), p. 10.
5. Jacques Ellul, *The Technological Society*, trans. John Wilkinson (New York: Alfred A. Knopf, Inc., 1964), p. 411.
6. Ibid., p. 417.
7. Ibid., p. 19–20.
8. Ibid., p. 20.
8a. Ibid., p. 21.
9. Ibid.
10. Ibid.
11. Ibid.
12. Ibid., p. 84.
13. Ibid., p. 97.
14. Daniel Callahan, cited in Samuel C. Florman, *The Existential Pleasures of Engineering* (New York: St. Martin's Press, 1976), pp. 58–59.
15. E. F. Schumacher, *Small is Beautiful* (New York: Harper & Row, 1973), p. 145.
16. Ibid., pp. 145–146.
17. Ibid., p. 146.
18. Florman, op. cit., pp. 103–104.

### Chapter Twelve

1. C. S. Lewis, *The Discarded Image* (Cambridge: Cambridge University Press, 1964), p. 218.
2. Ibid., p. 222. On the role of and changes in models, or paradigms, see also Thomas Kuhn, *The Structure of Scientific Revolutions* (Chicago: University of Chicago Press, 1962).
3. Adapted from G. Tyler Miller, Jr., *Living in the Environment: Concepts, Problems, and Alternatives* (Belmont, CA: Wadsworth Publishing Company, 1975), p. 212.

4. Ernest Hemingway, *The Green Hills of Africa* (New York: Charles Scribner's Sons, 1953), p. 284.

5. Ibid., p. 285.

6. Robinson Jeffers, "The Answer," in *The Selected Poetry of Robinson Jeffers* (1927; New York: Random House, 1933), p. 594.

7. Aldo Leopold, *A Sand County Almanac* (New York: Oxford University Press, 1949), pp. 109–110.

8. Ibid., p. 203.

9. Ibid.

10. Ibid., pp. 204–205.

### Chapter Thirteen

1. Ian L. McHarg, *Design with Nature* (Garden City, NY: The Natural History Press, 1969), p. 24.

2. Ibid., p. 26.

3. Robert Farrar Capon, *Hunting the Divine Fox: Images and Mystery in Christian Faith* (New York: The Seabury Press, 1974), pp. 114–115.

4. Augustine, *Soliloquies*, I, xiv, 24, in Erich Przywara, *An Augustine Synthesis* (New York: Sheed and Ward, 1945), p. 1.

5. From Augustine, *Confessions*, in *Augustine: Confessions and Enchiridion*, trans. Albert Outler (Philadelphia: The Westminster Press, 1955), p. 210.

6. Irenaeus, in *Against Heresies: Early Christian Fathers*, ed. and trans. Edward Rocie Hardy (Philadelphia: The Westminster Press, 1955), Vol. I, p. 385.

7. Thomas Celano, cited in Lawrence Cunningham, *Brother Francis* (New York: Harper and Row, 1972), p. 70.

8. Lynn White, "The Historic Roots of Our Ecologic Crisis," *Science*, 155, 3767 (1967):1204.

9. Alexander Schmemann, *For the Life of the World* (Crestwood, NY: St. Vladimir Seminary Press, 1973), p. 15.

10. Vladimir Lossky, *The Mystical Theology of the Eastern Church*, trans. members of the Fellowship of St. Alban and St. Sergius (London: James Clarke & Company, 1957), p. 111.

11. John of Damascus, cited in John Mydendorff, *Byzantine Theology: Historical Trends and Doctrinal Themes* (New York: Fordham University Press, 1974), p. 46.

12. St. Isaac the Syrian, cited in Lossky, op. cit., p. 111.

### Chapter Fourteen

1. G. C. Berkouwer, *Man: The Image of God*, trans. Dirk W. Jellema (Grand Rapids, MI: Wm. B. Eerdmans Publishing Company, 1962), p. 194. On the human relationship to God and the human task, see also Edwin D. Roels, *God's Mission* (Grand Rapids, MI: Wm. B. Eerdmans Publishing Company, 1962).

2. Gerard Manley Hopkins, "The Caged Skylark," in *A Hopkins Reader*, ed. John Pick (New York/London: Oxford University Press, 1953), p. 15.

3. Winston Churchill, cited in M. H. Lasky, "The English Ideology," *Encounter*, 39, No. 6 (1972), p. 25.

4. Ernst Haeckel, cited in John Black, *The Dominion of Man* (Edinburgh: University Press, 1970), p. 2.

5. Ronald Sider, *Rich Christians in an Age of Hunger* (Downers Grove, IL: InterVarsity Press, 1977), pp. 98–103, *passim*.

6. Ralph L. Smith, "Old Testament Concepts of Stewardship," *Southwestern Journal of Theology*, OS, 21, No. 2 (1971), p. 13.

**Chapter Fifteen**

1. John Rawls, *A Theory of Justice* (Cambridge, MA: Belknap Press of Harvard University Press, 1971), pp. 60–65; 302–303, passim.

**Chapter Sixteen**

1. St. Antony, cited in Charles Williams, *The Descent of the Dove* (Grand Rapids, MI: Wm. B. Eerdmans Publishing Company, and London: The Religious Book Club, 1939), p. 46.

2. Aldo Leopold, *A Sand County Almanac* (New York: Oxford University Press, 1949), pp. 176–177.

3. Ian L. McHarg, *Design with Nature* (Garden City, NY: The Natural History Press, 1969), pp. 72–73.

4. Leopold, op. cit., pp. 224–225.

# WHAT YOU CAN DO __

**ONE OF THE MOST DIFFICULT** aspects of writing this book has concerned the relationship of theory to practice and of generalities to specifics. We do not see theory as the opposite of practice, nor generalities as being opposed to specifics. Rather, theory and practice, generalities and specifics, work together—they ought to be viewed as parts of a continuum, rather than as disjointed, fundamentally different elements of human thought and behavior.

The emphasis in this book has been on understanding the reality of both the crisis around us and the principles and ideologies underlying that crisis. Thus, as Christians, we are confronted with problems in both spheres: we must act against environmental hazards and profligate, unjust consumption patterns, as well as against attitudes which encourage those hazards and patterns. Theory is not relegated to thinking about attitudes, nor is practice shunted toward cleaning up garbage and riding bicycles. We must *act* in theoretical matters and *think about* practical matters; we must, for instance, organize our voices so that we may speak out strongly against ingrained habits of mind, and we must, in another instance, think out carefully the complicated matters of changes in life-style.

What this comes down to, then, is that this book, with its emphasis on theory, would be incomplete without specific suggestions for practice. At the same time, it must be recognized—without apology—that this book is largely general and theoretical, and as such cannot aspire to being a handbook for action. (Not that the book ought to be considered impractical—its practicality, however, lies precisely in its attempt to promote a theoretical understanding of the problems and to encourage action in response.)

Why, then, do we include this appendix on what you can do? For two reasons: first, because of the need to show how theory can lead directly into practice; and second, to show that there are good theoretical reasons for many commonly advised actions (such as insulating your home).

We have divided this appendix into levels of participation—the individual and family, the political and economic structures, the educational structures, and the church. Such an organization stresses that the changes and (tentative) solutions to the problems we have described result neither from individual "change of heart" alone nor from massive "change of structure" alone. Rather, both individual and worldwide behavior—including all

the gradations between—must change. We should not view either individuals
or structures as the determinants of the paths followed by the world as we
know it. To assert that the former controls the direction that our planet takes
is to be blind to the immense power of the latter, but, at the same time, to
call the power of structures determinative is to deny the responsibility of the
individual.

One final word to put this appendix into context: we have to answer
the question of *why* we must examine and change our life-styles and *why*
we must urge governments and structures to examine and change their practices. The overriding motivation for such action rests, for Christians at least,
in *responsible stewardship* —the task of caring for God's creation. We must act
out of obedience to that task, not out of self-interest or even out of altruism.
Non-Christians may indeed act out of such motivations; some (as is often
the case and as Christians have often been slow to emulate) act out of genuine
love and concern. But Christians have an added urgency and richness to their
participation in stewardship and justice, and they also have less excuse for
their lack of such participation. Self-interest and concern for the wider realm
of human and nonhuman life are spurs to action which are of only secondary,
yet significant, importance.

*Responsible stewardship* means that Christians may not be unconcerned
or inactive in regard to their care of creation. These options of complacency
are not open to them. Yet the call to a stewardship which is responsible to
God and obedient to his Word entails a tremendously broad range of freedom. As specific as we would like to be, therefore, the possibilities for
stewardship listed below cannot be understood to be binding in all cases—
or binding for each Christian. What is binding is responsible stewardship;
how that stewardship might be worked out varies from situation to situation.

## INDIVIDUALS/FAMILIES

### Care of Nonhuman Creation

Perhaps the most important way in which we can exercise good stewardship over creation is by making such care a central concern of our own
families. The most important focus for such care is the training of children.
But since children have a nearly infallible way of reminding parents of their
own inconsistencies, these suggestions are as much for parents as for children.

1. It is important to be continually open to the wonder and beauty (as
well as to the complexity and the bewildering pain) of nonhuman creation.
Make sure that your family does not live in an entirely synthetic world. This
can be accomplished in the city as well as in the suburbs or the country, but
in all cases such openness to wonder requires a conscious and deliberate
effort. To see, and even potentially understand, the seasonal growth of plants,

the passing through of migratory birds, the kinds of insects on the screen at night, the changes in the weather, the planets and the phases of the moon; to recognize in the hills, valleys, and plains of today the moraines, uplifts, and lava flows of the past—all these are ways of learning to live in wonder and curiosity at the marvel and diversity of creation.

2. Gardens are—in addition to being an important supplement to diet and budget—an excellent way of learning (and teaching) lessons about the basic processes of life. Particularly if the garden is nourished by the composting of vegetable wastes, a family has the opportunity to observe and nurture photosynthesis, growth, and decay. In addition, eating lettuce and tomatoes from our own garden is a good way of reminding us that any food (homegrown or not) has to come from natural processess—it is not manufactured in the dairy, freezer plant, or supermarket.

3. Though pets eat food which could be eaten by people, their presence in a household is justifiable if they make people more prone to empathize with nonhuman life. Caring for a dog, a cat, or a goldfish is a good way of learning how to care for living things generally. And most important, living with animals helps to nudge us a little way from anthropomorphism by exposing us to a very different kind of created life.

4. In addition to these things which can all be done at home, it is important for a family occasionally to range more widely into places where the processes of life have proceeded with little human effort. Such excursions can range from a backpack trip in a wilderness area to a walk through a marsh. Such contact with relatively wild areas serves as a reminder of the raw material of natural processes out of which our society has been shaped.

5. There are a variety of books, magazines, and films which can greatly enrich a person's—or a family's—depth of appreciation for creation. *Ranger Rick* and *Owl* are excellent magazines for teaching children environmental awareness. For adults, perhaps no magazine accomplishes such education so well as the beautifully written and gorgeously illustrated *Audubon* magazine.

6. It is essential that the sensitivity to the material world which these activities generate not be just a private pleasure. They need to be channeled into action to preserve the possibility for future generations to develop a similar sensitivity. This usually involves the advocacy of causes—most often defensive causes against development (industrial or residential) projects which threaten a natural habitat. Advocacy of such causes is an excellent way of building a child's understanding of the importance of stewardship of all life, not only of human life and well-being.

### Resource Use

As was suggested above, care for nonhuman creation and patterns of resource use often conflict. This conflict will lessen when we adopt stewardly and conserving approaches to resource use such as the following:

1. Revise the habits we have adopted in moving ourselves and our goods from place to place—in other words, depend more on foot and pedal power, driving (less often) smaller cars and using public transit as much as possible.

2. Reduce the energy we consume for space heating and cooling by adequately insulating our homes, maintaining our furnaces at top efficiency, "dialing down" at night and during extended periods away from the home, installing alternative heating and cooling systems such as heat pumps and solar-heating devices, turning on furnaces and air conditioning only when really needed, and appropriately designing new homes to allow for maximum "passive" use of solar energy.

3. Do without labor-saving, but energy-consuming (and often simply unnecessary) appliances, and buy energy-efficient models of necessary appliances.

4. Install light fixtures which give maximum light per watt, and turn lights on only when necessary.

5. Recycle tin cans, glass bottles, and so forth.

6. Reduce consumption of prepacked and overpackaged goods.

7. Examine leisure-time activities. Begin vacationing nearer home, thus saving gasoline. Picnic in the parks nearest our homes, rather than traveling thirty miles to a marginally nicer park. Substitute swimming for water skiing, snow skiing for snowmobiling (even cross-country skiing for downhill skiing), bicycling for motorcycling, and jogging for going to a spa. An evening spent in the backyard with the family is often better than an evening spent traveling to a distant place for amusement.

8. Encourage churches, neighborhood supermarkets, and so forth to set up recycling centers on their parking lots to receive cans, bottles, and newspapers.

9. Work with municipal officials to develop comprehensive recycling programs for both materials and energy recovery.

10. Encourage employers to set up car- or van-pooling programs for getting employees to and from work.

11. Avoid drive-in facilities, such as drive-in banks. When stuck in severe traffic jams or slow queues, turn off the ignition if you think that you will stand for more than twenty seconds without moving.

12. Try to conserve materials by buying good-quality products and using them as long as possible. For example, buy (for non-growing feet) good shoes and resole them regularly, rather than continually buying new shoes.

13. Avoid use of disposable items as much as possible. Take reusable shopping bags to the supermarket. Avoid plastic forks, spoons, and knives

(they are made from petroleum), and other disposable goods. Get beverages in returnable bottles. Avoid paper towels.

### Other Life-Style Considerations

Responsible stewardship entails more than care for nonhuman creation and conserving resource use. When we engage in these activities we must do so with our fellow-stewards in mind. Thus, we must search for ways to eliminate the blocks to stewardship possibilities encountered by a large part of the world's population.

1. Exponential population growth is one of those blocks. As individuals we cannot do much to stop this growth in the developing nations, but even in Western society zero population growth has not been achieved. Accordingly, those of us who would like to raise children ought to consider the size of the world population in determining how many children to bring into the world.

2. Family size also bears on the economic problems outlined earlier in this book. The more children we Westerners have, the more our consumption will increase. There are other things families and individuals must keep in mind when examining consumption patterns: among other things, we must a) ask ourselves whether our buying habits satisfy real needs or whether they satisfy wants, b) be aware of the fact that our "development" needs are often fulfilled at the expense of other people's subsistence needs—the check that goes to paying for a new piano could also go toward helping a village in India install a new well for fresh water, even though a new piano may be necessary in promoting our child's or our own musical talents; c) support more strongly those agencies which work toward alleviating poverty or hunger—perhaps tithing is a practice which deserves inclusion when family and individual budget decisions are made, d) understand where and how we get the products we consume—do they waste resources, and thus take away from those resources available to the poor? Do they support agricultural practices which allow the rich to hold and buy huge sections of land, forcing small farmers to overcrowded and underemployed cities? Does boycotting bring about the purposes we want, or does it create new problems of its own? e) learn more about political and economic structures, so that we may wisely use our influence to help the poor and hungry (this is a suggestion which is also applicable in the contexts of care for nonhuman creation and resource use).

### And So Forth

There are many more ways in which individuals and families can help in alleviating the problems with which we are here concerned. And though we may despair, thinking our efforts do not help, we must remember that careful examination of our way of life and of appropriate changes is good—first of all because it is *right* to do so; secondly, because such changes provide examples to others and set new trends; and thirdly, because if we all stopped worrying about our insignificance and set to work, the total of our efforts would be enormous.

In the meantime, individuals and families seeking to understand and alleviate the problem of environmental degradation, natural resource shortages, population growth, poverty, and hunger (among others) ought to provide themselves with "support bases," perhaps by:

1. Finding ways to live in a more intensively communal way—*sharing* through communities which can be organized along various lines and to different degrees.

2. Joining or (where there is none) setting up study groups and action groups which direct themselves to the problems discussed in this book.

3. Becoming active agents in local, national, or international political, economic, educational, and ecclesiastical structures.

4. Arranging hunger awareness dinners to raise group consciousness about world hunger and profligate consumption patterns.

5. Supporting through prayer and finances the work of agencies which implement programs of greater stewardship and justice—for example, Bread for the World, Christian Reformed World Relief Committee (CRWRC), and Mennonite Central Committee, to name just a few.

## POLITICAL AND ECONOMIC STRUCTURES

As we said earlier, individuals and families are not the only determining factors in these problem situations. Governments and business corporations make decisions which have far greater effects than our own individual or family decisions can have. These structures have created such complex systems of behavior that we often wonder whether anyone is "in control." Yet it would be misleading to think that structures are moved by a dynamic which is separate from individuals. No *one* individual has much chance of changing structural problems, even from within the structure itself; but groups of individuals, considering the aggregated power they would wield, can change the direction followed by those structures. We must, therefore,

1. Understand the complex systemic mechanisms of structures which waste resources, contribute to environmental problems, and treat the poor and developing nations unjustly.

2. Elect leaders (or become leaders ourselves) in politics and business who are aware of systemic malpractices and injustices and who will use their

power to implement solutions to those problems: for example, to improve public transit systems, encourage energy conservation measures, set up food reserves, and promote equitable trade agreements.

3. Work toward equitable distribution of power. The argument is frequently used that entities such as business corporations, labor unions, or governments must be very big in order to be efficient or effective. This argument is frequently incorrect, but even where it may be correct, consideration must be given to the imbalance in power that large size creates. The same holds true for the distribution of wealth and education. One reason to avoid having too great a disparity in wealth or educational levels is that the wealthy and highly educated have a disproportionate influence on society.

4. Participate carefully. Systems require participation. Unjust systems, even when powerful, can be weakened by the failure of people of conscience to go along with them even when it is to their own selfish advantage to do so. Work for equitable taxes, fairer consumption patterns, adequate worker safety, and so on, even when it means the products we buy will cost more.

5. Be ready to protest. If everyone remains quiet, things will stay as they are. When people have the courage to raise their voices, sometimes in various forms of public assembly, their cause is noticed.

6. Support collective efforts to study, understand, and act to improve economic and political structures. We need to show insight, sponsor research, and show strength in order to get the job done. Individuals feel—and frequently are—impotent in the face of systemic problems. Collective effort is essential to the task.


## EDUCATIONAL STRUCTURES

Our educational institutions are important "behind-the-scenes" structural determinants of our local, national, and international societies. Their indirect influence often means they can hide behind the more "up front" political and economic structures. This societal institution which influences the direction of government, business, and labor must be called to responsibility. We can begin to do this if we:

1. Participate in school board decisions (attend meetings, secure positions of authority).

2. Support alternative educational institutions which teach children to treat the world, its resources, and peoples with care, respect, and love.

3. Examine curricular materials for the presence of attitudes which promote poor stewardship and/or injustice, and provide alternatives.

4. Determine whether or not adequate attention is paid in the curriculum to a) the philosophy and theology of nature; b) the philosophy and

theology of technology and technique; c) the presence and causes of world hunger and poor resource use; d) the practice of remanufacturing and repairing to curtail wasteful practices—for example, throwing things away as soon as they become slightly damaged.

5. Set up environmental studies programs.

6. Set up alternative food lines in the cafeteria, combining balanced diets, foods prepared and produced with less energy than usual, little waste, and concrete learning and discussion about food production and distribution.

7. Organize school or club projects such as: a) raising money for organizations promoting and engaging in proper stewardship and just practices; b) setting up a school vegetable and fruit garden for practical instruction in simplified food production; c) making school recycling stations and remanufacturing shops; d) experimenting with solar, wind, and other alternative energy sources; e) planting hedgerows and establishing sites off limits to humans to make it possible for wild animals to live on institutional grounds.

## CHURCH

Individuals and families can effect tremendous change if enough of them work for it, and educational, political, and economic structures have enormous powers which can be directed toward good purposes. But the best intentions and efforts must find direction and unity of purpose. It is here that Christians are especially equipped to lead the calls to and efforts for good stewardship and justice. Christians, while acknowledging the shortcomings of their own insights and the lessons to be learned from non-Christians, must take up positions of leadership in these areas: scholarship, education, politics, economics, and the family. The church, as the community of Christians, must take up a courageous role and work for the establishment of Christian principles of stewardship and justice in the lives of individuals, families, and structures. It may begin to do so by:

1. Awakening its own membership to an awareness of the problems outlined in this book and of the task and principles of stewardship and justice.

2. Raising the awareness of non-Christians to those same problems and principles.

3. Serving as a model in its own use of resources and care of God's human and nonhuman creation.

4. Performing its priestly and prophetic duties of praying for all God's people and of proclaiming all of God's Word.

5. Urging worship committees and pastors to regularly schedule services which focus, especially in the preaching of the Word, on stewardship

over nature, theology of the natural world, justice in the use of resources, and the call to obedience in *all* human activities.

6. Encouraging the use and discussion of church school materials which focus on issues of stewardship and justice in the use of resources.

7. Viewing the church building as usable for more than Sunday worship services.

8. Building new facilities only when necessary, and then with special attention to resource use.

---

There is so much more we must do, so much more we must learn. We must seek out those things by keeping our eyes and ears open and our minds alert to what goes on around us. The range of problems we have discussed—from the imported, foreign presence of dandelions to oil-slimed beaches twenty miles long; from temporary gasoline shortages to depletion of fossil-fuel resources; from the luxuries of bananas and coconuts to the starving of millions—makes an exhaustive list of "What You Can Do" untenable. Every reader, therefore, in whatever station of life he or she occupies, with whatever talents he or she is equipped, must join with others in determining problems—local, national, international—and in matching themselves to those problems. Outlining areas crying out for consideration is the best we can do in this book; we can also direct you toward other books which may help to provide more specifics. We invite you, therefore, to make use of Appendix B.

# FOR FURTHER READING

**THIS ANNOTATED BIBLIOGRAPHY IS** intended to help the readers of this book fill in whatever gaps may have occurred in the book, and also aid them as they respond to the challenges it presents. If *Christian Stewardship of Natural Resources* does no more than alert its readers to the basic issues and lead them on to further study in preparation for specific life-style and institutional restructuring, then it will already have done a great deal.

Not all the books listed here deal with the problems in the same way this one has; indeed, many lack a Christian orientation altogether. Such differences in perspective need not, however, eliminate the usefulness of these books, which often delve deeper into specifics than we have—indeed, sometimes they may be useful precisely because of their different bases and purposes.

But enough introduction; we will let the annotations themselves serve as guides in selecting those books which may best serve individual and communal interests and aspirations.

Barbour, Ian, ed. *Western Man and Environmental Ethics*. Reading, MA: Addison-Wesley Publishing Company, 1973. This collection of essays comprises a seminar-type response to Lynn White's thesis in "Historical Roots of Our Ecologic Crisis"—that Christianity bears "a huge burden of guilt" for current environmental problems. Many of the articles address White's article directly, but all consider, from a variety of perspectives, the implications of Christian civilization for the treatment of the earth.

Berry, Wendell. *The Unsettling of America*. San Francisco: Sierra Club Books, 1977. Berry describes and attacks the takeover of agriculture in America by large-scale, impersonal methods, and laments the replacement of husbandry by technique and the consequent loss of cultural values.

Biéler, André. *The Social Humanism of Calvin*. Richmond: John Knox Press, 1964. Though currently out of print, this book is the best introduction to the economic thought and teaching of John Calvin. Its powerful insight into Calvin's theology and its practical implications is not done (as is usually the case) to trace the "spirit of capitalism."

Daly, Herman. *Steady-State Economics*. San Francisco: W. H. Freeman,

1977. Daly explores what has seemed an impossibility to many others—the cessation of economic growth. He finds the steady-state to be possible, desirable, and even enjoyable.

*Energy and Power.* San Francisco: W. H. Freeman, 1971. This book is a reprint of a special issue of the *Scientific American* magazine which appeared in September 1971. It suffers slightly from being a collection of diverse articles, but it is an eminently readable and interesting discussion of many different topics relating to energy. Of particular interest are those essays dealing with the relationship of energy to different societies and also those discussing the earth's energy resources.

Florman, Samuel. *The Existential Pleasures of Engineering.* New York: St. Martin's Press, 1976. Florman, himself an engineer, defends engineers in particular, and technology in general, against the accusation that engineers are to blame for societal and environmental problems. Florman supports his case with much material from the *Odyssey* and from the Old Testament, showing that good workmanship is both honorable and ancient.

Fowler, John M. *Energy and the Environment.* New York: McGraw-Hill Book Company, 1975. This book discusses basic matters relating to energy, its use, and its environmental effects. A minimal knowledge of algebra is useful, but not essential, in understanding certain portions of the book.

Fritsch, Albert, et al. *Energy and Food.* Washington, D.C.: Center for Science in the Public Interest, 1977. Those who wish to make significant changes in life-style—especially eating—habits will find this book to be an excellent guide to understanding the relationship of energy use to food consumption. This study includes tables listing the various "energy contents" (not the caloric content usually listed on labels) of many common food items.

Glacken, Clarence. *Traces on the Rhodian Shore: Nature and Culture in Western Thought from Ancient Times to the End of the Eighteenth Century.* Berkeley: University of California Press, 1967. A careful, exhaustive, and impressive study of Western ideas about the relationship of humans to nature. The main theme is that three ideas have dominated Western thought: the earth is specially designed for human habitation; the earth—through its climate, topography, and so forth—creates a significant influence on human character and on culture; and humans may or ought to modify the earth in certain ways—by bringing order into it on behalf of God, for example.

Graham, W. Fred. *The Constructive Revolutionary.* Richmond: John Knox Press, 1971. About Calvin and Calvin's Geneva, this book also opens up some of Calvin's views of human society and economic activity.

Chapter IV, "Wealth and Poverty," and Chapter V, "Economic Activities," are especially appropriate.

Hayes, Denis. *Rays of Hope: The Transition to a Post-Petroleum World*. New York: Norton, 1977. The focus of this book is on basic energy politics and practices, especially those concerning solar energy. Hayes' enthusiasm (and perhaps overoptimism) for the possibilities for solar energy use puts his book on the "must-read" list of those interested in both current and future energy problems and solutions.

Heilbroner, Robert. *An Inquiry Into the Human Prospect*. New York: Norton, 1975. Heilbroner, a confessing secular humanist, searches for answers to the problems of overpopulation, resource depletion, and damage to the environment. His anthropocentric search comes up empty, and his faith in human capability is challenged. He ends with an appeal to mythology, revealing that, at one level, this is the story of a man searching for God and missing him.

Holdren, John, and Herrera, Philip. *Energy*. San Francisco: Sierra Club, 1971. This is an interesting and elementary book about energy, a good first book to read. (Though out of print, it may be available in public libraries.)

Koestler, Arthur. *The Sleepwalkers*. New York: Grosset & Dunlap, 1963. This book chronicles the changes in thought which led to the replacement of the earth-centered view of the earth's motion by the Copernican, or sun-centered, model. It reads like fiction, and is an excellent guide to the emergence of aspects of the scientific method which have had a profound effect on all our contemporary ways of knowing and using the earth.

Jegen, Mary Evelyn, and Manno, Bruno V., eds. *The Earth is the Lord's*. New York: Paulist Press, 1978. A collection of essays which deal with topics of stewardship, poverty, land reform, economic development, and economic systems—all from various Christian perspectives.

Leopold, Aldo. *A Sand County Almanac* and *Essays on Conservation from Round River*. New York: Oxford University Press, 1962. In this beautifully written and widely read collection of notes and essays Leopold conveys to his readers a stewardly view of the land and its living fabric. In the Almanac, Leopold brings us to appreciate the dynamic beauty of life month by month through the seasons; in the essays on conservation, he makes important contributions to an ecological view of the world, particularly in the essay, "The Land Ethic," in which he provides a basis for altering our view of humankind from one of conqueror of the land community to one of harmonious member of the biosphere.

Lovins, Amory. *Soft Energy Paths: Toward a Durable Peace*. Cambridge, MA: Ballinger Publishing Company, 1977. This is undoubtedly one of the most important books written about energy policy during the past decade. It has caused extensive debate about national energy policy, and has profoundly affected discussions in the White House and on Capitol Hill. Lovins argues that a complete rethinking of national energy policy is required, and strongly advocates abandoning nuclear energy and depending totally on solar energy in the future. A controversial book, its arguments are not always well supported but are certainly thought-provoking.

McHarg, Ian. *Design with Nature*. Garden City: Natural History Press, 1969. In this impassioned, eloquent, and highly influential statement, McHarg not only analyzes the main problems with our shaping of the landscape, but also outlines (in considerable detail) the principles of a more enlightened "design with nature." The book is abundantly illustrated, and is rich in historical example.

Myrdal, Gunnar. *Rich Lands and Poor: The Road to World Prosperity*. New York: Harper, 1958. Myrdal deals with causes of poverty in the Third World, and compares these situations to those in rich countries. He argues, for example, that there is a lack of "spread effects" in poor countries which results in the concentration of wealth and power in the hands of a few.

*National Energy Plan*. Washington, D.C.: United States Government Printing Office, 1977. This summarizes the national energy plan submitted by President Carter to Congress in the spring of 1977. Much of it was not adopted as policy, but the information contained in it is useful.

*Occasional Papers Series*. Written by the various members of the Calvin Center for Christian Scholarship (1977-78), the papers included in this series discuss in greater detail many of the topics touched on in this book. (To be released beginning in 1980.)

Phillips, Owen. *The Last Chance Energy Book*. Baltimore, MD: The Johns Hopkins University Press, 1979. Despite its sensationalist title, Phillips' book represents a serious effort to discuss energy resources. Written by a scholar, the book is academically respectable, and also, because of its clear and lucid style, is easily understandable by the layperson who wants a brief, up-to-date review of the energy crisis.

Pirsig, Robert M. *Zen and the Art of Motorcycle Maintenance*. New York: Morrow, 1974. The focus of this book is on the classic/romantic "split" and the tension it produces in the areas of art, science, and technology. Pirsig presents his own attempts to overcome this split through the positing of the existence of what he calls variously "Quality," "the Buddha," and "the Godhead." Basic divergences from biblically oriented critiques occur frequently throughout the book, but the autobiographical/fictional format makes it one of the most readable variations of non-Christian views of the ills of modern society.

Rawls, John. *A Theory of Justice*. New York: Basic Books, 1974. A controversial and influential treatise on justice within a nation. Rawls argues, in effect, that justice will reign in a nation if its institutions and common life are so arranged that each person has an equal right to the widest system of liberties compatible with like systems for everyone else, and that goods, services, and so forth are distributed equally to all unless an inequality benefits those who have the least in the society.

Schrotenboer, P. G., et al. *And He Had Compassion on Them: The Christian and World Hunger*. Grand Rapids, MI: Education Department of the CRC, 1978. This is a concise and understandable introduction to the topic of world hunger, presented by the Synodical (Christian Reformed) Task Force on World Hunger. Because it is written in the form of a study guide, it is very useful for group study and discussion.

Schumacher, E. F. *Small is Beautiful*. New York: Harper & Row, 1973. Among the very first and most eloquent calls for abandoning the mindset of "bigger is better" and the adopted attitudes and technologies which are inappropriate to humanized activities. Schumacher's thoughts on "intermediate technology" have been demonstrated to be practical and efficient in many locations in the world.

Sider, Ronald. *Rich Christians in an Age of Hunger*. Downers Grove, IL: InterVarsity Press, 1977. Sider, in a detailed and prophetic way, outlines what the Bible has to say to those Christians who ignore the plights of the poor and hungry in the world. He allows the texts which we have often "spiritualized" to take on their intended significances, thus becoming strongly pertinent to our Christian tasks and responsibilities. Sider also offers practical suggestions for individual and institutional change.

Spring, David, and Spring, Eileen, eds. *Ecology and Religion in History*. New York: Harper & Row, 1974. Like Barbour's *Western Man and Environmental Ethics*, the editors use Lynn White's essay as the focus for a collection of articles on the environmental consequences of a variety of religious views—including an article on the contrast between Franciscan and Dominican attitudes, and one comparing environmental attitudes and behaviors in Europe and China.

Steinhart, Carol, and Steinhart, John. *The Fires of Culture: Energy Yesterday and Tomorrow*. North Scituate, MA: Duxbury Press, 1974. This book is written at a nontechnical level, and provides a good range of introductory material on a wide variety of topics related to energy.

Van Beilen, Aileen. *Hunger Awareness Dinners*. Scottdale, PA: Herald Press, 1978. A planning manual especially written for those groups which want graphic illustrations of the world hunger problem. Also a product of the Calvin Center for Christian Scholarship (1977/78).

# CASE STUDY – RECYCLED PAPER

**AS WE HAVE POINTED OUT** in this book, making stewardly decisions is often a most difficult process. Answers are not always clear, and issues are complex. An excellent example of this occurred when the authors and publishers of this book were deciding whether or not to print it on recycled paper. Perhaps it seems self-evident that any book dealing with stewardly use of natural resources should, at least by way of example, be printed on recycled paper. After all, paper is made from trees, and shouldn't we recycle paper to save our forests? However, the issue is not that simple; perhaps a brief examination of the factors involved will reveal the complexity.

In making this decision, several factors must be considered. First, how does the *quality* of recycled paper compare to that of virgin materials? Secondly, how much *pollution*, both water and air, is caused by the recycling process as compared to the virgin-materials process? How does the *energy* consumption of the two processes compare? And finally, how does the *economic* factor enter in; i.e., how do the *prices* compare?

The quality of recycled paper is certainly different than that of virgin-material paper, but this is not to say that either one is better than the other. Quality can be defined in terms of many different factors. In general, virgin paper yields a higher tear and fold strength, while recycled paper has added opacity and a certain feel of suppleness. Recycled paper also tends to be more dimensionally stable and have better performance generally, but does have a disadvantage in terms of appearance if it is made of 100 percent recycled fibers. (Paper made only partially of recycled fibers can be made to look very much like "virgin sheet.") Overall, although there are differences in quality between virgin and recycled papers, it is more a matter of matching the paper used to the features desired than it is a matter of simply determining that recycled paper is superior to virgin paper (or vice versa).

Pollution has always been a major problem with paper manufacturing. For years paper mills have had the reputation of being major polluters, particularly of water, but also of air. Paper made of recycled fibers also results in pollution. Paper manufacturing is a very water-intensive process and substantial amounts of pollutants enter the waterstream. Formerly, because recycled paper requires de-inking and bleaching, the pollution generated in the recycling process was often greater than that for virgin paper. However, with environmental controls currently imposed upon discharge to waterways, both processes have become environmentally acceptable. Furthermore, with recent advances in production of recycled papers, it is possible to produce recycled paper with less air and water pollution than that produced during virgin-paper production. Although the issue is once again complex and not readily determined, it appears that, based on air and water pollution factors, recycling paper can be considered a more stewardly practice than using virgin paper. This conclusion is reinforced by major studies recently completed by both the United States Environmental Protection Agency and the Solid Waste Management Branch of Environment Canada.

Another pollution factor is the amount of waste paper disposed of in landfills. This paper decomposes in the soils and can release undesirable materials into the ground water if the landfill does not have environmental protection devices built into it. Currently, recycling used paper is clearly a better alternative than landfilling it.

Energy is another factor to be considered. Many cities are now constructing large incinerators to burn solid waste and extract energy from it, and solid waste consists of about 50 percent waste paper. While it is clearly better to recycle paper than landfill it, it is not obvious that it is better to recycle paper than to burn it and recover the energy. Once again, the analysis is complex. One must consider not only the energy recovered from burning the waste paper, but also the energy used in processing recycled paper in the plant. That net energy balance must then be compared to the energy used in producing new paper in the paper mill, including the energy consumed in chopping down additional trees, transporting them to the paper mill, pulverizing them, etc. If a careful analysis is performed, it appears that, from the energy standpoint, recycling paper is marginally better than burning it to extract the energy. As petroleum shortages increase and energy costs become higher, the energy issue becomes more important; indications are that higher energy costs will favor increased recycling of paper. In addition, we must recognize that as the population increases more wood must be devoted to the housing industry, rather than for the production of paper.

One final consideration: economics. Recycled papers are available in a wide variety of grades and qualities, just as are virgin papers. The variations of price depend more upon current market conditions for wood, waste paper, and finished paper products than they do upon the question of whether the paper is recycled or virgin. Thus, the price factor is a minor one, and depends very much upon the economic situation at the moment that the purchase is made. By and large, it appears that the prices are approximately equal for the two types of paper.

In summary, the use of recycled paper appears to be only slightly more stewardly than the use of virgin materials. However, since the use of recycled paper is rather new in the publishing industry, and since new manufacturing processes are likely to be developed with increased use of recycled paper, it appeared to the authors and publishers that printing this book on recycled paper would not only be a more stewardly use of resources, but would also encourage increased use of recycled paper in other instances.